While every precaution has been taken in the preparation of this book, the publisher assumes no responsibility for errors or omissions, or for damages resulting from the use of the information contained herein.

FODAY MUSA SUSO A VILLAGE GRIOT BOY AND THE WORLD

First edition. August 28, 2019.

Copyright © 2019 Foday Musa Suso and Emily Bishton.

ISBN: 978-1733044806

Written by Foday Musa Suso and Emily Bishton.

Dedicated to my father Saikou Suso

and to my mother Madame Jobarteh,

who always supported me

in everything I do.

Foday Musa Suso

A Village Griot Boy and the World
An Autobiography

As told to Emily Bishton

Table Of Contents

Foreword by Philip Glass	4
Preface	5
How I Came to be in the World	6
Receiving my Name	12
Village Life	18
Sare Hamadi and Foday Kunda	32
Hardheaded Leader of the Boys	53
Becoming a Man	59
Sutukoba	74
Life with my Teacher	83
In the City	107
Mandingo Griot Society Time	134
Meeting Bill and Herbie	160
I Get Married	170
Meeting Philip	191
Griot Traveling	200
Philip in Africa	204
Photos	216
On the Road, all the Time	245
In Many Worlds	268
The Flying Mijinko Band	287
A Citizen of the United States	297
Sakata in Africa	304
Jooka Time	310
A New Compound and Collaboration	321
Orion	332
Jooka II	337
Circling the Earth	352
Obama	374
Seattle	380
Emily and Uno in Gambia	394

East Coast Life	417
A Village Griot Boy	429
Acknowledgements	436
Discography	437
Photo Credits	442
Student Writings	444
Mandingo Glossary	448

Foreword

In my lifetime- say, the last 80 years- there is no doubt in my mind that the most durable and profound change in the music that we compose, perform, consume, and enjoy has come about through the globalization of music in our lifetime. And what a joy and privilege it has been for me to see the new ideas and energy that have poured into our lives- from Asia, India, Africa, China, Australia, and North and South America.

No one is more representative of this profound influence than the celebrated Mandingo griot, Foday Musa Suso. He arrived in the United States as a young man in his late 20s, and took up residence in Chicago. Already accepted as a master griot in his homeland of Gambia, West Africa, he began as a young professional, ready to share his great art, and opened himself to the currents and tides of Chicago- one of the most highly eclectic music communities in the United States.

We all were winners as we learned of his deep love and mastery of his own Mandingo traditions, and witnessed the ease and talent with which he absorbed the new music being born in contemporary American cities. Even as he became one with us, he has remained faithful and true to himself and his origins- forever African, and as American as the apple pie and music that he came to love.

For those who are meeting him for the first time, I am most happy and pleased to introduce you to my friend, inspiration, and often collaborator- Foday Musa Suso.
Philip Glass
New York City
June 2019

Preface

In 1979, I saw a Mandingo Griot Society concert poster tacked to a telephone pole in my Seattle neighborhood. On that day, I could never have imagined that this day would be a turning point, leading to a lifelong friendship and eventually to helping bring this book into the world. The bonds that began 40 years ago have made Jali Foday Musa Suso a true brother to my husband and myself, as close as any blood relative, and have united the members of the Suso and Bishton/Uno families through joy, laughter, and adventures.

From the summer of 2014 to the spring of 2019, we sat together and recorded over two hundred hours of interviews. Listening to him recount his life story, from his 1950s childhood in a traditional and remote Gambian village to traveling the world as a virtuoso musician and composer, was an experience that I will never forget. It is an honor for me to have helped put his incredible journey and his voice into book form, and to see as his story continues.

Life in West Africa has changed dramatically over the past 70 years, and that makes his journey unique in all the long history of Mandingo griots. His vivid descriptions of ancestral traditions are a gift to the current and future generations of all peoples, and a tribute to the elders who inspired and taught him. His words paint a picture that only an oral historian and master storyteller could ever do, so be prepared for an amazing experience.

Emily Bishton
Arivaca, Arizona
May 2, 2019

HOW I CAME TO BE IN THE WORLD

I come from the Mandingo tribe in the country of Gambia. Mandingos can be found in eleven West African countries: Niger, Northern Ghana, Ivory Coast, Liberia, Sierra Leone, Mali, Burkina Faso, Guinea, Guinea-Bissau, Senegal, and Gambia. I am from a Mandingo griot family, and we griots are found only in the last six of those countries. Among all the Mandingo people, there are many family clans: leatherworker families, blacksmith families, scholar families, trader families, griot families, and more. In Mandingo tradition, every young person growing up will follow in the footsteps of the family that they come from, whatever their job is. If you are from a trader family, your job is to be buying stuff and then traveling around and selling it. If you come from leatherworkers, your job is to be sewing things made from leather, and if you are from a blacksmith family, you will be manufacturing tools, knives, hoes, and anything else made out of iron. We griots are the oral historians of the people, and we follow in the footsteps of our families too. In our tradition, all Mandingo history is known by the griots, and passed from father to son, father to son, father to son for many hundreds of years. In times past, we didn't have things like books and libraries for reading about the history, and that is why sometimes griots are called, "walking libraries". We are the people who keep the history alive, and when you are born into a griot family, your main job is to learn the history and how to play your family instrument.

Traditionally, whenever griots start to play a song in the center of a village or in a family compound, all the people gather around them to listen. There will be a main griot reciting the history for the people to hear, other griot men playing their instuments, and griot women singing with them. The women griots play a kind of instument called a karinyang or newo, which is a small hollow pipe played with a small metal stick. Traditional griot songs can be about the history of a king or a kingdom, a warrior or a war between tribes, the families that founded villages and towns, or individual famous people. In my childhood time, I grew up in a traditional village way out in the bush, and even though I now travel the world playing music with some of the great composers and musicians of our time, I continue keeping the history of my people alive. So for me to write my autobiography, I have to start with the history and tradition of the griots and the Mandingo culture.

The very first Mandingo griot was Jali Nyanggumandua Kouyateh, who we call Jali Dua, and he was a singer griot that lived many, many hundreds of years ago. Jali is our word for griot, and it is like a title before our name. In the long history of the Mandingo griots, there are three traditional instruments that we play while reciting the stories and songs of our people's history. The first instrument was the balafon, which has wooden keys like a xylophone, and round gourds hanging underneath the keys. Jali Dua's son, whose name was Balla Fasiki Kouyateh, was the very first griot balafon player. He got the instrument from the Susu king named Sumanguru Kanteh. The king came from a blacksmith family, and he had big palace with a special room where he would keep his idols. In that room, he also had a balafon. One day, Balla snuck into that room and started playing it. The king heard him playing, and he rose from his sleeping area to go to that room. He opened the door to say, "Is this a human being here playing, or is this a spirit?" He couldn't believe it because Balla played the instrument so well! King Sumanguru had a lot of spriritual powers, and so Balla got scared that the king was going to do something bad to him, but the king liked Balla's playing so much. He said, "Keep playing. Play some more for me", and then he gave Balla the balafon and the playing sticks to keep.

The next griot instrument that was invented was the kontingo, which has a body made from a long, thin log, carved like a canoe and covered with a goat hide. It has a small neck and five strings, and it is played like a banjo. Over 200 years ago, my ancestor Jali Madi Wulen Suso invented the kora, a 21-stringed instrument with a body made from a half of a large, round calabash with a cowhide stretched across it, and a strong wooden neck made from a small tree. Balafon, kontingo, or kora can be the main instrument of any griot family.

Mandingo griots in Gambia come from the Suso, Kouyateh, Jobarteh, Konteh, and Sako families, and traditionally, griot men will only get married to a woman from another griot family. Also, only boys and girls who are born into a griot family can grow up to become griots themselves. Boys learn the history and how to play their family instrument from one of the elder men in his family, or can be sent to study under another griot teacher. Mothers teach their daughters how to sing the griot songs and how to play the karinyang or newo. But no one in a griot family is required to become a griot.

Also in Mandingo tradition, a musician and a griot are very different things, and it is very easy to spot who is a griot. Any person can play another instrument or drums, but whenever you see anybody holding a kora or balafon or kontingo in their hand, you will know right away that person is a griot. No other person will leave their family's trade to try to become a griot.

•••••

My father's grandfather was named Jali Mamudu Suso, and the kora was the griot instrument of his family. Jali Mamudu was a well-known kora player, and lived with his family in the village of Tambasansang, in the eastern part of Gambia and on the south side of the River Gambia. One of his sons was my father's father Jali Falai Suso, and he was a very heavy speaking griot who recited the history while other griots played the kora.

Jali Falai Suso married Luntanding Jobarteh, who was from a griot family in a village called Brifu, also in the eastern part of the country. My father Jali Saikou Suso was their eldest child, and was born in Tambasansang. He had two younger brothers, Lamin Suso and Surakata Suso, and two younger sisters, Fatoumata Sakiliba and Bintu Sakiliba. In eastern Gambia, the last name Sakiliba is the female version of the family name Suso. Other Mandingo families in eastern Gambia also have a different version of their last name for all the females in their family, but in the western parts of Gambia, women and men who are born into the same family have the same last name. . My father and both of his younger brothers became kora player griots, and one of his sisters became a griot singer.

While my father was growing up, my grandfather Jali Falai Suso moved the family to a small village in eastern Gambia called Sare Hamadi. This village is on the north side of River Gambia in the Wuli District, very close to the border with northern Senegal. After my grandfather moved his family to Sare Hamadi, many times his brothers would come from Tambasansang to visit him and his family. To get there, they had to walk to the town of Basse to cross the River Gambia in a canoe, with strong men paddling them. Then they would walk to Sare Hamadi and stay with my grandfather and his family in his compound, which is called Suso kunda.

My mother's father was Jali Demba Jobarteh, and he was the head of all the griots in the areas around the village of Dabia, in southwestern Mali. The griot instrument of his family was the kontingo. One day, King Kanda Kasse Juwara was traveling from his village of Borro Kanda Kasse in Gambia to the village of Kaaba in Mali, which is the most important village in Mandingo history and the Kingdom of Manding, also known as the Mali Empire. On his way, King Kanda Kasse stopped in Dabia. When he arrived, Jali Demba Jobarteh said to all the other griots, "Let's play for the king who is here." After Jali Demba and the other griots played for him, King Kanda Kasse went to Kaaba, then came back to Dabia on his way back to Borro Kanda Kasse. He told Jali Demba that he wanted him to be his personal griot and move to Borro Kanda Kasse. Jali Demba responded, "This is a very heavy request, because I have many people who depend on me in Dabia, and it would be very hard for them if I left." King Kanda Kasse said, "I can host how ever many people you bring with you. You are my griot and I can do that." Then Jali Demba replied, "I cannot go now because it is the beginning of the farming season, but if you are serious, then come back a year from now and we will go with you."

So King Kanda Kasse Juwara returned home to his village, and one year later he came back to Dabia to bring Jali Demba, his wife Mbajalla Sakiliba, and their first-born son back with him to Borro Kanda Kasse. Borro Kanda Kasse is on the north side of the River Gambia in the Wuli District, in an area of land that is nearly surrounded by a big horsehoe bend in the river. It is a very long way from Dabia, around 200 miles.

The King had a special compound built for the family of Jali Demba, right next to his own compound inside Borro Kanda Kasse. The rest of Jali Demba and Mbajalla's eight children were born in their compound, called Jobarteh kunda. My mother was their youngest child. Her name was Sarjo, and she was born after the birth of twins in her family, which is what her name means. But while she was a child, King Kanda Kasse Juwara gave her the nickname "Madame", because she was very beautiful and he liked to joke around with her. After that, everyone called her Madame for the rest of her life.

The following year after Jali Demba and his family moved to Borro Kanda Kasse, Jali Balake Suso said to his family, "Let's go to Gambia, because Jali Demba is there. My sister and brother are in Gambia now, so let's go." Jali Balake Suso was the brother of Jali Demba's wife, Mbajalla Sakliba, who is my mother's mother. To westerners, Jali Balake would be my great uncle, but in Mandingo tradition, he is the same as my grandfather. After he and his family came to Gambia, other big Mandingo families from Dabia also came: The Jarra family, Tarawally family, Touray family, and Konateh family. None of those are griot families, but because Jali Demba was so very respected in Dabia, they all wanted to go wherever he went. When they all arrived, Jali Demba said to King Kanda Kasse, "I told you, a lot of people will come here when I come!"

So the king said, "I will give the land for them to build a village", and gave all the other griots and townspeople from Dabia enough land to build a village very close to Borro Kanda Kasse. That new village was originally called Danfa Kunda, but is now called Manjan Kunda. Each family bult their own compound there, and Jali Balake was the head of the Suso compound because he was the elder man of the Suso family. His wife was Sulako Sakliba, and all of their eleven children were born there, nine boys and two girls. Nowadays, even though there are some people living in Manjan Kunda who have come from other parts of Mali, the root of that village is the people from Dabia. Even today, the dialect that these original families from Dabia speak is the same dialect they spoke in Mali.

King Kanda Kasse had a son named Kandara Juwara, who was very handsome and later became a great leader, even more powerful than his father. Long before Kandara Juwara became the chief of the Wuli District, my father Jali Saikou Suso used to travel frequently from his family compound in Sare Hamadi to Borro Kanda Kasse to play his kora for Kandara Juwara. That is where my father met my mother, and that is how I came to be in this world, a village griot boy. I am Foday Musa Suso and here is my story.

RECEIVING MY NAME

After my parents married, they began their family in Sare Hamadi, in my grandfather Jali Falai Suso's compound, called Suso kunda. In our tradition, the wife will always move to her husband's family compound. My brother Mahamadou Suso was their eldest child, and born around five years before me. Then my sister Nyama Sakiliba was born. I am the third child, and born in 1950. Traditionally, Mandingo people have celebrations for three big things in a person's life. The first celebration is when a child comes into the world. However, the day they are born is not the celebration day. In our tradition, we don't celebrate any of our birthdays, even when we are young children growing up. The first big celebration will be seven days after a baby is born, when they receive their name. For those first six days, they will either be called kekuta, which means new man, or musukuta, which means new woman. Then on the seventh day is the time for the baby-naming ceremony and a big celebration.

Traditionally, the firstborn child of the family is always named after one of the husband's parents. A boy child will be named after the husband's father, and a girl child will be named after the husband's mother. We have a saying that, "The first child's name belongs to the husband". The second child too, "belongs to the husband", and is named after someone from his side, maybe his father's brother or sister, or somebody else. The third child "belongs to the wife", and can be named after her father, mother, or whoever the wife chooses. The fourth child again "belongs to the husband", to name however he wants. It zig zags back and forth like that. If there are more kids, they can even be named after the parents' friends or after some famous person. Or it can be named after a member of the family. Today, people don't always do this. They might have only one child and name it after anybody they want.

In my case, my parents named me after a very heavy holy man and Imam named Fodaymusa Konteh. He is from a village called Gambisara, and is not related to my family. The reason I was named after him is that during the time my mother was close to giving birth to me, Fodaymusa Konteh's son Bakusa Konteh was traveling from Gambisara to a village at the border between Gambia and northern Senegal. When he was passing through our area and got to Sare Hamidi, he happened to spend the night in my family's compound. Bakusa Konteh was also a very heavy scholar and Imam like his father, and the night he arrived at our compound was the night I was born. He then continued his journey to the other village, and stopped at our compound again on his way back to Gambisara. He arrived in Sare Hamadi at nighttime, and the next day was the time for my baby-naming ceremony. So early that morning before the ceremony, he talked to my father and mother, saying. "This boy is my clear luck. When I am passing through this village, he was born. Now I happened to be passing through again, and it's his baby-naming time. Please give me the ability to name this child, so I can name him after someone I want." My father and mother said, "Yes, we will let you do that." And Bakusa Konteh chose to name me after his father.

On the day of a traditional baby-naming ceremony, a big crowd of family and friends will gather in the family compound. The parents have already decided the name of the child even before the people will gather, and have whispered it to the griot, and then the griot tells it to the Imam. But in my case, Bakusa Konteh was the Imam, so he already knew what my name was to be. At the beginning of the ceremony, the mother and baby are inside the house with a special woman. That woman will be carrying the baby when they bring it outside. When they sit down outside, the first thing they will do is to shave the baby's hair. Nowadays they only cut a lock of hair from the baby's head, but in those days they shaved the baby's head bald because we say, "The hair on the baby's head when it comes into the world was inside the blood for a long time, and now the baby should have all new hair". Once they shave that hair, they will give it to the father and mother. Then the hair is weighed in a traditional way, in a balance with some coins or paper money. However much money is equal to what the hair weighs, the father will give that amount of money away to someone at the ceremony. While all this is happening, men griots are playing the kora and women griots are singing.

Then the Imam will hold the baby and recite a prayer from the Holy Quran, and he will bless the baby. He will speak into the right ear of the baby and then the left ear, and he will call the baby's name. But he will not say it loud because the griot is the one who has the responsibility to make sure the whole crowd knows the name of the new child. Then the Imam will ask the crowd to say a special prayer for the baby to have a long life, good health, and wealth, and everybody raises their hands up to pray. In our tradition, when the first prayer is said for the baby, the number one prayer is for a long life, because this is the most important thing in a human life. Number two is for good health, because you can live for 100 years but if you are lying in a hospital bed, you can't do anything. Everything else in life is on top of that. On my baby-naming day, the moment they put me in Bakusa Konteh's hand, he prayed for me to have a long life.

Then the griot will stand and say "Everybody be quiet. We came here today to meet for the baby-naming ceremony for this man and this woman", and he will call out both of the parents' names. Then he will say, "They have a new child, and today is the day we will give the name to this child. We have shaved the baby's head, but I forget the name of the baby". He will actually say that! Then he says, "I forget the name of this baby, and I cannot remember the name of this baby until I see the baby's fathers and mothers and aunts." So all those people in the family get up and come to him bringing some money, meaning that they are paying something so they can hear the baby's name, even though some of them already know it. That's just our tradition. They each are giving and giving their money, and then the griot says, "Now I can remember the name of this baby!" And then he will tell the crowd, "This beautiful girl's (or beautiful boy's) name is such-and-such". For me, he said, "This beautiful boy's name is Fodaymusa".

During my baby-naming day, Bakusa Konteh told my father's brothers Lamin and Surakata something about me, saying, "This boy is going to be a world traveler when he grows up. He won't be living here in Gambia. Once he grows, he will be traveling. No one should be telling him to stay home. I can see it on him, he will be a traveler". But my family didn't know what kind of traveling he was talking about at that time. Maybe they thought I would just go to Senegal, or maybe some neighboring village or country, and then come back. Bakusa Konteh didn't tell them that I would go to western countries and all over the world, but he said that he could tell I would be a traveler by looking at my hand. Even though I was only one week old! A man who is from a holy family can do that.

After the baby's name is announced to everyone, the baby-naming ceremony ends and the celebration with music and dancing will begin. It's our tradition for the family to sacrifice either a goat or a sheep to feed all the people. We also make a millet cake called munko or senketo, that is similar to the special little round cakes called kitimo that we make for the Muslim New Year. First we pound the millet, then steam it and make it into little round balls. The moment the baby's name has been given is the time to bring those little munko cakes out with lots of kola nuts, so that every person in the crowd get one munko and one kola nut. The family must do a lot of work to gather and prepare everything for the celebration. There could be more than 100 people there, or even 200 people. Sometimes the family has to begin planning the celebration early in the pregnancy, and when the time is near for the baby to be born, they are really working hard and getting ready. On the sixth day after the baby is born, there might be 10-30 women cooking all day long to have enough food for everybody. They will use big giant cooking pots that have three iron legs and stand over the fire, and each pot will have enough food for dozens of people. At the celebration, people are all dressed up nice in traditional clothes. There will be dancing and drumming, and griot playing and singing going on the whole day and night, all the way until the next morning. If you don't have all the food and other things together for it, you should postpone the celebration until you do have it, but the baby always still has to be named on the seventh day. You can even postpone the celebration until the child is much older, but you do have to do it at some time, for the child.

Foday means "someone who listens", and Musa means Moses. There are a lot of Mandingo people named Foday, and a lot of Mandingo people named Musa, but to join those two names together is not common. When I was growing up, anytime you hear them together, your mind will go to Fodaymusa Konteh. There are not a whole lot of people with that name, and even today, people in Gambia still call me Fodaymusa. Besides me, only three others that I know of were ever named after Fodaymusa Konteh. Two of them are in Gambia, and one of them lives in Olympia, Washington. That Fodaymusa was originally from Guinea-Bissau, and his father was a student of Fodaymusa Konteh, and lived in his family compound. A very heavy Holy Quran scholar and Imam like Fodaymusa Konteh will sometimes have more than 100 students living in his compound and studying with him. When I was growing up, everybody knew of Konteh kunda. It is a big compound, and the people there have everything you can think of.

When I was growing up, I never met Fodaymusa Konteh. I went to his home village of Gambisara a long time ago after he had passed away, and I know that even today his grandchildren are there in Konteh kunda. None of his children are still alive today though. When I was growing up, I only saw Fodaymusa Konteh's photo, but I do know a lot of stories about him. One very important story is about how he passed away, because it wasn't in Gambisara. When he made the plan to go to Mecca for his pilgrimage, he actually prayed to God, "I am going to this pilgrimage, and if my prayer is going to be answered for you to put me in your heaven, I shouldn't come back from Mecca, I should die there". Fodaymusa Konteh prayed that to God with his eldest son, who was older than his son Bakusa who named me. Fodaymusa Konteh knew that his prayer was going to be answered, and he told his family to gather together and told them this. More than 50 people in his family lived in Konteh kunda at that time. He advised them about what to do after he left Gambisara, and settled everything with them. When he left with his eldest son to travel to Mecca, they even took two traditional burial cloths with them. A few days after they completed their pilgrimage, Fodaymusa Konteh died. A few days later, his eldest son died, and they both were buried in Mecca.

One thing I always say is, "There is everything in the world". Whether you see it or you never see it, whether you know it or you don't know it, whether you hear it or you never hear it, everything is in the world. In one second, the whole world can finish if it's meant to happen. No human being can know everything about the world, because it's too big for that. When you look at the world, there are billions and billions of different things about life, other places, and things. Our imagination cannot even go there. When you look at it, even just in Seattle or any city, with all the different kinds of things you can see, such as plants, people, grasses, stones, and worms, there are millions of different things. But it's just a drop in the bucket. Even scientists can't know it all, because there are so many things we cannot see.

And in our lives, it's the same. When I was growing up, we didn't know anything about the United States. We believed that all the white people lived in one small village, and that everybody there knows everybody else. We did not know anything about millions of people in the world, about snow and ice dropping from the sky, and even what is cold weather. I was born in a tiny village in Africa, and Emily was born in a big city in the United States, thousands of miles away. I could have stood there in my village and hollered "Emily" until I died, and she could never hear me. Yet one day we met, and have been friends for the rest of our lives.

VILLAGE LIFE

In our tradition, every dimbaya, which means family, will live together in one big compound. It is a round piece of land with a grass fence around it, and many grass huts inside. A typical compound would have an elder man and his wife, other wives if he has more than one, and all their children living there, plus the elder man's brothers, their wives, and all their children too. When the male children grow up and get married, their wives come to live there also, and so their children are born there too. Each compound usually has three generations of the family living there all together.

The elder man of the family has his own hut, and each of his wives also has their own hut. Each of his brothers has their own hut, and each of their wives also has a hut for themselves. In each wife's hut, she will live with her babies and young children. Sometimes all the wives in the whole family will share one very big grass hut with many beds inside, one for each woman. This is called musubungo, which means women's house. In some areas, they don't have musubungo though, and every woman always has her own hut. A girl child will always stay in her mother's house no matter how old she is, and they will add another bed in there for her as she grows up. When boys have completed their manhood training, they will all move out of their mother's hut into a big grass hut called a kanbanibungo, which means "young boys' room". In that hut, there might be two or three big beds, and two or three boys can fit into each one of them. When you come through the gate into the compound, the first huts you will come to are the kanbanibungos. Then you will reach the men's huts. The women's huts or the musubungo are always in the way back of the compound. You would have to pass through the area with all the boys and men's huts to get to them.

Traditionally, the elder man is the leader of the family, but the compound belongs to everybody in the family. The elder man's children, and all the children of his brothers, are treated equally no matter which parents they are born to. The elder man and woman are the head of the family, and they are most in charge when it comes to raising all the kids and making other important decisions. The elder man will consult his wife on all these things, but he will be the main one to say yes or no, as the leader of the family. When the elder man passes away, his elder son will become the leader of the family and compound. Even if one of the sons and his family doesn't get along with the others and decides to move away, there is never a meeting to say, "Let's sell the compound." That is not going to happen. It belongs to all of the children, even if they leave. Anytime they want to come back, they can come there to live again.

All the children in the whole family call all the men in the family by the name of father, and they will call all the women in the family by the name of mother. But there are different ways to call them father and mother: You will always call your own born father Baba or Mfama, which means father. If your born father is not the elder man of the family, you will call the elder man Bakeba, which means elder father. You will also call all your father's younger brothers Fanding, which means stepfather. You will always call your own born mother Na, which means mother. If your born father has more than one wife and your mother is not his first wife, you will call his first wife Nabba, which means elder mother, and you will call his other wives Nanding if they became a wife after your born mother. Nanding means stepmother, or younger mother. But when I say first wife, it's not about which wife is the eldest. It's about when they came into the family to be a wife. The first wife that a man marries might even be younger than his second wife. One thing about the Mandingo language is that it is very big and wide in West Africa, with different dialects. Sometimes people say Mbanding for younger mother, or Mbakeba for elder mother. But in our tradition, no matter which dialect we speak, the way we call them father and mother is all about respect.

You will also call your mother's parents and your father's parents either Mama Ke, which means grandfather, or Mama Muso, which means grandmother. When you are grown and married with your own children, you will call all the young children in the whole family Ndinke, which means son, or Ndinmuso, which means daughter. All the grandchildren in the family you will call Mamaring, which just means grandchild, whether they are a boy or a girl.

Kids will all call each other brother or sister, no matter which man and women in the compound are their own born father and mother. You will call all your elder brothers Nkotoke or Nkottoma, and your younger brothers Ndoma. You will call all your elder sisters Nkotomuso, and you will call your younger sisters Ndomamuso or Ndokomuso. You can call your younger brothers and younger sisters Ndomake also. If you share the same mother and father, you will call your sisters Mbarimuso, and you will call all your sisters' friends that too.

This is very different than in the western countries, where you call your father's and mother's brothers and sisters by the name uncle and aunt, and you call all their children cousins. In our tradition, your father's sisters are the only women you call Mbinki, which means aunt, and you call their children sanawo, which means cousin. Your mother's brothers are the only men you call Mbaring, which means uncle, and you call their children cousins too. But you will always call your mother's elder sisters Nabba, her younger sisters Nanding or stepmother, and call their children brother and sister. In Mandingo tradition, the whole family sticks together like this.

In our tradition, we also like to joke a lot with certain members of our family. Besides joking with your brothers and sisters, you are allowed to joke a lot with your cousins. You can tease them by saying, "I am your master, and you are my slave". The reason we tease this way is that your mother always leaves her family compound when she marries your father. Your father was born there, and because of your father, that compound is still there. Your cousin will tease you back by coming to your compound and saying, "I am your slave today." A boy might even go into the bush to get some firewood, bring it back to you and say, "Look, I am your slave, that's why I must bring you this firewood and work for you." A girl might go get some water, bring it back in a big jar on her head, and say, "Look, I am your slave, that's why I must bring you this water." These ways of joking around just make life sweet!

Certain families can also joke with each other, and we call those families our sanawo too. Every family has many sanawos, and the way the joking happens can be like this: Let's say it's a Saturday morning, and you are hanging out in your compound. Somebody from a sanawo family can say stuff about you to some other people in your village, like "Hey, that guy and his family ate so much food last night, they cannot even wake up!" Then anybody in your family who heard about that will say something about his family, such as, "Hey, I met with one elder man from that family on the street, and he cannot even walk because his stomach is big like a balloon!" If somebody asks you about a family that is sanawo to you, you will say, "Those are the worst people in the world!" Sanawo families will always be teasing something about each other, and they will be on each other all the time. If you hear anybody talking like that about you, then you know they are sanawo to you. When I was growing up, there are a lot of families that are sanawo to my Suso family. Some of the main ones are Darboe, Singhateh, Bayo, Touray, Jabbi, and Darameh families, but there are even way more than that. In our belief, if anyone who is sanawo to you gets injured in some way and has some bleeding, you must go to them and touch their blood and then touch your forehead. If you don't do that before sunset on that day, then you will get some kind of injury too. The connection is so very heavy between us. Two sanawos will never fight. If we would ever even get angry at each other, the whole village will come and ask us to sit down and work it out. Elder people will say, "Do you know what sanawo means? Do you think that's a joke? If you all don't cut this fighting off right now, you will hear from us what's happening".

You can go to a person's compound that is sanawo to you, even if you don't know them personally. If this happened and you were there visiting me that day, you wouldn't know they are sanawo. But as soon as I hear them, I will know. A sanawo man will say, "Hey, good morning Suso family, are you all up yet or is everybody still sleeping?" If he sees my wife Bobo, he will say, "Are you the wife here in the house? Where is your lazy husband?" When Bobo hears the guy talking crazy like that, she will automatically know he is our sanawo, because nobody else would ever come to your house and start talking like that who doesn't even know you. So she will say to him, "I don't think he's lazy more than you!" Then he will say, "Now I know you are a Suso too, because I see you are siding with your husband". Then I will fly in the room and say, "Hello, I decided to come and say hello to my son. Hello grandchild!" A person who is sanawo to us can even come to our compound while we are eating, and just sit down and start eating with us, or they can come to our house and say, "Where is my lunch?" Whatever food we have, we will bring it out for them. They will even ask us, ""How much money did you pay for that food?" Once they come, they are at home, they can do anything they like. It's still like that even today. We have a neighbor now in Brikama who is sanawo to us, and she will come to our compound right before lunch with a small bowl. She will tell us, "I gotta take mine and then I am going. I want to take mine now and then go. I cannot wait for you people, you people are so slow!" Bobo and me just smile at each other. Sometimes I will say, "You only come here for the food", and she will say, "I come here because you people think you are the only ones who can eat! Everybody has a stomach". Me and Bobo go to her compound too. Sometimes when I go there, I will say, "Hello, hello, where are the people here? You people are always in the house because when you cook the food, you always hide it under the bed." They will say, "No, we're not eating anything!"

You can also joke a lot with your grandparents, but not with your parents. Your grandparents might say things such as, "I like my grandchildren more than my own kids". They will call the grandchildren, "my friend". A grandfather might also tease his granddaughters and call her "my wife", and then the grandmother will tease back and say, "If you take her for a wife, you will starve to death, and the child will reply, "No, I will cook for my grandfather". Even today, I joke a lot with my eldest brother Mohammed's granddaughter Makuranding, because in our tradition she is my grandchild too. Whenever she comes to our compound or we talk on the phone, I like to always tease her and she will tease me right back. Your grandfather and grandmother's brothers and sisters are also your grandparents, and they can joke with you too. Even now, when brothers of my grandparents see my wife Bobo and me, they will say, "Why don't you leave that husband, he can't take care of you, and you will starve!" Then I will reply, " Go be a wrinkled guy" and Bobo will say, "No, your grandfather will take care of me!"

Grandparents also have the last word when you are raising your kids. If you discipline them too much, your kids will run to their grandparents and then their grandmother will come after you with a stick. They will say, "You have a problem! I never beat you, so you cannot beat your kids like they are a drum". When my daughter Nene was growing up, she would run to my mother's room anytime we were hard on her, and we could not go there to get her back. My mom would say, "Why do you do that?" but I can't say to her, "This is my child". If you do that, your parents will say, "What about you, who born you?" If your parents are alive, what they say is where it will stay. Even when you are 80 years old, you don't have any age over them.

If you have a wife, you and all your friends will call your wife, "my wife". Her friends will all call you "my husband". There is no sleeping together or anything like that, it's just joking that helps you stick together. If I am the eldest brother, all my brothers will also call my wife "my wife". They can joke with her and I can't do anything, it is none of my business. They can say anything to each other, or to me, about her. They can say, "Hey my brother, when are you going to get a new wife? How about a new wife who is much more beautiful than this wife?" Then she will say to them, "You're crazy! If your brother leaves me, he will never find a wife as beautiful as me." If this is going on, I can't say anything. We do lots of teasing with each other, but you can only do this kind of teasing with your elder brother's wife. You cannot do this with your younger brother's wife.

In our society, your elders will teach you the correct way to talk. There is a way to talk to people that are your same age, there is a way to talk to older people, and a way to talk to your parents. When you are talking to your parents or talking to other elder people it's the same, because you have to respect every single elder person as much as your parents. In our tradition, you also call all elder people father or grandfather, mother and grandmother, even if they are not part of your family. If the elder woman's name is Jalla, we would call her Mbajalla, which means Mother Jalla. If the elder man's name is Saikou, we would call him Basaikou which means Father Saikou. No child would ever call an elder man or a woman in the village by their first name alone. If they would do that, the child would get a whipping because of showing no respect. Today when I go to Gambia, many people call me father who I don't even know. We say, "People that are your father's age are your fathers, and people that are your mother's age are your mothers." You are not going to talk to your mom in a rude way, and you have to apply the same way to all elder women.

When I first came here to America in 1977, I learned that if you don't look people in their eye when you are talking to them, people think that something is wrong. They will think you have some evil plan, and that's why you don't look at them. In our tradition, it is a rude thing to look at an elder person straight in the eye. You can only do that to a person who is your same age. If you stare at an elder person in the eye, they will think that you are saying that you are equal to them, and not giving them any respect. And age is what counts for respect, not how much money you have. People who are older than you were in the world before you came, and so they are ahead of you. When you talk, you can bow your head down. We don't worry about looking each other in the eye, because our tradition says, "The eye doesn't hear, it's the ear which hears". We learn all this as we are growing up, and if you do this, people will know you have been raised up in a good way. If you don't, people will think that you don't know anything about life. So when I first came here, sometimes I have a little thing with people, where they are talking to me and want to know why I don't look at them.

Also, when somebody comes to visit you in your compound, we have a special way to greet. It's not just "Hey, hello" though. Our greeting can go on for a long time. You will ask and answer each other, "Good morning! How are you? How is everything? How is your family? How is your day? How was your way coming here?" It can keep going back and forth for a long, long time.

We also have a traditional way of communicating that is not talking. If you arrive inside a compound and stop to take your shoes off before entering a house there, you will need to pay attention to the other shoes that are lying at the doorstep. If you see a pair of shoes lying there and one shoe is lying across the other shoe like an X, it means, "We are having a heavy conversation in here, a secret talk, so don't come in". When you see that, you don't knock, you just leave and come back later on. If all the shoes are lying straight side-by-side, you are welcome to knock and come in. Here in America, it's a different place. We are always running like crazy. People wouldn't stop to look for this kind of thing here, because they are in a big hurry to get to the office. They will say, "Open the door, I got to get to work quick" and walk right past the shoes. In our tradition, there are hundreds of those kinds of things. There are hand signs, body language, and ways to look at people, all to communicate without saying a word. We call this secret language passingo. Today, most young people in Gambia don't know this language without words, and they would just say, "Why you looking at me like that?"

• • • • •

In traditional areas of Gambia, everything is based on a village system. Anything concerning the village is done together, and everybody is equal on that. In every village, there is always a family who was the first one to come and begin building there, because no village has all its inhabitants come in one day. The person who started the village will always be the mayor, and when that man passes away, his decendants will become the mayor. His eldest son will replace him, and then one of the younger brothers. When all those brothers pass away, the eldest child of the brothers will become mayor. Whenever you go to a village and you hear the mayor's last name, you will know right away whose family founded the village and are the ones who can become mayor. But if a man happens to pass away before any of his sons are grown up enough to be mayor, then somebody else can be chosen to be mayor for a while, just to hold it for the eldest boy until he grows up to become a man. Then they will give the mayorship to that son. Most of the time, the name of a village will have the family name in it, but not always. My childhood village of Sare Hamadi is a Fulani name: Sare means village, and the name of the founder of the village was Hamidi Baldeh. When he passed away, his eldest son Chewuto Baldeh became the mayor.

In the village, when people are building a house, it is done with teamwork, and the teamwork is free. No one person can build a house completely and finish it. Today people will help you, and tomorrow you will help them. All the houses in the village are built the same, with mud walls and a grass roof. When it's your turn to build a house, men will go out and help you dig a hole and wet the ground, to prepare the mud for building the walls. In our area, the earth is full of heavy clay. When we start digging the hole, we will first take off the top layer of dirt and put it aside, because the clay earth is usually deeper in the ground. We will dig a hole around six feet across, and then go to the well again and again to fetch a lot of water and pour it inside. Then we leave the hole and wait until the next day, when the earth will be much softer. That next day, we mix it up and bring the mud to the site where the house will be built. The way we mix it together makes the mud very strong. Then the builders make the round mud walls, piling a line of the mud on the ground in a big circle, rolling, pressing, smoothing, and shaping it, then adding another layer around and around until it is finished. When it dries, it becomes very, very hard and strong, and even the big summer rains won't do any damage.

Once the walls are done, it's time for you all to go to the bush and cut long bamboo poles to make the pillars of the roof. The roof is always built on the ground, and all the poles are tied together at the top, then spread out to stand on the ground. It looks kind of like a big tripod. Other strong sticks are tied to the bamboo poles to hold them in that shape, then you will all cut long grasses to wrap around the bamboo poles and sticks to finish the roof. You have to tie it all very well. Then everyone has to pick the roof up off the ground, and put it over the walls of the round house. It takes a lot of men to do that, because the house is usually around nine feet across, and there is a lot of moving it around to get it on top. People are yelling, "Move it west, move it north", and so on, before it's just right. Once the roof is put on top, the weight of the roof is all that is needed to hold it there. We don't use anything to attach it to the mud walls. During the rainy season thunderstorms, the wind can be very strong and sometimes tear off the grass part of the roof, and repairs have to be done. But on very rare occasions, the wind can be so strong that it blows the whole roof off of the walls. That is a big problem to fix, but we all do it together.

Once the grass hut is finished, we will make the floor level by smoothing and patting the dirt. Now it's time to make the tradional bed for the house. This bed is not meant to be moved around, and there is usually only one. To make it, we will go into the bush and cut six strong sticks that have a Y-shape in the top, and each of them will be around two feet long. Then we will cut more sticks that are five or six feet long, and bring all the wood back to the hut. We will dig six holes in the dirt floor for those Y-shaped sticks to go down into, and then lay the longer sticks across them. Then a bamboo mat goes on top that has been made to fit that particular bed. We call it a krinting mat, and sometimes people will just put that mat right on the ground to sleep on. Also, sometimes people will make a traditional mattress out of a peanut bag, which is woven from small jute rope. They will take the peanut bag out into the bush, and fill it with a certain type of dried grass that has a tiny stem, so it's very soft. After they fill the bag to make it plump up, they will sew it shut on top, then put it on their head to bring it back to the village and put it on the bed frame to be a mattress. That kind of mattress is called pasajo. People working together also make traditional seats called bentengo for the village square, which we call the bantaba.

Everyone in the compound helps to take care of all the grass huts inside to keep them nice, not just the hut that they live in. They will harvest all their crops together, and share the food. All the men and their grown sons will eat in one big calabash together, and all the women and their grown daughters will eat out of another big calabash. If there are young sons who are two to five years old, they will eat with their grandfather in his calabash, and if there are young daughters who are two to five years old, they will eat with their grandmother. In our tradition, children are always under the elders' care. It's our way to raise children. All your life, your elders will teach you what to do and what not to do, how to live, how to talk to people, how to look at people, where to sit when you arrive somewhere, how even to eat to prevent the food from dropping on the ground, how to eat so you share the calabash with all the other people, everything about life. You will need to learn that when you are eating, just be quiet and don't talk a lot, because it's just the time for eating. Your elders will show you how to sit by the calabash when you are in a crowd, so you leave room around you for everyone to fit. When you go out to other people's houses, they will teach you the way to go inside. There's a lot of stuff to learn.

A traditional village has no running water pipes, and all the people share the well. Some villages have only one well if they are small, but a bigger village might have three, four, or even five wells. In each area of the district, somebody who specializes in well-digging will come to do the work. Every well is dug by hand. One person is digging, digging, digging. Others at the top will lower the buckets for the digger to fill with dirt, and then haul it out. The well could be 20, 30, or 50 feet deep, depending on where the village is. If the ground is very dry, the well has to be deeper. Some villages might only have to dig 10-20 feet to reach the water. Once the well is becoming deep, they will lower the digger down into it by ropes, with a stick seat for him to sit on on the way down. Then he stands on the ground at the bottom of the well and digs for a while, and then signals to the people that he wants to come up. Everybody at the top pulls on the ropes to bring him up. Digging a well can take a week or more.

During the end of dry season in January, February, or March, people will also work together to clean the grass behind the village and make a fire break, like a big belt around the whole village to keep the fire away from it. You need a lot of people to help for all that, and everybody is equal, so if there is a wildfire, it cannot jump and get inside the village. If a fire happens to come inside the village, it's everybody's job to help put it out. We don't have any fire-fighting machines. If anything comes on your side, everybody will stand for you and help. Not for you to pay them the money, but because that's how life is, you help them and they help you. Both men and women will run to the village wells and fill big giant pots, put them on their head, and run to the house where the fire broke out. Other men are there, and they will take the pot of water and throw it on the fire. Sometimes that fire will do a lot of damage, and the whole family's house will be burned. If that happens, all the people in that village will accommodate that family until they can stand on their feet again, even if it takes a whole year or more. Sometimes the family might have lost all of their seeds in the fire, and they won't have anything to plant during the next farming season. They might lose all their food, clothing, and everything else. We don't have any banks or anything like that, for people to go and get a loan. Everything is just based on the people themselves, so other people in the village will give them all the things they need.

Everything in the village is done together, such as building the grass huts and fencing your compound with a grass fence. That will work for everybody. Everything in the village is about teamwork, and no one can be living a lonely life. You won't be lonely for nothing. We don't have that. Everybody knows each other very well, and everybody is into each other, so there is no such thing as living alone.

If you say, "I am on my own, I am by myself", then you cannot live there in the village, and you cannot survive. If you say that, people will leave you alone if anything comes to your side and you need help. They will think, "Since he says he wants to be alone, we will leave him". Then you will have loneliness. This is how it is in the villages, even now.

In our tradition, there is a way people live. This way to live is that men and women do different things. Some will be similar, but most of them will be very different. A man's job is first to marry a wife, and second to have a house. Men are responsible for building the compounds and the village, the grass huts inside the compound, and grass fences. They also must feed the family by farming the crops they need to eat. No matter whether you come from a trader family, blacksmith family, leatherworker family, scholar family, or griot family, every family will farm. Farming is for everybody. There are big fields outside the village where four different kinds of millet are grown during the rainy season, in a public farm for the whole family to eat from, and to store for the dry season. Other big fields have peanuts to grow for food and for selling. There are also crops such as cotton, pumpkins, squash, sweet potatoes, and corn. The yellow corn we grow is called mako or toubanyo, which is short for Toubab-nyo, and means, "Toubab's millet". Toubab is our word for a white person. This corn is cooked in the fire or in water, dried in the sun, the seed coat peeled coat off, and then pounded into flour. The white corn we grow is called saata, and multicolored corn is called wlubobasang. Today young people don't know these words, and you just have to say, "White corn". Many foods we eat are wild crops that are picked out in the countryside and then brought to the village for all the people to share. One of my favorites was the bush yam, because it was so sweet. Many years later, I was so surprised when I found them for sale in New York City, in a market in Chinatown! Men are also responsible for harvesting crops and bringing the food to the compound for it to be cooked. In the area I grew up in, I have also seen men and women working together on these big farms, and I have seen other places where men leave the hard work of farming for the women to do.

In our tradition, women will also grow food in their own little farm, which is for their private family use. Her farm is outside the village too, and will be based on what she needs for cooking stews and soups for the family. There could be tomatoes and onions, and other vegetables too. Women will grow and harvest the peanut also, sell part of the crop so that they can earn some money, and use the rest of the peanut harvest for making peanut sauce for her own family cooking. It's her private farm. Even if the woman of the family is making more money than the man, it makes no difference. It is her money. The husband cannot say, "Split it 50/50" or anything like that. Women are also responsible for raising the kids from the time the baby is born, breast feeding and bathing them every day, fetching water from the well for drinking, washing the clothes, and cooking food every day.

Traditionally, men usually do the weaving and making of clothes. Men grow the cotton and harvest it, then bring it to the house. Women will take the cotton and work on it, softening it, and spinning it to make thread. Women and men can both dye the thread to make it different colors, but men will take the thread and weave it to make the clothes.

This is just how it is in my part of Africa. In the village, men and women know where they stand. In the village, there is no one who gets up in the morning and says, "What am I going to do?" You already know what part you will be taking. The jobs of girls and boys are different too. The boys will do what their fathers do, and that is what they will learn. The girls will do what their mothers do, and that is what they will learn. In traditional places, there is nothing like going to a school to learn how to work in an office, because there is no office. Also, there is no system to say that you must get up and go to school. There is no such thing as shopping, because there are no stores. People live on the land and are growing their own food, making their own clothes and other things they need, and they share everything. This way of life, it works for us.

Almost all people in Gambia are Muslim, and prayers come five times every day: at dawn, in the early afternoon, in the late afternoon, at sunset, and in the late evening. Breakfast is always after morning prayers, lunch is always after the early-afternoon prayers, and dinner is always after sunset. People gather together in the bantaba for special occasions and village meetings. Everything is based on tradition. In my time of growing up, whether you are traveling, working, riding a donkey or a horse, that's it.

In the village, someone might not even have twenty dollars after a whole year of work. In fact, in two years you might not have more than twenty dollars. But it's OK. You might buy a bag of salt for three cents, and it's a big bag, enough for three or four months. And when it is finished, you don't have to go buy a bag right away that day. You can send your daughter to the neighbor and say, "Go ask Mary to give us some salt", and they bring it. They don't ask, "Why didn't you buy your own salt?" It's not like that. Sharing is going on and on and on, until you go buy a bag of salt. And then when someone asks you for salt, you go and get your bag and give some to them. In a traditional place, it's like that. Very sweet. If somebody doesn't know village life, they might think, "How can I rest, because people are around me all the time?" But that's how the village is, that's our style. Village life is something else.

SARE HAMADI AND FODAY KUNDA

At the time I was born, Sare Hamadi was a small Mandingo and Fulani village. It had only around nine Mandingo family compounds and around seven Fulani family compounds. The Fulani boys and Mandingo boys played together every day. In fact, we would do everything together. While I was growing up, I could speak Fulani just like the Fulani people themselves. Now I can still speak it, but not like that. The Mandingo boys I grew up with are named Madi Touray, who passed away a few years ago, Mamudou Danjo, and his elder brother Filly Danjo. The Fulani boys I grew up with are named Donfo Sowe, his brother Yerro Sowe, Wuridado Baldeh the mayor's son, Ngaibotel Baldeh the mayor's brother's son, and other Fulani boys too. We small boys all played together under the trees in the village, but we were not allowed to go out in the bush by ourselves yet.

The main thing we like to do is a game we call toronkoso. It's a little bit similar to a game the British call cricket, and a little bit like the game hockey. We boys will divide ourselves into two teams, and each boy will have a stick in their hands that looks like a curved club. We make our sticks from digging and cutting the root and stem of bamboo. We also carve wood to make a small ball, or sometimes we might use a small calabash. To start the game, each team will face each other from one side of a middle line, with all boys pounding their sticks on the ground. Then we drop the ball on the middle line in a little hole, and each boy tries to hit it towards the other team's side, where there are two big stones set a few feet apart. It's kind of like a hockey goal. We try to block each other's sticks whenever we try to hit the ball. In fact, toronkoso is a lot like hockey with a ball, on dry land. Whenever I think about that game, I remember that one time, a fingernail on my left hand came off because of being hit by a stick. Something like that happened also one day I was cutting the grain we call findo in our farm outside Sare Hamadi, and I hit my own finger with the tool we call woroto, a curved knife with small teeth that looks kind of like a hand sythe.

In those days, my father did a whole lot of traveling to Senegal and Sierra Leone. Usually, farming is done in the rainy season and griot traveling is done only in the dry season, but my father traveled at any time of year. While he was gone, his two brothers Lamin and Surakata took care of the farming. Sometimes Surakata went with my father to these places too, but my mother and us kids didn't go.

During the time when I was growing up, many times people told me stories about when I was very, very young, and I would reach for my father's kora to try to play. They said that the kora would be standing up against the wall, and I would try to come and play it, pulling the strings and stuff like that. Then I would fall down with the kora, because it was big and I was so small. I would start crying, and they would run over and pick me up, and put the kora back. But being hardheaded, I would go back to the kora again, pulling on the strings to try to play, and then fall over again. Over and over I did that, all the time!

My father's father Jali Falai Suso was alive when I was born, but I never met my mother's father Jali Demba Jobarteh, because he had already passed away. One day when I was small, me and my grandfather Suso walked together from Sare Hamidi to a village called Barrow Kunda. It is a long walk for hours, down a small footpath through the woods. At the beginning, I ran ahead of him all around, but after we were walking for a long time, I got very tired. I was crying to him, "Grandpa, I am hungry" over and over. When we got close to the village, he called out in a loud voice to the people there, "Barrow Kunda people, it's me, Falai Suso. Bring the lunch, bring us food". So the people all came out of their compounds, each with a small calabash full of food for us. The mayor of that village was my grandfather's good friend. By the time we got to the bantaba in the mididile of the village, the streets were full of women with the food for us. When we got to the mayor's compound, they put all the food out for us to eat. My grandfather greeted everyone and didn't eat right away, but he said to me, "Look at all this food. Go ahead and eat, you can even rub it on your body if you want!" He started doing the greeting with the mayor and everybody, but me, I did not want to do any greeting. And when I started eating, I never wanted to stop - ha ha! I went from one calabash to the other. When my grandfather finished the greeting time, he began to eat. After being there for a while, we continued our journey back to our village, and by that time I was strong and had my energy back.

A long time later when I was a grown man, I was traveling in Gambia from Brikama to Foday Kunda with my wife Bobo and my daughter Nene, who was still very small. We crossed the River Gambia at the town of Basse, and we stopped in a small Fulani village near Barrow Kunda. It was evening time, and because I know that the Fulani milk their cows at night, I stopped there to get some milk for Nene. At one house in the village, I asked a woman for milk, and she said that the cow milker would be coming back in a few minutes. He came back with the milk in a big calabash, and she asked me how much I would like to buy. While we were talking, there was a very old man lying on a cot in the house. He asked me where I was from, and I told him Sare Hamadi. He said, " I know that village very well, what is your name." When I told him my first and last name, he asked me, "Are you a relative of Jali Falai Suso?" I replied, "That is my grandfather". Then he got up from his cot, and sat down on a chair and said to me, "Falai is your grandfather? He is our great griot, and a good friend of mine. You are never going to buy milk from me, you must take it. It is yours. You are like a grandson to me, because your grandfather and I are heavy friends. Take it, this is your milk". He was a very old man, but still I was surprised that he knew my grandfather. That year it was 1988 and my grandfather died in 1961 or 1962, and people say he was 111 years old.

•••••

When I was four or five years old, my mother took me and my sister Nyama Sakliba to move from Sare Hamadi to a village called Foday Kunda. It is in the easternmost part of the Wuli District, near where the River Gambia flows into eastern Senegal. The reason that happened is because when I was growing up, my father was always traveling a lot and gone for a long time. My mother did not go, and because of that she decided to divorce him. Then she married a griot named Mamadi Kanuteh, who was from a village called Foday Kunda, around 23 miles away from Sare

Hamadi. She moved to his compound with my sister Nyama and me, and my brother Mahamadou stayed in Sare Hamadi along with my father and the rest of the Suso family. Later on, my mother and Mamadi Kanuteh had two children together: my sister Tita and my brother Dembo.

The village of Foday Kunda is named after its founder, a man named Foday Singhateh. Everybody who lived there were Mandingo people, and there were a lot of griot families: The Suso family, Kouyateh family, Jobarteh family, and Kanuteh family. There were also a lot of trader families there: The Singhateh family, Camateh family, Kebbeh family, Ketta family, and Danso family. The leatherworker families were the Jagne family, Sisawo family, and Sillah family. There was only one blacksmith family, the Kanteh family, but I don't think there is any Kanteh compound there today. Foday Kunda was a small village, and all the people would gather at one of the trader family's compounds when griots would perform.

In a traditional village, almost every elder woman knows how to be a midwife. When women are young, they watch the elder women and learn from them. When I was growing up in Foday Kunda, my mom became a midwife too. When a new baby would come, every morning for the first two or three weeks, the mother would bring the baby to my mom to wash and clean it in our traditional way. In some cases, my mom would go to their house twice a day: around 7am and around 3pm. To clean the baby, first she warmed up the water a little and put it in a little clay jar called a fenkengo. Then my mom washed the baby outside in front of her grass hut. She laid the baby face down on her hand and forearm. The baby's head was resting on her forearm, and my mom's hand was holding the baby's legs. She washed the baby all over its back, and then she turned it over to wash the front too, and rinsed the whole baby with the water from the fenkengo. Then she would blow air into the baby's ear in case there was any remaining water there that should not stay.

My mom did more than just to wash the baby, she also gave it our traditional exercise. First, my mom would sit up and straighten her legs, and put the baby in her lap so it is sitting up straight and facing left or right. Then she put one of her hands under the baby's chin and the other hand behind the baby's head and picked the baby up by its head. Lifting it up and down a few times. I don't know why she did that, but the babies like it! They never cry. Then she put the baby down and turned the baby to face her. She put her hands on each side of the baby's head and turned it one way and then the other, back and forth a few times. Then while the baby was still sitting in her lap, she laid it face down on its stomach and took one of the baby's arms to bring it behind its back a few times. Then she did the same with the other arm a few times. Then she turned the baby upside down and held both legs near the feet, and moved the child up and down gently. The babies like this too! There was no crying, just natural baby noise. The last thing she did was to lay the baby in her lap and use shea butter, which is made from nuts of a tree in our area, to rub the baby's body and massage it. Then she wrapped the baby up and gave it back to its mother. She did all this washing and exercise twice a day every day, for two or three weeks! It's not for any payment, or nothing like that. It's our tradition.

One thing I have noticed in the U.S is that a baby walks a lot younger here than a typical baby did when I was growing up. Here, I see even little tiny babies who are walking. In our village, a baby has to learn how to sit up by itself on the ground without falling, and to roll over onto their back or their side. That takes a long time. Then they learn how to crawl, and they will crawl for a long time before they stand up. Then after that, they will learn how to stand up and not fall down right away. From there, they will try to learn how to walk. We had no baby walkers and don't use baby shoes, so a baby has to learn on their own without that help. When they first start to walk, it is so slow before they can clearly walk and not fall down.

•••••

When I was growing up in Foday Kunda, I saw some small fires that burned only one grass hut, but two very big fires happened that burned almost half of our village. The first big fire happened when I was eight or nine years old. It started during the time right before the rainy season, when people rake up all the sticks in their fields to clean the ground and prepare for farming. Once the fields are all cleaned, they will burn those sticks. One man who was the father of a friend of mine, had a corn farm close to the village, and he was doing this. Corn farms are always closer to the village than any other farms. I think this is because we make a lot of food from corn, and they become ripe sooner than any other crop. Our corn plants are very tall with big corncobs that are very high on the stalk, and on the day he burned his corn stalks, a big wind started coming. Typically, we will have three or four winds like this at the beginning of the rainy season. The wind that came that day was so big, and brought a big dust storm. If you were there, you couldn't even open your eyes. The man went to his field to see if all his fire was out, and he thought it was. But there was cow dung there that had caught on fire, and it burns for a long time. The wind blew some of the cow dung into somebody's grass fence at the western edge of the village, and the fire grew so fast that it burned every single house in that half of the village. The wind was so strong that the fire almost cut the village in two. People were rushing around to try to put the fire out, but once they saw that the fire was too big for that, they rushed to the houses that weren't burning yet and just tried to get everything important out of them. Carrying wooden boxes, big bags of peanuts, duffle bags, suitcases, and running to set them outside the village. Everyone who can work was helping drag these things out of the houses. Many animals were lost- goats, donkeys, and sheep- because they couldn't get away. My family lived in the eastern part of the village, so our house didn't burn. No one could do anything to put this fire out because the dust storm and wind was so bad. The fire just went through our village and kept going past, until it burned itself out.

One little girl also died. She was a beautiful little girl around six or seven years old, named Makumba Jagne. When the fire started, she was with her mother and her older brother Musa out in their farm, which was a little ways away from the village. When her mother saw the big black cloud of the dust storm coming from far away, she told the brother, "Take your sister and go to our house, and I will follow you". So they began walking on the road back to the village, but the dust storm arrived just before they entered the village. The boy was holding his sister's hand, but he got confused and her hand slipped away from him. So the little girl went and stood under the verada of a nearby grass hut to try to get out of the wind. No one can see her there, because the dust is so thick. During that time, the fire started on the grass fence, and then started to spread from one hut to the other. Soon it became very intense and reached the place where she was standing. She fell there and was burned to death. When we went there, you could see the mark of her body like a shadow on the ground, as if somebody had poured oil there. That's all that was left. It was very heavy.

The second major fire I saw was four or five years later, and it happened in a similar way, but wasn't so bad. No one lost their life there, and no animals were lost. Other fires will break out in the village from time to time, but 90% of the time it is a small fire and people can put it out quickly, so it will burn only one or two grass huts. When I came to the United States, I used to think about that. Living in Chicago, every day I saw fire trucks going to two or three fires, sometimes more. And many times, people die in those fires, so I will always be wondering, "How can this be?" In Africa, our houses are made out of grass, our fences are grass, and people are cooking with fire all the time, but we don't have so many house fires like this. Also, it's very rare for people in our villlage to die in a fire. In fact, it might be many years in between anything like that happening.

Some traditional villages have a big, wide drum called a tabunlo, with a single head made from a cow's hide. They make a big leather strap handle to carry it, and they play it with a special stick that is shaped like a baseball bat, but not as long. The stick for tabunlo is not made of wood though. It is also made from a cow's hide that is twisted together in a braid and tied. I call tabunlo a "news drum", because it will only be played for special occasions, not for dancing and entertainment. It has a very, very deep bass sound, and people who hear it will be counting the beats because they all have a meaning. The sound carries for a long way, and whole village will hear it. When something is coming to harm the village, such as invaders or war, if a fire breaks out, or any other emergency, they will hit that drum three times very speedy, over and over. That beat means, "There is no time to waste". If a very important person in the village passes away, they will hit that drum six times. On Fridays, they will hit that drum to announce the time to go to the mosque to pray. First they will beat the drum three times slowly, then stop, so that people will know that it's time to go and wash. Around 15 minutes later, they will beat it three more times and stop, so that people know it's time to go to the mosque. To call the people to gather in the bantaba for a regular meeting, five beats are done very slowly. The tabunlo will always be kept at the village mayor's house, because the mayor will always be the first to hear about anything big that everyone else in the village needs to know about. Important messages will always come to the mayor first.

•••••

During my time growing up in Foday Kunda, it might be two years in between seeing any trucks or cars, so we became fascinated whenever one of them came to the village. The dirt road that passed by our village was very full of holes and ruts, so it would have to go very slow. When we would hear the sound of it coming, everybody would come and run to the village square to look at it, adults and kids too. When it was leaving, we would all run and follow it, trying to see who can run fast and grab the back. Then the driver would push on the gas and leave everybody behind. At that time in my village, there were also no bikes, radios, watches and clocks, or record players. Any sound you will hear is a village sound.

I remember when one of my uncles got an alarm clock. When he first got it, the clock was set to go off at six o'clock every evening. I don't know if he set it that way, or if that's how it came, because he could not read or write. Whatever time it said when he got the clock, that's what time it is. Every time it reached six o'clock, the alarm would go off with a loud ring, ring, ring. My uncle made us believe that he was controlling the sound, because he told everybody, "I'm going to tell my clock how many times he can holler. Once I tell him to stop, he cannot pass that!" So every day a few minutes before it was going to ring, he would bring the clock outside and sit on his doorstep, waiting for us all to arrive. Everyone would run and gather at his house, and he would tell us, "Now I'm going to tell it how many times it can holler." When the alarm went off, we boys would count each ring, "1, 2, 3, 4, 5, 6", and then he would say, "Stop! Don't say nothing!" We believed that the alarm clock was hearing him and he was controlling it, because the alarm always rang only six times! Later on, we learned that this is just the way an alarm clock works, but we didn't know that at the time. This uncle was my father's cousin, and we called him Happy Man, because everywhere he went in the village, he was always doing something to make people laugh.

After that, the first time we saw a record player was when a guy whose name is Abdou Cani brought it to our village. It was in the mid or late 1950s. Abdou Cani was a very famous hippo hunter in Gambia, and he could shoot very well. He was in Burma in World War II as part of the West African regiment from the British colonies of Gambia, Sierra Leone, Ghana, and Nigeria. When all those soldiers came back after the war, since Abdou Cani was a hunter, the British even let him keep his rifle. His record player was a gramaphone, and he had only one record. That record was of a griot named Jali Kunye Sako playing the kora, and it was made in Sierra Leone at the home of a very rich Gambian man who made his money in the diamond business.

When Abdou Cani came to Foday Kunda, he wound up the crank on the gramaphone and played that record. The whole village was stunned, because no one had ever seen anything like that. We children were all kneeling down looking at it. All we could see was the round record on top of a little box, a tiny little needle that has a bend like a snake, and a big horn on top. We were hearing the voice and the music, and Jali Kunye Sako saying, "We are the griots playing in the house of Alhaji Abu Sisay, in Freetown". We kids and everybody else in the village were saying, "How can they put somebody in this box and make that person so small?" We were bending down and looking, to see how can that be possible. That gramaphone kept the whole village wondering the whole three days that Abdou Cani was there. We called the record player "machine jallo", which means machine singer, because we didn't have any word in our language for it. Any time we saw western stuff that we didn't know, we made our own name for it. Abdou Cani couldn't explain the gramaphone to us all because he didn't really know how it worked either. Later on in 1971, when I grew up and left the rural areas to come to Brikama, I met the griot Jali Kunye Sako where he was living in Serekunda, and got to know him.

After that, radios started coming to our village. I remember this one radio called a Phillips, which was big like a box. In my village, only one man had it. That man I called Uncle Barasa Camateh, because he was a friend of my uncle. I remember that he could get radio stations from far away in Sierra Leone or Nigeria. Then another thing like that came to our village, called transistor radios. They were a very tiny little box, and came in many colors: white, blue, green, and red. There was only two buttons on this little radio: one to turn it on and off, and one to set the station. The transistor radios maybe came from Europe, and you could even see the things working inside it. And when it started going, there was heavy, heavy static! Ever since that time, I have always been fascinated with any western thing.

I also remember the first time I saw a motorcycle. A British guy who was one of those anthropologists came to my village on a motorcycle. When he came to the bantaba, that was the first time most everyone there saw anything like that. In our village, we also didn't see very many white people at all, which we call toubabs. When that British guy got off the motorcycle and put the kickstand down, it was just standing there alone. Everybody in the whole village came and gathered all around it to look. Later on when he left, I was crying that whole day to my mom, "Tell that guy to bring the putu-putu for me." At that time, we didn't have any name for the motorbike, because it's not our invention. So we just called it by the sound it makes: putu-putu. And when I was crying, my mom called out, "Toubabo, toubabo, bring the putu-putu to my son, bring the putu-putu to Fodaymusa." Anytime my mom said that, I got happy, because I was thinking that the guy will be coming back to bring the motorbike to me, and so I stopped crying. I was thinking, "It's my mom who called him, so he has to come!" But the man had already left. She would even holler, "Bring the bike, bring the bike, my son wants your bike." I would wait a little while, and then I didn't hear any sound of the putu-putu or see that guy. So I started crying again, "Mother, mother, he didn't come." Then my mother would say to me, "I told you, he will come", and then she hollered, "Toubab, I told you to come! Bring the bike!" The whole day it was going on and off like that, until I got tired of crying. After that guy left, I never saw him any more in my village.

But it's funny, many years later when I was living in the United States, I went to San Francisco to play a solo kora concert at a place called Fort Mason. That place was jam-packed with people coming to my concert, and that same British guy happened to be in the crowd. He would always go to any Gambian stuff he heard about, so when he saw that a Gambian kora player was coming to play at Fort Mason, he went. I played the whole concert, and then I announced to the crowd that I would play one last song, and that would be it. I played that last song, and when I finished it, everybody clapped and I said, "OK, good night everybody, thank you for coming". Right then, that guy stood up in the audience and said to me in Mandingo, "Griot, you are not finished playing yet, because you did not play a song called Masaneh Sisay." There were a lot of people in the crowd, and I didn't see him at first, so I said, "Who is talking to me in my language here?" He said, "It's me. My name is Sambujan Sisay. I looked at him and said, "Whoa!" because that is a typical Gambian name and he is a toubab. Masaneh Sisay is a famous kora piece, so I played that song for him. In our tradition, people will come down and put money in the sound hole of the griot's kora while that song is played, or they will put it on the griot's lap. That guy came down to the stage and put his money inside the kora, and then he told the crowd about this tradition. So right away people started coming down to put money in my kora, until it was getting full!

After the concert, he came backstage to visit me. He told me his name was Dr. David Gamble, and he was teaching anthropology at San Francisco State University. The reason he said his name was Sambujan Sisay is that during the time he was in Gambia, that was his Gambian name. The people named him that. Even today, if you ask older people in Gambia, "Do you know any toubab named Sambujan Sisay?" they will say yes. But if you say, "Do you know Dr. David Gamble?" they will say no. He told me that he lived in Gambia for 15 years, and during that time he went to almost every single village in the whole country. When I was talking to him, he was telling me about all the places he went, and I couldn't even believe it. He knew the whole place. He asked me where I lived, and I told him I lived in Chicago. Then he asked when I was going back there, and I told him that I was leaving in two or three days. He told me that he has a Gambian friend there in San Francisco named Kebba Fatty, and said that he would like to send Kebba to pick me at my hotel the next day. I said OK, and the next day Kebba came and took me to Dr. Gamble's house.

When I arrived there, I came in and sat down, and we talked about Gambia some more. He showed me a whole lot of old photographs from Gambia, and handmade movies he took there. I was thinking, "Nothing stays the same in the world. If you showed those pictures to young Gambians today, they wouldn't believe that this is Gambia. They will say no". The people in those movies, compared to the way people dress in Gambia now, it's very different, so they would say, "These are not Gambian people". When Dr. Gamble started telling me about how he traveled from village to village, right away my mind came to think about that first toubab I saw on the putu- putu. So I asked him, "Have you ever been to any village called Foday Kunda?" He said yes, so I asked him, "How did you get there?" When he answered, "I had a motorbike", I said, "Aha. You might be the toubab I saw there when I was a little child". He said, "Yes, that was me", and then he showed me a picture of him on an old green Ducati motorbike. It was a funny looking motorbike, and very different than the ones they have today. In the picture, he was wearing khaki pants and a white t-shirt because it was so hot that day, and not exactly the same clothes he had on when I first saw him in Foday Kunda. But as soon as he showed me that picture, I knew he was that same guy. He said that picture was the only photo he had of himself at that time, to put in any paper. It even used to be posted on the internet with the caption, "Dr. Gamble and his motorbike in Gambia", but now it has been taken down.

After that meeting, me and Sambujan Sisay became good friends. We exchanged phone numbers, and for many years, we would talk on the phone from time to time. We always spoke in the Mandingo language, because he could speak that language very well. When I was talking to him, it was just like I was talking to a Gambian. We talked about the families, the villages, and all about the country. Any time I was in the San Francisco area, I called him and he came to see me. One time I was playing at the University of California at Berkely, and he came there too. And one time around 1983 or 1984, I was in my house in Gambia sitting under the Mango tree with my friends, and Sambujan showed up. When he first got to the town of Brikama, he asked people, "Where is Fodaymusa's house?' and since everybody knows me there, they told him. A boy came with him to show him the way, and Sambujan was dressed in the same kind of way those anthropologists always dress: a khaki shirt and pants, shoes with thick socks pulled way up, pens sticking down in the top of the sock, and a round cloth hat, that we call kasketo. I don't know if it's because it looks like a casket, or what. We just call it that. If you look at the old movies or old pictures of toubabs that are "discovering" Africa, they dress like that. He came there to Gambia for a visit, because he lived there for so many years. He knows the people, the villages, the traditions, and a lot about Gambia. In fact, he is also a Gambian citizen. The government gave him that and a passport too, and he has a Gambian flag in his house. They have an Independence Day celebration in Gambia on February 18th, just like here in America on July 4th, and every year Sambujan Sisay will celebrate that day with a party, and invite all the Gambians there to his house in San Francisco. From that time on, I called his house every few months to check on him and talk to him. Even after I moved to Seattle in 2009, I talked to him. But in 2011 when I called his number, I got a recording that it was disconnected. I was worried, so I went to the internet to check on him, and I saw that he had passed away. All those books he wrote about Gambia, and the old pictures, movies, and his whole archive, he gave it to UCLA. They also have a lot of his writings online at St. Mary's College of Maryland. The way he knows Gambia, I don't think there is any toubab who knows it like him. He knows some special things very well, such as how a kafo works, because he was in a lot of them. Even now, if somebody goes to the internet and searches for Dr. Gamble, they will see so many things there about him.

While I was growing up, the only other time I saw a white person was two or three years after Dr. Gamble first came to our village. I was at the farm of Jali Madi Suso, one of my mother's brothers, in Manjan Kunda. Jali Madi was the firstborn child of Jali Balake Suso, who was the brother of my of my mother's mother, and came with his family to follow Jali

Demba Jobarteh from Dabia, Mali to Manjan Kunda. Westerners would call Jali Balake Suso my mother's uncle and Jali Madi my mother's cousin, but in Mandingo tradition she will call Jali Madi her brother, and I will call him my uncle.

Uncle Madi had a corn farm by the river. Sometimes farmers who are close by the river in that part of Gambia like to grow what is called "last corn", because the wetter area around the river makes it possible to plant and harvest later in the year. We went to his cornfield above the river cliff to pick the corn, and we saw a boat going up the river, not speeding but going strong. That's the only time I saw a big boat like that. It was about 35-40 ft long, with a big round fence around it on top, and inside that little fence there were two toubab boys playing football, which people in the U.S. call soccer. We did not see any other people or the boat driver, just the two boys playing football on top. My uncle had never seen anything like that either. We just stood and looked, and said, "Aha, toubabs." Everything about them was so different: their color, hair, and the shape of their face, and we wondered if they were human beings like us. Whenever white people came into our village, people would go to the mayor's house to announce it, and the whole village would gather in the bantaba to see them. Now when I see white people, it's an everyday thing. But today, when I think about those boys playing football on top of that boat, it's still like I've never seen a white person before in my life. Maybe because I was so young and so fascinated at that time.

When I was a little boy, I also became very fascinated with airplanes. We called them kulungtilla, which means "flying boat", because that's what it looked like to us. Whenever I saw a kulungtilla in the sky, I would just stop no matter where I was, to look at it. Then I would start singing a song I made up, with words that mean, "A big bird is passing, making a wind sound". Also, we have a big bird in Gambia that we call Kunku Duntung, and whenever I saw an airplane I called it by that name too. I would sing, "Kunku Duntung is passing, flapping his wings". The whole song goes like this: "Tambita, Kunku Duntung, tambita, kulanyi, kulanyi. Tambita, Kunku Duntung, tambita, kulanyi, kulanyi." This is just my song, the one I made up as a child. When I was working in the farm with my mom during the rainy season time from June to October, any day I saw an airplane passing overhead, thousands of feet up, I would stop working. Then I would get into heavy dancing and singing this song. I would tell my mother, "When I grow up, this is the thing that will be my transportation". She would take a handful of dirt and throw it at me, telling me, "Stop dreaming, you must be crazy, bend down and let's work! You are wasting time! How can you get inside this crazy thing? You don't even know what it is". That was very true, because we didn't know anything about an airplane. We never saw one on the ground, only just far away in the sky and very small like a finger. We didn't know anybody who had ever seen one close up, and nobody could tell us anything about it or how it works. All we heard was that there can only be one person inside of it, the driver. And this driver has to be laying down on his stomach while he is holding the steering wheel, because there is no room in there for him to sit or stand. That's our theory about the airplane! In fact, you could never convince anybody that even two people could fit inside the airplane, because it's so small. But this fascination was just in my head so strong, and so my tongue and my mouth just said I wanted to be the person inside. I didn't care where I had to go, I would even go to the North Pole as long as I could get inside the flying boat. That's all. I wanted so bad to be up in the air, and it was a very big thing for me. That's why, when I started traveling all over the world, I would talk about my childhood with my mother and she would say, "I almost have to call you a psychic, because you predicted these things about the airplanes, and now it happens".

When I was a child, the only flying thing I did get to see up close was a helicopter. This too happened in the rainy season while I was out in the farm with my mom. The helicopter didn't fly very high off the ground, and when it was going, its nose was kind of pointing towards the ground. When I saw it passing over my village and going in the direction of another village, I threw down the hoe that I was weeding with, and started running towards that village. My mother called after me, "Fodaymusa, Fodaymusa, what's happened? Where are you going?" I didn't even listen to her, I just started running. I think I was about 10 or 12 years old at that time, and I could run very fast. I thought that because its nose was pointing down and it passed our village, that meant the helicopter had to land at the nearby village of Brifu. My goal was to get there before it arrived, and once the helicopter landed, even if the toubabs inside of it wouldn't let me in, I would jump up and grab the legs of the helicopter and hold on so it can't leave me behind. I was thinking that once I grabbed on, even the wind could not blow me off! I was running and running. Brifu was about a mile and a half from my village of Foday Kunda. About halfway there, I met one man and one woman who were traveling on foot. I was breathing hard like crazy, and I asked those people, "Did you see a flying boat passing?" They said, "Yes, we saw it and it's going to land in Brifu." But they didn't know it was going to land, they just made that up. So I took off again like I'm insane, I wanted to see it so bad.

When I got to Brifu, I came to the bantaba where there is a big tree. A few boys I knew were playing under that tree. I was breathing so heavy, because I was running to the death to catch these toubabs and their helicopter before they could leave. The moment I arrived, I asked those boys, "Have you all seen a flying boat come here?" They too fooled me, and said, "A flying boat came and landed, and then one of the toubabs opened the door and looked at us. Then he said that they had landed in the wrong place, so the toubabs closed the door and they took off again". Those boys just made that up, because the helicopter never even landed there! So I came back to Foday Kunda, and my mother said, "See, you wasted your time. You've been gone for a long, long time with this crazy flying boat thing". Even now, I think that one thing about this particular western invention, no matter how many times you see an airplane with your eye, a helicopter is a whole different thing. It doesn't look like anything else, and you can clearly see the people inside. All these years later, I have flown in an airplane thousands of times, but I've still never been inside a helicopter.

•••••

When I was around seven or eight years old, a disease came to all of Gambia, including my village of Foday Kunda. Our word for it is alibala, which means, "the destroyer". One day, there were four girls and one boy just in one family that died from it. Only children from around 5-11 years old died from alibala, not little babies. When this sickness came, nobody knew what to do about it. When you catch it, you could die in just a few hours. In my village, nobody could even cry anymore because of so much crying about the death of so many children. Every day, men were just digging graves all the time, because so many children were dying. Alibala would come into a village, and if it got you, in a few minutes your body will be hot. Your stomach will get a bunch of small bumps on it, kind of white and very small like sand. Then your tongue becomes like it was burned, with whitish bumps on it too. A second way you can get alibala is for your body to become hot, and your tongue gets the small white bumps, but your stomach has bumps only on the inside. If you got the bumps on the outside of your stomach you will live, but if the bumps are only on the inside of your stomach you will die.

When the sickness came all over our areas, they passed a law that nobody should travel. Nobody can leave any village and go to any other village. Every village was so quiet you would think it was just a ruin. In every village, you could hear a pin drop. No one was making any noise, no celebrations, no ceremonies, no nothing. Everywhere you would go, people were just waiting for death. Even with all the traveling stopped, the whole of Gambia and other countries in West Africa were coming down with it anyway. Traditionally, we don't wait for burial like they do in western countries, and in those days of alibala, people went to bury back and forth all day long. Within two weeks, everybody who was going to get it had gotten it, and either died or survived. Only lucky ones will survive it, maybe even only 2% of the people who got it. People didn't want to even talk about what was happening with each other, because there was nothing that could be done. Almost every family lost children, and one other Suso family lost two sons.

My elder sister was a beautiful girl named Nyama, and we two got the sickness the same day. My younger sister Tita and younger brother Dembo were not born yet. I remember that when me and Nyama got up that morning, we had it. Later in the morning, mine got much worse. Then in the middle of the night, mine was calming down a little, but hers got worse about one o'cock in the morning. By seven in the morning that next day, she died. Everybody was running and coming to our compound, thinking it was me who died, because mine was worse that first day. But by that next day, my sickness was getting a lot better and was leaving me. That's why we call alibala the destroyer. This sickness just happened so fast and there was no medicine for it. Even today, we just don't know about it and why it happened. Alibala came back again to our village around five or seven years later, but that time only a few kids died.

In the years after alibala first came to our village, my mother used to take me with her whenever she went to the town of Sutukoba. We would walk there from Foday Kunda, which was around six or seven miles away. In Sutukoba there was a holy man called Alhaji Mba Jaiteh, and his wife Tamaratou was a good friend of my mother. Since my mother is a griot woman, she would travel there to visit and sing for Tamaratou. Also during that time, my mother's elder sister Sendin Jobarteh lived a few miles away in Borro Kanda Kasse, the same village where my mother was born. They were very close, and Sendin's son Mohammed Suso, who was much older than me, also used to come to our compound in Foday Kunda a lot, just to say hello to my mother. Sometimes in the farming season, he would also come to help her in her farm. Many years later, Mohammed lived in Brikama and brought his mother there to live in his family compound, and when I bought my first compound in Brikama, I brought my mother to live there too, so she could be close to her sister.

•••••

During all the time I was growing up, Gambia was always just a farming country. Gambia's chief crop was the peanut, and the peanut companies were really happening in those days. The harvest happens in October and November, and once the farmers harvest their crop, they need to get their peanuts to certain towns by the River Gambia to sell them. Those towns have to be located in areas where the river is very deep, so that big boats can come to the docks there. Each of those towns might have two or three different places for selling your peanuts, and they kind of compete with each other for clients. Besides their buying place in the river town, the boss companies of the peanut buyers have a main office in the Banjul area, and three or four big trucks for picking up peanuts from the farmers. If you are a farmer who has been selling your peanuts to a certain buyer for a while, you just get in touch with them after you have harvested your peanuts, and tell them that your peanuts are ready. The peanut buyers will provide you with big bags to put your peanuts in once you tell them how many bags you need. When they have loaned you the bags, it means you will sell your peanuts only to them, and they will come to pick up your peanuts. The buyer's trucks will cross both sides of the river and pick up the peanuts at the farms that are ready for them. They will be traveling mostly on the roads, but sometimes they will also just drive where there is just some open space to get to the farms.

Let's say that, my brothers and me, and our wives, all have big bags full of peanuts. Each bag is filled with around 100 lbs., and looks almost like a big barrel. We might have 40 or 50 bags of peanuts from our farm. When we contact the buyer to come and get our peanuts, they will also ask us to tell all the other people in our village that they are coming. When they come, they will load our peanut bags first, and then go to the other families who have their peanuts ready too. The driver will always come with his apprentice, and we will throw the peanut bags up to the apprentice because he knows how to pack them all in the back of the truck. The truck will be so full, and the bags will even be stacked higher than the sides, so they will have long ropes to tie all the bags down. That time will be a big festivity for you and your family. All the men, brothers, sons, wives, even the kids, will climb up on the truck and sit on those bags to go to the place for selling. Sometimes we would get there late in the day, and have to stay in the town overnight until the selling place opened the next day. When you get to that place, there is a big round thing that they put the peanuts in to clean them. They roll that thing so that all the dirt, little stones, leaves, and stems come off. Then after the peanuts are clean, the peanut buyers put them back in the bags again, and weigh them on a big balance. Then they will pay us. Also, there are a bunch of men standing there, waiting to carry the bags. They are laborer workers, and they will put a peanut bag on their head and carry it inside a big fence, open the bag, and pour it on the ground. Over and over they do this, until a month or two later, the peanuts are so high that they look like a mountain.

Once you are paid, it's the time to go and do a little shopping for families back home. Sometimes people will buy some new clothes or some cloth for sewing, some bread, shoes, presents, or other special things. Then we will tell the truck driver to take us back to our village. A lot of children like to go to the trading post because once your parents get the money from their peanuts, you like for them to buy you some pound cake. Our pound cake is a round thing, and we call it panketo. I'm laughing now because at the time in my village of Foday Kunda, a man lived near us who was going to sell his peanuts in a nearby town called Koina, and his little girl wanted to come. But he said, "No you cannot come, you stay here", and then he left. The girl was crying so loud, and we could all hear her. I teased her, "Your father will be eating all the sweet stuff and you won't get any". That made her cry more. She stood in one spot saying "Ba, Ba, wait for me". Then I said, "Right about now, your dad is putting the sweet cake in his mouth", or "Koina is going to be sweet today", and stuff like that, and she cried even more. Now she is a grown woman, and I saw her in Serekunda a few years ago and teased her by saying, "You're not going to Koina", and she said, "Get away from me! You, Fodaymusa, you are no good!"

By the time the peanut-selling season ends, you can see the peanut mountains from way far away. Then the big boats would come to the river town. They were long and hollow, with a big place to fill with the peanuts. There is nothing fancy on those boats. The laborer workers load the peanuts back into bags, and fill the ships. Then the ships begin their travel back to the Banjul area. Some of those peanut mountains were so big that it took two or three trips with a big boat to carry them all! Once the boats brought all the peanuts to Banjul, some of the peanuts would be loaded onto other big ships to be taken to some western countries. Also, there is a big factory in a place called Saaro, near Banjul, where they press the peanuts to get the oil out of them. They sell it for cooking in Gambia, and sell it all around the world. Anytime you get near Saaro, you can smell the peanut oil in the air. After they press the peanuts, the leftover part is what we call peanut powder, and a lot of different things are made out of that powder at the factory too. Farmers in Gambia live on peanuts too. They also roast the peanuts to eat, and the women in the villages will press their own peanut oil by pounding the peanuts until it comes out. Then the women will take the leftover peanut powder and cook it down to make a kind of washing soap out of it. That soap is not made as a commercial product at the factory, but all the village women know what it is and how to make it.

Peanuts were the cash crop of all of Gambia at that time, but now the peanut farming has decreased a lot. Things changed because other countries are not demanding the peanuts the way they use to. People tell me that, in a way, the peanut industry is falling apart. They don't have the big trading posts in the river towns anymore. That's hard for the farmers, who have depended on this for so many years. The government is now encouraging the farmers to plant more other crops that can become a source of money. Millet, peanuts, and rice have always been the main things for the farmers to grow for themselves and to sell, and there are four kinds of millet we grow. Each one tastes different. A lot of people are now turning to farming Cashew Trees too. When I was growing up, we didn't even eat the cashew nuts. We harvested the fruit from the tree to eat, and threw away the nut. There are also a whole lot of vegetables and fruits being grown in big amounts now: tomatoes, sweet, potatoes, yams, bananas, oranges, and many others.

HARDHEADED LEADER OF THE BOYS

In my childhood time, I was hardheaded. I was very, very hardheaded, especially in the way of an African village. In the village, if you are a young boy, it's very important to be brave, to fight, and to stand up for yourself. Otherwise, other boys can look down on you. Boys in the village are left to themselves, and parents don't intervene in between them. If you are beaten, you just cry, but you don't run to parents to have them sue the other parents. Unless it is a big, big thing, parents don't get involved. Boys will physically fight each other, but there are no guns or knives. If your child is beat today, they will beat somebody else tomorrow. This is just the life of the young boys in the village, and then when you grow up, you grow out of that.

Also in my childhood time, I was always the leader. Every day, all the village boys would gather in front of my mother's hut, even before I got up. Then we all went to the batanba together, and I would tell them to go sit 30-40 yards away from me, under a big tree. One by one, I called the boys that I wanted to play with, to come to me. The boys I did not call had to stay behind, and I would say "Tetuluna" to them, which means, "not to play". Then those boys would run back to their compound, crying to their moms. Mothers would bring their sons by the hand to come back and beg me, "Please play with him, he's your brother and friend". I would say, "Yeah, yeah, yeah", but as soon as the moms left, I told those boys, "If you follow us, we will beat hell out of you. You cannot play with us". This went on, back and forth with the moms and kids. I also might say to them: "If you want to come play with us, you must bring a penny". If they brought the penny, then I would let them play. The boys I always picked to play with me were brave boys. I liked the boys who said "Yes" whenever I told them what we were going to do. I didn't like anybody who was scared, so I wouldn't pick them.

In that time, to show the village that you are a strong man to everyone, there are certain things you need to do: Be a good wrestler, be brave to go to the bush to hunt, be ready to fight when challenged without being scared, be good at bringing honey home, digging wild yams and other foods to eat, not to be scared of the night, be a good fisherman, carry a heavy load from bush to the house, and be a hard worker, not lazy. Now there are very few people that follow these things. Many things they cannot do. In my childhood group, all my friends knew that to hang with Fodaymusa, you must be into these things. Boys who aren't into this wouldn't even try to hang with me.

Our village of Foday Kunda is about a mile and a half from another village called Brifu, and from Foday Kunda you can see Brifu in the distance because it is a bigger village. In between the two villages there is one big Wolo Tree, with a lot of leaves and a lot of sand underneath it. When I was 11 to 13 years old, boys from my village and boys from Brifu would meet under this big tree and wrestle each other. We always met after lunch, and only during the dry season. During the rainy season from June to October, all the families have a busy farming time, but in the dry season from November to April, most of the work is fixing fences, roofs, and cutting wood. So during that time, kids are free to do what they want, so that is when we do the wrestling. Before we decided on the day to meet, we sent messages to each other. When we Foday Kunda boys came to the bantaba and met under the big tree in the morning, I would say, "Today we are going to wrestle the Brifu boys". Then a messenger would go to Brifu with the news.

In Foday Kunda, I was the champion wrestler and leader among my guys. In Brifu, the champion wrestler was Solo Wally. Me and Solo are very good friends also. Solo passed away a few years ago in Serekunda, but before that, any time I was in Gambia over the past 15-20 years, he would come to my house to see me and talk about this wrestling. Then we would jump up to grab each other like we will wrestle again!

Whenever we Foday Kunda boys all started walking to Brifu, we brought a cart that we made. The top was made out of planks, and underneath it had a long pole, around one inch in diameter, with a calabash on each end like wheels. There was a long rope attached to the front of the cart, pulled by the other boys. I rode on the cart, because I was the champion! The boys pulled me all the way to Brifu, but we always had to stop many times along the way to fix it because the calabash kept coming off the pole. The Brifu boys also made a cart like this, and pulled their champion too. We didn't see each other until we all met under the big Wolo Tree. When we all arrived there, the Brifu boys would sit on one side and we Foday Kunda boys sat on the other side. Since Brifu is bigger, more boys always came from Brifu than from Foday Kunda.

Traditional wrestling always has drummers, and a special song called, The Wrestling Song. The boys from Foday Kunda made 3 small drums out of tin cans, and the boys from Brifu made them too, to imitate the traditional Mandingo drums called kutiros. Once we all sat down, the drummers would start playing hard. Automatically, it was known that me and Solo would wrestle, but that didn't happen until after all the other boys wrestled each other. First, me and Solo choose which boys from our side will wrestle, and we tell them to go to the ring. They must first dance around in the ring, then they must look at each other and give a sign with their arms out straight, which means they are now ready to wrestle. Then they go back to their side to get ready. We wore a wrestling belt made from woven cloth around our waist to hold our pants close to the body, so there was nothing to grab. Soon everybody was very excited and cheering. All were thinking about strength and braveness, and how to wrestle. Those two people chosen will wrestle once or twice, and then sit down. Then I would call a new person and Solo would call a new person to get up to fight. The main rule is, beat the guy on the ground!

When I was growing up, my other favorite things were to go to the bush to pull wild honey, dig wild yams, and gather fruits. We have a fruit called kunjeh that looks like a small pear and tastes sweet. We also have a fruit we call bembo, which is smaller than a grape and also very sweet, and grows on a vine. The fruit called kutifingo or simbong grows on a tree, and it is round and bigger than a grape, with a big seed inside too that we don't eat. There are many other wild fruits too. So very many! During the end of the rainy season time in October and November, we will also have wild pumpkins behind every house in the village, along with calabash. They are very sweet pumpkins. So at night, while everybody is sleeping, we boys would be clunking around the cooking pots, picking pumpkins and steaming them to eat. We did this with corn, during the corn harvesting time too. No one gave us a bad time, because the adults knew that they were like that one day too! I also did a lot of hunting with the other boys, using a slingshot. We shot pigeons and doves, but if we didn't get one, we might shoot somebody's chicken at night after they went home to their compound.

Once there was a man in the village who had a big rooster. We boys came back from hunting on a day when we didn't get anything, and we saw the rooster under a big Mango tree. I had a slingshot, and hit the rooster on his comb and killed it. Then I divided the boys, saying, "You go get salt, you go get a match", etc. Outside our village, there is a big rocky hill, and we had a place there where we would cook the things we raided. There was a big giant rock there too, shaped like a lounge chair, and behind it was a big hole so deep you could die if you fell in. I leaned back on that rock like a king with my throne, ordering all the boys.

At that time of year, the grasses were very tall and dry. The guy who owned the rooster knew about that place on the big, rocky hill, because he went there as a child too. He made a whip rope out of some grasses to take with him to catch us. The other boys were making noise in the dry grass gathering things, and the guy was tip-toing so nobody could hear him, and I was leaning on the rock so I didn't see him. Then one of my guys saw the man and yelled, "Karang Kutubo is here", which means Teacher Kutubo, because he was the Imam of the village. The man raised his hand and tried to beat me around my chest with the whip. I was just lucky because I heard the boy yell, and leaned forward and jumped off the rock right before the guy could strike me. Everybody ran and scattered, and left everything behind. The guy's son was part of my group, and he was there too, but the guy followed me because he knew I was the leader and that it was my idea to kill the rooster. I looked back to see him flying behind me. I could run fast, just like air, and so if I get one foot in front of you I cannot be caught! I flew fast, and I looked back to see him stopped and standing. Then he went back home and visited my mom. He said, "I want you to advise Fodaymusa, because he and his guys killed my rooster. If I catch him, I will beat hell out of him." My mom is not a quiet person, and if she says, "Do it", you will do it with no wicky-wacky thing going on. My mom replied to Karang Kutubo, "I wish you would get him. If you get him, I will be happy, because there is no advising in the world that I have not done already. So try to catch him, and from now on, whatever he does, just beat hell out of him, I am fine with that".

Another time during the dry season in February or March, the mangos were ripening but still green. We boys picked them from a Mango tree on the roadside, a little ways outside the village, and we chewed them even though they were sour. One day I told the boys, "Let's go cut fruit from that tree again." When we got there, I climbed the tree because I am very good at climbing, and I cut the mangos to drop down to my guys to eat. Alhaji Jagne was the owner of the Mango tree, and a man named Landing was his guest, but Landing had been there so long he was part of the family. Landing only had one eye, but he saw us go over there, and came to check on the tree. He heard the boys under the tree before they saw him coming. When the boys saw him, they said, "Oh, Landing is here!" and ran away to stand under a big Baobab tree. But I was way up in the tree. Landing looked up with his one eye, and I looked down on him. He said, "OK, come down, I will kill you good. Today, Foday Kunda will be free from your troubles, because today you will die. Today will be the last day anybody will see you alive. Everything has an end." I told him that I was coming down. He said, "Good. I know today I am lucky. I will just wait for you to come down and then kill you, and I don't have to run after you." He picked up a giant mud rock and said, "Just come, you come down, I kill you and it's finished. I am glad I am standing under you here." I said, "OK, OK, I am coming down." Then I came down all the way to a main branch junction, and said, "Get away from the trunk, and I will come down. " He said, "Just come down, and today will be the last of you." I tried to go on other branches, but any branch I went to, he ran and got under it. Then I went back and forth, running from one branch to another while he chased me. I finally jumped down, lifting my hands and arms, and I could feel that big mud rock brush under my armpit as it passed by when he threw it. Then I ran like hell and he couldn't catch me!

Another thing I did, since I was the hardheaded leader of the boys, is to climb far up a tree that had a lot of leaves. Then I would tell the boys to take an axe to cut the tree under me. When they chopped it, I rode the tree down! The tree must have a lot of leaves, and you have to climb to the opposite side of where they are cutting, so when it falls down you don't go on your back. The leaves will cushion the tree when it hits the ground, and it even bounces up from the ground, so you get to fly up again. Very sweet stuff!

BECOMING A MAN

The second big celebration time in a person's life is when a boy becomes a man, or a girl becomes a woman. In my time growing up, there was a celebration for boys just before they go to the circumcision ceremony, and another celebration when they came back. Traditional circumcision happened for boys when they were 10 to 13 years old, but could be done even up to when they were 18, and once someone had gone through the circumcision ceremony, they were called men even if they were still one of those young ages. Those who had not been circumcised yet were called boys. That is why some people also call this tradition manhood training. Our circumcisions were not done by a doctor in a hospital, though. They were done by an older man called a numo, because he comes from a numoli, which means blacksmith family. Since not every village had a numo, and there might only be one in the whole area, families in all the villages would send the numo a message one or two months in advance of the date that they wanted their boys to be circumcised. Nowadays, circumcision typically happens earlier in life, and some people even do it in a hospital when the child is a new baby. My two sons did not go through it the way I did, but I have heard that in some of the rural areas they are trying to bring back the traditional way.

In my childhood time, there were many preparations for the family to do before the circumcision and manhood training could happen. Every family who had a boy must prepare by putting together rice, peanuts, and other food, which could take one to three years to do. These families had to make sure there was a whole lot of food ready when the boys came back from the manhood training, because it is a big, big celebration for the whole village, with relatives from other villages coming to attend also. All the families will prepare for all of this the same way, whether they are from a trader family or griot family, or whatever, and boys from all families are equal in how the circumcision and manhood training is done.

Traditionally, the circumcision date will be on a Saturday. In the two or three days before the ceremony, relatives of the boys will arrive in the village, and on Friday, there will be a big gathering in the village. By that time, all boys that are to be circumcised will be dressed in a special way. Women will take a white cloth and dye it with the bark from a tree to make it a yellow color, and then hang it up to dry. Then that yellow cloth will be wrapped around the boys and worn with a long sleeveless robe, so that everyone who sees them will know. Sometimes each family will also tie some beads around their boy's neck, or give them some other special thing to wear. Then all of the boys go to the house of one older man from the village, that is the leader for watching over all the boys who are to be circumcised. In eastern Gambia, this leader is called seema, and in western Gambia he is called ansimba. A lot of Mandingo words are like that, different in east and west. Families will bring traditional bamboo mats to lie on the ground in the middle of the seema's compound for all the boys to sit. There might be only four boys or there might be a crowd of 40 boys there, depending on the size of the village. Everybody knows that tomorrow will be the circumcision day.

After dinner, the dancing and drumming will begin in the bantaba, and last that whole night. Women can dance too, but the boys will be the main dancers. It's a kind of dancing called barungo, which means strong dance. All the young men and older men who have already been circumcised are there too, and the uncircumcised boys are the ones dancing the barungo. They do the dance to show all the people, "I am very, very strong, and I can dance all night long, and I am not afraid of being circumcised".

Every village will have one big tree way around a half-mile away from the village, that we call the Waana Tree, where the circumcisions will take place. Waana means "the place where the new men will be". Some people call this place jujuo. Traditionally, it is a very heavy secret place. In the very early morning, the numo will go behind the village with the crowd of elder men, and then they will all walk to that place to wait for the boys.

While that's happening, the crowd is still drumming and dancing and the bantaba is jam-packed. The people will have become one big giant round crowd, and the drummers are drumming and circling around them all. Then the strong young men will run up to the boys who are to be circumcised, and do what we call chamfuro. All of a sudden they will pick somebody up, sit him up on their shoulders to carry him, and start running into the bush towards the secret place. One by one, they are picking up the boys, picking up the boys, until all have been taken. Some of the boys are 16 or 17 years old, and very big and grown. Those are big boys! They don't have to ride on anybody's shoulders, but they have to walk and dance all the way to the secret place, with the music and all the dancers and drummers behind them.

No women can be there in that circumcising place, though. When they pick up your son and carry him away, you can only go to a certain point, which is around halfway to the secret place. You can't follow them past that point, no way.

•••••

When you get to the secret place, the numo is there and his knife is ready. No numbing is given, you just come and they circumcise you. But traditionally, older boys will have something to do to the numo to show him that they are not scared. Those boys will chew a lot of kola nuts in their mouth, grinding them up very, very small, but they don't swallow it. When they come to the numo and he circumcises them, they spray that stuff right into his face! This is to show him that they are a brave man now. They will even hold up their little finger and point it to him, to show that they are not afraid and they are not going to run, even if he cuts them on their finger or on another part of their body. But the numo doesn't cut them in any other place, it's just our tradition.

In that secret place, there will also be young men who are carrying a traditional, black powder gun, and every time a boy is circumcised, they will fire that gun, boom! So if you are in the village, you will know how many boys have been circumcised by counting the number of times they fire the gun, and you can hear it even though they are way deep in the bush. Once we boys were circumcised, the men would dress our wound in a certain leaf from our area. These leaves are ground up, and they put them on the wound and tie it there. It hurts, but you gotta be strong, because in that time, everything is about being strong. I was 12 years old, and for me, I didn't care about it because I was a hardheaded boy. I'm talking about it now because I am writing this book, but otherwise from 1962 until today, I never discussed this with a woman because in our tradition, this is something that is a secret society with men and kept secret from women. Even your mom, you don't tell her. If she would ever ask you about it, you can't just tell her "No", but you can just say, "Oh I am busy and I gotta go now".

After the circumcision is done in the morning, a group of men will work together to build a big grass fence in a circle around the big Waana Tree. Sometimes they will cover the top of the fence with a grass roof, but sometimes there is no roof. Inside the grass fence is where the new men will be living day and night for two or three months, especially in long ago times if the crowd of boys is very big. It's not because it takes that long for your wound to be cured, it's because in this waana place, you will all be learning how to be a man. To be there all the way to three months is so there is enough time for the older men to teach us all how to be a man.

In the waana, there will be little seats made out of a termite mound. In my village area, we have very big termite mounds, but also small ones, and you can shape the small ones with an axe to be like a little stool. That is where we sit when the men dress our wounds every morning and evening, a few feet away from the Waana Tree, until we become well. Everybody will be sitting on one of those mounds when they are dressing our wounds. They first wash and clean our wound, and then put the traditional medicines on it. Some kids don't even care, and some kids can get scared and maybe even holler a lot. This is why you will hear drumming sounds coming from the waana every morning and evening, to cover up that hollering.

During this time, all the men in the village who are around 30 or 40 years old will go and stay in the waana too. Even if they spend the day doing work in the village, they will always come back to the waana the moment the sun is going down, and they will sleep there too. Even if you don't have a son in the waana, you have to be there. All the young men in the village who have already been circumcised but are not married yet, will live all day in the waana with the new men. They are not going to go back to the village to sleep either, because they are the guardians of this group of new men. They have to accompany everything the new men will do, even to go out into the bush to pee. These young men also are the ones who go to pick up the food from the women of the village. Every day, the family of every boy who is there in the waana has to bring food three times, for breakfast, lunch, and dinner. Women will cook the food and put it in a big calabash to carry on their head, and come out of the village to that certain point, around halfway between the village and the waana. It's too far away from the waana for any of them to see and recognize their own son, though. Whenever the guardians see the women coming with the food, they always make all the young men come inside the waana, because they don't want any of them to see their mother or for their mothers to see them. At that halfway place, the women all take their calabashes off and set them on the ground, and then go back home to the village. Then the guardians will go to that place to pick up the food and take it back to the waana for the boys.

When we are out there in the waana, sometimes some boys' moms will cook some extra good food, but they cannot cook enough for everybody and they want their son to be eating the food they made. That is because of the mother's love for their child. The moms cannot go to the waana themselves, so they will get in touch with their own son's guardian to make arrangements. Then the mom will put their food in a special calabash, or tie it with a hankerchief, and the guardian will come to the village to get it. Then the guardian will hide it in the woods or some other place in the bush. When it's time for everybody to eat in the waana and all the food is brought there, the guardian will give a secret sign to the boy, and the boy will say, "I need to go in the bush, I have to use the toilet". Then the guardian will take the son to find the place that their mom's food is hidden, because the guardian has to go everywhere with the boy they are in charge of. When they get to that place, they will sit down and eat their mom's food, then hide the empty calabash there. But they can't come back to the waana with food or oil on their mouth, so they take dirt and rub it on their lips before they go back so their mouth looks the same as when they left. Some time later that night, the guardian will go back to the hiding place and get that empty calabash and cloth, and take it back to the mom in the village.

The whole time we are in the waana, we sleep on grass mats that were made for us, and we put them down side-by-side on the ground, jam-packed. The men only want you to sleep on your back, so you don't roll over on your stomach while your wound is healing. Also, so that when your wound heals, your private parts hang straight down and don't lean to one side. Once a lot of the boys are getting well, small groups of five to seven of them, with two or three guardians, will go dog hunting, which we call wulu deemo. They will bring our hunting dogs there from the village, and every day after breakfast, we will go hunting. When there are a lot of boys in the waana, each of the small groups leaves and goes a different way to hunt, one group at a time. Some groups will hunt deer, some rabbits, and some other animals. We try to come home just a little after two in the afternoon, and then it's time for lunch. All the calabashes will be full from our moms' cooking when we arrive, but we all wait until every group is back in the waana before any of us can eat. We clean all the animals, and then those are cooked for our dinner. And every other thing that we need to learn about going out into the bush, we will learn there.

•••••

During this time also, the men's secret society will make something that is a masked dancer called Kankuran. In our tradition, we believe that the Kankuran are the protectors, to protect the boys in the waana from evil spirits or from bad, evil people. There are three different Kankuran: one is called Kankuran Wulen, which means red, because its outfit is made from the bark of the Faara tree. Men will go to the bush with a piece of wood almost like a club, and they will beat the Faara tree for a long time to get the black bark out of it, so they can get the red bark underneath. Then they pull that red bark off, and put it on the Kankuran Wulen to cover his whole body. There is also the Bassang Kankuran, which means mixed, because this Kankuran's outfit is the red bark of the Faara tree from his head to his waist, mixed with the leaves of the Jallo tree from the waist to the knees. And there is the Jamba Kankuran, which means leaves, and his whole outfit is made from leaves of the Jallo tree or from the Kulukulo tree, covering his whole body.

In our tradition, Kankuran Wulen is the very serious one. Women are not even allowed to see it. If a younger woman sees the Kankuran Wulen, they might not be able to produce a child because of the power it has. The Bassang Kankuran and Jamba Kankuran are mostly about entertainment, singing, and dancing. When they make Kankuran Wulen, it is also to drive evil spirits out of the village. While the boys are out in the waana, it is our belief that this is a time when some things can go wrong. Some people might try to use their evil stuff to harm the kids, and the Kankuran Wulen knows this. So on the day that the Kankuran Wulen will come to the village, there will be an announcer who goes down every street about three or four hours before they come, saying. "All women in this village, if you are cooking the food today, you should try to get your cooking done early because the Kankuran Wulen are coming. Before they come, we want everyone to finish. Kankurans are coming today". So the village women will all finish their cooking earlier, and take all the food out to the bush for the boys in the waana. The whole time this is going on, the boys will all still be out in the waana with their guardians. They don't come to the village until much later, when it's time to come back as a new man.

On that day, there will be older men who have already gone to the bush to make the Kankuran Wulen. In traditional areas, only older men make the Kankuran Wulen, not the young men. Those older men might make four or five, or even seven of them. Also, you have to have some kind of spiritual powers to be the Kankuran Wulen, and you have to know more than many people. You can't be just a regular guy in the village. Because the things these Kankurans do, the miracle things, are unbelievable. Once the Kankurans are made, in the afternoon they will come to the village. In every single house, people will go inside the grass huts and lock the doors. Women always go inside with all the little kids, but some men will go inside too, if they didn't already go through a special ceremony called sondiro, which means, "To show you something about the Kankuran". Even if you are a grown man, if you haven't gone through the sondiro, you can't be outside. You have to go inside the house. Sondiro is a symbol language that the Kankuran will ask you without talking. He will make marks on the ground, and make another sign or movement, and you have to answer it by making signs too. If you never went through sondiro, then don't go outside. The whole village is quiet because everyone is inside with the doors locked. Kankurans will each go into their own street, carrying a cutlass in each hand, with two or three men following them. Those men are called Kankuran Joobo. The Kankuran run really fast, and if you are one of the Kankuran Joobo, you gotta keep up because otherwise the Kankuran will come back and beat hell out of you. Anything they do, they want you to do. But it is very difficult, and it gets to the point where you don't think they are even regular human beings. They all have some kind of power that is not like a regular human being.

Once all the Kankurans are in each of their streets, drummers will come to the center of the village and pull their drums very tight together. They don't talk, they don't touch, or nothing. While everything is quiet like a ghost town, the drummers come up and all hit the drums together at one time, with a speeding beat. The Kankurans are hollering on every street, "Kill all of them, cut all of them into pieces!" and the Kankuran Joobo following them are hollering too. The Kankuran are running and hitting the cutlasses on everything as they pass by, pow, pow, pow! They will stick one of their cutlasses into the ground, and then jump on the handle and dance on it. You know that the Kankuran could fly and jump on the roof of somebody's hut, and that's not going to be a joke. The whole village feels like the world is coming to an end, and it's very scary. When the Kankuran come, they don't stay a long time. They come and do their thing, and then leave after only 35-40 minutes. But that's enough time. I remember it when I was a small boy, being inside the hut with my mom when they were doing this. This is the part no woman will see, and nobody will explain that to a woman. Except here I am, explaining it to you. It is called kewulo, the men's secret society. When I was a young man, I was the Kankuran Joobo too. But even when it is somebody you know who they make into Kankuran Wulen, by the time they finish making him, you will be very scared right there. They tie the person down and make them into Kankuran Wulen, and the whole thing changes the inside of him, and so you will be scared. Today, you won't see this kind of thing though.

While we are in the waana, we also have to learn the correct way to talk to our mom and our dad. When you come home to your village as a new man, you will never sit in your mother's bed again, and you will never sit in your father's bed. In the morning when you get up from your own bed in your room, you have to come and say hello to your father and your mother. You learn that when you go into someone's house, especially people who are older than you, take off your shoes. When you are in a place where everybody is sitting and you are sitting there too, if somebody comes in the room that is older than you, you stand up and they sit down. Anybody who is older than you can also send you to go and do things for them. They can say, "Let me send you to the market to buy this thing for me", or "Go and do this or that for me." The person doesn't even have to know you. You will never say, "No I'm not your son or daughter." The only thing you have to see is that the person is older than you. Look at them, and then you will see. They can come into your village from anywhere, and stand in the village square and say to you, "Young man, come, I want you to go do this for me." And you go, with no question to them like, "Who are you and what's your name?" Nothing like that. You have to go and do for them, and you will do those things without any payment.

If you are a hardheaded boy who is crazy, wait until you go to the waana, you will be fixed. No matter how you are when you go in, you will be cool when you come out. When you finally do go home as a new man, everyone will be surprised and see that you have changed, because of the way the elder men deal with all of us. It's a heavy discipline about how to talk, how to look at the people who are your elders, and more. It's so heavy that even if your father is sitting there watching, he won't say a word. If the elder men say, "Do this", that's what you do. If they knock on your head, your father might move away, or turn his back and start talking to somebody else, because he doesn't want to see it, but he won't say a word. He knows that he went through that too. You can't say, "My father is here, so I can depend on that", because he won't even look at your face whether he likes it or not. He might even go back to the village if it gets really heavy.

They will hit you too, if you need to learn. So you learn very quickly about how to talk, how to be respectful, and how to share. When they bring the food, everybody will share it. There are always a lot of people sitting around each of the big calabashes, but no chairs. Everybody is sitting on the ground or kneeling. You have to hold the edge of the bowl with your left hand, and take a little bit of food with your right hand, but there is no looking around a lot while you are eating. And when you are finished, you can't jump up and say, "Now I am full". You just say the Mandingo words that mean, "My hand is bitter". That lets other people know that you are finished, but you must still stay there at the calabash until everyone else is finished too. People eat in that way, and then the guardians return the bowls to the village so the women can use them for the next food. You also have to learn the correct way to get ready to eat. When they bring the food to the waana, if you see something that you want to eat, don't say a word. Just go to that area and sit down or stand, but don't jump and say, "That's what I want". If you say that, they will say, "OK", and then they will take a handful of dirt and throw it in with the food, mix it up and say to you, "Now you can eat it". That food and dirt is not going to kill you, but that's what you will have to eat. If you stop eating and say you are full, they will say, "No you have to eat it all, because you said this is what you want."

The elder men want everybody to act correct. If even one boy does some crazy thing, they beat everybody. So sometimes you will tell that boy who acted crazy, "When we get out of here, I will kill you!" because he made them beat hell out of everybody. I remember one boy who was so hardheaded, and he made everybody get beat a lot. Every few days he did something crazy, so we all got beat. I told him, "When we get out of this place, I'll be the first one to kill you." We all told him that. They used special sticks to beat us, called marango. As soon as we get there to the waana, the guardians will start cutting the wood and carving it to make those sticks. They make two sticks for every boy, and we see them. Marango are two round sticks about one foot long, and the way they beat you with them is to lay one stick on top of you and then hit that stick with the other one. The places they will do this are your shinbone, your head, and your back. You go crazy when that happens, because it hurts so much. Sometimes they don't beat everybody right away when one boy is acting crazy. They might wait until three in the morning, to surprise you. They will tell the drummers, "Get up and play", and the drummers will start playing a fast rhythm like they do when the Kankuran Wulen is coming. Sometimes there is even already a Kankuran that has been made and hidden away. They tell all of us, "Bend down on the ground!" and while everybody is lying there face down, the Kankuran will start running on top of our backs, back and forth. Sometimes they even take cold water and pour it on us. It's a heavy discipline thing when somebody does something crazy.

Now comes the sweet part. Every evening, just a little bit after eating dinner, and every day early in the morning before breakfast, it's the singing time. The songs are about Mandingo proverbs that mean something about being a man, and all about life. All the men who have been through it already know all of these songs, and they teach us their meaning. At the beginning of the singing time, everybody stands up around the Waana Tree, and we start greeting the tree, singing, "Good evening tree, parent tree, we greet you for hosting us". Then a grown man will start singing, and we new men will all respond to answer. We also all will tap our marangos together with a steady beat while we sing. All of the songs mean something, and they happen every evening and every morning that we are at the waana, so we know them all very well. I don't know if this thing still happens out in the rural areas, but it was a heavy, heavy thing when I was growing up. It is a very sweet time that no new man will ever forget.

All the time we are in the waana, we new men are all together, no matter which family we come from. And no one will take a shower or bath until after our wounds are healed, which can take one or two months after circumcision. Once all of us are healed, they will take us to a river or pond for bulukuo, which means, "This is the day they are going to wash". If there is no river or pond close by, our guardians can go and get a whole lot of water from the village well. Then after that, every Saturday we will wash. But while you are in the waana, you don't ever think, "I won't touch this or that while I am out in the bush, because I don't want to have it on my hand when I eat". You are grabbing everything. There is nothing wrong with the dirt, no chemical on it, nothing. During that time, your body will develop a shininess on it like silver, because of the dirt. Sometimes toubab people will say, "Dirt will kill you", but that's not true. Natural dirt, you can eat it and nothing bad will happen to you.

●●●●●

After we do everything we need to do to become a man, the time will come to leave the waana. The day we leave is usually on a Saturday. That day is called ansimbo, which means "new men coming home", and there is a big celebration, with cooking the whole day. Families will kill a goat or a sheep or cow, and there will be a big feast. In the morning that day, we are all washed clean. Before all of us new men come back to the village, our parents will have sewn us a special new shirt and pants, and the guardians will bring it to the waana for us to put on. We all walk together back to the village, with drummers playing and walking behind us, and the guardians dancing around us. Anybody who sees us will know that we have just come from the waana by the way we are dressed, what we are carrying, and even by what our faces will look like. After all the new men come out of the waana, the elder men will destroy it. They will put everything together that is supposed to come to the village, and bring that back. Everything that is supposed to stay behind, they will leave there. They will take down the fence and everything else, and when they are finished, only the Waana Tree is left there.

When we get to the village, we all go to the bantaba and gather in a big circle. Each new man will go to the center of the circle and dance in front of everybody, one by one. It's a special dance that we learn while we are in the waana, called ansindong, which means "new men's dance". There are two different dance pieces we have to learn: kingo and sampintango. They are very different from each other. To dance the kingo, you have to criss-cross your legs back and forth, with the left one in front of the right, and then the right one in front of the left. To dance the sampintango is to jump and turn your whole body one way, and then jump and turn around to face the other way again. While you are dancing, you hold a special stick that is decorated, and painted blue, black, and white, with something on the head of the stick that we call kotoro.

While you are doing those dances, all the people in the village are there, all the families and even some people from other villages. They are all there gathered around under the big tree in the bantaba, watching the new men dance one after the other. Even if you cannot dance well, you have to jump in the circle and do a little bit. As soon as you jump in, your family members will start giving you money. Then you will leap out and another boy leaps in. The money they give you, you will hand it to your guardian who was there with you in the waana. He will hold all the money. Then the celebration is over, and the seema will lead all the new men to go to every single boy's house, one by one. The whole crowd will go too, and at each house the seema will say, "Now I bring your new man back", and then the new man's parents and relatives will give the seema a gift to tell him, "Thank you for taking care of our son for all that time". After that, each new man will stay at his family compound.

When all the new men come home to the village, they will also have a week or two when they are special, hanging out all over the village and eating at each other's houses. Everybody is looking up to them now and saying, "Now we have new men, our new men are here", and it's a happy time. Once you have come back from the waana, you are considered to be a man now, and to live in the society with everybody else until you get to the age to become married.

Women have their own traditional thing, and I don't know much about that. What I do know is, there might be 10 or 15 girls together who go to a special place for this. They too have a woman seema who watches over them, takes care of them, and heals them. They will stay in one grass hut in the seema's compound inside the village. I think it might only be for a few weeks, though. When the new women come home, there is a big celebration for them too. While they are in their special place, no man or boy is allowed there, and if a man made a mistake and tried to open the door to come inside, he would pay the price. Those girls and women would scratch his face and his body very bad, and make him leave.

Sometimes when we new men first come back from the waana, we will have an issue with the girls. They will be testing us to find out if we know more now, or if we know nothing, and we have been taught in the waana about how to respond. Usually, once we come back, the girls will want to be hanging with us. A bunch of us new men will get together and say something like, "We are going to Momadou's house", and when we go there, some girls will come too. The girls will not ask us out loud about what happened to us, but they have a way of asking with sign language called passing. But sometimes the passing can turn into a crazy thing. We have to be watching while we are talking to each other too. In fact, everybody is watching each other. We new men won't stop talking to each other, and the girls won't stop talking to other girls, but you have to be watching everybody's movement because passing is a symbol language between us. Maybe a girl will touch her face in the middle of her forehead, then touch the top of her head, and then the back. That means she is asking the question, "Is it in the morning time that they circumcised you, or is it in the middle of the day, or is it at evening time?" The boys stay talking to each other, but one of us will rub the front of his head to say, "It was in the morning time". The front of your head means east, because that is where the sun comes up.

Or sometimes the girl will be sitting down, and she will cross her legs. That means the question, "The time they want to circumcise you, are you so scared that you close your legs to stop them?" When I first came to the United States, anytime I would see people crossing their legs, I was thinking that they are asking this! Or sometimes I was thinking, "That's the style here? If you don't do this you're not a businessman?" or "Damn, they don't know what they are doing here." In the passing, when the girls cross their legs, one of us will answer by stomping his feet with his legs apart, meaning, "No, I am like this! Here I am, not afraid." You have to keep watching everybody all the time even while you are talking to each other, because if you don't answer a question, it means you don't know anything!

Also, if somebody's hand is in a certain way, they are asking, "When they circumcise you, did the skin close back up or is it open?" Then you have to answer by the way your hand is. So once this all has been going on for a while, one of us new men will make a sign by rubbing the whole front of their face to say, "You should stop now, because we are shy to be talking to you about this thing." But sometimes the girls are hardheaded, and they don't want to stop. And we are prepared for this, because while we are in the waana, the older men will make something for us called bunkun passing. It's made from the wood of the Bunkun tree, which is very soft, and easy for carving. The bunkun passing is a secret thing, carved to look like a woman's private parts, and the older men even put some black hairs on it. But they might only make three or four of the bunkun passing, even if there are 30 or 40 boys who have been through the circumcision. Usually, one of us new men will have a bunkun passing in their pocket, and we will check with each other to make sure one of us has it. When we want the girls to stop asking questions and they won't stop, whoever has the bunkun passing will pull it out of his pocket and wave it at the girls. That stops them right away! The girls will run away crying to their mom and dad, but when people ask them what happened, the girls can't explain it to them. The older people, they know what's happening, and they say to the girls, "Hey, we don't want to hear about this nonsense any more!" But sometimes no one in our group will have a bunkun passing in their pocket, and we all are trying to ask each other, "Do you have it, who has it?" and so on. Somebody might have to run and go find the one who has it and say, "Give me that thing, because we need to use it." In Gambia today, many people won't know what bunkun passing is. If you ask them, they won't have any idea. And when I remember about all those things, I think, "Wow". I don't think there is anything like this done now, even in the area I grew up in.

SUTUKOBA

In the time when I was growing up, what I like and what I know about, is dog hunting. What got me into gun hunting was living with the Yaffa family in the vlllage of Sutukoba. The reason I went there is, I was thinking I wanted to go to an English school, and the only English school in the far eastern part of Gambia was in Sutukoba. It was around six miles away from Foday Kunda, and I walked there. There were a lot of boys in Sutukoba like me, who came from a long way for that school, but when that English school was built, they didn't build any dormatories for boys to live in. Anytime a boy came there to be a student, the town mayor Banjara Jabai would call one of the local families to ask them to be a host. These host families never got paid to do that, and sometimes they hosted a boy for four or five years! I was lucky to be matched along with another boy from the school, to live with Bilal Yaffa's family.

Bilal Yaffa was the eldest brother of the Yaffa family, and his compound was big. His brothers Jabello and Balla Yaffa also lived in Yaffa kunda with their wives and children. All three brothers shared the same father, but Bilal had a different mother. Balla Yaffa was my favorite friend of all the older persons. We call each other "Toma", which means namesake, because we have the same name. My mother also always called me Balla, which means Musa in the Mandingo language. In fact, the names Balla, Bangaly, Lalo, and Musa all have the same meaning.

Balla was a gun hunter, a strong man, and all the things I like about being in the bush. When he saw someone who liked these things too, he knew they are "right on his footprint". Besides me, there were six other boys in Yaffa kunda too, and four of them were from the Yaffa family. But I'm the only one that became addicted to the hunting with Balla. Our favorite time to go gun hunting is in the last part of the dry season, from February to June. Even when the rainy season starts in July is a favorite time. We hunt at nighttime, when it is pitch black, and just after the rain is over and the sky has thick clouds. In times that the moon is out all night, we will wait until the full and bright moon days are over. We use flashlights with three D-cell batteries, so the darker it is the brighter our flashlight will be.

A time will come when it will rain all day very hard. That night, while I'm in the boys' hut in our compound, I know Toma will come to wake me up to go hunt. I cannot sleep because I am so excited! Just lying in the bed without sleeping. At ten or eleven o'clock at night, I will hear heavy footprints and know Balla is coming. I hear his big voice say "Toma, are you ready?" and I say, "Yes!" Then we will go out without any shoes because we say, "A shoe will slow you down". He will have a gun and flashlight, and he ties the flashlight to his head on one side, facing the front. His gun was a traditional handmade African gun that uses gunpowder, like the American civil war guns. You put gunpowder inside and some steel balls that blacksmiths make. When you fire the gun, it could be one and a half minutes for the smoke to clear, and then you will know if you hit the target or not. That gun makes a big noise too. Balla will have the gun, a flashlight, cutlass, and a small bag. I will just have a cutlass.

One has to be very brave to hunt like this. It's pitch black in the bush, you cannot see anything, and I have to stay twenty yards behind him so animals don't know that there are two people. If you are into hunting, it comes with a price. Sometimes you can be in the bush using the flashlight, and the bulb will blow. When that happens, we will take the head part off the flashlight and put a little piece of metal to hit the bulb on the side, and sometimes it will come on again. Sometimes not, but if we have an extra bulb we can change it. If not, you gotta come home because it's too dark to hunt. Sometimes we see an animal, and Balla aims to shoot and pulls the trigger, but the gun doesn't fire because it is too moist inside. But I don't care. Anytime Balla comes to get me, I gotta go!

One night, we went from Sutakoba to an area called Mori Kunda Road, because it went a long way to Mori Kunda village. There is a place there with old farmland that nobody farmed for many years, so the trees started to grow up tall like a forest. Those young trees were about ten feet tall with lots of leaves. That night was after a big rain, so the trees had lot of dew on the leaves also. We were walking, and I was behind Balla like always. He spotted an antelope, which we call mankaro, and shined the light on his eye. Balla was turning his head back and forth, and when the light hit the mankaro eyes, it was like a red ball. Balla made a hand motion for me to stop. No noise, just a hand motion. So that moment I stopped, and he aimed and shot at the mankaro, it fell down. We ran to where it was, and Balla put his gun down and pulled out his knife to cut the throat. Suddenly the mankaro jumped up and ran! Balla ran after it, breaking smaller trees as he went. It's hard to believe he is a human being! The mankaro disappeared. We looked, but we couldn't find it. In the early morning around four o'clock, he said, "Toma, maybe we should go home", and I said OK.

It was very far to walk back to the village. We found our way to Mori Kunda Road, and every few feet we cut some leaves and put them on the ground to mark our path. I got so tired and sleepy from walking so far. We got back to Yaffa kunda at five o'clock in the morning, and I went inside the boys' hut to sleep. But Balla did not sleep. He waited until the sun came up, and went back to exactly where he shot the mankaro, following the bloodstains. He found the mankaro near a giant termite mound in the thick bush, dying. Right before it died, he killed it and brought it back on his shoulder to the village. I heard people talking about it, and right away I opened my eye and ran outside!

Another night we went round and round to an area called Jonkotolo, a fishing area near the River Gambia where there is a pond. We walked for a long time in the bush. Suddenly Balla shined the light in my direction to say, "Let's go", and there was a hyena right behind me, following me. He said, "Toma, a hyena", and right away it left and ran away. Hunting and hunting that day, we got a porcupine and brought it home.

•••••

Balla is my good friend, because all the time I am growing up, he is the champion of all the things I like. He was a famous wrestler, so good at being in the bush, and hunting too. Many years later when I wrote the songs for my first Jooka cassette, the wrestling song called Bantabato is about Balla. Balla and his elder brother Jabello were very good wrestlers. God gave them strength and structure that is very rare. Jabello was even stronger than Balla, and very tall. He had a donkey, and he put peanut bags on it to take to the trading post called Fata Tenda. It was not too far from Sutokoba, so in one day he could take two or three trips to Fata Tenda and back. If the donkey didn't want to go, he picked it up like a pet cat! For some reason, donkeys don't like the dark, so if the donkey wouldn't go because of that, Jabello could pick it up and carry it for a block or more, and that would make it go.

Balla was smaller than Jabello, and did carpentry and farming as his main work. He made doors, chairs, and tables for people. Of the traditional wood called duto or keno, he preferred duto, because it is very, very strong wood. When Balla was bringing the duto wood to his workshop, he could pick up a whole tree trunk on his head and carry it a long, long way. You would be thinking, "What kind of human being is this?" He could carry such a big section of tree trunk! A lot of men would come to visit Yaffa kunda, because that was the favorite conversation place of the whole village. Balla's workshop was under a big Mango tree in the compound, and while he would be under that tree doing his carpentry job, lots of people came to see him.

One day Jabello Yaffa had an argument with his wife, but whatever it was about did not come out to the public. After the argument, Jabello came and sat on a jarri benteng under the Mango tree, where all the men were sitting. A jarri benteng is a big traditional couch that is woven from bamboo, with a frame that holds it off the ground. It is very common in village life, and so big that a lot of people can fit on it. Even today, there is a jarri benteng under that Mango tree. Jabello's wife's name was Kumba, and she was a small woman but very, very brave. While Jabello was sitting there, Kumba came with a big stick, tiptoeing behind him, and hit him hard in the back! Then she ran back inside the house, locked the door, and hid under the bed. Jabello didn't even look back to see what happened, because he already knew. He just kept on as if nothing was going on. But people started getting up and going back to their houses, because they didn't want to be there to witness what would happen. Once everybody left, Jabello got up and came to the door of the house and grabbed it, lifted it off the house, and threw it to the side. The bed inside had a traditional mattress on it, made with grass. He grabbed all that and the bedframe, and just threw it outside. Kumba was yelling and going crazy.

He bent down and grabbed her with one hand, like she was a baby, so her feet were not on the ground. He stepped outside with her, and hit her with one index finger, and then she fell down and cried. His finger was big like a toe, and his hand was very big. Jabello and Balla were bigger than American football players. No fat on them, and they did not do any bodybuilding to get that way. Strength, they have it.

Kumba visited my compound in Brikama a few years ago. She now has passed away, and Jabello passed away a long time ago, but the first wife of Bilal Yaffa is still alive. Her name is Kanku but everyone calls her Daadu. She was more than 40 years old back when I was living in Sutukoba, which was in around 1966 or 1967. I think Daadu is now over 100 years old. She is the oldest person living in Sutukoba, and has many grandchildren and great-grandchildren there now.

While I was living at Yaffa kunda, I also had an older friend in Sutukoba who was a Muslim scholar, a holy man, and Imam. His name is Alhaji Mba Jaiteh. He comes from a holy man family, and I know their history so heavy because I have known them since I was a little boy. The reason I know him is because when I was a young child, my mother would take me with her to travel from Foday Kunda to Sutukoba to do griot singing for his wife Tamaratou. Jaiteh kunda was not far from Yaffa kunda, and so I used to go to their house a lot on weekends and after school. I liked to go there. Alhaji Mba Jaiteh was a heavy scholar, and had a lot of Quran students in his house, sometimes even 50 or 60 at one time. At night during the rainy season, when it's hot like fire outside, I would fan him with a cloth in a traditional way. I liked to do that a lot. But the school had a rule that no student could be going out at night, and they would write your name down if you did, and punish you. But that didn't stop me. I just zig zagged from Yaffa kunda to Jaiteh kunda real quick.

One day Alhaji Mba Jaiteh said to me, "You should leave the school and go learn the kora." When he told me that, I heard the words but they did not go in my head, becaue I was thinking that the scholars who teach traditional Quran just didn't like the English school and a western education. But at the same time, whenever griot travelers came to Sutukoba and I went to hear them, I would think, "I could leave here right away and go with them." After a while, it came to me that Alhaji was right. A few months later, he told me again, "If you go learn how to play the kora, it will be good for you." I never asked him why, and just said OK, but I was thinking, "Maybe there is something to this". The next day, I came home from school and said, "Father Bilal, I am going back to my village Foday Kunda." He said, "No, don't go". Even when I told this to Balla, he did not want me to leave. But I took my clothes and put them in a bundle, and started walking back to Foday Kunda because I decided, "No, I am a kora player. That is what I know, and that is what I will do."

When I got back to Foday Kunda, the word went out that I had left school in Sutokoba. My blood brother Mahamadou rode on his bike all the way from Sare Hamadi to Foday Kunda to tell me, "You gotta go back to school." A couple of days later, he forced me to go back. He put me on his bike and he pedaled me back to Sutukoba. I knew that they did not allow any cigarette smoking at the school, so I got two cigarettes while I was in Foday Kunda. When we got to Sutukoba, school was out for the day, and three or four of the teachers were sitting there under the veranda along with the headmaster Kai Jabang, who was from Brikama. Before we got close to them, I pulled out a cigarette and start smoking it, even though I didn't even smoke cigarettes at that time. Mahamadou did not see me because he was still pedaling. When we arrived where the teachers were, he said, "I brought your student back." Then the headmaster Kai Jabang said, "We welcome our student back, but I want to make it clear that right now that he is doing something that is not allowed in our school. No student can smoke here." When he said that, I replied, "Well, if I am here, then I am going to smoke. I'm not going to stop smoking for nobody." My brother didn't like that. He threw the bike down and jumped on me to try to stop me from smoking. We were fighting right there in front of the teachers. They pulled us apart, and then he pedaled his bike back over 15 miles back to Sare Hamadi. That night, I went to Yaffa kunda to stay, but the next morning I walked back to Foday Kunda. I told my mother, "I am not going to school, I am going to study and learn the kora." She asked me where I wanted to go, and I said that I wanted to study with my Uncle Saikou Suso in Passamasi village. My mom said, "OK, since that's what you want to do".

⬤⬤⬤⬤⬤

Even though I wouldn't go to the school in Sutukoba, it is a great village, and I like it so much! It is the village of the holy men, and the man who founded Sutukoba is a great man. His name was Foday Kaniman Jatta, and he is now buried there. He was a hunter, and he had some hunting dogs, and he liked to come to that area because was very thick with big trees, so a lot of animals can be found there. He came there to hunt with his dogs, but with no gun, just an axe and maybe a cutlass. One day while he was hunting in that area, he was lying under a tree resting and sleeping. His dogs were lying down all around him, and one of the dogs got up. That dog went away a little ways from him and started scratching the soil there. The dog scratched and scratched, and in a little while, water came out and started flowing. That was a miracle, because that area is a very dry place. Foday Kaniman Jatta opened his eye and heard his dog barking, so he got up and walked to that area. Dogs typically bark for only a few reasons: they saw an animal but cannot get it because it is so big, or they cannot get it because it is up in a tree. They will also bark so that their master can come and kill the animal. But that dog barked because he wanted Foday Kanniman Jatta to get up. When he saw the water, he decided to build a village there called Sutuko. The word sutuko mean thick forest, and Sutukoba means inside a thick forest. Today, there are not many forests like that, but in those days there were a lot of them. Foday Kanniman Jatta moved his family to that forest to make a village, and quickly it became very big. Later on, Foday Kaniman Jatta traveled another 15 miles away and built a smaller village called Sutukoding, which means inside a small forest. Even today, the Jatta family leaders are the mayors of that village.

There are three great things about Sutukoba: the first is the founder Foday Kaniman Jatta, the second is Karan Saikou Aljali Jaiteh, a heavy holy man who was the head of all the Jaiteh families in Sutukoba, and the third is another great holy man, Fatty Fin, who was an Imam. He was also the tallest human being anyone can ever talk about in all of Africa. Every Friday in Sutukoba, Fatty Fin led the jumas, which means Friday prayer. Then he would go to Sammeh village to lead their prayers too.

He is a kind of human being that might be one in a billion, because he was so tall. Here is one example: The River Gambia is between Sutukoba and Sammeh village, and when he was traveling, he had to go to the Sammeh Tenda, which means the crossing point of the river. When he got there, he just jumped over the River Gambia! Fatty Fin's father was from Sammeh and his mother from Sutukoba, and at one point before he died, these two villages were debating where he should be buried. But Fatty said, "Just bury me in whichever village I am in when I die". He died in Sutukoba, and so his grave is there. Even now, people will go there to check it out. There are three big stones there to mark his burying place: one is above his head, one at his waist, and the last stone at his feet. Those rocks are so big that they cannot be moved, even in the rainy season or floods. Anyone who grows up there knows where his grave is. People will bring some small things with them, such as a kola nut or a few dollars, and ask for his blessing for anything they are about to do. From time to time now, something will come into my mind about Fatty Fin, because he seems to be somebody that no westerners have ever heard about or studied. Even in Gambia, some people have never heard of him or talk about him. In my childhood area of Gambia, the people know about him and think he is surprising, but we say, "God created him, so that's how it is".

•••••

In 1979, I happened to see Balla Yaffa for the first time since I was living at Yaffa kunda as a young man. At that time, I was living in Chicago, and went back to Gambia to visit. I was staying in a small place in Banjul called the Government Rest House, on the second floor. I didn't know that Balla had traveled to Banjul and was staying there too. One day when I was coming up to my room, I heard him talking with another friend from Sutukoba named Saara Kamaso. The compound of Saara's family is very close to Yaffa Kunda, and Saara was a friend of mine ever since I lived there. Sometimes when me and Balla would go hunting, Saara went with us too. He was much older than me, but much younger than Balla. One thing to know is that in the Passamasi area, the Mandingo dialect is very different from the dialect they speak in Banjul or Brikama. I heard them talking, and I knew right away they were from my area. I couldn't believe it sounded just like Balla. I went closer, and their door was open just a little bit. I peeped in the door, and saw it was Balla and Saara! We grabbed each other to greet, and I asked, "Why are you here?" He said, "To get a shotgun, because the old fashioned gunpowder gun is such trouble". At that time, you had to come all the way to Banjul to get a license to buy a gun. And the only guns in Gambia are shotguns, except for the army. There are no handguns, and no people killing each other with a gun, even now.

That was the last time I saw Balla. He has now passed away, but Saara is still alive and living in Sutukoba. Saara didn't wrestle, but he liked hunting so much. When I saw them in Banjul that day, the excitement was something else. In fact, that got me into hunting again myself, though I didn't buy my own guns until 1986. Right now, anytime I am in Gambia, my favorite thing is to go hunting. That's what I like, and that's what I do. While I am hunting, I think to myself, "All my friends around the world, if you told them where I was right now, they wouldn't believe it!"

LIFE WITH MY TEACHER

In our griot tradition, even though my father was a master kora player, a father does not teach his own child the instrument. So I studied under my Uncle Saikou Suso, a master kora player in the village of Passamasi. Uncle Saikou's mother and my father's mother were sisters, with the same mother and father. My father's mother was the elder one, and her name was Luntanding. My teacher's mother was the younger one, and her name was Kankunding. When I was born, my grandmother Luntanding was alive, but Kankunding had already passed away. Because in Mandingo tradition we call our mother's sisters by the name of mother also, and we call their children brother and sister, Uncle Saikou and my father are brothers.

In our tradition, we also name our children after our elders, and so Luntanding and Kankunding both named their first-born sons after their father, Jali Saikou Jobarteh. They also named both of their second sons Lamin, after one of their father's brothers, and named their third sons Surakata after another of their father's brothers. Since all these children in our family have the same name, we have a traditional way to make it clear, which is to add the mother's name to the son's name. Since my father was Luntanding's son he would be called Luntanding Saikou, my teacher would be called Kankunding Saikou, and so on with the other sons too. Because my father was born before my Uncle Saikou, he would also call my father nkotoke, which means elder brother. Sometimes people would also call my father Saikou Jango, which means tall Saikou, because of how tall he was. Ever since I came to the United States, I have never seen anyone taller than my father. Even when I saw Wilt Chamberlain on TV in a Volkswagen ad, I didn't think he was taller than my father. In any crowd, my father was always the first one you would see, because his head was up high above everyone.

When you go to get a teacher and learn the kora, you don't pay any money for that. You have to take ten kola nuts and present those to your teacher. That means you have come to be a student. Your teacher will take those ten kola nuts and divide them between his family members, and say, "Now we have a new student". I remember the day when my mother gave me the money to buy the kola nuts, and I walked so fast to get to Passamasi. From Foday Kunda to Passamasi is around five miles, and I arrived there around three o'clock in the afternoon. Right away, I went to Suso kunda to ask for my Uncle Saikou. There were only three people in Suso kunda that day: Uncle Saikou's father Jali Nfamara Suso who I call grandfather, his wife Jalisira Sakliba who I call grandmother, and one young girl. Grandfather Nfamara Suso was an old man at that time. After we greeted, I asked him, "Where is my Uncle Saikou? I came to learn the kora". Then he told me that my Uncle Saikou, along with his three brothers and all their wives, were not there because they had gone griot traveling. He said, "Today, they are in a village called Sabi, in another state called Kantora District". At first I said, "Wow", because there are three villages called Sabi in Gambia, and I thought they were in the big Sabi village that was far away from Passamsi. But the Sabi village they were in was within walking distance, only around 10 miles. To get there, you have to cross the River Gambia in a big canoe, at a town called Fatoto. Then you go down the hill and walk two more miles, and before you get to the village of Kusunu you will see a tiny village with only one or two compounds. That is Sabi. So I said to myself, "I can walk", and I started walking fast. Soon I found the tiny village.

When I arrived there, I asked about my Uncle Saikou and his family, and because it is a very small village, everybody knew that they were staying in Sillah kunda. So I went there and met them, and we greeted. Then I told my Uncle Saikou, "I want to learn the kora", and he said, "That's good, you have come to the right place because you are our son. Your father is my elder brother, so when you come here you are home." So I went with them to do griot traveling, which is called jalya taamo. It always begins in the dry season, usually around January or February. After griot families harvest all their crops and bring everything back to their compounds, we go traveling from one village to another for one, two, or even three months. Whenever my teacher's family went on jalya taamo, it was my teacher and his three wives, his second brother Lamin and his two wives, his third brother Surakata and his wife, and the youngest brother Karunka and his wife. All their kids will go too, including two young boys who were my teacher's kids, but I was the only kora student. We were 22 people in all. One or two griots can go on jalya taamo by themselves too, but our heavy tradition is that the whole griot family goes together in a big group.

When we come to a village, if my teacher knows anybody there, we will all go to that person's compound right away. If not, we will walk to the village mayor's compound first. All the people who see us carrying the koras know right away that we are griots, and don't have to ask. They also know that it is Mandingo tradition for them to welcome us, even if they have never seen us before. At the first compound we enter, my teacher will say to the elder man, "We are griots from Passamasi, and we are traveling and just arrived here to visit you." That man is honored to have a griot come to his house, so his family will fetch water to give to us to drink and to wash our feet. At any place we go, they can see that our feet are dusty because all our traveling is done on foot. Then they will divide us among each compound in the village, so that every single person has a host family. We will go together to each host family compound to say hello, and they are very happy because they know we are bringing them a griot. It could be a man, woman, a child, or even a baby who cannot even walk yet. It doesn't matter to the host family, as long as it is someone from our group, and they will welcome that baby as their griot. In many cases, the baby will stay with them from the morning to nighttime, except when it cries and they bring it to its mother for breastfeeding.

We know that no single host family alone can care for all of us griots, because they are responsible for our breakfast, lunch, and dinner. The host family is honored to provide us with those meals, and to watch over us. For every meal, they will bring calabashes full of the food that they cooked for their griot, into the compound where Uncle Saikou is staying, so we can all eat together. Even the host family of a baby who is still breastfeeding will cook food and bring it to that compound. After a while, Uncle Saikou's host family won't even have to cook for their own family, because there is so much food arriving there for every meal. We three young griot boys will quickly become friends with some of the other boys in the village, and then sometimes invite them to have lunch or dinner with us. This way of griot traveling works well, because there is no one person or family in any village who is carrying the whole load.

The first day when we arrive in a village, we don't play any music. Since we have been walking a long time to get there, we will rest for the remainder of that day. That first day, we can even hear some of the villagers talking to each other, saying, "What's happening tonight, will they play?" But we need to rest. The next night, my teacher will tell his host, "We want to play some music". By then, the villagers can hardly wait, because they are in such a hurry for us to play. They will bring a bunch of bamboo mats to the bantaba or to my teacher's host compound, and lay them on the ground for us to sit on while we play. There might be three or four kora players there, and all of them will sit in the front row. Standing beside them, the teacher will be reciting the history. Women griots will be standing behind the row of kora players and singing. My teacher, who knows the history more than anybody else, will introduce every song to the villagers, telling them who the song is about, where that person is from, what they did, how long ago they lived, how long they lived, who his children were, what they did too. While this is happening, the kora students will be sitting in front of the kora players. Each kora has a nail used for tuning the strings, and we will pull that nail out of its spot inside the sound hole of the kora, and then we will tap the bottom of a kora with the nail to provide a rhythm. Every song has a special way of tapping that goes with it, and we students have to know that too. While they are singing, women also will play the metal scraper that we call newo, which they play almost like a bell. They too, will all know the special beats to use for each song.

That whole night will be about music and history, and as soon as it starts, villagers will all come quickly and sit down to listen. Boys and girls, women and men, young or old, they don't want to hear any other sound besides us. The whole crowd will be so quiet that if you came into that village, you would think that only the griots are there. You won't hear anything but the griot music and the griot voices. Everyone is so quiet, and no one talks between each other, they just listen. The griot that is reciting the history will be mentioning family names, and the villagers will be listening to hear what their ancestors have done. Mandingos have a lot of different last names, and the griot will talk about who was the first person to ever have that name, how and where they lived, and when they lived. He will also start mentioning some family names of people who are in the crowd. Then those people will come and give us whatever they can give. They will come to our teacher and say, "My griot, I am very happy that you mentioned the name of my great, great grandfather and I am proud of what you I heard from you". Then he might give a cow, a sheep, a goat, money, clothing, or other stuff. People can come up right in the middle of the show to do this, or sometimes tell us where the animal is, and to come and get it later. Or they will just come up while we are playing and drop a rope there in front of my teacher. That's the sign for giving some kind of animal. The next day when you go visit them, they will give that animal to you.

Our show will go on all through the night, and we might stay in the village for two or three days, then move on to another village. That's why jalya taamo will take a long time. We will be going to a bunch of villages, as many as we can. We can easily spend two or three months doing that. Sometimes people will like it so much that they won't want us to leave their village. They will say, "Please stay for more time". We might stay there longer, or we might tell them, "We are on a long road to many, many places, and cannot stay". In any case, when it's time for us to go, the villagers will bring all their gifts to one place, and my teacher will tell the mayor, "Right now, we can't take everything with us. Please hold all these things here for us until we return back to our home village, then we will send a message to you."

By the month of May, we have to be going back to our home village to start cleaning our fields to prepare for the rainy season farming time. We have to be ready to start farming as soon as the rainy season starts in June. During the rainy season, we might go on jalya taamo for two or three days, but then we have to get back to our crops or go hunting. During the dry season is when we have the time for long griot traveling. Once we are back in our home village, we will send a message to the mayor of all those villages, telling them that we are back. Then each mayor will send two of his sons and some other boys to bring all the village gifts to us. Before I was born, those sons would bring these things on the back of a donkey or in a basket on their head, but when I was growing up, I also saw them bring these things to us on a bicycle. I went on jalya taamo many times with my teacher and his family. Of all the adults who were in the family then, only a few are still alive today: Lamin's first wife, Surakata's wife, and Karunka and his wife.

Kora learning can be done anytime you are there with your teacher, or part of his family. You can take the kora in your hands any time your hands are free. Nothing is written down, everything is by ear. Your best bet to learn is to be listening all the time. You will bring the kora and come sit next to your teacher. He will tell you how to hold the kora, how to play it, do this, and do that. He talks to you, and you follow in his footprint. My teacher was the head of his family and the head of all the jalya taamo time. Before I learned the kora with him, I could already play it a little bit because since the day I was born, I saw and heard my father play. The other person in my teacher's family who also helped me learn was his youngest brother Karunka Suso. He will always be teaching me, and helping me to learn too. I did a lot of griot traveling for a few days at a time with Karunka, just the two of us. He liked to do that kind of traveling, and he liked me to be with him. While he was playing, I would be tapping the bottom of the kora with the tuning nail. He is an old man now, and lives with his family between Brikama and Banjul in a village called Lamin.

•••••

When I was growing up in my teacher's compound in Passamasi, I also had strength for men's work, and I wanted to do it so much. In a traditional village, hunting, wrestling, and fishing is how people become great, not for being best at school. I enjoy hunting very much, starting with dog hunting. The way we use the dogs for hunting is different than in America. Our dogs run after the animal and catch the animal, and we don't use a gun. I had some hunting dogs, and when it comes to hunting, those were my best friends. Even when I was at my teacher's family farm, those dogs would stay with me until I went home. We also hunted rabbits and other animals. Once those dogs jumped and started chasing an animal, they wouldn't stop until they caught them, and I followed them running. They never got lost from me, because one dog was always barking while they ran like hell. I always had four or five dogs. I had a female dog that was very small, but she was my favorite. Her name was Sinkoi, which means white leg, and she was something else. Muriti was one of the male dogs, and he reminds me of a pit bull because he was short but very strong and fast. I called him Muriti, which means "stray", because one day he came to me as a grown dog and decided to stay. Another male dog I named Kulanjan, after an eagle. And Samirong was named after a crocodile because once he grabbed something he never let go. For a long time I kept these four dogs, because they were #1 hunting dogs. I liked them so much because they were so good at bringing me the kill, and I would be so happy that I would give them my whole lunch.

I hunted for ground squirrels, which we call duma kereng. Those squirrels are big, the same size as tree squirrels in America. In Gambia, our tree squirrels are called santo kereng, but we don't hunt them much because they are so small. I also hunted rabbit, which are similar to American rabbits, but all are a brown color. Another animal we hunted is called a kansolo, which means grass cutter. It looks like a beaver, but with a tail that is small like a finger, and eats tall grasses but not trees. We also hunted taye, which is in the same family as raccoon, but doesn't climb trees. It's all black, and has a bushy tail with white spots, and big hair. The wato is in the same family as a cat, with big neck and spotted body like a leapard, and it climbs trees. It likes to live in the hollow part of a tree that has a lot of vines twisting together on it. That is how I knew to look for the wato there. The dogs knew that too. The sunkang is an animal that looks kind of like a raccoon, but much bigger and with a longer tail. It also has a spotted body, with long hair, and lives in an underground burrow or inside a termite mound. That animal is very difficult for the dogs to kill because its hair is hard for them to grab, and has a very bad taste, like pepper. That hair burns the dogs' mouth when they bite it, so they can't get a hold of its body for long.

One early morning in the dry season, I got up and said, "I am going hunting." In the dry season, sometimes a bush fire will burn our farming area. Then the hunting is sweet, because you can see a long distance, and there is nowhere for animals to hide. Around six in the morning, I went out to a big open place where a bush fire had burned. Way at the other end of it, I saw a sunkang with its tail dragging behind it. I signaled my dogs to go chase it by saying, "Amuta!" three or four times quickly, which means, "catch him"! They knew just what I meant, so all four of them took off running so fast. They saw the sunkang and went faster, and I was running fast after them. I could run fast when I was that young, and for a long distance without stopping. Just in bare feet too, because my feet are used to the rocks and rough wood. All I had was my hunting knife in a sheath at my waist, plus my hunting axe. The sunkang just stood there, and the dogs would bite it and leave it, bite and leave. I tried to chop the sunkang with the ax, and it tried to bite me when I rushed in. There were porcupine burrows all around us, but they were really anteater burrows that the porcupines took over. The sunkang went inside one of those burrows, but my female dog Sinkoi followed it inside and they came flying out the other side. It was heavy fighting before I got him. In and out of the burrows they were flying, Sinkoi and the sunkang. The fighting went on a long time before I killed the sunkang. I tied him up and put him on my head, and went back to the village. That was the only time in my life that I killed a sunkang.

When hunting in that area, I learned a lot of things about it. Whenever the dogs came to a termite mound with lots of burrow holes in it, Sinkoi would come there and start hollering, digging and wagging her tail. She wouldn't come when I called, so I would know that something was there. Then I will come with my axe and start chopping on it and digging. Sometimes I will have to go get a bunch of dry grasses and stuff them in the holes, then set them on fire to smoke them out. When the animal came flying out of a hole, the dogs would run and get it. Sometimes a big cobra or python or puff adder will come out of the hole, and the dogs will know not to get it. Today, the search dogs in the airport remind me of my dogs. Dog hunters also know traditional things to do to give their dogs heavy strength. Whenever I was getting ready to go hunting, I would go out to the bush to find the plant we call kupanpang. When you cut a kupanpang leaf, it drips a white liquid like milk. I cut some of those leaves and mixed them with some ants. We have a black ant called manyafing that bites, and when you pull it out of your skin, the head sticks inside. We also have red ants called manya wulen. We mix seven black ants and seven red ants, seven pieces of hot pepper, and seven bees, and pound them all together along with leaves to make what we call wulenmindo. Then we put this in the dogs' food just before we went hunting. Dogs usually eat what we eat, and we make a wooden, canoe-like trough for their bowl. But after feeding the dogs with wulenmindo, you have to be ready to go, because it makes them want to hunt right away. They would grab a goat or a sheep if you don't take them hunting, and you have to try hard and hunt a long time, because the dogs don't want to come back home. After eating wulenmindo, they want to just stay and hunt.

One day I gave my dogs the wulenmindo on the way to my hunting area. From Passamasi to my hunting area, there is a Fulani village we call Chinchota, but its actual name is Banibakali. In those days, it was a small village with only three compounds. Fulani people always have cattle, and that day there were some calves there too. The moment the dogs saw the calves, they could not be stopped, they didn't listen, and jumped on a calf and started biting. I ran and tried to stop them, and the Fulanis ran out yelling at me. The calf fell down, and the people said if it died, I would have to pay. I got my dogs off of the calf and we went hunting. That night when I came home, I told my teacher's brother Lamin what had happened. He said, "OK, let's see what happens. If the calf dies, I will pay". Uncle Lamin told that to the Fulanis the next day too, but he also said, "You people have to watch out too, because your cows always come to our farm. If your cows damage our crops, you will have to pay too". Luckily, the calf did not die. When farming time came, we planted our crops, and one day I was sitting in the guard tower above our millet field. The Fulani's cows came into the field. The boy following the cows was named Monde, and when I saw that, I ran out to see whose cows they are. I told Monde, "Aha, you see what your cows did?" He left the cows and ran back to the house to tell his family that I said I would beat him because of it. My Uncle Lamin went to the Fulanis to say, "You cannot say this", and they apologized. In our tradition, we know that people have to forgive each other many, many things. Our saying is, "The foot is on the ground and the snake is on the ground, but they are prevented from harming each other because each is on the ground." That means, whatever happens, we should figure things out.

•••••

While I was studying the kora and living with my teacher's family, I was also out a lot at nighttime to guard the farm. I would work in the farm during the day with the family, then remain behind there while they went back to the village, to make sure no wild pigs, monkeys, or baboons came to eat all the crops. In our tradition, we make a place in the middle of the farm for guards to stay, with two buildings. The first is a small grass tent with no walls that we call a buko, for us to sit in when it's raining. It has pegs holding it to the ground for when the wind is blowing hard, and lots of ashes all over the ground around it because of our cooking there. The second is a kantary benteng, which means guarding tower. It is built out of long poles that have a big "Y" branch at the end. We dig a deep hole for the poles, and build a wooden structure on top of them. It looks like a big table in the sky. The kantary benteng is very tall, and it might need to be remade every year. Once it is built, we will go into the bush to cut some wood and bring it back to carve three log drums, which we call bombolos. We carve them with different sounds and pitches, and then climb the guard tower with them to play. Those drums stay up there on the guard tower all the time. We play them to entertain ourselves, to make the animals know we are there, and to communicate to people who are on another tower or in another farm. The sound goes for miles. We say things to each other with the drums, like calling someone's name, asking how they are doing, and telling them, "Here is what I am doing", "I am going to the river", "Yes I am coming", "Did you hear from so and so in his farm?" or "I'm going home". We can talk to each other about all kinds of things with these drums!

A bombolo is a common drum in central Africa. Some areas will even use this drum for entertainment in the village, but in my village we just use them during farming season from mid-June to October. When farming season is over, we tie them to a tree until next year, and then come back to play them. We might find that one is rough on the inside, so we leave it on the ground for termites to eat, then come back later and knock the termites out, and the drum will be very sweet. This is a typical village thing. If you come from the city, you won't know what I am talking about. But every boy who does all the things of a traditional village will know how to carve a bombolo, or they will know at least what a bombolo is.

There are drums all over Africa, and some might look similar to each other, but you can't tell the difference just by looking at them. You have to touch them to know, because then you will hear that the drums are tuned to match the language and tone of the people's voices and the way they sing. The reason for this is that we have a whole lot of languages in Africa, and each group of people will tune their instruments to match the tone of their language. For example, Mandingo people, Wolof people, Dagomba people in Ghana, and Hausa and Yoruba people in Nigeria, we all have talking drums. Many other places also have them, and the tones are very different in each area. Just like hearing a language, when I hear the talking drums played by the Hausa or Yoruba people, I know that these are Nigerian drums even if the people playing don't sing anything. It's the same thing with balafons and xylophones, and kontingos. They are common instruments in many places in Africa, and you might see one that looks like another, but when you touch the keys or strings, you will find out that it sounds completely different because of the tuning. That tuning will match the language that the people are speaking. Sometimes I can see a balafon and know exactly where it is from, but not always. A Mandingo balafon is built to be low to the ground, but there are other people who build them that same way and yet they sound very different. Also, in the Cassamance area of Senegal, the xylophones look the same as the ones in Burkina Faso, but their sounds are completely different. In Mozambique they have a xylophone that looks so different, and in fact I have never seen a xylophone that looks like that anywhere else in Africa. They make many different sizes of this instrument, and some have big, wide keys and a very deep bass sound, even deeper than the xylophones played by the Shona people of Zimbabwe. All these Mozambique xylophones are tuned the same, but some have a higher pitch and some a lower pitch. Even the nyanye instument of the Fulani people, which only has one string, is tuned different in each place it is played.

Bolon is another big instrument in Mandingo tradition, but nowadays it is disappearing. It was invented before the kora, but is not a griot instrument. It was made to be a war instrument, and there is a lot of mystery about it. A bolon is made from a big round calabash, covered in cowhide. The bolon makers would go into the bush to choose a tree branch to use for the neck, with a big bend in it like a bow for shooting arrows. Then they attached three big bass strings. When warriors would be going into war, the bolon players would be following them, and playing and singing for them. Even though the bolon has only three strings, it makes a deep, deep sound that carries a long way, even if only one bolon is playing. Later on, bolon players would sometimes travel and play just for the people to dance to also.

•••••

In the Passamasi area, we also had a lot of wild bees and hives, and I was very good at pulling the hot honey from the hive. For us, we do not have any beekeeping, but when we see a tree with a hole, and bees going in and out, we make plans to pull the honey. At night, we build a fire on the ground, climb the tree with a torch made of millet sticks, smoke the bees when they come out, and then pull the honey out. We reach in with our bare hand and the bees sting us. We swing the honeycomb over the bucket to make the bees go away, then put the comb in the bucket. When we come home, our hand is so swollen from 50 bee stings that it is numb. It can be swollen all the way to the armpit sometimes. The cure for this is to boil water in a bucket, then put your arm in the hot water and scrape it with a bamboo stick to get the stingers out. By the end of the day, your hand and arm will be just like normal. We also have an herb that you boil and wash your body with, and drink some of it too. Once you do that, when bees sting you it will hurt, but it will not swell your body. If you want to be a pure man, you have to be able to pull the honey. You have to know too that African bees will defend their hive so much if there is a lot of honey. If they are laid back when you come, you will know there is not much honey there. But if they are going crazy on you and very aggressive, then you will know there is a lot of honey there.

Our farms were pretty far from Passamasi village, and next to the River Gambia. One day while I was by the edge of the farms, I saw bees on a tree that was not very big. Even though people always pull honey at night when bees cannot see them, I said, "OK, I am going to pull this honey but not wait until nighttime." I just put some firewood together with dry grasses, and built a fire under the tree. The bees were up about 13 or 14 ft. high in the tree. I put a torch together with millet grasses, grabbed my sharp axe, and climbed up. Then I put the torch under the hole to make all the bees to go down and leave the hive. I took the axe and started chopping the hole to make it wider, so I could put my hand in and pull the honeycomb out with no problem. The bees waited until they felt me chop the hole two times, and on the third chop they all came out by the millions. They started stinging me like crazy! I remember that this day I was bald because I just shaved my hair. Also, I was not wearing a shirt, because we believe it is better if the bees can't fly under your shirt and get stuck there. I still believe that idea works if you are pulling the honey at nighttime, but that idea did not work during the daytime. It was not a good idea at all!

The bees were coming out, stinging me all over my face, back, hands, stomach, and my head, every place except my pants. There was no chance to do anything, because it was one sting after the other. So I didn't take my time to come down the way I went up. Instead, I threw my axe on the ground and jumped all the way down. There were bushes all around where I landed, and I threw myself into the bushes to see if that would stop the bees. I threw sand at them, but they didn't care about that one bit. There was no slowing them down. So I knew, "There is nothing I can do, I cannot outrun them, and I have nothing to cover me". I threw myself into the bushes many times, but they stayed with me. Now, the only option for me was to run to the river, two or three blocks away. I ran as fast as I could, and when I got to the riverside, all the bees were still following me, stinging my head and stuck to my head. I jumped and flew off the cliff into the water. Going down in the water, some bees were even stuck to my hand and my head while I was smashing them! Even under the water, some were stuck to my head, and I was so mad I was squishing them with my fingers under the water. Finally they left me to go back to their hive. Then I swam to a place I could get out of the river, and found the road back to our farm.

Normally when you challenge bees but cannot get them, they will go back to their hive, drink all their honey, and fly away to make a new hive. So I made a plan to go back to get the honey that night. I waited until sunset, and then I walked back to that tree. I was thinking, "Now bees, I am going to pay you back". Whenever I am in the bush, I always have a water bucket with me for drinking, and so I took this bucket to the tree. I built a fire under the tree and cut the whole tree down with the axe. I chopped the bee entry hole bigger. The bees were there but they didn't come out. I filled my bucket with the honey and brought it home.

Whenever we bring honey home, it is for everybody. We also chew the honeycomb. When it is big honey-pulling time, villagers will put it in a big steel barrel, build a fire, and cook it for a long time. When the honeycomb floats on top, we take that off, and put the honey in bottles and jars. A big honey bottle that was about one liter would sell for 25 cents, but most times its not even sold, just given away to others. In the morning, people like to eat porridge that we call mono, and put honey on top. And in those days, we did not have any sugar in our villages.

•••••

I also like fishing. While I was growing up in Passamasi, there were several traditional ways of fishing: with a spear, or a hook, or with a net. Spearfishing is done during the rainy season, when the River Gambia is flooding all the way up and over the edge, supplying all the ponds connected to the river. At that time of year, we will be watching to see when the ponds fill up. When that happens, fish will be in every one of those ponds, and swimming in the long channel that connects them with the River Gambia. To get those fish, we use a long, double-headed spear called a sorro. It's made from two bamboo sticks tied together with a special rope, with the spear attached to the end. A blacksmith makes the spear for you, and it is very sharp. You just throw it in the water to try to hit something. When throwing it, some fish will begin running in the water, and then other people will gather to try to spear those fish too. It is very dangerous.

At nighttime during the summer flooding season, everybody in the village goes to the channel to fish for daa. We call this nighttime fishing bulufilo, and it starts at sunset and lasts until morning. When we go to the riverside, we gather under one big tree, which we call Jungo. All our spears are stuck straight down in the ground for safety, because of how sharp they are. No one can just lay a spear down. If you left them down on the ground, somebody could step on them in the night and get hurt bad. Then we build a fire and sit around it under the tree until nine or ten o'clock. Then we go get ready to catch the daa, which is a big catfish, as big as a human! They have a great big head and long whiskers, and the bones in their head are as hard as a rock. If you try to spear them in the head, it will be like stabbing concrete. Your spear has to hit on their neck or body to catch them.

At night, the daa will swim from the River Gambia into a channel that leads to a very big pond. All the men will stand in the channel about 20 ft. away from each other. No talking is allowed. Everyone is silent, moving slowly without splashing the water, because the daa will know and then disappear. Everybody is holding a spear in the air. The only light is the stars and moon. When the daa come, they are floating, not swimming, and they look just like a log going by. When you see their silver reflection, you gotta throw your spear as hard as you can. When you hit the daa, people around you have to run and help you, because a daa can break your spear and swim away. On man cannot hold it down. Everybody who fishes for daa has to be very strong. We will also have some 6-10 ft long ropes with a stick on the end, called sunjulo. When the daa is speared, we put the sunjulo through its gills and tie a knot, then everybody helps each other drag it out of the water all the way to the Jungo tree. It is very hard work! We rest there too, in between fishing. Late in the night, between one and five o'clock in the morning, is when the big big daa come. We think it's because they know we are all tired. They stop coming when it gets light out, and then it gets very quiet with no more daa coming until the next nighttime. They just disappear completely.

Another fish called kosso is also in that water. They are small, only about a foot long, but they are a dangerous fish that wounds people a lot. There are three different kinds of kosso, and all have very good meat: Kosso Wulen is the red kosso, Kosso Koyo is the white kosso, and the tiny one is called Kosso Konkon. All of those fish have fins on their sides and top that are very sharp and can break off in your skin, and sometimes people accidentally step on one and it hurts to get it out. It is a very dangerous fish to be around. Sometimes in the early part of the night when we are waiting for the daas to come, we just fish for the Kosso Koyo. When they come, they always come floating in the floodwater on their back, with two kossos grabbing each other by the fin. All you have to do to get them is tie a bag to your waist with a rope, and stand there without moving, and you will see the light reflecting off their stomachs. Then you just stab them and put them in your bag, stab and put in your bag, over and over. It seems like millions are going by! Then you drag the whole bag from the water to the Jungo tree, pour out your kossos, and go back to the water. You can catch 50-60 lbs of them in one night. They also stop as soon as the light comes, so by six o'clock, we all go under the big Jungo tree and build more fire to dry ourselves off. People who have been fishing for kossos have to prepare them by breaking off their fins. The way they do that is to grab it, put the dorsal fin between the two spearpoints on the double-headed spear, twist and break it. Then they break off the side fins, pack all the fish in a bag, and put the whole load on their head. People who catch kossos have that big load on their head all the way back to the village. People who catch daa have to stick the spear in the gill and lay that fish over their shoulder to carry it. A daa is so big that its head will be up over your head, and its tail could be touching the ground behind you. When we come back to the village around eight or nine o'clock in the morning, everybody will be eating fish, even if not every family had a man who went fishing. Everyone gets a share.

When you cut open the daa, you will see two big egg sacs inside that are yellow, and look like corn on the cob. When any fisherman sees them, he wants to cook those eggs and ask his friends to come eat with him. Then we will talk about the story of the fishing night, and all the details. We will cut the daa into pieces, and smoke it before eating. First we make a thing like a table, with four legs and sticks across the top. Then we lay the fish across the sticks and build a fire under it. I don't like to eat fried catfish because it's so slippery, but it is very good tasting after you smoke it over the fire. When you go to our villages during the rainy season time, you will see smoke flying everywhere over the whole village because people have caught the daa.

Fishing with a hook is very different. Our word for a fishing hook is dolingo, and there are two different ways we use them. Nammo fishing is when you use a 20-40 ft long rope, with a bunch of one-foot-long lines hung on it. Each line is about one foot apart, and each one has a hook tied to the end of it. Then the rope is stretched across a lake, and attached to poles on each end. A one-foot-long millet stick is also attached to the rope, with a chicken feather stuck inside it as a marker for when any fish is caught on a hook. After tying the rope, you just go home and then come back later to check it. If the feather is down all the way under the water, you will know a big fish has been caught. You bring your spear with you, and lift one hook after another until you reach the fish. When you find it, you try to stab it with the spear, and then get your hook out of the fish.

Another way of fishing is to use one big hook, taken to the river at nighttime. This kind of fishing is called suto doling fayo, which means night hook fishing. It's very hard to do because in our area, there is a big cliff going straight down to the water. First we each dig a hole into the side of the cliff in the shape of a seat, around two or three feet up from the edge of the river. Then we dig two smaller holes, left and right in front of the seat, to put our heels in to stop us from sliding into the water. We might build a small fire there too. We attach a hook to a rope by wrapping it with a wire, because the fish we are trying to catch have very sharp teeth like a knife, and would cut the hook off if we didn't do that. Everybody is sitting side-by-side on the riverbank, with a dried palm leaf laid on the ground in front of each person. We will tie a weight on the rope, and tie a small fish on the hook for bait. Then we will throw the rope far out in the water, and lay the rest of it down on the dried palm leaf so it will make a sound when the fish bites. When you hear the rope scratching on the palm leaf, you gotta grab it and jerk hard to set the hook, then start reeling it in by hand. We don't have any gloves, so we need to have strong hands! The fish we catch this way are sokoro, binteko, and kulun domo. Also the tikingo, which is an electric fish that is round like a blowfish but doesn't have any spines. When you reel in the tikingo, you can feel the electric shock on your hands. Even the rope feels electric! We don't eat the tikingo though, we just knock them on the head with a stick and take the hook out, because even when it's dead it can shock you.

We do net fishing in three different ways. One way is with a big net, usually 30-40 yards long, that you tie with each end on long pole out in the water. Then you go home and come back the next day to get the fish trapped there. I know how to make this net with big spools of twine. Another way is with a faijo, a big round net that has a rope in the middle. A fisherman can take it and throw it out into the water. In eastern Gambia, we usually take it to some kind of lake, but in the west, people use it out in the ocean. The third way is with a wusungo net, which is like a long basket, made from woven bamboo. It's about two feet tall with an opening on top. A wusungo can be used for group fishing, with everyone in a line pushing their wusungo into the water where they think fish are. Then you put your hand inside to get the fish, but you gotta be careful cause there could be a snake or iguana inside!

When I was about 15 or 16 years old, I had a fishing time that I will never forget. The source of the River Gambia is a long, long way from Passamasi, in the Futa Jalon Islands in Guinea, and every year during the month of August, a big flood comes down the river into Gambia. In the Passamasi area, the River Gambia is in a valley surrounded by 25-30 foot tall cliffs, and the flooding fills it up to the top and even goes over the edge! When this happens, the trees that are growing on the edge of the cliff will now be leaning right over the water. When those floods happen, we go fishing instead of farming. One day, I was sitting on a long branch that was ten or twelve feet out over the water, fishing with a hook and line. I was catching fish, and I had a small bag that I hung on the branch to put my fish inside. While I was busy fishing, a hippo came swimming under me, but it did not see me and I did not see it. Unexpectedly, the hippo lifted his head and sprayed the water from its mouth straight up under me and through the branches. I was not expecting that, and I was so frightened that I fell in the water, right next to the hippo's mouth! The hippo also was scared and swam away quickly down the river. I was so lucky that I could swim very well and reached the shore to get out, and that I did not fall in his mouth.

•••••

I still liked to wrestle in those days too, and the villages in our area would organize the festivals and matches. The young men and girls gather in their kafos to pick a date for the festival. Every village has its own kafo groups, which are a group of boys or men, or a group of girls and women. Beginning from around age 10 or 11, you will join a kafo with others who are around your same age until you are around 13, and then you will join a different kafo to be in from ages 14 until around 20, and so on. No matter what family you come from in the village, you will be all together. You will stay in your kafo for your whole life, even after you are grown, with the same people in it the whole time. When women marry, they might go to a different village, but they are still in their same kafo. If your village is small, then your kafo will be small, but if your village is large, there may be 30, 50, or more people in it.

The girls' kafo would provide futo for our wrestling festivals, which is made from millet powder. The young men's kafo would provide a bull to kill, putting their money together to buy it. The meat would be divided between all the compounds where the grils were cooking, or it would all be done in one big compound. Then they would send a message to all the other villages to tell them, and to invite wrestlers from all over our area. Villagers will come with their wrestlers, and when they get there, they can go into any family's house and somebody there will let the kafo people know. Hundreds of people are cooked for, the food is divided between everybody at the festival, and the match always starts at nighttime.

I know how wrestling is. Your body gets used to it if you do it every day, but after taking a long break, you will really feel it the next day. One year, wrestling season started while it was still sanjano, which means time for digging the peanuts and harvesting other crops. I saw that there was a wrestling festival in a village called Mori Kunda, and a lot of people were going there so I wanted to go. Uncle Lamin Suso, my teacher's brother, said, "Don't go, because we are going to be working in the farm in the morning". I replied, "No problem, I will come back". We had to ride bicycles to get there, and I took my teacher's brother's bike. Lamin said to me, "You can't come back and say you are sleepy. When we go to the farm, you gotta go too". That night, I went and jumped in the ring and started dancing. Somebody came in and we wrestled. I wrestled all night until 5:30 in the morning, then everybody started scattering back to their own villages. I rode the bicycle back with all the others from my village. While riding, I started sleeping and trouble came. All the roadside grasses were dry and the road was small, and when I fell asleep I would go into the grass. Whenever I heard the grasses rustle, I would wake up and get back on the road. By the time we arrived in Passamasi, it was eight o'clock in the morning. The food was already made, and the men had eaten and were ready to farm.

I put the bike down and my Uncle Lamin said, "See, you look so sleepy". I sat down to eat mono out of a calabash, and I even fell asleep while eating, and forget to chew! I pretended that I was so fine. Then they all said, "Now we go to the farm". We use a special tool to dig peanuts, which is called a simba, and we bend down while digging. I took my simba to the farm, but when I was digging, I bent down and fell asleep like a statue. I heard my uncle say, "Move, move, move!" real loud, so I woke up and started digging again, but again I fell asleep. I started whistling like I was OK, then my whistle stopped. He started throwing dirt at me to keep me moving. One time when I stopped, he yelled and threw dirt at me, but still I fell down. The sun was hot, but I went right to sleep. Women brought lunch from the village to the farm for all to eat under one big tree, but when the lunch came, I still could not open my eye, and I missed it. They kept farming until four o'clock in the afternon, but I slept. Then they all went home. My hunting dogs stayed and made a circle around me. I woke up at seven o'clock, and started walking back to the village with the dogs following. When I arrived, my teacher's brother Lamin and another brother started yelling at me, "You will never go to a wrestling place again during farming season!" But when dinner came, I ate with everybody.

FODAY MUSA SUSO A VILLAGE GRIOT BOY AND THE WORLD

•••••

In our tradition, every young griot studies with their teacher for a few years, until they feel like you can play the kora well. Then it's time for you to take your teacher's kora and go alone to villages all around the area to do a kind of special griot traveling. Any time you get to a village, you will talk to the men's kafo, tell them who you are, and that your teacher will soon build you a kora, and that you will play for them. At every village you go to, they will know right away what you are doing. All the men from that kafo will gather in the middle of the village at the bantaba, and the leader will say, "We have a young griot here from such-and-such village, and we should help him to build his own kora". Everybody will say, "OK, we will do that". The men's kafo will make sure you have a place to stay for a few days, and the people will feed you the whole time you are there. You might stay at the compound of the leader of the men's kafo, or some other place, and you will play for the villagers every night. All the people in the men's kafo will always be there to listen to your playing. At the end of your stay, they will help you with the materials you need to build a kora: either a cow so that you can use the skin, or a big calabash for the kora body, some food for your travel, or a little money so you can buy the things you will need. You will go to as many villages as you can, to play for the people on your own, and to receive gifts from them. When you finish traveling, you will come back to your teacher's village with everything you have received.

Then it's the time for your teacher and his brothers to build your kora. You can help out a little bit, or just sit and watch them, but it's their job to build it for you. Griot women will gather all around, and they will be singing while the kora-building is happening. It takes a long time to build a kora. First, your teacher and his brothers will cut a big gourd in half to make the body. Our word for the gourd is mirango, but we will call it calabash when talking to toubabs because they understand that word. Then they cut the sound hole, which we call buludundula. That word means hand entrance, because that's the place where you will store your spare strings and the tuning nail, and you will have to put your hand in there to get them out. Then they cut the top and bottom holes for the neck of the kora, which we call the falo, but they cannot put the falo in until the body of the kora is completely dry. Some time before the day they start building the kora body, the men will have already killed the cow and prepared the skin, which we call kulo. They will also have made the two handles, which we call bulakalo, and the wooden braces which we call bantan bilo. Once those handles and braces are attached inside the body of the kora, they stretch the cowhide over it. It is stretched even over the sound hole and neck holes.

Then the kora will have to be brought out into the sun every day to dry. Nowadays, people can take it inside a house to dry it faster, but in those days it was all done outside in the traditional way. The cowhide starts out being black, but when they bring it outside, the sun is very hot on it. They will spray water on it every hour or so all day long, which will make it gradually and slowly turn from black to white. Once it is is completely dry, it's easy to see the place where the holes were cut, and to cut that part open. While the cowhide is drying, they will get a wood pole to make the neck.

Once the neck is attached inside the body of the kora, then the men can start to decorate the outside of the kora. They also have to carve the wood for the bridge, which we call batakungo, and put the little kora pillow under it, which we call kunlarango. Then we attach the jutunewo, which is a big iron ring at the bottom of the falo that the strings are attached to. Each of the 21 strings is also attached to the top of the falo with their own konso, which are the leather tuning rings. Then the kora is finished. But a new kora will never be sweet when it is first built. It has to be played a whole lot before the sweetness comes out. When a new kora is finished, you don't even want to listen to it. So when the teacher and his brothers finish building the new kora, they will have all their students play on it all the time, just hitting it in all kinds of ways to bring the sound out. Once the kora sound is sweet, then it will be time for your test.

Every kora song has a big history behind it that goes way, way, back, and even people who are not griots will know what each song is about. They can be about kings, empires, a friend, a famous person, a spiritual person, or other things. For your test, you will sit down in front of all the elder men in your teacher's village and play a song, then your teacher will ask you what it means. All the elder men will know the answers even if they are not a griot themselves, since they have been hearing these songs all of their lives. They will know if you say something crazy or mistaken about the song. And they will know if you can play or if you cannot play, if you know the history or if you don't know it. They will look at how your fingers are playing, and ask you how long ago the song was written. After that, you will play another song and your teacher will ask you those questions again. You don't have to play all the traditional songs, because each one can take a long time, maybe three or more hours. No one can play all the songs in one night! Nowadays, nobody will do this test, but in those days, that's how it was. Then the people will all tell your teacher what they think about your playing, and he will listen. If they say, "Your student can play well", then you will pass the test. When I finished playing, all the people told my teacher, "He can play very well".

My teacher showed me a whole lot about the kora, but I could play it even before I came to live with him and do all the griot traveling. All the time I was growing up, I was learning the kora. I was listening to my father play and I learned from that, even though my style is very different than his style. Even early in my life, I would always listen very well to all the griot travelers playing in my village. As soon as they finished, I would go straight back home and try to play those songs myself. When I was studying the kora, I could even play a song well after just hearing it one time. People would tell me that I play them even better than the griot traveler, because I was adding more strings and parts to the song. It was just like that for me with the kora. Kora playing was a gift to me from God, and I know that is 100% true. I never was struggling to learn it, and by the time I was leaving my teacher, I was playing very well.

A few days after you pass the test, it will be time for you to leave your teacher's compound. Then he will bring you back to your home village, or he will send somebody to go there with you. From that day on, you are ready to hit the road and be a griot. My teacher took me back to Foday Kunda, and soon after that, I decided to start traveling. At that time, I was around 21 years old, and it would be a long time before I was in my home village again.

One day in 2014, I was talking to my childhood friend Mohammed Suso. He is one of my cousin's brothers, and still lives in Pasamassi. He said, "We are doing traditional work right now, cutting findo". Findo is a very small grain that tastes so good when you cook it, but they don't grow a whole lot of findo now, because everything about harvesting and preparing it is a lot of work. Mohammed also said that the river didn't flood to supply the big ponds and lakes with water, so they did not do the traditional fishing this year. I told him, "I have to come to our village next time I go to Gambia, just to feel all those places again. Those old trees may not be there!" I was thinking of one big Silk Cotton tree that was in the village. Bantang is our word for Silk Cotton tree, and Bantang Ba is big Silk Cotton tree. Now over 40 years after I first left Passamasi, I was thinking that maybe those trees were gone. Then Mohammed said, "Do you remember the Baobab tree that was in the village? That tree just fell down, but the Bantang Ba is still there". I replied to him, "Today, it is like I am there with you right now".

IN THE CITY

Around four miles from Passamasi, and on the south side of the River Gambia, is a small trading town called Fatoto. I have a good childhood friend there named Demba Camara. We like each other so much. Whenever I go to visit him in Camara kunda, everybody is my friend there, but especially Demba. So a short time after I left my teacher's house in Passamasi village and came back to Foday Kunda, I decided to go to Fatoto to visit Camera kunda. The Camara family comes from Guinea-Bissau, and there are around 110 people in their compound: aunts, uncles, cousins, grandparents, and more! I always play a kora concert there when I come.

It was the year 1971, and after being there for a while, one day during the month of Ramadan, I decided to go to the town of Brikama. It is in the western part of Gambia in the Kombo District, near the Atlantic coast. So I talked to Demba's elder brother Lasana Camara, who was a driver for someone else's taxi car, a Puegot station wagon that held seven passengers. The man who owned that taxi was well off. His name was Alhaji Amara Gumaneh, and he had a shop where the car was kept. Every morning, Lasana would go to that shop, and the people who wanted to travel in the taxi would come there and pay. On that day, Lasana was driving from Fototo to the large town of Basse.

Because I am Demba's friend, Lasana wanted to give me a ride for free, but the car was already full, with first come first serve passengers. So Lasana told me, "Walk ahead of me, way down the road up to a rocky hill, and stand on the roadside and wait for me to arrive". I went ahead there and waited, with my kora on my shoulder and a fudo cloth wrapped around my clothes to make a bundle. Lasana saw me and stopped. He said "There are seven passengers inside so the taxi is full, but I will put your kora in the trunk. You have to ride on the roof of the car and hold onto the siderails. If you can hold on, you can ride". So I got up on the roof, facing backwards so the wind would not hit me in the face. The road was gravel and very bumpy in those days, and I had to hold on very tight so the bouncing around wouldn't throw me off. Sometimes the car hit a pothole and I went flying in the air. Lasana was driving, driving, driving, his normal speed. Sometimes I wondered if he remembered that I was on top! Dust was flying, and wind was hitting my back, picking my shirt up like an umbrella. People on the side of the road were all looking as we went by. I was worried that the siderails would come off in my hand! Just before getting to Basse, Lasana stopped to let me off so no one in town would see me on top. It is 22 miles from Fatoto to Basse, but since the road was not good and the car was flying, riding on top felt like way more miles than that to me!

Then I walked to the Basse market, and was sitting there to see how I could get transportation to Brikama. I had never been to Brikama, and in those days it was very hard to know even one person who owned a car. So people will use every kind of transportation, whatever they can get. It takes a whole day of traveling from Basse to Brikama because the dirt roads are rough with potholes, and the road zigzags a lot back and forth through villages all the way. Not like today! While I was sitting in the market, I recognized a guy named Mukumba, who is from the village of Kartong. That village is also in the Kombo District of Gambia, and right on the Atlantic Ocean. Mukumba worked as a driver for a man who bought peanuts at trading season time. Their agent was stationed in Fatoto, and it was the time of year that they were picking up the peanuts, so Mukumba had already driven from Fatoto to Basse that day too. I went over to talk with Mukumba, and he said to me, "I am going to Kartong today". I replied, "That is where I am going", because I knew that the main road went through Brikama to get to Kartong. He said, "Stay here, because I am going to give you a ride." So I waited for Mukumba and his apprentice to be ready to go. Mukumba drove a big truck, around the size of a dump truck. The apprentice sat in back, and I rode in front with Mukumba and my kora. We left Basse around ten o'clock in the morning and arrived in Brikama around nine o'clock at night, at the area near where today there is a very big market. But at that time, nothing was there except the big junction where the road from Basse meets all the roads that go to the capital city of Banjul, and to Gunjur, Kartong, and other places. When we got to that big junction, I asked Mukumba, "Where is the police station here?" because I knew that my brother

Mohammed Suso's compound was opposite the police station. Mukumba dropped me at the junction, and told me, "Walk on the road towards the Banjul way. Your brother's compound will be on the left side".

I never forgot what Mukumba did for me. Around 1984 or 1985 when I was home in Brikama, I was sitting with some mechanic friends of mine not far from my compound, and Makumba came there. He was talking to someone next to us, and told that guy, "I need you to loan me 250 dalasi to pay my kids school fee". But the guy replied, "I'm sorry, I don't have it". When I saw Mukumba, I recognized him even though I had not seen him since that day he dropped me in Brikama, but he did not recognize me. I called to him, "Hey, I want to talk to you". Mukumba was always a fast walker, mover, talker, and always in a hurry. So he followed me to my compound, all the way to my living room. Still, he didn't know who I am or what I was going to say. Then I said to him, "Sit down. I heard you talking about needing 250 dalasi", and he said, "My kids are starting school on Monday and I need it for that". I went inside my house and brought out 500 dalasi, and then I said, "Take this, I give you this. You don't know me but I know you". We Mandingos have a saying that a young person can recognize an elder person even after a long, long time, but an elder person cannot recognize a young person. That is because the young person grows up and changes, but the elder person doesn't. I said to Mukumba, "Do you remember many years ago, you used to be a truck driver in Wuli? Do you remember bringing one young griot all they way from Basse to Brikama? Do you remember that day when you brought me, my payment to you should be 7.50 dalasi but you said I don't need to pay anything?" Then I said, "The payment for that day is 500 dalasi because you did a good thing that day. You can take the 500 dalasi and pay your kids' school fee and keep the rest for yourself. Anytime you come to Brikama, you are welcome to visit here." After that, I only saw him one more time. His name was Momadou Camara, but everyone called him Makumba. He passed away around the time I came to live in Seattle, and he has a relative in Seattle that I still keep in touch with, and one of his sons is living in Sweden.

When Mukumba first dropped me at the Brikama junction that day in 1971, it was just after sunset. During the month of Ramadan, every day after sunset there is a special prayer added to the normal prayers that people do in the mosque or at their compound. When I arrived at Mohammed's family compound, I could hear them all offering that prayer. So I decided to sit there at the gate, because I knew if I walked in, the children would all run and greet me right away. So I waited until the prayer was done. When I walked in, we all greeted, and then I began to live there with Mohammed and his family. Because our mothers are sisters, we call each other brother, but because Mohammed is older than me I call him nkotoke, which means elder brother. His mother Sendin Jobarteh was the elder sister of my mother, and they were very close. Mohammed had brought his mother from Borro Kanda Kasse to live in his family compound in Brikama, and years later when I bought my first compound in Brikama, I brought my mother from Foday Kunda to Brikama to live there with us, so she could be near Sendin.

In those days, I would go to play my kora at a lot of ceremonies, marriages, and baby-naming ceremonies in Brikama. But when I first got there, it was not easy for me because I come from the eastern part of Gambia, and the kora songs we play there are Mali and Guinea griot style, in the sauta and haridino tunings. Brikama is in the west, and the kora music in that area is the Cassamance style of southern Senegal. The songs and style of singing are very different, and the tuning they use is called tomora or silaba. I could see that it was hard for people to understand my playing, so I said to myself, "I have to adapt, to change so I can learn". Very quickly, I picked up the Cassamance style, with the tomora tuning, playing and singing. I was lucky to be quick to learn.

Quickly, people started recognizing me in Brikama, and there I was also reunited with my friend Mohammed Camara, who I first met in Sutokoba. He was a Quranic student with an Imam in Sutukoba when I was living there at Yaffa kunda and going to the English school. Mohammed Camara comes from a Fina family. Fina are like a griot because they can sing praises, but they don't play an instrument. During traditional ceremonies, they will recite from the Holy Quran or recite sayings from the prophet Mohammed, while kora players play and sing. Fina have a way of singing God's praises and reciting the Holy Quran that is something else. One day I went to a baby-naming ceremony in Brikama, and I saw

Mohammed! We always called each other "boy" while we were growing up, so after we greeted each other very well, I said, "Boy what are you doing here?" He told me, "This is the place I am originally from. My family had sent me to Sutukoba to learn the Quran". Then he asked me, "Boy, how long have you been here?" and I told him, "I have been here about a month, and I am in my brother Mohammed's house in the compound opposite the police station". So that's when we got together in Brikama and became very heavy friends. Later on, Mohammed became in a wheelchair, but he still did a lot of work to build and take care of his family compound in Brikama. He was such a very hard-working man to do all that.

So every time I was going to play my kora, I went with Mohammed Camara. We played all over Gambia, down to Cassamance, and up to the northern part of Senegal. Sometimes I would play and sing, and Mohammed would tap the bottom of my kora with the tuning nail. Sometimes I would play and he would recite from the Quran, and sometimes we would sing together while I played. We played with another griot man and his wife sometimes too.

In those days, there was another new style of playing the kora that came up. Young griots liked to make the biggest kora, so that people who come to see you play can only see your head! Some people also added two or three more bass strings on top to make it 23 or 24 strings. The way the kora sounded with more bass notes made the people start dancing more, and it was very popular. This new style came from the Cassamance area, which is the Mandingo part of southern Senegal, and it used syncopated beats with a lot of 6/8 rhythms. The Cassamance kind of dancing went with that style of playing. It was so popular that people would always ask me, "Can you play Cassamance songs?" The first famous songs were called Yenyengo, Mama Manneh, and Musu Balanto. I had a small-size kora, so quickly I told my friend, "I need to make a new kora. I can build it, but I will need help pulling the skin over the calabash, because it is very big". So he helped me. I also added extra strings to it. That is the kora that I am holding in the photo of the 1st National Troupe of Gambia. Quickly after I finished building that kora, I changed my way of playing, because I knew I had to change or my thing wouldn't be happening there.

After I became recognized as a good Cassamance style kora player, women's groups in Brikama and other villages in the Kombo District started inviting me to play and be their Jali. At that time, the women called me Jalinding, which means young griot. Sometimes even now, when I see some of those women in Brikama, they still call me Jalinding. Now when I play, I can sound like I am from any of these regional styles: Mali, Guinea, Guinea-Bissau, Gambia, and Senegal. Whenever I hear anybody say, "Such and such is the best kora player", it is just wind over my ears, because only kora players know who is the best. If somebody is a good kora player in Gambia but they can only play Gambia style, and then they go to Mali, people would not know what they are singing about. They would think, "They are only hitting strings" and the audience will not be moved. If you are going to be a kora player, it's good to learn all the styles of the Mandingo areas, so that everywhere you go, you can satisfy the people and they will appreciate your sound. Kora music is a very complicated music. In our tradition, kora songs are not written music, but even if they were, the main rhythm is the only thing that would be written down. When improvising, that variation makes a big difference. When griots are playing, there can be 10 or 20 of them playing together, each of them taking turns improvising while others hold down the main rhythm. A teacher can teach you how to make the main rhythm on the kora, but not how to improvise. The improvisation cannot be written down, and not everyone can improvise.

•••••

Sometime in 1972, I left Brikama. My blood brother Mahamadou was going to fly from the capital city of Dakar, Senegal to Paris, and he asked me to go with him to the airport. I took my kora with me to Dakar, and right away I saw that people liked that Cassamance style from southern Senegal. A few months later, after Mahamadou had already come back from Paris, I returned to Brikama temporarily. I told my family there that

I was going back to live in Dakar, and I remained there for two years, playing the kora and going to baby-naming ceremonies and other events.

I also got a job playing the kora every night to entertain the tourists in a Dakar restaurant called Kerebaimbarik Faal. It was a traditional African restaurant, specializing in lamb and cous-cous, with a lot of western people coming in because it was near the airport and the ocean, and the food was very, very good. The way I got the restaurant job was this: One day I went to talk to the restraurant's owner, a wealthy Senegalese man named Baimbarik Faal. I proposed to him to hire me to play for the people there, and he gave me one day to do it, to see if the tourists would like it. On the day for my show, the owner offered to pick me and bring me to the place, which was jam-packed with people. I was carrying my kora and wearing a traditional Mandingo griot hat and clothes. As soon as I began to play, all the tourists stopped eating to listen to me. I walked through the place playing my kora, and approached each table to ask, "What is your name?" in French. Then I started singing their names in my songs, and whoever name I sang would be so happy. I had a friend write down "Please put money in kora" in French on a piece of paper, and people put lots of money in my kora. Then the owner said to me, "You must come here every day". So I began to play there every day except Monday, starting at four or five o'clock and going for the rest of evening. This is where I first saw currency from all over the world, and heard a lot of western languages.

At that time, there was also a weekly program on Radio Senegal with a producer and host called Alhaji Muktar Jallow. The name of his program was Histoire de Cassamance, a French phrase that means History of Cassamance, but his program was about Mandingo people from all over West Africa. On the program, a man called Mamadou Sillah was the main speaker, talking with Alhaji Muktar Jallow about many different warriors, kings, and tribes in our history, while a very famous kora player named Jali Lalo Kebba Drammeh accompanied him. Jali Lalo played only solo kora, and on that show he always played traditional griot songs, but he wrote orginal songs too.

Two things happened for Jali Lalo Kebba that had never happened before for any kora player: his voice knows the Mandingo wording and puts the words together without making any mistakes, and the strength of his hands was very aggressive in every part of a song, with perfect volume of hand and voice. We have a saying, "Hand is ahead of mouth", meaning that the singing cannot keep up with the kora playing, or "Mouth is ahead of hand" meaning that the kora playing cannot keep up with the singing. But Jali Lalo Kebba had mouth and hand equally great. In any city or village he played, everyone would always gather in the village square or mayor's compound to hear him. Every Mandingo also listened to the Radio Senegal broadcast of Histoire de Cassamance, which reached all the way to Guinea-Bissau and Sierra Leone. So all the people heard Jali Lalo Kebba playing every week.

One of the big things that Jali Lalo Kebba was known for happened in 1972. A Manding Conference on kora music was held in London at a place called The School of Oriental and Africa Studies, but we Mandingos call it the Africa Center. At this conference, kora players from Senegal, Gambia, and Mali were showcasing their playing and having a competition to see which country had the best kora player. Each country was sending two or three griots to go. President Senghor of Senegal, as well as many griots, wanted Jali Lalo Kebba to represent Senegal. Jali Lalo Kebba was raised in the Cassamance area of Senegal, so a lot of people thought he was from Senegal. But at the time his mother was pregnant with Lalo, his mother and father were griot traveling and came to the village of Bondaly in the southern part of Gambia to visit King Bondaly Fatty. While they were there, the labor came to his mother, and Lalo was born.

Gambian President Jawara was also planning to send a troupe to the Manding Conference, and everyone in all of Gambia was happy when Jali Lalo Kebba decided to represent Gambia there. Dignitaries from Senegal, Gambia, and Mali were there to judge the kora playing, along with some British people who knew kora music. Jali Lalo Kebba played last. No one there could match him for the kora at that time, because he played very strongly and sang very well. He won the competition because he had more variations of playing the kora than any other griot there. He played in a style that young griots today do not play. Still today, I have never heard another player come close to playing like Lalo ever in my lifetime. He was so heavy. The way he played the kora, you cannot find anybody to play kora like that. He played with a heavy strength and his playing was very loud. The way he touched the kora, and his singing too, is the same thing. When he plays, you don't want him to stop. When he is singing, you don't want him to stop. If he was alive today, he alone could fill a big stadium with people coming to see him play. It's unbelieveable in a way that is hard to describe with words.

Jali Lalo Kebba was a friend of my father, and used to come and visit him a lot in Banjul. Lalo came there to stay with Basiru Jawara, another friend of his who was a very wealthy businessman, and in fact is still alive today. During the daytime, Lalo didn't have much to do, and so he would come to my father's apartment and spend a lot of time there. Lalo and my father knew each other for many years, even before I was born. When I was growing up, I would sit and listen to them talking with each other about things that happened a long, long time ago. That's why I know Lalo so heavy. When I heard him play, right away it became my favorite way of playing, and I looked up to him. Sometimes even now, I sit down and change the tuning of my kora, and I play all those old songs for a while.

I was already living in Dakar when Jali Lalo Kebba passed away there. Soon afterward, Alhaji Muktar Jallow wanted someone to play the song of a man named Jula Jekereh Bayo while Mamadou Sillah recited the history. There were a bunch of griots living in Dakar who are from Cassamance, but Alhaji Muktar Jallow and Mamadou Sillah couldn't find anyone who knew how to play the song well. Jula Jekereh Bayo lived a long, long ago, and was a famous man from Passamasi, the same village where I learned the kora from my teacher. He went and built his own village called Dutabasi near the border of Gambia and eastern Senegal. He was from a Gambian trader family, and was very wealthy and powerful. He was a very heavy guy, and he passed away when my teacher's father, Jali Mfamara Suso, was a little child. Since my teacher's family lived in Passamasi for a long time, all the griots in that family knew a whole lot about Jula Jekereh Bayo and the song that was composed for him. The first song every young griot learns to play on the kora is called Kelefa, but one of the first songs I learned from my teacher was Jekereh Bayo, so I know how to play it very well also.

Mamadou Sillah knew a lot about Jekereh Bayo too, because he is from a leatherworker family in Brifu, the same village where the family of my father's mother Luntanding Jobarteh was from. Mamadou Sillah also knew my father when they were growing up, and called him Nkoto Saikou, which means elder brother Saikou. Mamadou Sillah knew all the other kora players in that area too. I never knew him in Brifu though, because he came to Dakar when I was just a small child. I heard his program on the air when I first came to Dakar from Brikama, but I didn't know who he was or where he was from.

One morning while I was at a baby-naming ceremony in Dakar, Mamadou Sillah came to that compound for the celebration. He heard me playing the kora, and came up to say hello. He asked my name and where I was from, and when I said, "Gambia", right away he asked me which area. When I told him my village Foday Kunda, he said, "What? You are the one I am looking for!" I asked him why, and he told me his name and that he was the one with the Histoire de Cassamance radio show with Alhaji Muktar Jallow. Then he said, "We are getting ready to do the history of Jekereh Bayo, and since you are a griot from eastern Gambia, I know that you will know about him". Mamadou Sillah knew that all griots that are born and raised in my area of Gambia have to learn to play Jekereh Bayo, and that it's one of the songs we specialize in. That's when he told me, "We tried some other kora players to play that song, but they could not play it. I want to take you to the radio studio to meet the host of the show". He asked where I lived, and I told him I was renting a place at 950 Nyari Tally. In that area of Dakar, two big streets meet in the center of the neighborhood with a long boulevard between them, and Nyari Tally means "two roads" in the Wolof language. Then he said, "I will come and pick you up next Wednesday, and we will go together to the Radio Senegal studio".

When we got there that day, I started warming up with the kora, and right away Alhaji Muktar Jallow said, "Oh, you can play". Then he asked me to play the Jekereh Bayo song. I started playing, and after only two or three seconds he said, "This is exactly what we are looking for". So I played my kora while Mamadou Sillah recited the history of Jekereh Bayo. That first recording was played on the following Sunday, and on Monday, several kora players came to the radio station to say, "Fodaymusa Suso is from Gambia and not from Cassamance, so it shouldn't be him playing". But Alhaji Muktar Jallow replied to them, "When we say Histoire de Cassamance, we mean it to be the history of the Mandingo people in every part of West Africa, not just Cassamance. I tried you people first, and none of you people can play the Jekereh Bayo song clearly. Fodaymusa can play it clearly, so it should be him. No more complaining! No more jealousy". The next Wednesday when I came back to the studio to do the taping again, Alhaji Muktar Jallow and Mamadou Sillah told me about what happened. After that, whenever I saw those other griots in Dakar and said, " My uncle, how are you?" they would not reply anything to me. So I left them alone. After that, I played for eight months of the Histoire de Cassamance radio program. The show was broadcast on Sundays, but they recorded it every Wednesday at one o'clock in the afternoon. So every time they began the taping, they would always say, "Tonight, our Sunday program is..." That was funny to me because I never knew about that kind of thing. That Histoire de Cassamance program kept going for long, long time after I left, and I think maybe it just ended only twenty years ago.

One year after Lalo died, Alhaji Muktar Jallow also decided that he wanted to do a traditional kora concert for the anniversary. He called all the griots in Dakar to meet, and told them his plan. The concert would be at the Daniel Sorano Performing Arts Center, a big place in Dakar, and he would invite a lot of people to attend. For each song, he wanted there to be two kora players playing together on stage. The griots there, most who were from Cassamance, refused to play together with me, because the jealousy was still there about the radio show. I told Alhaji Muktar Jallow, "If nobody wants to play with me, can't I play alone?" so he said, "OK, that's what we will do." All the other griots played in pairs, but I played solo. At that time, I was becoming very well known in Dakar, and everybody knew me. So I got in touch with a lot of people who were from Gambia, Mali, and Cassamance but were living in Dakar, to let them know about the date for the show. Hundreds of Mandingo and Wolof people came to the show all dressed up in traditional clothes.

There were some very wealthy Wolof women in Dakar too, and Jali Lalo Kebba had written some songs that were popular with them for dancing.

Lalo was my mentor and role model. I like his style and I learned his songs, and patterned my playing after his playing. So I decided to play his songs at this concert. After all the other griots played two at a time, they called my name to come onstage. When I got up there, I took the microphone and stuck it inside the sound hole of my kora, because in those days they didn't have the kind of little microphones that clip onto a kora. The first song I played and sang was Chedo, which is about warriors from Guinea-Bissau. Then I played Jimbasingo, which is a highlife-style song about fishermen. Lalo didn't compose those songs, but anytime he touched the kora, he could play them better than the people who composed them. Then I played a song that Lalo composed called Musubalanto, which was also a highlife-style song about a woman. My last song was Lalo's most famous song before he died, called Kuran Mbisaan. It's a love song written to his wife, sung in the Wolof language, and it gave Lalo a big name. When I played that song, I mentioned some people in the crowd while singing. When they heard their name in my song, they were very honored, and people started running up to the stage and bringing money to stuff like crazy into my kora. So that night, I made more money than any other griot there. After the concert, Alhaji Muktar Jallow told all the griots to come back to the concert hall the next day to get paid. When we all got there, I heard other griots telling him, "Fodaymusa should not be paid today because he made so much more than anybody else yesterday". Alhaji Muktar Jallow said, "I will pay him the same as I pay you. You all said no when I asked each of you to play with him, so now everyone will be paid equally".

•••••

Around this time, my father founded the Gambian National Troupe. Senegal, Guinea, and Mali, all had a national troup of musicians at that time, but Gambia didn't have one. My father had been in Sierra Leone and traveling for a very long time, and knew about those troupes. When he came back to Gambia in 1973, he went to the office of the President of Gambia, Dawda Jawara. He knew the President well, so he could meet with him. My father said, "All our area countries have a national troupe, but we don't have one. I want to talk to you about that, because I would like Gambia to have a troupe here". Then President Jawara said, "Well, I have known you for a long time, and now you are back from Sierra Leone, so what I would like to see is for you to put the griots together here. You will organize everything, and once I see that, I will know what my government can do". At that time, Lalo was still alive, but he was living in Senegal and did not join the Gambian National Troupe.

While all that was happening, there was also a balafon player from Gambia named Banna Kanuteh, who was living in Dakar and performing with the Senegal National Troupe. He moved to Senegal because he had some big political differences with President Jawara. When my father talked to President Jawara, he said, "Our Banna is in Dakar. Banna is my friend. I know he fell apart with your government, and that's why he left Gambia and moved to Senegal, but I want you to forgive him so I can bring him back to be in our national troupe". The President told my father, "OK, I will do that on your behalf, but if you people are serious, you will advise him to stay away from politics when he comes back. He is not a politician, and he didn't go to an English school to have any kind of political career or anything like that. The reason he left Gambia is that he was interfering with my government. Griots are always griots, and should stay the way they are. On your behalf, I will do this if you tell him to please, please stay away from politics". My father said, "No problem, Banna is my friend. When I talk to him, he will listen to me. But he is scared to come back to Gambia, so to make sure that he knows he will be safe here, I want you to provide me with some government transportation to go and get him. When he sees me arrive in that transportation, he will know that it is safe to come back with me to Gambia". So the President sent my father with a big truck to go get Banna. The day my father went to Dakar, he was with three other griots: Jali Yaya Jassey, Jali Kebba Suso, and Jali Madi Suso. I think he is still alive today, but he is a different griot than my Uncle Jali Madi Suso from Manjan Kunda, who I was with as a child when we saw toubab boys playing football on a boat. My father and those griots all went to Banna's house. When they arrived, they all greeted, and then Banna said, "What's happening? Why are all you people here?" My father said, "Nothing to worry about, everything is cool. The reason I came with all these people is that we are coming to take you to Gambia today". Banna said, "But hey, how can that be?" and my father said, "I already met with President Jawara and got his word, and he got my word. You are forgiven, and we will go back to Gambia today".

By this time, I was already in Dakar, playing my kora at the Kerebaimbarik Faal restaurant. When my father got to Dakar, he told the people to ask Mamadou Sillah to go to my house to tell me that he has come to get Banna. Also to tell me that I should pack all my things, because we will all go back to Gambia together that day. I was in my house when Mamadou Sillah arrived. He said, "Brother Saikou is here to collect Banna and his things, and he told me to come and get you because they don't want to leave you behind here". I said OK and got ready to go, and put some money in my pocket that was paid to me by the restuarant. When Mamadou Sillah and I arrived at Banna's house, the people were taking all the tables and chairs, bowls and beds, and everything out from the house, and loading it all into the big truck. Banna had a wife and children, and a whole household full of furniture. I went to my father and asked him to come and talk with me. We walked out away from the people and into the street, and I said, "I know you want me to come back to Gambia today with you, but please let me stay here. I have a very good job playing in a hotel and restaurant, and I am making good money." Then I took the money out of my pocket and told him, "I want you to take this. Please let me stay here, and I will come to Gambia later on". He said OK, and took the money inside and divided it among all the people there. He gave everything to them. That's how he is. So they kept packing and packing, and then they all went back to Gambia.

My father continued leading the Gambian National Troupe until he passed away many years later. After that, other people tried to keep the troupe together, but it didn't keep going. My father always had very heavy respect from the people. Everybody who looks at him will bow their head down in respect. He is that kind of man. Even many times when President Juwara himself had things going on, such as politics or arguments between his ministers and government people, somebody would run and tell my father, "The President wants to see you". It could be in the middle of while we were eating dinner, and it meant that those people were talking about something heavy, and my father needed to be the mediator between them in a traditional griot way. We Mandingos have a saying of, "They need someone with a strong mouth to fix this", and my father is number one for that. My father is a very quiet person. He doesn't talk a lot, but when he talks you will listen.

When they first built the Radio Senegal station in Dakar, the first griot music that was played on the radio was my father and two other griots named Kunye Sako and Baskala Suso. This was when I was a small baby, long before Alhaji Muktar Jallow and Mamadou Sillah had the History of Cassamance radio show. My father was a very famous griot throughout all of West Africa. My father's brother Sunjulu Suso was born in Cassamance and became a very famous griot also, and he was on that radio station too. My father's father and Sunjulu Suso's father were brothers, so we call my father and Sunjulu brothers too. Thinking of this reminds me of a time around 1979, when a Senegalese guy named Amadou Cham came to visit me in Chicago. He was living in Indianapolis, and he showed me a copy of a magazine called West Africa, with some old, old pictures of griots playing their koras in Senegal. While I was looking at the magazine, I saw a picture of my father with Kunye Sako, Baskala Suso, and a griot woman. So right away, I bought that magazine from Amadou Cham. I knew that this picture was taken before I was born because the kora my father was playing in the picture was a kora he had a long, long time ago. The handles of this kora were made out of silver. When I was a small boy, my father used to tell me about that kora, and that he paid the silversmith who made those handles with a bull. Later on, my father gave the silver handles to his younger brother Lamin Suso for his kora, and when that kora broke, my Uncle Lamin took them and gave them to me. I never used those silver handles on my kora, because today the koras are made differently, but I keep them in my house in Brikama. Even though I won't use them, I can look at them.

•••••

Later on in 1973 or 1974, while I was still renting my place at 950 Nyari Tally in Dakar, I got to see something I never saw before. My place was only two blocks from a stadium called Stadium Dembajobe, and at that time, the whole city was talking about how a great American musician was going to play a concert there. That musician was James Brown. In those days, the stadium was used only for football (called soccer in the U.S.), so I said, "No, I'm not going to any football stadium." I didn't know about James Brown at that time. People were lining up to buy tickets to go to the show, and a lot of people were coming down the streets. I could hear them outside talking, and the crowd noise becoming very loud. I layed down on my bed and turned my light off, and then the music started. A heavy funk beat started, then the guitar and horns, and then James Brown started hollering! There was no roof on the stadium, and there were doors all around the outside of it. It sounded like he was standing right next to my bed! So I said to myself, "I gotta go see what's happening". I got dressed and walked to the stadium. The outside was full with the people, and the inside was jam-packed. Everyone was standing around to listen, and I tried to get a ticket but it was sold out. I saw somebody I knew who was working at the show, and asked, "Wow, how is it inside?" He said, "The tickets are finished, but one thing I can do for you is this: go around the stadium to this one door. Scratch at the door, and if I hear you I will scratch, and if you hear me scratch back, then I will let you in". So he snuck me in to the concert. When I came in, James Brown was firing up so much, doing all his style: tiptoing on his toes, pushing the mic stand over and catching it. He was something else!

Being a musician myself, I know that those kinds of people are made to be like that. God made you to be that way, your way is different than everybody, and no one can do exactly what you do. You can do it as soon as you wake up in the morning. People such as James Brown, Jimi Hendrix, Mick Jagger, and Michael Jackson, somebody else could practice 100 years and not do it their way. The way Jimi Hendrix played, everything he did came to him easy compared to other people. He was perfect on that. Many musicians, comedians, boxers, basketball players, all are like that too. I always say, "Just do what you do, and don't try to be like them". The next year, the Jackson 5 came to Senegal and played a different place than James Brown. Michael was a small boy then, singing in front of his brothers. No one can do it like him, he was meant to be that kind of singer. I went to see the Jackson 5 too, but the one that really takes me is James Brown.

•••••

While I was still living in Dakar, there was going to be a big Gambian Independence Day celebration on Feb 18th, 1974, so I went to Gambia to attend the celebration. The Gambian government invited the Ghana government to participate in the festivities too, because Ghana, Sierra Leone, and Nigeria were all former English colonies like Gambia. The President of Gambia had gone to school in Ghana too, so he was extra close with that country. The President of Ghana did not attend the celebration himself, but he sent a delegation that included the founder and director of the Institute of African Studies at the University of Ghana, a famous ethnomusicologist named Kwabena Nketia. At the celebration, Kwabena Nketia saw the griots playing kora and became very interested in having someone teach the kora at the University of Ghana at Lagon. So he asked Mamadou Cham, the Gambian Minister of Culture, who he should invite to Ghana to do that.

The Gambian National Troup was rehearsing in Banjul at that time, and the minister went there to talk to my father Jali Saikou Suso, the leader of the troupe. My father told Mamadou Cham, "You should talk to many other people here", because he did not want to choose his own son. But the other elders who were there told Mamadou Cham, "We wish Fodaymusa was here because he could do this, but he is in Senegal". Then others in the crowd told them, "Fodaymusa is here for the celebration, because we saw him yesterday!" and my father said, "Yes, he is here at my apartment". Mamadou Cham told my father, "Let's go look for him", and they went driving around and around, looking for me. They found me walking down the street and asked me to get in the car to go with them. They said, "We are going to the Atlantic Hotel to talk to some people from Ghana". They dreopped me off at the hotel, and Kwabena Nketia came down from his room to talk to me. I answered all the questions he asked, such as how to build the kora, how many strings it has, how to tune it, and more. Then he told me he wanted to bring me to Ghana to teach, and said, "We have music from all over Africa there, but no one to teach the kora". After meeting with Nketia, I came to teach at the University of Ghana, which is just outside the capital city of Accra. The university asked me to stay three months, but I ended up staying there for close to three years.

It took a long time for all the paperwork to be done before I could go to teach in Ghana though. From February to April, I was in Gambia waiting while negotiating was done between Gambia and Ghana, without going back to my work in Dakar. Finally an appointment letter came, and I had to be examined for health by a man named Dr. Samba. Everything was OK with me, so I told my father, "I have to go back to Senegal to settle my apartment". When I got back to Dakar, I talked to my childhood friend and kora player Surakata Kouyeteh about replacing me at the restaurant. He is a griot and my same age, and we are good friends ever since we were kids growing up together in Foday Kunda. He was living in Dakar at that time, and I knew he could play the kora very well, so I took him to see the owner of the restaurant. I introduced them and asked Baimbarik Faal to allow Surakata to replace me, and play for the people. Baimbarik agreed, and from 1974 to 1979, Surakata played there. Then some French people took him to Paris with a six-month contract to play in France, but Surakata stayed there. Even today, he is still living in Paris with his family. We talk to each other a lot on the phone now, and laugh about our childhood days.

The name Surakata is very common among the griots. In our tradition, we say that Surakata was the first griot of the Prophet Mohammed. The Prophet had many followers who traveled with him, and Surakata was the one who did the talking for the whole group in any village they arrived in. As soon as they got to a new place, Surakata will say, "Villagers come out, come out. A prophet of God is coming to your village, come out to hear him". And the villagers would all come out to meet the Prophet Mohammed, and he would talk and pray for them, and then the villagers would give him some charity. Later on while continuing the traveling, the Prophet Mohammed would take that charity and divide it among all the followers, but he would always give more money to Surakata. One day, a follower asked him, "Why do you give more money to Surakata than everybody else? We should all be given the same, because we all are going with you". The Prophet Mohammed said OK, and then he told Surakata, "From now on in any place we go to, don't say anything". So when they came to the next village, nobody living there came to hear the Prophet Mohammed speak, or gave anything to his followers. The same thing happened at the following village, so at the end of the day there was nothing to divide. Then the Prophet told his followers, "Aha, now you see that the reason why I always give Surakata more, it's because of his mouth that people are coming out. When I told him to say nothing, then nothing came to us". That's why the name Surakata is common among the griots.

In 1979, when Surakata Kouyeteh was going to leave Kerebaimbarik Faal restaurant to go to Paris, he took his elder brother Jalikeh Kouyeteh to meet the owner, and he replaced Surakata there. Later on, Jalikeh made enough money to even buy his own house in Dakar. Some time later, Baimbarika Faal passed away and his son Ousman Faal took on the business. Then he too died, and the place kept going for a while, but later Surakata told me it was not there anymore. I went there only two times after coming to the United States, and the second time I was wearing a cowboy hat and no one recognized me. I sat in a covered, grass-roofed area of the restaurant, ordered and ate food, and paid my bill. When I was leaving, I stopped and lifted my cowboy hat up and showed them my face! Then they made me take my money back for the bill.

•••••

In the months when I was preparing to leave for Ghana, there was also jealousy from other griots of me going there. When I told them I was going, no one said, "Safe journey" to me. At that time, there was only one newspaper in Gambia, called The Bulletin, and it had an article about me going to Ghana. Some people sent that copy of The Bulletin to some Gambian students who were in Ghana, to show them what day I was going to arrive, and those students came to the airport to meet me. It was a Sunday when I arrived in Accra, and the three students I remember are Mamu Konteh, Bakary Ketta, and Lamin Komma, but there were others too, and they were all holding a copy of The Bulletin. Not far away was a hostel where some of the Gambian students were living, and they took me there because they said, "No one is working who can drive you to Lagon today". The next morning at nine o'clock, the students took me to the University of Ghana African Studies Department to meet all the people there. We went to Kwabena Nketia's office, and I found out that all my accommodations were ready in South Lagon, which is between the university campus and the city of Accra. I began to settle in there, and my apartment was very nice, with two bedrooms and a living room. Then some food was brought to me called kenke, which I like a lot. It is a Ghanian food made from corn dough wrapped to make it sour, and eaten with fried fish, and pepper and onion ground together for a sauce. This was first time I ever saw that kind of food, and it became my favorite.

In all the years that I was teaching at the University of Lagon, some days a well-known driver came named Glofast would come to pick me at my apartment and take me to the university campus. If not, I would walk to campus along the back roads, and I liked that better. It was good to see the people, compounds, and shops on foot. In those days, a kind of music called highlife was very, very big in Ghana, and there were a lot of clubs and highlife music being played everywhere in Accra. There were also a lot of people from all over Europe and America who came to the university to learn to play African instruments, and most of my kora students were from Germany or Scandanavia. Besides teaching my students, the Institute of African Studies Department had me perform kora concerts there, and sent me to the Ashanti area and other places inside Ghana to play, and the French Embassy brought me to the neighboring countries of Togo and Benin. I always traveled with a famous musician named Kakaraba Lobi. He was the very best player of the gyil, the traditional instument of his people, the Lobi tribe from Northern Ghana. The gyil has wooden keys with calabashes beneath, similar to the balafon. Kakaraba Lobi had been invited by Kwabena Nketia to be a teacher at the Institute of African Studies when it was first being formed in 1962, and he stayed there a long time. When we traveled together, we performed our music at the same concerts, but we did not perform together because our tunings are very different. Kakaraba was much older than me, and later on he traveled all over the world playing his music and taught many students. He passed away in 2007. During those years I was teaching in Ghana, I also traveled on my own to other countries just to visit, but I never traveled back home to Gambia.

Later on, I found out that Kwabena Nketia was invited to be a visiting professor at UCLA, and spent around three months of every year teaching there for quite a few years. He was also Professor of Music at the University of Pittsburgh, and brought his whole family to live there. He became very famous because of how well he knew the traditional music of all West Africa, and because of all the music he himself wrote. I never saw him at either of these two universities, but I did see him in New York City in the mid 1980's. At that time, Robert Browning had put together the World Music Conference, and brought me there from Chicago along with a whole lot of other musicians. I performed at Town Hall and also taught some classes for students, and one day Kwabena Nketia came to one of my classes. He had come to New York all the way from Ghana. We talked with each other for a long time. He lived to be almost 100 years old! And as I remember when I looked at him face to face back then, I think he looks like somebody who could live a very long time.

While I was teaching in Ghana, I also met the very first American friend I ever had, black or white. It was a guy named Richard Hill from New Haven, Connecticut, and he was studying music at the University of Ghana. While he was there, he recorded me playing kora on some traditional griot songs, and a young Ghanaian named Joseph Kobum playing traditional Dagarti songs on the balafon. After Richard came back to the U.S., he contacted Lyrichord Discs about this music, and in 1977 they put out those songs on an album called Sounds of West Africa: The Kora and the Xylophone. During my time in Ghana, I also became very good friends with two British guys that were around my same age too: One was a student named Stuart Sutton-Jones, and the other was a guy named Tony Grilly who was traveling around and happened to visit Ghana. I don't think Stuart and Tony knew each other there or in London, because I didn't ever see them hanging out together back then, and they are very, very different from each other.

Tony is a good guy, but he is also wild and crazy, and he is hardheaded just like me! He came to Ghana with his wife Balbear Balbeia, who was from India. Tony had a crazy truck and a shotgun too. He was not a hunter, but he likes guns. He came and showed me the truck, and we rode all over Accra in it. I went crazy and said, "I know how to hunt, so let's go". So we got ready to go night hunting, and brought a big flashlight with us, the kind with three D-cell batteries. I told him, "Let's go to the farm area in case there are rabbits coming there to eat the vegetables". That was our big mistake. He drove us out to the Laateh village area, flying on the road from Accra even though neither of us knew that area. I put the flashlight on my head like my good friend Balla Yaffa used to do, and Tony was following me around. We went to a yam farm, and I was walking and swinging the light, so people saw me from a far distance. They thought, "These people are coming to steal our yams", so they called the police. Very soon, three, four, or five trucks full of police came from Accra, with their guns pointed to us. The next thing that happened is they grabbed us and put us in the trucks. We said, "We got a truck here", but they replied, "No, you gotta leave it and go to police station for questioning". I told them, "I teach the kora at the University of Ghana in Lagon", and they asked Tony, but he was talking fast with his heavy British accent, so they did not believe it. They did not find any yams in our hands because we did not steal anything, and luckily Tony had the paperwork for the gun. We were at the police station for a long time, but they finally released us. That was the first and last time Tony and me wanted to go hunting! We used to write to each other a lot when I was first in the United States, but since he left Ghana, I have only seen him one time. It was in London at the end of 1984, and I was touring with my band Mandingo after the release of the Watto Sitta album. He and his wife were living there, and I went to their place to see him.

I met Stuart Sutton-Jones after I was living in Ghana for a while, and we were hanging out a lot after that. He had a car, and we went driving around in it. Stuart is one of the greatest men I have ever met. He has to walk with crutches and big braces on his legs because he got polio when he was a child. But in his car, he had all the controls for his hands to do the driving. Later on, Stuart even learned how to fly airplanes like that, and he still flies back and forth across the United States from New York to California! Stuart is something else. Whenever he wants to sit down, he just pushes a little button on the side of his braces, and poom! they bend so he can sit. When we met, right away we became very good friends. He was at the University of Ghana studying, but not in the ethnomusicology department. And he is very heavy smart, wow. His speaking and his thinking are very good, and any place he goes, he can fit into a heavy job. Anytime he arrives at a new place, the next thing I know is that he will be working for the government. He can do many things that even if people had ten legs they cannot do. He's that kind of person, a very heavy human being.

While me and Stuart were hanging out in Accra, we went out to the bars to hear music. Even though I don't ever drink alcohol and Stuart doesn't drink a lot, in those days the bars and clubs were filled with live bands and music all the time. Ghana was a party place, and every weekend the hotel and club owners would host something they called "afternoon jump". Bands from all over Ghana who played highlife music would be there, and people would dress up nice to go and listen. One day, we went to the Starr Hotel, and were sitting at the bar together. I was talking to some people on my right hand side, and Stuart was talking to some people on his left hand side. I didn't know it, but Stuart started to argue with somebody there, and the next thing I knew he was hollering and punching the guy, hard! The guy pulled him down and they both fell on the ground. When I jumped up and grabbed Stuart to start pulling him off, he was going crazy and yelling, "Suso, Suso, I'll kill him!" I said, "No, no, Stuart, let's go!" because I had to stop the fight. He said that the guy was trying to play some foolish thing on him. I will never forget that day.

Stuart also introduced me to Adam Rudolph. One day, Stuart went from the university campus into Accra, and there he happened to meet Adam. That day, Adam told Stuart that he just came to Ghana a short time before, and was trying to find a way to learn to play the Mandingo drums we call kutiros. So Stuart told him about me, and said that he would introduce us. Later when we met, Adam told me that he wanted to go to Gambia to learn how to play. Right away, I thought of the guy I wanted to introduce Adam to. I told him, "I know a very good kutiro drummer in Brikama whose name is Fakary Badji, but he is called Jallo Badji. His younger brother Touray Badji is my very good friend". I wrote a letter to Jallo Badji to introduce Adam, and to ask him to teach Adam to play kutiro. Jallo Badji wrote back to say, "Yes, when he comes I will teach him." Soon after that, Stuart went back to England, and was living in Brighton.

• • • • •

After Stuart left Ghana, Adam and me started hanging out together a lot in South Lagon where I lived, and I told him he could come and stay with me there. I also told him, "You say you are going to Gambia, and I want to go to Germany." In those days, a lot of Gambians traveled to Germany, France, and Scandinavia. So I went to the German embassy, but the people there told me, "The visa person is not here, you must come back later on." Later that day, me and Adam had dinner together, and I told him that maybe I would like to come to United States instead. He asked me why, and I said, "I would like to go there and start a band". I already knew at that time that I wanted to name my band Mandingo Griot Society, because of Alex Hailey's book and movie, called "Roots". I thought my band could get work because since that movie came out, the word griot was now recognized by many people in the United States. Adam asked if he could play in the band, and I said yes. So me and Adam, and a friend of his named Lieberman, went to the U.S. Embassy to get a visa for me. Adam and Lieberman asked the embassy people if they could speak on my behalf, but the embassy people wanted to speak to me directly. They asked me why and how long I wanted to visit the U.S., and what I was doing in Ghana. I told them about teaching for the university, and that I wanted to visit the U.S. for two months. They said they wanted a letter from the university to verify my job, and for me to bring it back with the $8.00 visa fee. So I went to the African Studies Dept and Nketia wrote me a letter, and then I went back to the embassy with $8.00

and they stamped my passport. Things were so much simpler back then in 1977!

Later I met up with Adam again and told him that I got the visa. He asked me, "What kind of band do you want?" I said there should be kora, bass, drums, and percussion. Adam said, "I know a drummer friend in Chicago named Hank Drake. I still want to go to Mali, but I will not go to Gambia on this trip". By that time, I had contacted Stuart Sutton-Jones to tell him that I was coming to the U.S., and he said, "On your way, you should pass through London, and come to visit me here". So I told Adam, "By the time you come back from Mali, I will be leaving Ghana and stopping in London to visit Stuart on my way to the United States".

I left Ghana on British-Caledonia Airlines at around two o'cock in the morning on August 30th, 1977, and arrived at Gatwick Airport in London at around seven o'clock. Stuart drove all the way to the airport from his home in Brighton to pick me. At the time I arrived in England, Stuart knew a woman named Lucy Duran who was living in London and had been to Gambia to visit a griot named Jali Amadou Jobarteh. He is a relative to me on my father's side, and I call him grandfather. Stuart had gotten in touch with Lucy to let her know I was stopping there on my way to the United States, and she had arranged some concerts for me to do in London. When I arrived at the airport, they stamped my passport and asked me where I was going, and how long I would be there. I had my visa, but I didn't have any work permit and I didn't know anything about immigration stuff. So I made a mistake to mention that I had some concerts to do. They asked me, "What kind of concert?" and I said that I was going to play my kora. Then they said, "I hope they are going to pay you something for that". I said yes. So right away they told me, "You go over there and sit". Two passengers remained beside me who also had a problem with the immigration thing: a man from Chile and a lady from Nigeria. We stayed there all the way from seven in the morning until three o'clock in the afternoon!

All day long, Stuart was looking for me in the airport and asking everybody, "Did you all see somebody wearing a big African dress and holding an African instrument?" Somebody finally said yes, and told him what was happening. When he found out, Stuart called some office people in downtown London to asko them to try to fix it, and they called the airport people to try to arrange things. Stuart tried very hard, but it didn't work. Finally, he told the immigration officials that he was my host, and I had been mistaken about the concerts when I told them that. He told them that he tried to get me some gigs but it didn't happen, and I wasn't going to play anywhere. It took him a long time to convince them of that, but they finally let me go. After that, he drove me to his home in Brighton. But he had told many friends I was coming, and they were all waiting there to see me. When we arrived, I was so tired that I just layed down on the bed to go to sleep. His friends kept coming over to me to say, "Hello, hello", and talking a lot while I was trying to sleep. But I was so tired that I just slept right through that, and it was around five or six hours until I could open my eye.

I stayed in Brighton with Stuart for two weeks, and then went to London, where I stayed with Lucy Duran. The solo kora concerts she had arranged for me to do were at the Africa Center, where the Manding Conference had been held in 1972, and two other places. By that time, Adam had arrived in London from Mali. A guy named Mike Tangent came to tape record my show at the Africa Center, and afterward said he wanted to release my music on his label, Tangent Records. The next day me and Adam, Lucy Duran, and Mike met in his house. He gave me a simple one or two-page contract that was to pay me 500 British pounds. At that time, I didn't know anything about recording contracts and how to read one, so I asked Adam to read it for me. Adam read the contract, and I asked him what was written there. As soon as he told me that it said, "For next five years you cannot record for anyone else", I said, "If I get something in the United States, what can I do? I am not going to sign this!" Then Lucy Duran told Mike Tangent, "If he doesn't sign this, my teacher Jali Amadou Jobarteh is coming and he will sign it". Even though Amadou is my grandfather, I didn't say anything about that to her. I just said, "That's OK, if your teacher comes and wants to record for free, that's OK, but I am not going to sign this".

After I came to the United States, I did not see Stuart Sutton-Jones for a long, long time. We would get in touch to talk on the phone or write letters, but then I didn't hear from him for many years. During that time, Stuart came to the United States and was working for the United Nations in New York City. One day in 1991, he was talking to some people from Gambia and telling them about me: who I am and what I do, and that he has known me ever since I was teaching in Ghana. He told them that in fact, he knows that I am living in Chicago, and he decided to call me right then. When he called my home phone, he had to leave a message on my answering machine because I was not there. In those days, we didn't have any cell phones or anything like that. And on that same day, something told me that I should check my message machine, so I called it and heard his voice. His message said, "Hey Suso, my brother! I am here in New York at the United Nations". I couldn't believe! I was in New York myself, working on a recording project with Bill Laswell, and I was walking down 14th Street with a big crowd of people all around! When I heard his voice, I just stopped and right away I called him and said, "Wait for me, I am coming now, now, now!" Whatever I had to do that day, I just left it. I jumped in a taxi and went to his big building with a doorman and everything. When I got up to his place, we just talked and talked for a long time. Today, Stuart lives in Vancouver, British Ccolumbia, and I went and visited him there in 2016 before I left Seattle to move to the east coat. It was a very good visit. We talked and talked then too, and I stayed at his house.

MANDINGO GRIOT SOCIETY TIME

On Sept 28th, 1977, me and Adam flew from London to Boston. Adam's brother Denny was in school in Williamstown Pennsylvania, and was keeping Adam's car for him, so Denny drove it to Boston to pick us up. We all went back to Williamstown to spend the night, and the next day, Adam and I drove to Oberlin College in Ohio. Adam had gone to school there, and wanted to visit one of his professors, Roderic Knight. This professor had gone to Gambia around 1972 to study the kora with two of my uncles, Jali Suntu Suso and Jali Nyama Suso. When we got to Professor Knight's house and Adam introduced me, the professor said, "Oh, you are the one who did the recording for Verna Gilles. She just sent it to me, for me to write liner notes for the album release".

Verna Gilles had come to Lagon in July 1976, while I was teaching at the University of Ghana. She wanted to do field recordings with musicians in Ghana, and my American friend Richard Hill had heard about her and told me, "There is a lady here from my county, and she is recording people all over Ghana and not paying them much of anything". When Verna found out a kora player was there, she came to see me with a mutual friend from Sweden named Bengt Berger, who was living near the university and studying the balafon. Verna asked me to record some kora music for her. I said, "OK, let's talk about the fee. For me to do the recording for you, I have to get $200.00." She said, "What? I am recording the whole Ghana Ensemble for $50.00". I asked her, "What is the recording for?" and she said, "It is just for me, I like kora music to listen to in the U.S." We went back and forth about it, and I still held on to wanting a $200.00 fee, because Richard told me that record companies sometimes take those recordings and release them. She kept trying, but I didn't listen. We did not come to an agreement, and then she left Accra and went around to some other West Africa places.

After a while, she came back to Accra and contacted me again. She came to my apartment in South Lagon, and she tried to get Bengt Berger to convince me too. I told him that I needed $200.00 for my recording, and later on she agreed to that, but I told her "Before I do the recording,

I want to know exactly what you are going to use it for. You said you are going to use it just for yourself. Don't go and sell my music and not tell me", and she said, "No I won't do that, it's just for me." So I recorded some songs for her at Bengt's house in Medina. But that day in 1977 at Oberlin College, I said nothing to Professor Knight about my agreement with Verna. The following day, me and Adam drove from Oberlin College to his parents' home in Chicago. When we arrived, Adam invited me to stay with him and his family, in the house where he grew up in the Hyde Park neighborhood. Adam is the eldest child in his family, and has two brothers. Denny follows him, and his youngest brother is Alex. I stayed with them for nine months. Adam's mother and father, Judy and Robert Rudolph, were very nice to let me live in their house for so long.

A few days after we arrived, I found Verna's phone number that I had saved, and called her in New York. I said "Verna, how are you, this is Fodaymusa Suso." and she said, "Oh my God, where are you?" and told me about the record. I said, "I am in Chicago". She said, "When the Folkways record company people heard your music, they liked it so much and wanted to put a record out". Then I replied, "When you recorded me, you said you just wanted to listen to my music for yourself. You cannot put my music out, because I did not sign any agreement with you to do that". That was the end of our conversation. After that, I started asking other people there in Chicago what I should do, and I was advised to contact the people at Folkways Records myself, which is part of the Smithsonian.

So I called them, and talked to a guy named Bob Muso. I told him that I knew they had a tape of my music from Verna Gilles that they were going to put out, but that they couldn't do it without me agreeing to it. Then I took the whole thing in my hands. The record company told me that they were not going to work with Verna on it anymore, but they still wanted to put my music out on a record. They told me they would pay $500.00, and sent me a contract with the money. That record came out in 1978 and was called "Kora Music from the Gambia- Foday Musa Suso". That was the first time my name was written in that way, with my first name divided into two separate names. I thought to myself, "Maybe toubabs like it that way", so I left like that from then on. But in Gambia, everybody still calls me Fodaymusa, and that's the way it will always be for the rest of my life.

Verna also had a club called Soundscape, in New York City. We kept in contact after that Folkways record came out, and I even played with Mandingo Griot Society once or twice at Soundscape events. In 1981, Verna also asked me to play a solo kora concert at the Lincoln Center Summer Festival. She said she would pay for my plane ticket and around $200.00 or $250.00 for the concert. She said that Lincoln Center was supposed to also pay me $250.00, but after the concert she told me that they didn't give her the money yet, so I went home to Chicago. Then she never sent me any money. I like Verna. She is a strong lady. Years later, when she heard that I was going to Gambia, she asked me to bring back a kora for her to give to Bengt Berger as a present. I told her it would cost $350.00, and she gave that money to me. I took that money to Gambia but I didn't bring back a kora! When I came back, I didn't call her for a long time. Then she called me to ask, "Why no kora?" She talks very fast too. I told her, "The baggage handlers broke the kora and I threw the empty stick away in the airport." She said "OK, but don't forget next time". When I started working with Herbie in 1984, we played at the Pier in New York City, and I was staying at the Mayflower Hotel. Verna called and came to see me, and said, "I want to be your manager now." I said, "But Verna, you still owe me $250.00 from Lincoln Center, how can I trust you?" She took $250.00 from her wallet right there, put it on the table and said, "Here's your money". Since that day, I never saw her again. That was that.

Me and Adam also started putting together the band soon after we arrived in Chicago. He called his drummer friend Hank Drake, who is now known as Hamid, and we met. After a while we all said, "Yes, we will form the band Mandingo Griot Society, and now we should get a bass player". Adam and Hamid had played with a lot of jazz people in Chicago and around the United States before I met them. Adam played the congas and other percussion instruments, and Hamid played trap drums and tablas. We were ready to play, but it took a while to get a bass player. Sometime when bass players came to audition and try the music, they would say, "This music is strange", because it's a different kind of music between the western and African beat. The African rhythm goes with the up-beat, and western is with the down-beat. Sometimes they would say, "This is wrong", and I would say "No, it's not". But we are both right. It took me a while to see that clearly. Now I can go with the up-beat or the down-beat, and I like to play with a down-beat now even by myself sometimes. After checking out a bunch of bass players, we met Joe Thomas. He came for the audition, and after one rehearsal he said, "I'm glad you called me, because I want to play something different". When he said that, I said "OK, we got it". Joe had played in a lot of bands with a bunch of famous people too. We rehearsed a lot until we had some music we could play, and all the songs we played were traditional kora songs. Then the four of us started playing in clubs in Chicago.

Our first concert ever was in the Daley Center in early 1978. It is downtown, in a big glass building. We had contacted the Daley Center people to tell them that we had a band, and wanted to play for their lunchtime concert program. They said they had $500.00 budget per band for that, and we said OK. When I came to U.S., I also brought a lot of traditional African dresses with me, so when we were going to play, I made sure we all had some of those clothes to wear. We set up our amps and started to play, and right away people started coming around to see and hear us. Nobody there had ever heard any kind of kora band at that time, or seen people dressed like us. Quickly the whole lobby was jam-packed with people, and more people were outside looking in. Chicago TV channels 5 and 11 were there, and later that night we were on the news. The newspaper said, "There is a new happening in Chicago! A band called Mandingo Griot Society, with the leader playing an instrument called the kora, with a bunch of strings hanging down and decorated with a bunch of grasses". That was from Howard Mandel, a jazz critic who worked for the Chicago Daily News, and he was trying to describe the kora for his article. He later went to work for DownBeat and moved to New York, and became famous as a writer and a teacher. We have kept in touch from time to time for all these years.

•••••

There were also some people at our Daley Center show who were from the Illinois Art Council, including a lady named Grace Moore who worked to bring artists-in-residence to different schools. After the show was over, she came to talk to me, to ask if I would work with kids in schools. I said yes, so later on, we met at the Illinois Art Council office in downtown Chicago, and all the people there said they wanted me to work with them. They said they would help me get a work permit, and they wrote to the immigration people. Immigration told them my visa was called a B-2 visitor's visa, and that I did not come to the U.S. with a work permit so I had to leave. The Illinois Arts Council wrote back and forth to them, and finally immigration said I could stay in the U.S. only for three months, and that I could work. After that, I started working in School District 65 in Evanston, Illinois. Every day, I would go to a different school in the morning time, and play for their assembly. Then I would go from room to room in the school, to play a little bit in each one for the rest of the morning. One of the School District people named David would take me to those different schools, then he would take me to Chute Elementary School for the whole afternoon. When I first started going to that school, I went from classroom to classroom there too, playing the kora and balafon, and finding the kids who were not shy about learning to play the music. When I would invite kids to come up and play a little bit, the kids who raised their hands and wanted to come up and try it were the ones I picked to teach how to play drums, balafon, and percussion. Every afternoon, I worked with those special kids in the school auditorium. After three months, we organized a special show at Chute Elementary for the kids to play for all their parents.

After that, the Arts Council had me worked in schools in Springfield and Champaign-Urbana in the same way, for three months at a time. I would work from 9am to 3pm every day for three months each time, and they paid me $100.00 per day. Sometimes I would have to miss one or two school days to do a Mandingo Griot Society concert, but they let me make up those days later. I ended up doing this type of thing for five years. Besides the Illinois Art Council, I also worked for a place called Urban Gateways, and The Young Audiences Program to teach a whole lot of kids. The Young Audiences Program bought a bunch of drums and balafones for the kids to play in school and in the after-school programs. During that time and afterward, schoolchildren all over those towns would recognize me when I was walking around, and say, "Look, it's Mr. Suso!" to their parents.

•••••

At that same time, Mandingo Griot Society was playing a lot of clubs in Chicago. We didn't have any agent, so a club would call me or Adam, then we would talk to all the other bandmembers. We had no competition, and there was nobody in Chicago doing anything like us. We played a whole lot at two places, Wise Fools and Quiet Night, and anytime we played at Wise Fools, there was a guy named Bruce Kaplan who would always come to our show. He was the president of Flying Fish Records. One day when we were taking a break between sets, Bruce was sitting by the bar. He said to me, "Hello, I want to talk to you. I have been coming to see you almost every time you play here, and I want you and your band to do a record for me." I said, "OK, let me talk to my friends". I called Adam to come over, and told him what Bruce had said. None of us knew anything about the record business, so we talked among ourselves. Flying Fish was a small record company, and at that time, Bruce was the only one who was doing that kind of thing in Chicago. Later on, there was Alligator Records and some other stuff, but for that time, he was the one. Bruce has passed away now, and the record company was sold. He was a very honest man, and not into any wicky-wacky thing. When working with him, everything was up front. When we went to his office, he was there with his assistant Jim Needer. Bruce said, "I can give you $2500.00 for recording in a studio", and then we signed the contract.

When this was happening, the famous trumpet player Don Cherry was living in Sweden. I didn't know much about him then, but Adam and Hamid had already done some playing with him in the U.S., and Hamid had gone to West Africa with him. I heard his music, and even though he wasn't playing traditional songs, he was the first westerner I heard that was into the instrument called dusungoni, which means hunter's harp in my language. We talked about bringing Don Cherry to come and play on our first record, and told this to Flying Fish. Bruce liked the idea, and said he would get the ticket for Don to come to Chicago. When he arrived, we went to the studio with him. The first day we recorded was June 29th, 1978 and the whole recording took only two or three days. But instead of having Don play dusungoni, I asked him to play trumpet, and I played his dusungoni. Don did a great job on our first record. In fact even today, the tracks he played on are my favorite tracks he ever played, especially on the songs called Fasu Barra and Apollo. We also recorded three of the songs I played at the one-year anniversary concert for Jali Lalo Kebba: Jimbasin, Chedo, and Musubalanto. During the week we did the recording, we also did a concert with Don at a Chicago club called Amazing Grace. Later on that same year, our first Mandingo Griot Society record came out.

•••••

In 1978, I also had my first chance to go home to Gambia. By this time, I was living in my own apartment on Harper Street in Hyde Park, not too far from Adam's parents' house. On August 7th while I was getting ready to leave for Gambia, I was in my apartment and a guy from LA named Abulai Sumare called me. He said, "Are you the kora player? I am from Senegal, but I live in LA and work with Stevie Wonder. Stevie is getting ready to do a record, and he is looking for a kora player to play on it." I said, "OK, but you caught me at a bad time because I am leaving tomorrow to go to Gambia". He tried to convince me to cancel my flight, and said, "We will pay to fly you here, blah blah blah". But I said, "No, my bags are packed and I am only waiting for tomorrow to come so I can fly". He replied, "If you cancel your flight, it will only take a few days". But I wanted to go home so bad! I had not been in Gambia for three years, since before I went to Ghana. So I told him, "I will be back in the U.S. in two or three months, so give me your phone number and I will call you then. And I will come there to LA if you are not finished with the recording".

The next day on August 8th, I left Chicago and flew to Paris, and stayed there a few days before I continued to Dakar. During the time I was in Paris, I sent a message to my childhood friend Mohammed Camara that I was coming, so he met me at the Dakar airport. When I arrived, I was wearing the kind of jeans with the chrome studs up and down the pant leg, a jean jacket to match, and a leather cowboy hat, and I was carrying a leather shoulder bag. I was also wearing sunglasses. Mohammed never saw me dressed like that, only wearing a traditional African dress. He was standing there at the arrival place, but he didn't even recognize me at all. I passed him and grabbed his dress to surprise him. He said, "Boy!" and then we grabbed each other and greeted.

We came to the customs place, and I had three or four suitcases with me, plus a big boom box and garment bag. Customs was looking for me to pay tax on something, so they told me, "The boom box needs a tax". I told them, "I am not staying here, I am going to Gambia, so I don't need to pay a tax". We pushed back and forth, back and forth on that. Then some old man who was into that wicky-wacky stuff started siding with them and saying stuff. Finally I said, "I don't have any money with me here now." Then they said, 'What if somebody goes with you to the hotel?" and so I said OK. But I knew it was a scam. This old guy and the taxi driver sat in the front seat, and me and Mohammed sat in back. We went to the Hotel Independence in downtown Dakar, the workers took all my bags inside, and I registered two rooms for Mohammed and me. I told the old guy, "I am not going to give you one dime. I am not a trader, and I am not going to sell the boombox, so I'm not giving one penny". Then the old guy tried to follow me into the dining room, but the hotel people stopped him. After me and Mohammed spent the night there, we went to the main Dakar car place in the morning to get a ride, and I hired a driver to take us all the way to Gambia. The car held seven passengers, so I paid seven fees to keep the whole car just for us.

At that time my father was living in Banjul, and he was very sick. For many years before that, he had been living in Sierra Leone and he also married another wife named Kani, but they never had any children together. I knew he was not well, so before I left Chicago, I wrote a letter to my blood brother Mahamadou who was in Sierra Leone with his wife and daughter, to say, "Father is very sick. I am coming to Gambia from the United States, and I want you to come there from Sierra Leone too". So Mahamadou came, and he arrived in Banjul on Thursday, August 17th. At that time, I was staying at the Rest House and taking care of my father, and my brother was staying with other friends in Banjul. I decided I wanted to find a compound to buy for my home, and I told Mahamadou, "Go around and look for a place, and any compound you like, I will pay for it. Then we will have our own compound, so nobody will be renting and we can all stay together." Also, I told Mahamadou, "You already left your family, so I will buy a one-way ticket for your wife and daughter to come to Banjul from Sierra Leone too. I will send it with some people I know who are traveling there". So on Friday October 6th, his wife and daughter arrived from Sierra Leone.

Mahamadou found a place for me to buy in the town of Serekunda, from a man named Allie Kebbeh. The cost was 3050 dalasi. I didn't tell my father I bought it because of something that had happened a few years before in early 1974, when I was living in Dakar. I came down to Gambia with enough money to buy a compound, and I even spoke with a man named Bunja Bayo, who wanted 2400 dalasi for his compound. I told him, "I can give you half of the money now, and I will come back in one month to give you the rest". Bunja Bayo's father owned two compounds and had passed away, and that's why Bunja wanted to sell one of them. At that time, my father was in good health and very laid back. After I gave Bunja Bayo 1200 dalasi, he told a friend of my father's about it, and that friend then told my father. My father said, "Fodaymusa is too young to do this", so he and his friend went to Bunja Bayo and said, "No purchase, because Fodaymusa did not tell us". Bunja Bayo gave him back the 1200 dalasi, and my father told his friend to keep the money for him. Then when I came back to Gambia for the big Independence Day celebration in February 1974, I went to Bunja Bayo to pay the second half of the payment for the compound. He took me inside to tell me that my father came with his friend to take the money back. So then I went to my father's house. When we were eating lunch, I asked him why, and he told me. Then he said, "My friend has the money, so you can get it back". At that time, my father's friend owned a house but my father did not. I said, "Father, you are paying rent and he is not". Later on that day, I went and asked my father's friend about the money, and he told me, "The money is with your father." The next day I told my father, "If God keeps me alive in my body, I will buy a house for you to live. I promise you, you will see yourself inside that house, but you won't know when or where, or nothing". After that, every day my father's friend would come to his apartment, and anytime that guy arrived, I would leave. If I came there and heard his voice inside, I didn't go in. One day I was in a taxi to Haddington Street to go to see one of my uncles. I gave money to the taxi driver when I sat down. That guy was standing on the street and stopped the taxi, and he came inside. He sat in front with the driver, and said, "Use his change to pay my fare, he is my son". Then I got out and picked up a big rock or brick, and I stood in front of the taxi. I said to the driver, "If you try to move, I will smash your windshield". A few days later my father said to me, "You are very angry with my friend", and I told him, "Even in heaven, I will never talk to this man".

After all that happened in 1974, the chance came for me to teach in Ghana, and then to go to the United States. But I kept this idea in my mind all the time, until this next opportunity came in 1979. So when I bought the compound in Serekunda, I told Mahamadou, "Don't tell anyone, or I will cancel the sale". He found the compound in three or four days after starting to look, and told me how much it cost. I said, "Let's go there. I am the one buying it, but you are the one who will be living there all the time, so I want to make sure you want to live there". We took a taxi together and my brother said, "Yes, I like it". So I bought the compound, and we went to the mayor's house in Serekunda to sign the papers. I gave Mahamadou money for him to fix the compound up too, and nobody knew about it but him and me. By the time everything was ready, my father was very sick and in bed all the time. Nobody knew about the compound, not even Kani or my father's brothers Lamin and Surakata. When the moving day came, I told Mahamadou, "Go get me a rental truck and tell our father that we are going to my house". He went to my father and said, "Today we are going to our house. Ah, Fodaymusa has a house", and my father started to cry. I went to my father's landlord Mr. Sisay, and I said, "Thank you, today I am taking my father to my own house. I want to settle all his debts too if he owes anything". Mr. Sisay said, "Very good, only this month he has not yet paid 60 dalasi rent". I paid that, and we shook hands. Then I told my father that we were going, and said, "Father, if you remember, this is what I told you would happen". I put my father in a taxi to Serekunda, and my brother took everything from his apartment in the truck. My father's younger brothers Lamin and Surakata also helped with all the moving.

The next day, my father's friend who took the compound money came by his Banjul apartment to say hello. He asked the people there where my father was, and they told him I that had bought a compound in Serekunda and took my father there. That man actually lived in Serekunda too, so he turned back and went to my new compound, and met my father there. I told Mahamadou and my father's brothers Lamin and Surakata, "That guy is not a good human being". At that time, they thought I was just being hard on him, but later on they all came to believe that about him too. By the time I left Serekunda on Nov 11th, 1978, everything was set up and working well in the new compound. My father remained sick though, and around six weeks later he died. My father's brother Lamin continued to live in the compound with his family for the rest of his life, and Mahamadou lived there for the rest of his life too.

●●●●●

Earlier in 1978, during the same trip to San Francisco when Dr. Gamble called my name from the audience and we became friends, another big thing happened: Some people were making the movie called Roots: the Next Generations, and looking for a kora player. They tried to get in touch with me in Chicago, and found out I was in San Francisco, so they contacted me there. They said they wanted to fly me to Burbank Studio to play my kora for the soundtrack music. I told them my price, which was $2500.00 or something like that, and they just said yes. Those people in Hollywood didn't waste any time. As soon as they knew I was in San Francisco, they flew me to LA the very next day. They sent a limousine to the airport to pick me, and took me right to the movie studio. When they showed me the part of the movie that showed a griot playing a kora, I saw that another Gambian guy was filmed who was not even a kora player. The moment I saw his face, I started laughing! They said to me, "Why are you laughing?" and I said, "Because I know this guy." His name is Bossy Korra and he is from a traditional trader family, and was living in LA, selling African woodcarvings and other art. I know that guy's family, and traditionally they don't even touch the kora. When the movie people told him they wanted him to play the kora in the movie, he told them, "I cannot do this, because I am not a kora player. I can hold it, but I cannot play it". But he went ahead and held the kora, wearing the typical African dress and rolling his fingers on it to act like a kora player. After the Hollywood people first showed me that movie scene, they said there was a little time before they would record me playing, and asked me if I wanted to eat something. I said yes, so they put me back in the limousine and took me to Chinatown to a tiny resturant that is my favorite. I don't know if it is still there, but it was called The Chinese Friends. It's very small, but there is always a line because it's the best Chinese food anyplace in the world! After I ate, the limousine took me back to the studio. They showed me the movie scene again while I was playing, and it only took me four or five minutes to finish playing. So even though they filmed the movie with Bossy holding the instrument, it is my sound that is coming out of the kora. After I did that, I didn't even spend the night there in LA. I just flew back to San Francisco, and then the next day I took a flight back to Chicago.

While I was in Gambia later that year, after I bought the compound for my father, I decided to go to Bossy Korra's house. In our tradition, my family and his family are sanawo to each other, so we can joke a lot with everybody in each other's family. When I got to his house on October 29th, Bossy was sitting there with his family. Everybody said to me, "Hey Fodaymusa, how is everything in America?" and we were greeting. Nobody knew what I had up my sleeve! After a while, I stood up and turned to Bossy, and I held my hand out and said, "Put my money here". He looked up at me and asked, "What are you talking about, what do you mean?" I just said again, "Put my money here". Then he said, "I don't owe you any money", and I replied, "I am going to talk". He said, "What are you talking about?" and I said, "Oh, are you a kora player in Los Angeles now?" The minute I said that, he jumped up and grabbed my mouth, squeezed my neck, and dragged me into his room, saying, "I know you're crazy, but please don't mention anything about that". I said, "Ha ha, then put the money here." He said, "Yes, look I'm going to give it to you, but please don't say anything about that for my family to hear." I said, "OK, but I know that because you are into the money, that's why you jumped and said yes you will do it. When you told them, "No I cannot do this", they convinced you the moment they said they would pay you. You said OK, and that means you only did it for the money". I was joking with him a lot, but he was worried! He gave me some dalasi, so I said, "OK, now you bribed me, I'm not going to say anything". Now if somebody buys that movie today and sees him, they won't know he is from a trader family and not a kora player, unless they know him or his family. He is sitting there, his fingers are going, and my sound is playing. If you didn't know him, you would think he was playing!

When I arrived back in Chicago from Gambia, I called Abulai Sumare in LA to tell him I was back. He said, "We already got a kora player from France named Lamin Konteh, and brought him to play on the record". I told that to my friend Spencer Bibbs, and right away he jumped and said, "Oh you blew it! You should never have gone back to Africa and left that opportunity here for playing with Stevie Wonder. There will be no more opportunity now". I said, "I want you to listen. My belief and your belief is a whole different type of thing. My belief is that, if it was meant to happen, it wouldn't come on the day I was supposed to leave. My belief is that when God made me, he didn't say that my life is hanging on whether or not I play with Stevie Wonder. I take everything in a simple way, with a heavy faith. In fact, it would not be good for me to play with him because it was not meant to be". Spencer argued, "You only have one chance for things like that", and I said, "Then maybe it is not meant to be". That Stevie Wonder record was called The Secret Life of Plants. It did not make Lamin Konteh's life change a lot or anything though. He was the first kora player to settle in the west, and was already in France when I arrived in the U.S. He was older than me so I did not know him, but I know that his playing is very, very good. Before I came to the U.S. in 1977, I heard his music, combining kora with merengue Cuban music and South American music. He was from Cassamance and after he left, he never went back there to live. I looked him up recently on the internet, and it said he passed away around 10 years ago in France.

•••••

By this time, I had been in the U.S. for over two years, and my visa had been extended a few times. Back in 1978, the U.S. Immigration people had extended my original visa so I could work with the Illinois Art Council. By the time the next letter came from them to tell me to leave the country, I had already signed the contract with Flying Fish Records for the first Mandingo Griot Society record. So Flying Fish wrote a letter to immigration, telling them that "Suso just finished a record for us, and we need him to tour here in the U.S. to promote the record". Then the writing happened back and forth between them, and back and forth again, and finally the immigration people extended my visa. At the end of that second visa extension, people advised me that I should get an immigration lawyer to try to extend my visa more. They also said that if I married a U.S. citizen, it would be cheaper for me to extend it. But I said, "No, I won't marry". From day one when I came to the U.S., I didn't want to lie and marry somebody just to have a paper. I wanted to marry for real, to somebody that I like and who likes me. I'm not part of all those people who marry just for the paper.

So at that point, I started talking to a lawyer named Malcolm Gerber. He listened to my situation in his office downtown, and looked at all my papers. He said, "Yes, I can get you the visa extension, but it will cost you $170.00". I paid him, and then he sent me a letter to say that he was checking on it, but I would have to pay another $300.00. I said, "OK, I am going to New York City for two or three days, and then I will come to your office". When I flew back, I called him from O' Hare Airport to say I was coming to see him. When I arrived, I gave him the $300.00 and took a taxi to my apartment in Hyde Park. Two or three weeks later, he sent another letter saying I have to pay $130.00. That's the day I became angry, and I called him and said, "This is Mr. Suso. Do you think I am crazy? You never tell me what's happening, so I'm not going to send you nothing".

Later on, I was talking to someone else about this, and they suggested that I call Nick England, who was the head of the World Music Department at the California Art Institute. They said, "Explain your problem to him, because he has a lot of experience with artists from foreign countries". So I called him to introduce myself, and he helped me get in touch with a lawyer named Ellen Armstrong. She is the best immigration lawyer, and we became friends. I called her to explain my situation, and where I was living. She laughed and said, "Yes I am a lawyer in LA, and my husband and sons are immigration lawyers too. But a lot of Chicago immigration lawyers are shady. If you marry a U.S. citizen, the cost will be $1500.00, but otherwise it will be $3000.00. Malcolm Gerber was afraid to tell you that, so instead he was doing dink, dink, dink, a little money at a time".

By this time, Adam had already moved to LA, but I stayed in Chicago along with Hamid and Joe. I liked my apartment and I liked Hyde Park a lot, so I wanted to stay there. Ellen said, "You don't have to pay the whole $3000.00 at once, just make some payments every month. I will call immigration and tell them to send all your papers to LA, and we will do it all as if you lived in LA too". She sent me forms to sign. The moment I saw them, I knew she was going to do something. I sent her $700.00, and then I called Adam, because he is the first person I knew very, very well in the U.S., and he knew me very well too. I told Adam, "My lawyer is in LA. She said since my visa has already expired, I should go someplace outside the U.S., and she will have my visa renewed while I am there. She said I could go to Canada or Mexico, or some place like that". Then I said, "I want to go to Canada", so I went to Toronto and spent the night in a hotel. The next morning when the U.S. Embassy opened, I took the papers she gave me and they stamped them. They let me back in the U.S. with new one-year visa that didn't expire until June 10, 1981, and then I went back to Chicago.

During all that time, I was playing a lot, either in solo concerts or with Mandingo Griot Society. Traveling all around the country, playing colleges and clubs, and eventually going to Europe. While I was teaching in the artist-in-residence program, Mandingo Griot Society was playing in clubs in Chicago, but when I wasn't teaching we would go to the east coast, New York City, Detroit, California, and so on. We went to play in New Orleans at the Jazz Festival, and we went up and down the west coast every year. Because Adam was living in LA, me, Hamid, and Joe would fly there, then we would all get in Adam's station wagon and go on tour. We went to San Diego, Santa Barbara, San Luis Obispo, Santa Cruz, San Francisco, and up Highway 101 to Ashland, Eugene, and Portland, Oregon. We would also go all the way up to Washington State. In Seattle, we played in a world music place called The Bahamas, and the furthest north we went was Bellingham. Then we would turn and go back down the coast to LA again.

We had a whole lot of fun and crazy times together! In a San Francisco club, a guy came up to us who lived in Angel's Camp, which was a small town nearby. He said he wanted us to play in his club, but we said we were on our way north. So he said, "Please come on your way back", and we agreed on $300.00 for the gig. When we came back, we found that Angel's Camp was just one small main road and just a few houses. We came to his club, we did soundcheck, and then we played. There were only three people there for the whole first set: the guy, one friend, and his wife! Usually we play two sets, so after the first one I told Adam and the band, "Maybe we should tell the guy to keep the money and we will just go". We told the guy that, but he said, "Please keep playing". We asked him, "Where are the people?" and he said, "We are here, it's OK. Please play, we like it." So we played another set full and loud, pumping all the energy as if it was a full house. After we finished, he had some rooms upstairs above the club where he let us stay.

One of our favorite places to play in California was Santa Barbara. Our friend Scott Clayton, who was the head of Santa Barbara Jazz Society, invited us all to stay at his house, no hotel needed. Scott was a very good friend. Later he moved to San Francisco, and we lost all contact. I have looked for him online, but none of us can find him. A retired guy named Vernon, who used to fly jets for the army, came to every concert we did in Santa Barbara. Then he would throw us a big party every time after the show, with lots of people in his big backyard. In Santa Cruz, there was a guy named Greg who was very into African music. We would call in advance to tell him we were coming, and he and his friends would cook Ghanian food called fufu or banku for us, no matter what time we arrived day or night. We played in a club that I saw last year is still there in Santa Cruz, called the Kumba Jazz Club. Later on, Greg moved to Philadelphia or Washington, DC. In a small town called Forestville, another favorite club was by the roadside. Free lifestyle people lived around there and liked us a lot. Ashland, Oregon was another favorite place, and we played in one or two different clubs there.

One time, we were driving on Highway 101 and happened to spend the night in a small village along the roadside. There was a motel there, and we got rooms. In the morning before we left, I went to a nearby store to buy food for our trip. I was wearing typical African clothes, and as soon as I went inside the store, everybody stopped right away and started looking at me. So I said to myself, "You have to get used to this, because you are a musician and traveling". Even now sometimes, I am the only black person or African on a plane, or in a hotel. That day, I picked out my food and came to the cashier to pay, and walked out. The moment I stepped outside, I saw that someone was following me. Then he asked me, "Are you the king of someplace?" So I asked, "What do you mean?" He said "I saw it on TV, people who dress exactly like you are the king". So I said, "Yes, I am the king of something". And right away he turned to his friends and said, "I told you so, I told you so, just like on TV". They were all there watching. So when I left there to go back to our motel, I was laughing inside my mind about this. I was thinking about the world, and about how traveling gives you an education that no one can teach you or show you. You have to travel to learn this. Your knowledge will increase, so that once you come to a city, you can know how it all came to be, the trees, the city, and the land. In Gambia, we say, "Traveling can give you knowledge that cannot come from a book". You can walk the streets and hills, and learn. You will know people in that place, both good and bad, and you will have that knowledge. You can get knowledge there that you can't get anywhere else. It can earn you money, friendships, and much more than you can get sitting home in your house. We have another Mandingo saying that is, "The old man who lives to be 100 years old and a young man who travels to 100 cities, their knowledge is the same". The old man's knowledge is not more than the younger man, and maybe the young man's knowledge is even more. If you don't travel, you will think everything is the same all over. If you travel, your system will know much about life, and it will be easier to get along with any kind of human being. It doesn't matter if you are rich, beautiful, or anything. You won't meet anyone who can freak you out. Traveling is it's own school.

Near the end of 1979, Emily came to our show at the Seattle club called The Bahamas, and our friendship began. The next year on our second trip to Seattle, we also met her roommates Karen and Torre, and the whole band stayed at their place then, and again in 1981. We were always jamming and playing all kinds of instruments in their big living room with the tall ceiling and pillars: kora, congas and other drums, xylophone, bells, and even some crazy horns made from kelp. I cooked a lot of peanut stew in that kitchen too, so everybody could have a feast. I remember that a lady committed suicide from the Space Needle sometime around then, and we were all saying, "Wow" about that. Our second trip to Seattle was also the same year Mt. Saint Helens blew. Right after we left Seattle, the mountain blew up while we were driving down the coast to California, and we were saying, "We are so lucky to have passed by it before that!" We also played at the New Orleans Jazz Festival that year. After our friendship began, I contacted Emily whenever Mandingo Griot Society came to Seattle, or when I came for a solo concert. After she and Uno got together, I would always stay with them in their house any time I was in that area.

After playing those west coast places for many years, a long time passed before I was there again. Then a few years ago, I came to the west coast with Philip Glass to play, and we went to several of those towns: LA, Carmel-by-the-Sea, the University of California at Davis, and Ashland, Oregon. There were people hollering in the audience, "Hey we remember you! Mandingo Griot Society!" even after over 20 years had passed! I was so surprised.

In 1980, Mandingo Griot Society also went to New York City on an east coast tour, and went to Creative Music Studio out in Woodstock, NY. It was way out in the countryside. In that studio, they would bring professional musicians to perform, and to teach students who were there. Karl Berger was the owner, and he lived there for a long time. Besides us, there were some other musicians and bands there too: a jazz ensemble, the Senegalese drummer Aïyb Dieng, and some others. The whole Mandingo Griot Society band was there for a week. In 1981, I also remember seeing the Reagan assassination attempt on TV in my apartment on March 30th. That same year, Mandingo Griot Society recorded a second album called "Mighty Rhythm", that was released on Flying Fish Records. The band changed to add John Markiss on electric guitar, along with a backup singer named Isatou Walker. The rest of the band was the same: Adam, Hamid, Joe, and me.

A very funny thing happened when Mandingo Griot Society went to Grinnell, Iowa in the winter, to play at a university there. When we were getting ready to go to Grinnell, I showed Adam the address of some friends who were living in that area, that I had met a long time before at the University of Ghana in Lagon. Adam said this was close to our playing spot, so I called one those friends named Carol, to tell them all that we were coming. The club put the band up in a motel, and the weather was very cold at that time. After we played the gig, Carol and the other friends invited me to their house. We ate some food and hung out a while, and then I said, "I have to go back to the hotel". I told them it was on the roadside, but I didn't know its name because I just stopped there for a minute with the band, to drop our bags before the gig. They took me to one motel and asked me, "Is this the right one?" I said yes, so they dropped me and left. All I remembered was that my room was #6B or #6A, or something. Nobody was at the reception desk because it was so late at night. So I started looking for my room, and I knocked on a door and heard someone inside. I said, "Get up, get up, you are in my room!" The guy in there was asleep, but he pulled himself together and came out.

I jumped in the bed and went to sleep. It was about two or three in the morning, and I went right to sleep.

When I got up in the morning, I went to the reception desk and looked for Adam and the others. I asked the reception guy, "Where are the people who are guests from Chicago?" and told him their names. He said, "There's nobody here by that name, when did you check in here?" I said, "Yesterday. Don't you have a group here called Mandingo Griot Society? We came here to play at the university, and they gave us this place to stay". He said, "You stayed here? You have to pay!" I said, "Wow, I think the university paid for us", but he said, "I have no booking for you!" I didn't have any money with me, so I told him that I would go look for my people, and he said OK. By this time, Adam and the band were driving the streets of Grinell, looking all over for me. They did not know where my friends there were living, so when they got up and didn't see me, they were worried and all packed up to go looking. They found me standing in front of that motel. Adam said, "Where were you?" and I said, "I went to the motel". He said, "Man, you went to the wrong motel. Now we have to pay them". So we went inside and paid, then went on our way. The reception guy also told us that he got a complaint from the guy who was in that room, who said that someone woke him up in the middle of the night and made him leave, but that the person sounded like he was right about whose room it was.

That guy I woke up was a blues musician from Chicago, who was in Grinnell playing that same night too. I never saw him before or after that, until many years later when I went to Santa Fe, New Mexico to play at a festival with Mandingo Griot Society. We were staying in a place where somebody had a lot of small houses on top of a hill. It was very fancy. That blues musician knew Joe Thomas and the rest of the band, but not me. We were all talking and hanging out together, and when I left the room, that guy told the band, "This guy doesn't remember me, but I remember him. This is the guy who woke me up at three am in my hotel room, and kicked me out in the cold". Later on, I came back in the room, and that guy asked me, "Have you ever been in Grinnell, Iowa? Did you ever wake up somebody in the middle of the night in a motel?" I said, "Oh man, sorry, sorry, sorry!" but he was OK, and we all continued laughing about it for a long time that night. Even now, this makes me laugh a lot!

••••

Mandingo Griot Society also went to Europe a few times. The first time we went, we were based in Copenhagen Denmark, and we all bought a Eurail Pass that cost $600.00 to travel anywhere by train for a month. We went to Norway, Sweden, and Germany to play, and every time we would go to one of those countries, we would come back to Denmark. Back and forth like that between every country. Later, on the 1982 Europe trip, we had to change bass players because Joe had moved to Petaluma, California to do other stuff. John Marsh was our new bass player. He is a very good bass player, just unbelievable in fact, but traveling with him was a difficult thing. We had to show to him a lot about traveling. He also gets lost easily.

One day in Germany, we left Hamburg to go to Berlin, and then to Cologne and Hildershine, to play in a club. We found out that the trains always leave on time there. Then one day, we had to go from Copenhagen to Helsinki, to play in a festival downtown in big park. I told everybody to be at the train station by six o'clock in the morning. I warned them to be on time, because the train wouldn't wait. At six, Adam, Hamid, and me were there, but no John Marsh. I called the number where he was staying, and a friend picked it up and gave to John. I said, "What's happening? We are here at the train station". He told me, "I am not going today", and I said, "What? We came to play!" So I told Hamid to stay in Copenhagen to make sure John came the next day. Then me and Adam took the train to Stockholm with all the instruments, took the ferry to the Helsinki side, and stayed overnight in the hotel. The next day was the gig. We were waiting, waiting, in the hotel for Hamid and John to arrive. The time is coming close, and calls were coming from the guy at the festival to say, "It's time to come for soundcheck!" Our road manager Ken Day came to get us, and they were still not arrived. At the last minute, Hamid and John put their bags down at the hotel and got to the festival grounds to play. We didn't have any soundcheck time, but we played and the soundman got it right. The people liked it so much. We played one song, but in the middle of the second song all of a sudden I had to pee so bad. That day I learned that it was good to have a wireless microphone on your instrument! There was a portable bathroom behind the stage, and I went in there to pee with one hand and kept playing the kora with the other. People thought it was part of the show, and started hollering when I came back on stage. After that, Adam called me "Crazy Man" all the time, instead of my name. I will not dispute that!

After that concert, we went to the Hamburg train station, and we only had three minutes to get our amps, drums, and everything to transfer to another train. We were rushing and got everything out. Then John Marsh went back inside the train to make sure he didn't leave anything behind his chair, and the train took off with him trying to get out! I told the train station people about it, and described John to them. They said the first stop was not for 35 minutes, and for him to get off there and come back. This ruined our schedule. John got off that train at the first stop, and got on another train to come back. When he arrived, I said, "OK, you are great musician but it's very difficult to travel with you, so I can say you will never travel with Mandingo Griot Society again". When we came back to Copenhagen at the end of the tour, I told Hamid, "I am going to Africa now, but you have to make sure John gets back to Chicago". Later on, John moved from Chicago to LA to be with a friend. After that, I did not see him for over 30 years, until I located him through the internet. He told me he moved from LA to a town near St. Louis called Hilltop, or something like that. I talked to him on the phone, and he said he is still doing the music.

Once we got back to Copenhagen, me and Adam met up with his girlfriend Nancy Jackson and went to Africa together. But the reason this happened was very crazy: Years before, Nancy was Adam's girlfriend at Oberlin College in Ohio. When me and Adam met each other in Ghana, he and Nancy were writing each other, but when we came back to the U.S., they broke up. Then Nancy got together with someone else and got married, and she and her husband lived in Oberlin. But Adam and Nancy kept in touch. During one of our Mandingo Griot Society tours on the west coast, Adam, Hamid, John and me all left Seattle to drive to

Portland. Adam was driving, Hamid was in front, and John and me were in the back seat. I was sleeping, and I dreamed that Adam and Nancy got back together and married, and came to Gambia with me to visit my brother's house in Serekunda. When I woke up and opened my eye, I sat up and I told Adam, "Crazy Man, I just dreamed something now that you will not believe". Then I told him the dream, and he said, "Hey Crazy Man, you are crazy". I told him everything that happened in the dream: people dancing under the Mango tree in the compound and everything. It was very clear to me. And then this did happen! They got together and got married. At the end of the European tour, me and Adam met Nancy in Copenhagen, and flew stand-up, bus-style on Russian Aerofloft Airlines from Copenhagen to Leningrad, from Leningrad to Moscow, and from Moscow to Dakar. We were so lucky, because that flight from Moscow to Dakar was the last one on that airline before the next one crashed. We went to Gambia and stayed with my family, then came home to Chicago. From that time on until today, anytime I tell Adam that I dreamed something, he says, "That will be".

•••••

During all our touring years, we usually booked our shows ourselves, by word of mouth, and by contact with people we met. But we had an American friend named Ken Day, who had moved to Scandinavia and then Copenhagen, and for a while he was our agent. The first year of WOMAD (The World of Music and Dance Festival), a guy named Nick Houb, who organized the festival, called me in Chicago to ask Mandingo Griot Society to play. I told Nick that they should pay us cash, and our fee was 1000 English pounds. It was July 1982, and that festival was in a small town called Bath, England. The whole stage and everything was in a big cornfield. They had Chinese musicians, a Burundi drumming troupe, and more people from all over the world. At that time, there was a Nigerian musician named Prince Niko Mbarga, who had a very famous song called 'Sweet Mother'. Before the festival, we were hanging out together in London, and he was also a performer at that first WOMAD. I remember that when we played, the band called The Police was going to play after us, but the people liked our music so much they didn't want us to stop. The festival people had to pull the plug on us at the end so that The Police could play.

Afterward, the hotel they put us in was very full, with all the musicians staying there. I told Ken, "I cannot stay here", and he found a bed and breakfast for me out of town in the countryside. The rest of the band stayed there at the hotel in Bath. Later on, Ken came to me with 400 pounds cash and a check for 600 pounds, and said that I could cash the check the next day. I told him, "You shouldn't take a check" because I knew that sometimes it's good to start a festival small and grow bigger, but not to get big right away the way WOMAD did. I told Ken, "Tomorrow early, we must get the money". So in the morning, Ken was first at line at the bank, and after him the rest of the musicians did not get paid. We heard that the organizers flew to London and nobody knew their address. People were looking for them all over but could not find them, and that was the only time we ever played at WOMAD.

Another big thing that happened for me in 1982 was that I bought a compound in Brikama, to live in any time I am home in Gambia. When I had bought my first compound in 1978 in Serekunda for my father to live in with his brother Lamin and my blood brother Mahamadou, my mother was still living in our village of Foday Kunda with my sister Tita and my brother Dembo. My mother's elder sister Sendin Jobarteh was already in Brikama, living in the compound of her son Mohammed Suso, where I first came to when I left Passamasi in 1971. When he bought his compound in Brikama, he brought his mother there from Borro Kanda Kasse to live with him and his family. In fact, we also sometimes call him Mohammed Sendin, the same way my father was sometimes called Saikou Luntanding for his mother's name. So when I decided that I was going to buy a second compound, I asked my mother where I should buy it, so that she and Tita and Dembo could come live with me since her husband Mamadi Kanuteh had passed away. I asked her, "Should I buy it in Serekunda or Brikama?" She told me, "If you are going to buy a compound, you should buy it in Brikama so I can be close to my sister Sendin", so that's why I bought my compound there. After that, my mother and her sister got to see each other every day, and were always going back and forth to each other's compounds.

In 1983, Mandingo Griot Society did another Europe tour, from March 14th to April 20th with Ken Day as our agent. We played at the University of Warwick in Coventry, England on March 17th, and the next day we drove and took the train to Reims, France to play at a big festival called Carnival. On the 22nd and 23rd, we played at the Westside Club in Leon, then traveled to the University of Nancy to play a show on the 25th. Then we went to Paris to do a live performance on a TV show on the 29th. That show was called Banana Split, and we played four songs: Jarabe jeh, Fasu barra, Jimbasing, and Demba Tenkeren. Our tours were like this: we traveled by day, and played at night. People there liked our music a lot, and no one had heard kora music played like this along with western instruments. After England and France, we went to Germany, Austria, and Yugoslavia, and came back to Chicago on April 20th. Later that month, we played again at the New Orleans Jazz Festival, and then I went to Gambia for another visit.

The first tour Ken Day did for us that year was good, but the second time didn't go well. Ken got a flight to Belgium for Adam, Hamid, Joe, Isatou, and me. He said he would come to meet us there, and then we would drive through Germany to Denmark. Our tickets were on Icelandic Airlines, so we flew to Iceland, and then to Belgium. We flew all night, and our plane landed there in the early morning. When we got off at the gate, we heard an announcement on the loudspeaker saying, "Mandingo Griot Society, Ken Day will be late to pick you up". So we waited there at the Belgium airport. After two hours, Ken called to say he was in Antwerp, Holland, but his bus broke down and he was trying to fix it. We waited a long time. Another call came at around one o'clock in the afternoon, to say the bus was broke again. Then no more calls all day! That night, we had to sleep on the airport chairs. We called the place that Ken was, and they said he was gone. When we got up the second morning, I told the band, "We cannot stay here, we must go to town to shower, eat some food, and rest in a hotel. Tomorrow we should go back to the airport and fly home". So we took a train into town, checked into a hotel, and the next morning early we came back to the airport. I told the people at Icelandic Air that the whole band needed to go back to Chicago, and they said they would have to look for standby flights for us. We were there until afternoon before they said they had one open seat. I sent Isatou on that flight. Between five and six o'clock that evening, two seats opened on another flight, and I sent Joe and Hamid on that one. Me and Adam stayed, and finally at one o'clock in the morning of the third day, there were seats for both of us so we flew home. Ken Day never called us that whole time. But some clubs had paid a deposit already for us to play, and he had to pay them back. He told those people that we came to Europe, but our bus had an accident so we couldn't make it to the clubs to play. Some people even sent us a get-well card! That tour fell apart, so we never worked with Ken Day again. He's a nice guy, an easy-going person, but he didn't know the business well at that time.

In all those touring times with Mandingo Griot Society, and even ever since then, I didn't have one favorite town, but I can say that my favorite country to play in is the United States. It's a very difficult place too, because there are so many different kinds of music. A lot of things can be happening with the music, and if you can do your art, you can do very well. And once you have something happening and become known, it is the best place for you, and you can do stuff here that you cannot do in any other place.

MEETING BILL AND HERBIE

Around the middle of 1983, I recorded a solo album called Hand Power for Flying Fish Records. I composed all the songs for it, including a song about my good friend Demba Camara's family compound in Fatoto, and a song about the President of Gambia, Dawda Jawara. It was recorded at Acme Studio in Chicago, and I played all the instruments on it, including kora, balafon, dusungoni, nyanye, electric guitar, kalimba, harmonica, shekere, and African drums called kutiro, tamo, sabaro, dundungo, belengo, and junkura. Mandingo Griot Society backup singer Isatou Walker recorded on two of the songs also.

Around that same time, Mandingo Griot Society had also gone to a recording studio to make a demo. At end of 1983, I decided to take that demo to New York City, but I didn't know anybody there, so I just started to look up New York record company addresses and copy them down. I bought a ticket for my flight to New York, but then I happened to see Herbie Hancock's video called RockIt, that was produced by Bill Laswell. I said to myself, "When I am in New York, I would like to talk to that guy who produced this. I will call him". I got Bill's number, but I didn't call him right away. Every time I was going to call, I would pick up the phone but then put it back down. I didn't dial, because I was thinking, "This guy won't know anything about my music or what I am talking about". Finally on the third day, I just called him, thinking, "Well, whatever happens is OK". Then I was so lucky that he picked up the phone. I introduced myself and said, "This is Foday Suso. I am calling you from Chicago but I am coming to New York soon, and I would like to meet you. I have some demo tapes that I would also like to give you to listen to". He replied, "Are you the one who plays dusungoni? I have one of your records". I was thinking that he might not know anything about African music, let alone anything about me. But he was way ahead of any other music producer in America when it comes to African music and world music. The reason that the dusungoni instrument stuck out for Bill is because he is a bass player, and the dusungoni is kind of like a bass. I said, "Yes, I am that guy". He said that he was going to Japan for two weeks and would be back around January 9th or 10th, and that he wanted to meet me when he came back. So I canceled my airline ticket, and bought a new one for Tuesday, January 10th.

My Hand Power CD was released on January 1st, 1984. On January 10th, I flew into LaGuardia airport, and a very good friend named Asher Delerme came to pick me. We had met long before in Ghana, when Asher was visiting there to study drumming and dance, along with some other students from his school, Wesleyan University in Connecticut. We hung out together a whole lot while he was in Ghana, but we didn't play together then. Ever since that time though, we kept in touch with each other, and I always call him up anytime I am in New York and say, "Hey, let's go eat some Indian food!" Then he will come into the city, and we will go and eat and hang out together. He is a very good percussionist and has done a lot of touring with other people too. On this trip, we stayed at his sister's house in the Bronx. The next day, I went with Asher to his rehearsal place. Then he drove me to where my friend John Crowley was working as a carpenter at somebody's house, and that night I stayed with John at his house in Queens. On Thursday the 12th, John took me into Manhattan, where all the record companies were. I took a bunch of my cassettes, and went from one record company to another with another friend of mine named Jim Quinlan, to ask each one of them to listen to it. They all had a big basket by the door, so whenever people came in and gave them a cassette, they would say, "Oh, yeah, we will listen to it and then get back to you". But then the moment you leave, those people just throw your cassette in that basket. Unless you have a heavy name or you know somebody with a heavy name, they don't want to listen. So all those people threw my cassette in that basket too.

After a while, we happened to go into Celluloid Records, which was owned by Jean Karakos. I said to him, "I would like you to hear this cassette", and he said, "I've heard about you. A friend of mine in France told me that you played in a festival there, and he liked your music so much". Right away, he played my cassette and was even dancing to it while I was sitting there! Then he said, "I work with a producer here also, named Bill

Laswell. Do you know him?" and I was thinking, "Wow". He called up Bill and said, "I want us to have a meeting with this guy in my office because his cassette sounds good". That night, Jean Karakos, Bill Laswell and his girlfriend Thi-Linh Le, and me all went to eat some food together. Bill said, "Yes, I think we can do something with you. Would you like to play on somebody else's record?" I said, "Yes, if the music is good". Bill didn't tell me whose record that would be, though. And for me, I look at music very different than a lot of other people do. I don't know if it's because music is in my blood for hundreds of years, but I have to be serious about it. No joke. I cannot just run and do any music just for the money. I have to see if I am adding to somebody's music, or making good music. I can't just do a gimmick. I hate that. At our meeting, while we were at dinner together, we talked a lot but there was only a short conversation about the music. I was learning a lot then too, and I knew that when people talk, talk, talk the whole night about doing something together, then nothing is going to happen. But if the talk is quick, then it will happen.

The next day was Friday January 13th, and Jim Quinlan arranged for us to go to Harry Belefonte's studio to try to meet him. When we got there, we met a a South African composer named Paifa, who told us that Harry Belafonte was not there, so we left. Later on, I went back to my friend John Crowley's house, and on January 17th, I flew back to Chicago. Soon after that, Bill told his assistant Roger Trilling to call me, and say that they wanted to bring me to New York to play on Herbie Hancock's track for the 1984 Los Angeles Olympics. Roger said, "Since the Olympics is an international event, Bill would like to have an international sound. We will pay for your plane ticket and your hotel too". I asked my friend Jim Quinlan to book my hotel, and he booked the Madison Hotel on 38th St. in Manhattan. On the night of Tuesday February 7th, I flew back to New York. Bill's driver named Hassan picked me at the airport, and took me to the hotel. Then around eleven o'clock, he took me and Jim Quinlan to Evergreen Recording Studio. The break dance style was going strong then, and Bill had programmed the drum machine sound, but that's all they had. I tuned my kora and dusungoni, went into the room to plug in, and told them I was ready for them to play the track.

I played my idea to it to see if it would fit, with the kora in the first section, the dusungoni in the second section, and then back to the kora. Then I said, "OK, now you can record me". But Bill just said, "This is it! We got it!" after that first take. I said, "Are you sure?" and he said, "Yes, yes, this is it!" Then he called Jean Karakos to tell him that he should sign me to his label. Jean came right over to the studio with a contract, and I put it in my bag to look at later. Then Hassan took Bill and me, Jim Quinlan, and Roger Trilling back to the Madison Hotel. Bill said, "Who put him here? We always put our guests in the Mayflower!" Then I said to myself, "Now things will get rolling". They sent the Madision Hotel guys upstairs for my bags, let the hotel keep the money for the five days reserved, and took me to the Mayflower Hotel.

•••••

A couple of months later, Bill brought me back to New York. From April 11th to the 15th, I recorded some tracks at Evergreen Studios for Herbie Hancock's Sound System album, which Bill also produced. Then I came back to Chicago without ever meeting Herbie. Bill was recording all the basic tracks in New York, with drums, bass, and other instruments, and then he would take them to Herbie in California to overdub keyboards. After I came back to Chicago, I signed the record deal with Jean Karakos and Celluloid Records. The contract was for the band Mandingo, which was Adam, Hamid, Joe, Isatou and another singer named Nora Harris, and me. On May 2nd, I flew back to New York to start recording our new CD. There were no other band members in the studio at that time, just Bill and me. For about four days, I recorded the basic tracks, and then we flew to Chicago to record with the rest of the band at Studio Media in Evanston, Illinois. That was the same studio where Mandingo Griot Society recorded our second album, Mighty Rhythm. From May 9th to the 14th, we recorded the rest of the album with the whole band and some guest stars: the drummer Aïyb Dieng, a guitar player named Abdul Hakeem, and a guy named Reymond Sillah who played the African drum called dundungo. After that, me and Bill went to LA and mixed the record at El Dorado Studio in Hollywood for the next few days. While we were in the studio, Herbie came and played on one of the songs. It is called Harima. He listened to the track, he created parts for it that worked very well, and recorded them. He was very happy that we met after I played kora on his Olympics track. After our mixing was finished on Sunday May 20th, I went to Santa Barbara to visit my friend Scott Clayton, who was the head of the Jazz Society there. Then I came back to LA, and Bill was working on some other people's music in the studio. On May 29th, I left to go back to Chicago, and on June 3rd, Mandingo did a concert inside the Chicago Field Museum as part of their summer music program. By that time, Abdul was a member of the band too.

Soon after that concert, Herbie was getting ready to go on tour with his band, The Rockit Band. At first, they were trying to see if their keyboard player could play the kora and dusungoni parts that I played on his Olympics record, because they wanted exactly the right sound. But kora sounds a lot different than keyboard, and the way my fingers were flying is hard to do. Later on, I heard they were discussing whether or not they should ask me to come on tour, because they thought I wouldn't do it since I had my own band. But one day, a guy named Tony Meilandt, who was the assistant to Herbie's manager David Robinson, called me. Tony was a go-getter. Very agressive, and never wasted any time! He said, "Foday, we want you to come tour in Japan and the U.S." Then he put Herbie on the phone to talk about everything, and we agreed on the price and tour details. They flew me to New York on Thursday July 12th, and we rehearsed for the tour in a Manhattan studio from the 13th to the 22nd. On the 25th, we all flew from Kennedy Airport to Tokyo, and we were billed as "Herbie Hancock and the RockIt Band, featuring Foday Musa Suso". The jazz musician Gil Evans was on that flight too, and in his band he had the trombone player Jack Lewis and the bass player Jaco Pastorius. I met them all for the first time at Kennedy Airport when we all flew out together. The reggae bands Black Uhuru and Steel Pulse were also on that tour, and I met them after we landed in Tokyo. All four bands played at the same festivals and cities on that tour, and at every show, Herbie's band was always the last to play.

That was a time I will never forget for many reasons, including hanging with Jaco Pastorius. Jaco was only wearing shorts and no shirt when we all got on the plane, and he tied a bunch of grasses around his arms and legs and called himself a Hawaiian dancer. He wore this outfit the whole time on the plane! Also, he was drinking from the time we got on the flight all the way to Tokyo. When we arrived, the tour people took us to the Prince Hotel, and that night they had a big welcome party for us. After more drinking at the welcome party, Jaco was in the Prince Hotel bar and broke a bunch of glasses there. The people in the bar called the police, and they took him to jail. Then the manager of the band bailed him out. The next night, Jaco went out drinking again. In those days, Japan was not as open to the west as today, and nobody locked anything. Jaco stole a motorbike and took off weaving down the street. Police followed him, and he hit a light pole and fell down. He was not very injured, and they took him to jail. Again the manager bailed him out. Every time I saw him on that whole tour he was drunk, and it didn't matter if it was day or night. Yet he still played so very well at all the concerts! That always amazed me because I never drink alcohol. One time when I was talking to Jack Lewis, I asked him why they brought Jaco on the tour. He said, "The promoters said we have to bring him. He is a big, big star". Ever since I first met Jaco, I liked the way he played so much. No one can play like he did. And he was a direct guy. Those are the kinds of people that I can become close to. He called everybody "cheap ass" also. Before we parted at the end of the tour, me and Jaco laughed together a lot, and it was very sad that he passed away so young just a few years later. In fact, one night only three or four weeks before he died, I was walking back to my hotel in New York and I happened to go past CBGB's on my way. Jaco was standing out in front, kind of drunk. As I got close to him, I said, "Hey, cheap ass!" and he recognized my voice and said "Susu! Susu!" I stopped and we talked a little bit, then I continued walking. Later on after I was back in Chicago, I was so surprised when Bill called me to tell me that Jaco died, and about how it happened.

The first show we played in Japan was on Saturday, July 28th. We went to Nagoya on the bullet train to play a daytime show outside on a stage that was set up in front of a kind of castle. It started raining very heavy, and rain was just pouring down. We left the stage and the rain stopped. We went back on and the rain started again. This happened three or four times! People in the audience just stayed out there in the rain, because Herbie was very famous in Japan and everybody knew him, even the little kids. The third or fourth time we went back out and had to stop again, we said, "No we gotta go, we're not going to play". All the audience came and stood in front of the bus saying, "No, no, don't go! Then the tour people had to call security to help us leave. We went back to Tokyo that night, and the next night we played a show in a big concert hall. On Monday the 30th, they arranged a CBS disco party for us in Tokyo. On Tuesday, we traveled to Sendai and played a concert, and on Wednesday we left and flew to Sapphoro to do a show on Thursday August 2nd. The next day, we went back to Tokyo and played a show at a place called Music Park. On Saturday August 4th, we played in Nagasaki and stayed in the Unzen Konko Hotel. The next day, we traveled to Osaka and played our last show of the tour, then came back to Tokyo again.

I also had a Japanese friend in Tokyo named Takenari Simisu, who took me to a lot of places there. I had met him while on one of the European tours with Mandingo Griot Society, because we happened to be staying in the same hotel in London. He was a young man just traveling around for vacation. In the morning when I was in the hotel lobby, I had my hair braided with a lot of beads in it, and I had a red beret on too. I could see from the way he was looking at me that he had not been around black people. He would look at me, but when I turned to look at him, he would look away. He was holding a camera, and I knew he wanted to take my picture but he couldn't ask. So I went over to him and said, "Hi, how are you?" He said, "Fine", and then I asked him where he was from. He told me, "Japan", so I asked, "Do you all have some black people in Japan?" and he said no. Then I said, "I can see that by the way you are looking at me. I know you want to take my picture because you looked at me, then you looked at your camera". He laughed, and I said, "Just tell me the truth". He asked, "Can I please?" and I replied, "I have one condition before you take it, because we have to agree on something. You have to send me a copy". I told him that I am from Africa but I was living in Chicago, and we exchanged addresses. He took the picture, and I continued my tour with Mandingo Griot Society.

Around three or four weeks later, he sent me a copy of the picture with a little letter that said, "I am happy to meet you. I was interested and fascinated by your hair braids". I replied with a letter back to him, and he wrote again asking me about the place I come from in Africa. I wrote back and explained, and after that we wrote each other back and forth many times. I told him how people live in Gambia, the weather, and other stuff. One time he wrote to say, "I can't believe the stories you told me about history and tradition, and that people can go and stay for free with somebody in Gambia even if they don't know them. I would like to visit your country. Can I stay at your house?" I wrote back to tell him, "Yes, you can stay there, even if I am not there myself. When you are ready to go, just let me know. But I have to tell you that Gambia is not like Tokyo". So when I knew I was going to tour Japan with Herbie, I wrote to him. The day we arrived in Tokyo, he came to my hotel and took more pictures of me, next to a Samurai costume they had on display in the lobby. And anytime I was in town during that tour, we hung out and walked around together. Later on, he told me he was ready to go to Gambia, and I contacted my brother Dembo to welcome him and show him around. Takenari went and stayed in my compound in Brikama for four weeks. Then he told us his friend Usamo all about me too, and so he too wanted to go and stay in my house. I said yes to that, and Usamo stayed there for three or four weeks too. My mother and brothers and all my friends got to know them, and even today my friends ask me about them. We have kept in touch all these years.

After the last show on the Japan tour, the rest of the band members flew back to New York while me and Herbie remained behind in Tokyo. On Tuesday August 7th and Wednesday August 8th, we recorded our duet record called "Village Life" for CBS/Sony Records. The original plan was for Wayne Shorter to come to Japan, and for the three of us to record together. But Wayne didn't make it there, so it ended up just Herbie and me. Herbie told me that he didn't have songs to record, but I told him that I had lots of songs. That is why the kora is at the front of most of the songs on the record, except for the song Herbie played solo piano. That recording was done live, with us two playing together. No rehearsal. Herbie is a one-of-a-kind special person. He knows how to listen, and he can play something on top of anything he hears to make it work. I like him so much in that way.

Herbie was always using a Yamaha keyboard called a DX-7 at that time. He made that keyboard sound very famous, and every other keyboard player wanted to have one. Since it came from Japan, musicians in the U.S. had to be on a waiting list for four or five months to get one. During the time we were in Tokyo, the tour people took us to the Yamaha factory and all the band members were given a new DX-7 with a case. They also gave Herbie a brand new DX-1 in the studio when we were recording our CD. After we finished recording, me and Herbie flew back to New York, and when we landed at Kennedy Airport, a guy there saw that I had a DX-7. He came up to me and said, "Oh man, where did you get this? I want to get one, but I have to be on the waiting list, so will you please sell it to me?" I said OK, and went back to the Mayflower Hotel. I went up to my room on the 9th floor, and the bellhop brought my bags. Before the bellhop even got back down to the lobby, that guy arrived with $2500.00 for the keyboard and bought it right in my hotel room!

On August 18th, I went back to Chicago so I could go to Detroit with Mandingo to play at the African World Festival. Afterward, the rest of the band flew back to Chicago, but I flew to Virginia to play with Herbie at the Virginia Beach Pavilion. We stayed there for a few days and then we played the Merriweather Post Pavilion in Columbia, Maryland on Aug 29th. The next day, we went back to New York to play at The Pier, and on Friday the 31st we went upstate to play at the Saratoga Performing Art Center. After that, it was good to go back to New York for a few days off, because from September 4th to the 30th, we were on the road playing in big concert halls and amphitheaters from New York State to LA. On October 1st while we were in LA, we also performed on the Solid Gold TV show. Then that tour with Herbie was over, and I flew back to Chicago on October 4th.

•••••

On November 30th the Watto Sitta record was released, which in the Mandingo language means, "The Time is Right". Celluloid Records wanted me to do a bunch of promo for it in England, so I flew from Chicago to New York. Then on Sunday December 2nd, my friend John Crowley took me to the Newark airport to fly to London. A promo guy from Celluloid named Mike Knute came and met me at the airport, and we went to dinner with some people from the BBC to talk about a lot of stuff. On December 4th, I did a taping for BBC-TV, playing some songs and getting interviewed. That night, Mike Knute and another guy from Celluloid named Chris May took me to an Indian restaurant to talk over the taping I did, then we all went to Mike Knute's apartment to hang out. The next day, a guy named David Lane came from one of the London newspapers to my room at the Columbia Hotel to interview me, and Chris picked me to go back to BBC for more taping and interviewing, and back to Mike's apartment to hang. On December 7th, Chris May picked me again to go to Mike's for more interviews with media people. That was a lot of talking for just a few days! That same night, my very good friend Stuart Sutton-Jones came with his friend to meet us, and we all went out to a Greek restaurant. I saw my good friend Tony Grilly too, in the middle of running, running, running around London.

Then on Saturday December 8th, it was time for a very big thing. Chris May picked me at my hotel and took me to Heathrow airport so I could fly to Paris, then Dakar, and then back home to Gambia. On Friday December 14th, I went with my close childhood friend Mohammed Camara from Brikama to Ziguinchor, the biggest town in Cassamance.

I GET MARRIED

Me and Mohammed stayed in Ziguinchor from December 15th - 17th, 1984 for my wife Bobo and me to get married. Then we all came back to Brikama. For the first three days after we arrived, Bobo stayed with Mohammed's family in their compound, and then on Thursday Dec 20th, she came to my compound for the first time. On Friday was our Mandingo traditional marriage celebration called manyo tulungo, which we do in honor of a new wife. There was drumming and dancing, other griots and musicians, and lots of people coming to my compound. My family from all over the world came there too. It was a very big thing.

However, our wedding was begun long before that. We met in 1982 when I saw her at the compound where her aunt lived, in an area called Pikine, which is part of Dakar. She was very nice and very beautiful, and even today she is still that way. We did all the traditional marriage arrangements, and because Mohammed is my very good friend, he was a big part of the whole marriage planning and preparing from the beginning. Earlier in the book, I mentioned the first two big celebrations in a person's life: receiving your name, and becoming a man or becoming a woman. The third big celebration is when two people are getting married. In our tradition, the courtship leading to the marriage takes a long time, and the wedding ceremony itself goes on much longer than a typical wedding in western countries. When a man wants to marry somebody, he doesn't just go himself to ask the woman. There are many things to do first, especially to send a message to her family. Whether you are from a griot family, a leatherworker family, or any other family, it is the same way. When you want to begin the marriage process, you have to send somebody to the woman's family that you trust very much. That person is called a songharo, which means messenger or negotiator, and Mohammed Camara was my songharo.

To get started on the marriage plan, you must first buy five or ten kola nuts, and give them to your songharo. Then your songharo will take them to the woman's family compound to talk to the elder man and his brothers there. That songharo does not just come alone with the kola nuts though. When he gets to the village where the woman lives, he will stay with a host family, and his host will go with him to her family compound. When they get there, they will tell the elder man in the family that you are interested in marrying her. Then the elder man will call all his brothers together in a meeting to say, "So-and-so wants to marry our daughter". Before anything can go further, you will try to find out something more about the woman, and her family will try to find out more about you. Sometimes you and she don't live in the same village. You, or your friends and brothers, or even your son himself, will come to the woman's village. Then you will all go to another compound to ask the people there, "What do you think about this woman? We have a person who wants to marry her". The woman's side is also doing this to find out more about the man. If you don't ask, then you won't know. Knowing about the whole family is important too. Sometimes a family can come and talk sweet to you, but you have to find out how they are from other people. The neighbors could say, "This family is very nice, and any man who marries a woman from this family will always stay well. " Or they could say, "This family is very crazy, and anytime anybody gets married there, they always end up getting divorced." This whole process takes a long time, not like two people who see each other and then quickly decide to get married. Nobody wants their daughter to get married and then have them get divorced. Because the elder people know this, they want to take a lot of time to investigate the other person.

•••••

Marrying is a heavy job. Imagine this: two people, they aren't born in the same place, they don't have the same background, they don't know each other, and they try to live together forever. It doesn't always work out. It is a heavy thing to work it out. Only lucky people can stay married for the rest of their life. If two people who don't know each other talk about getting married, here is an example about what happens in the time they are talking and going through the process: Each one of them has 50 habits. While they are talking together, each one of them only shows the other person 25 of those habits. The other 25 habits, each one of them hides "under the bed". They go back and forth, they're calling each other honey and sweet, and all that. They make sure that the habits under the bed don't come out. But from day one after they say, "I do", the habits under the bed start coming out one by one. The first 25 habits that they showed each other are nothing much, but the 25 habits that come out from under the bed are the difficult ones. Then they will say to each other, "You didn't tell me this before. I didn't know this was going to happen." Such as, "When I sleep, you pull all the covers over my head, don't do that." Sometimes the habits can even make a big problem because it's a surprise. That's why we call marriage "futuo", which is very hard to translate to English, but it kind of means, "It comes with a heavy burden, and one has to be ready because it's not an easy thing to carry".

In fact, marriage is a very heavy thing to carry. It can have stress, and is not always sweet, sweet, sweet, to work it out for both the man's and the women's sides. Sometimes people say, "I am your wife now, and anything I say, that's what you have to do", or the same with "I am your husband now." The time they were first seeing each other and calling each other honey, nobody would say those things because their whole thing would break apart. Once you start pushing at each other, that's when the trouble happens.

•••••

After both of the families do all the investigating and are ready to start negotiating the marriage, the man's family will buy another ten kola nuts to give to the songharo, who will again bring those kola nuts to the woman's family. The man's family has to be the first to make a move with this, and the woman's family is just waiting. Once the songharo and his host bring those kola nuts to the woman's family compound, all the men of the family will welcome them. The songharo will say, "We are from such-and-such village, and we came from such-and-such family, and a son there named such-and-such wants to marry your daughter." When that happens, the father of the woman won't say anything yet to reply. He will tell the songharo to leave the kola nuts there and then to go back to the host's house, and that the family will contact him when they have made a decision. It might be two or three, or even five days that the woman's family will talk among themselves about it. Men and women don't ever stand with their parents and talk with them about the marriage thing. You will never hear them say, "Dad, that's my girlfriend", or "Mom, that's my boyfriend." It's a whole different thing in Mandingo tradition.

If the woman's born father is the elder brother of the family, he will say to the songharo, "I must gather my younger brothers together, because she was born to me, and so my brothers must be the ones to make the decision. Whatever they say, that is what is going to happen". Then the eldest one of the younger brothers will lead the decision-making. This is how it works for the daughters, and for the sons, of the elder brother. They are all under the decision-making of the younger brothers. But if the woman's born father is not the elder brother, that younger brother will say to the songharo, "My elder brother is here, and you will have to talk to him", because the elder is in charge of calling the meeting and making the decision if it is any of his younger brothers' daughters or sons getting married.

But before anything else can happen, the brothers now have to ask the woman. The way they ask is not to talk to her directly though. They will call one of her girlfriends and tell her, "Some people came here from such-and-such village, and asked if the man named such-and-such can marry her. You are her friend, and we want you to ask her what she thinks about marrying him." The girlfriend then will ask the woman. She might reply, "I don't know this man, but because my mother and father are looking out for me and want me to marry him, I will go for it." If that happens, the girlfriend will tell the family and the marriage plans will continue. But if the woman says "No, I don't want to marry that guy", then that will be that, and the marriage plans are all over. They will send somebody to take those ten kola nuts back to the songharo and he will give them back to the man's family.

No matter which brother is the woman's father though, all the brothers have to agree on the marriage for it to happen. These things are to keep the family together. This is why: If one elder brother made the decision on their own and said, "Yes, I agree to this marriage", and then the man and woman go ahead and get married, no one will like that. Especially if later on, they get divorced, and the woman will come back to her family's compound, very upset and crying. If the elder brother is not alive at that time and his younger brothers have to take his place as leader of the compound, they will say to her, "The way it happened, you pushed us away when you got married, so we don't have anything to say now."

Sometimes people think that in Africa, people are always forced to get married, but that's not how it is. If sometimes people do force their son or their daughter to get married, they will find out that it doesn't work out. I have seen this, and it can become terrible stuff. I saw one time when a woman said no, but the family forced the marriage and sent the girl to the husband in Sierra Leone. After two or three weeks, she decided to put no food in her mouth any more, even if she would die. Every day, the husband and wife also fought hand-to-hand. Later on, the wife's girlfriends said, "This is not going to work. We know her. If she says no, she will never change. Even if you take a knife and put it to her throat, she will never change. If things keep going and you don't stop this, we know that she will die. And when she dies, the blame will be on us". So the family brought her back to Gambia.

Traditionally, even after a woman says yes to the marriage, things don't happen right away. It takes a long time. The songharo goes back to the man's family and tells them, "Yes, the woman's family accepts the ten kola nuts". That's the sign that says yes to the man's family. Then the kola nuts are divided by the woman's family. No matter how big the family is, they will first divide the kola nuts between all the men and women of the compound. Then the men's side and the women's side will each divide their kola nuts and give them to all the other men and women in the neighborhood. Even if it's just a little piece of kola nut to put in your mouth, everyone is a part of it, and everyone will learn all the details of who is going to get married. The reason for everyone to know about the marriage is that every child born and raised in that village calls every man in the village father if he is old enough to be their father, and calls every woman in the village mother if she is old enough to be their mother. So they are all family in this way.

Once everyone knows that the marriage will be happening, it is the time for the man to come to the woman's family compound for a visit. But first, a friend of the man, who lives in the same village as the woman's family, will host the man to stay in their house. If the man does not have a friend in that village, it will be arranged for the man to have a host family there. When the man arrives in the host's compound, the host will send a message to the woman's family to tell them he is there. Then the host family will cook dinner and eat together with the man before saying, "Now we should go to the woman's family compound." That host will come with the man every time they visit it. When they get to the woman's family compound, the man will pull off his shoes at the gate to show respect. Then the host will pick up the shoes, take them to the door of the family's house, and put them down there. When they come inside and meet the woman's family, everyone will greet each other, but the man won't talk a lot. When the talking starts, it will be the host who speaks for him, and when he has anything to say, he will tell it to the host. The woman is there too, but the whole time the man and his host come to visit, you wouldn't think she is even there. She knows the man who wants to marry her is there, but she ignores him. The host might talk to the woman directly, but she doesn't even answer him much. You will never see her talking with the man, and they cannot be alone together. If you don't know that they are going to be married, you would think, "This woman don't like this man", but that's just our tradition. This is very serious stuff. Nowadays, it doesn't always happen like this though.

After they visit, the man and his host will go back to the host's house. Later that night between ten o'clock and one o'clock in the morning, they will do something we call sunkutumuto, which means, "going to get the bride". We also call it musukammo, which means to "go bring the woman". Traditionally, the way it works is that the host will go back to the woman's family compound by himself, to try to convince ther woman to come back to his house so that she and the man can talk to each other. When the woman comes to the host's compound, he will bring her to the grass hut where the man is staying. The host will be there in the hut too, and sometimes another a friend of the man will be there also. A friend of the woman might be there sometimes too. So the man and woman just talk, talk, and talk together for a long, long time, to try to get to know each other. They might talk for two or three hours, then the host and the man will bring the woman back to her family compound. This kind of thing can go on for a long time. The next night of the musukammo, the man might go back to his home village for one or two months, and then come back to the woman's family compound again. It goes back and forth, with many trips. Sometimes musukammo goes very well, but sometimes it takes a lot of time. Sometimes the woman will go over to her girlfriend's house when musukammo happens, instead of going to the host house to talk to the man. But that does not discourage us. Taking time is just part of our tradition.

•••••

I remember one time that a friend and I were the hosts in Suso kunda for a man, and we went to do musukammo and get the woman to come. That woman's name is Mbanding, and she lived in our same village. That day, she knew that the man who wanted to marry her was in town. In her family compound, there was only her, and her grandfather and grandmother. There was a big Mango tree in the center of her family compound, and we came to that tree to talk to the grandmother. The grandmother said, "Mbanding left earlier", but she didn't really leave. So me and my friend went to every single compound in the village, even looking in the backyards and under the beds, but we didn't see her. So we went back to her family coumpound and asked the grandmother, who said again, "She left. I don't know where she went." Our village was around one mile away from a village called Tabanding, and I said to my friend, "Mbanding is not a scared person, maybe we should go there and look for her." It was nighttime, and we walked all the way to Tabanding to look for her, and asked everyone. By that time it was almost two o'clock in the morning, so we came back to the her family's compound and said, "Grandmother why won't you tell us where she is?" She said, "I told you, Mbanding left. Since after dinnertime, I don't know where she is."

Then I told my friend, "Let's just sit down here and wait for her. Between now to tomorrow, she will have to come back home." So we took two wooden stools and we sat down. The moon was bright, and we were sitting there under the big Mango tree. The reason this makes me laugh, even today, is that Mbanding was sitting in the top of that tree! We didn't see her there, but she got tired and fell asleep, and nearly fell completely out of the tree. While she was falling, she tried to grab some branches and we heard the sound of the branches, clack clack clack! I said, "Oh, is this chickens?" My friend said, "No, chickens don't like to be up there, this is something else." There is always a flashlight in every compound, so I went and found it, and shined the flashlight up in the tree and saw her. She yelled, "Leave me alone!" but I said, "Come on down". She said, "OK, I'm coming", but she was like a devil because when she came down, she grabbed my friend's shirt and tore the whole thing! My friend was fast and he jumped on her, but she started hollering and kicking too, and scratching us both. Even though it's two o'clock in the morning, people knew that musukammo was going on so nobody was worried. We picked her up and we brought her to my compound. The man who wanted to marry her was already sleeping by that time, so she slipped away and went back home again. Later on, they got married and had a bunch of kids! In 1981 or 1982, after I was living in the U.S. for a few years, I came to Dakar, Senegal and was staying in a hotel. The husband happened to be a security guard there, and when I was leaving the hotel, I saw him looking at me. I called his name and we greeted. Then he said, "I don't live far from here", so we went to his house. I teased Mbanding and she was laughing so much! I said, "That day you are like a lion woman, scratching us like you never want to see your new husband's face. And now look at all the kids you have!" I never saw another musukammo like that. But no matter how it goes, musukammo always takes a long time.

•••••

After musukammo is finished, the woman's family says, "Easilobula", which means, "Now we open the road for you." That means it's the time to open the negotiations for what is to be done to make the marriage happen. The first thing they do is called nonkonla, which means, "The day we will announce the marriage plans to the public". It is also called futusito in some parts of Gambia, which means, "Tying the marriage tight." The woman's whole family and the man's whole family will come together in the man's family compound or in the mosque. But the man and woman are not present for any of this. The man's family will bring a floor mat and a big basket filled with salt, which they give to the woman's family. After the marriage is announced to the public, the families will begin talking about futunafulo, which means marriage money, which the husband's family has to pay the wife's family. Traditionally in the olden days, it's very small amount, only naninintala, which is 4 dalasi and 50 bututus. If the new husband has more money, it's good for him to pay more than that. Nowadays, it can even be hundreds or thousand of dalasi.

In our language, the new wife is called manyo, and the new husband is called manyoke. After the futunafalo is negotiated, there is also other money given by the manyoke's family to the manyo's family: The first is faadomoro, which means fathers' spending, and baadomoro, which means mothers' spending. This money is given to all the fathers and to all the mothers in the manyo's family compound. There is also something called faadondiko, which means father's dress. This money is given to the manyo's father, and is used to buy material to make a special shirt for him. Or they can bring him a new big shirt to wear instead of giving the money. Then there is baarinkekido, which means brothers' gun. It is only a small amount, sometimes just 25 cents, and it is not used for buying a gun. Baarinkekido is associated with the time when the manyo is going to the manyoke's compound, and there is heavy dancing and firing of guns into the air during the celebration.

If the manyoke's family has the money together for all these things, they can give it to the manyo's family at the nonkonla. If not, they can pay it a small amount at a time until it is paid in full. No matter how they pay it, the manyoke's family always gives all money to the songharo, and he is the one who gives it directly to the manyo's family. Of all these monies, the most important among all of them is the futunafulo, the marriage money. It's best for it to be paid at the nankonla. But even if you cannot pay it that day, in our tradition it must be paid sometime, even if it is forty years later. You cannot owe this money. If you don't pay it, the marriage is not completed.

When a man wants to marry, most of the time the woman he chooses is already grown up. But sometimes a girl is chosen for marriage that is still young. We call that, "watering the onion". In that case though, everything about the marriage preparations waits until the girl is old enough to get married. That waiting process takes a long time, and nowadays people don't usually do this, but it happened sometimes when I was growing up. It could happen when a boy might be only 12 or 15 years old, and his parents will choose a new girl baby for him to marry much, much later on. Another example is if parents have a baby son, and one of their brothers and his wife has a baby daughter. That being the case, the parents might want the son to marry the brother's daughter. If so, they would take a little piece of cloth and put it on the daughter's hand like a bracelet. That cloth signals that this is the parents' intention, but nothing happens on it for many, many years. If somebody else comes along in those years and wants to marry this daughter, the parents will tell them what is already planned. When the girl becomes grown up, she will be hearing from her parents that she is meant to marry that boy. But if the girl wants to say no, or the boy wants to say no, they can say, "Mom I don't think I want to marry them". The parents might try to change their boy or girl's mind about that, but if that doesn't happen, then all the marriage arrangements are ended. But if they say they do want to marry, then things go in the same traditional way with the kola nuts and all that. This kind of thing happened a lot in the old days, and could be very sweet. It could help the family stick together, because your father's brothers are your father too, and your mother's sisters are your mother too. The new husband and the new wife respect them in the same way as their own born mother and father, and are treated equally by all of them. A marriage like this can mean that all the planning goes smooth, the new bride's family won't make the marriage money too high for the new husband's family, and there will not be a big "taking sides" thing in the marriage. Today, it doesn't happen very much though, because if any trouble happens in the marriage it can become a big problem in the whole family, which is no good.

•••••

In all marriage preparations, once all the musukammo and marriage money negotiations are done, the new husband will begin working a lot for the new bride's family for two, three, or even five years. Every year when the farming season comes, he will come and work on her family's farm. The villagers will all gather at their kafos to make the preparations. When you get to be an older person, your kafo won't be active anymore in working for the new bride's family farm, but you will always still recognize each other as being in the same kafo. When it's time to inform everybody that it's time to gather, each mens' kafo will have its own horn to call everyone. Those kafos each have a different sounding horn, and each man in that kafo knows the particular sound of their horn. When the horn is calling for you to gather, you gotta come no matter what you are doing, even if you are eating dinner. If you don't come, they will fine you, maybe five kola nuts or even maybe ten kola nuts. When a kafo is meeting as part of marriage preparations, someone will announce, "We got everybody here because we got a message that its time for the new husband to go work on his new bride's family farm". Then all the kafo members will start discussing it, to choose a date when they all will go there to work. This kafo gathering and discussion is always done many days in advance, because all the kafos who will go there will have to choose the date to go to work. Once that date is chosen, the kafos will send a messenger to the new bride's family to tell them when the kafos are coming.

When they arrive at her family's farm, the younger men's kafos do the farming jobs that are heavy work and hard to do. The heavy work that is done can be to clean up all the grasses around the village to prevent fire from coming close. The older men's kafos go along just to thank them and encourage them. The kafos of girls and women do a lot too, such as the food cooking and bringing water to the men, and supporting each other. There is also a special friendship between the boys and girls kafos that are the same age. For example, when you are working in the new bride's family farm, the girls in the kafo that is around the same age as your kafo will be the ones that are bringing you food and water.

The whole village thing is about that. Also, the new bride's family must put everything together so they can feed their future son-in-law and all these people who are coming from his village. Many women in her family come join, to help get the food for breakfast and lunch for all these people. There is no way to accommodate all these people for sleeping, so people will bring woven mats to the host's compound in the village, and cloths, old bags, and other things to lay down on the ground in the center of the big yard for people to sleep on. When the new husband's people are arriving on the night before they will start working on the farm, they are already in their work clothes, ready to farm. The men don't even sleep that night, because they are in a hurry to see that farmland. In the early morning, everybody is up, sharpening their hoes and other tools. As soon as it's light enough to see the crops that are growing, they start working. They work so hard, sometimes they finish and they even begin to work on the neighbors' farms. They have a lot of energy, and some people are playing drums behind them and singing songs to give them even more energy.

This is how it is growing up. You are in a kafo, and when it's time to go work on someone's farm, you go. By the time it's your turn to get married, you have done this many times. It's not about the money, this is just how it is in the village. Everybody benefits, and there is no money paid. The new bride's family is working right next to the kafos from the new husband's village, and also they cook a lot of food. They don't want anybody to be working so hard and be hungry. Usually, the people finish the farming day quick, in the early or middle afternoon, and then go back to their village for dinner. The proud nature of the kafo is to jump on the work and finish quickly. Teamwork. It works out very heavy in that way for everybody. This kafo farming work can be done during planting season or during harvesting season. For every man in the kafo who is going to get married, everybody will do this for them, just like we work together to build a house in the village. This kind of work can be going on for several years, planting and harvesting peanuts, rice, and other things, until both families are ready now for the marriage.

In my case, because my village and my kafo is a long, long way from Ziguinchor, the city in Cassamance where Bobo's family is from, we didn't do any of the kafo farming as part of our wedding preparations. Also, Ziguinchor is not a typical village, it's more like a big city, so people living there didn't have big farms for us to even be able to do that. Also because when Bobo was very young, she went to live with her aunt in the section of Dakar called Pikine, and they didn't have farms there either. But our families did all the rest of the traditional marriage planning, preparations, and celebrations.

•••••

After that, the next thing that happens will be a few months later, or sometime during that year, or even the following year. That is the time for the new husband's family to go ask for the wife. To do that, they send the songharo to tell her family that they are ready for her. Sometimes her family will say, "Yes, we are ready" but sometimes they will say, "We are not quite ready. Can we do it next year?" That might mean that her family wants to buy a whole lot of things for her before she goes, but they don't have all those things yet. This is said in good faith, so everybody understands. The mother's side of the new bride's family wants to buy all the things a woman will need for her own household: clothing, cooking pots, bowls, mortars for pounding the food, many calabash, bedsheets, suits, beads, bracelets, and more. Sometimes just the new bride's mother is doing this buying, but usually all the women in the compound are helping too. Even the mother's sisters from other villages and compounds are helping. But the mother will never bring those things into the compound for her daughter to see. Instead, she will hide them in other women's houses in other compounds in the village. The new bride's mother is also not going to tell her daughter exactly when the marriage will be, but the rest of the family will know.

Traditionally, if the new husband and new bride happen to live in the same village, the families will do all of the marriage celebration together there. But if they live in two different villages, the new bride's family will do their own celebration in their village for everybody, and after that is over, the new husband's family will go back to their own village to have a big celebration there too. On the day they have chosen for the marriage, the new bride's family will secretly send somebody to go to the home of one particular old woman. That old woman will already know that this is the date that has been chosen, so she will be ready. They will say to her, "It's time for our daughter to go and get married, so it's time for you to play the water drum".

This is always done on a Wednesday, in the evening after dinner, when the new bride is out somewhere, hanging with her girlfriends. The old woman will come to her family compound, and they will put water in a big pan, then put a big calabash upside down on top. There are two big sticks to play that water drum with, and the old woman will start to play. It has a very big bass sound, and that sound travels far. When the old woman starts hitting that water drum, everybody in the village can hear it. She starts playing a continuous beat, but not a specific song, and everybody in the village knows that this sound means there is a new bride in this village that is going to get married soon. When all the girls in the village who are in the ages of getting married hear that sound, they will run to their own family compound to check whether it is being played for them, or for somebody else. Whoever finds out that the drum is being played for her, she will start crying, jump into her mother's room and jump on the bed. Her girlfriends will follow, and everybody will be crying. The crying will not be happening because she doesn't want to get married, though. It's just because she knows she was born and raised in that house and now she is leaving her mother and father, brothers and sisters, and friends. It's a big step. Some hardheaded boys will run into that room too, put their finger in their mouth, and put saliva on their cheek to pretend they are crying, just to tease the girls. Then the girls will all get up and beat them to make them leave!

The family will all let the new bride cry with her friends, then the old woman will come into the room with a big white cloth, which we call manyo fanno, which means "bride's cloth". That's a heavy thing, that piece of cloth, and it will be what they cover the new bride's head with. When the manyo fanno is put on a woman's head, it's known by everyone that she is a new bride, and will be going to her new husband tomorrow. We Mandingos also have a funny saying about the manyo fanno. Mothers will say to their young girl children who misbehave: " If you disobey me, you will remember what I will do until they put the manyo fanno on your head!" Meaning that, "When I discipline you, it will be so much that you will remember it for many, many years!"

•••••

New brides always go to their new husbands on a Thursday, and early in the morning on that day, many people will come to her family compound. The women will gather and loosen her hair, wash her body and her hair, and work on her. After lunchtime, a women specializing in braiding a new bride's hair will come. The braiding can be done in her family compound, but usually it is done right in the middle of the bantaba under a big tree. Everybody in the village will come there too. The women will sing while the braiding happens, and drummers will be playing. Griots will also be playing koras or balafons, and singing the praises of the new bride's family and the new husband's family. People will be dancing all around. It's a big, big festivity! Those people want the woman braiding the new bride's hair to be stretching out the time so it takes a long, long time before it's all finished. The pattern of that braiding is six rows from the front of the head to the back. They don't put any kind of extensions on the new bride's hair for the braids, they just use her natural hair. People from the new husband's family village also come to witness the braiding on behalf of his family. In fact, each family from the new husband's village sends a representative or two, even if the whole family cannot go. The families of the new husband and new bride are also giving the griots money while they play. Doing all these things together is important for everybody there.

When the braiding is finished, it is usually around four or five o'clock in the afternoon. Everybody leaves the bantaba and goes back to the new bride's family compound. Now her family is preparing to bring out all the things that they bought for her. They will show them to the crowd and say, "This is what we bought for our daughter". People are bringing those things out from all the places where the mother had hid them, and putting them in the center of the compound to make a big display. Then the father himself, or one of his younger brothers will talk. But the new bride's father or his brother will be talking quiet, and a griot will be the one to proclaim it all in a loud voice so everyone can hear. The griot also makes sure everybody stops talking among themselves, and listens to the whole announcement. They will say, "OK, we are here today, we gather here today because our daughter is going to get married to such-and-such family from such-and-such village. The new husband's family are here from that place, and we are going to show you all the things we got for our daughter." Then they will count everything on display while they announce it to the crowd, so everyone will see it. For example: 150 cloths, 75 shirts, 8 pairs of shoes, 27 calabashes, 5 gold pieces, and on and on, until they have announced everything they have gotten for the new bride.

By the time all that is done, sunset will be happening. When the new bride is ready to go to the new husband's compound, everyone will start getting ready to go, but before they leave, the leader of her family will gather everyone to give advice to the new husband's family and representatives. That person will say, "Here we give our daughter for your son. So we advise you all to take it easy with each other because both of them are new to the marriage. This is their first time. We're not saying, they should not argue, because no one can stay together and never argue". They will also say this proverb: "Inside your mouth, your tongue and your teeth are there. Sometimes you will make a mistake, and your teeth will bite your tongue". Then they will say, "Both of them have to know that they should be guarding each other's side, and not to be starting any problem. Our daughter is sitting here getting ready to be married. We didn't tell her to go to be a wrestler with her husband. Husband too, you must remember this same thing. We did not give you our daughter to sell her to you, we gave her to you to respect our culture, and this is why we agreed. People should get married. But for every human being, the house they were born and raised in is the house they will like more than any other place. The reason we give our daughter to you is because of this natural understanding". Only the new bride's family will have the chance to do some advising like this. After this advising is done, all the representatives from her family will say, "People shall get ready now". Then the representatives for her family will start gathering all the things that were bought for her, and putting them on their heads to carry to the new husband's family compound. Later on, when everyone arrives at his family compound, the new bride's family advisor will repeat all of this advice to everyone gathered there too.

In the new husband's village, the family has been preparing for this for many months, with the amount of food they will gather to cook, and the cows they will kill. On the marriage day, they will be all set. The new bride now will walk to the new husband's compound with the people from her village. They are called manyo dingoli, which means, "bride's children". There will also be one old woman who will accompany them, but she is different than the woman who played the water drum. She is called manyo makan, which means, "the person who will be the new bride's comforter". The new bride's mother doesn't go on the walk though, and the manyo makan is kind of like her representative, to show the new bride how everything should be in the marriage. There will also be a girl walking with them called dalindrila, which means, "someone to help you get used to a new place". She could be the new bride's young sister, or some other young girl around 12 or 15 years old, and she will help the new bride to not miss her family so much. These two people will be very, very close to the new bride, to travel with her all the way to her new husband's family compound with all the manyo dingoli, and they will stay with her for a while there too.

The new bride will have the manyo fanno covering her whole head, even her eyes. The manyo makan will be in front of her in the crowd, holding the manyo fanno and guiding her. The dalindrila will be walking next to the new bride, and she will have a little clay jar filled with incense that she will be carrying, but it is not lit. During the whole walk, the new bride doesn't talk to the other people who are all around her. If the new bride and new husband live in the same village, the traveling won't be that far. But at any junction the whole crowd gets to, the manyo makan will say, "Everybody stop! We are not going to pass through here until we get silifata nonkong", which is six cents. This is money that must be paid by the new husband's family and the family respresentatives. Until they pay that silifata nonkong to anybody on the new bride's side, the whole group cannot keep going. The new bride's people will give all the money they get to the manyo makan. Also, sometimes the manyo makan can stop everybody and say, "The new bride need a horse, she is tired of walking" and then one of the new husband's friends will have to stop and bend down, and the new bride will climb up and ride on his back. That man gets tired, but all the people will say, "We want to go as slow as we can, and if you put her down, we are not going to go anywhere." We call that kind of walking manyo yenyengo, which means, "walking very slow with the bride". Sometimes to make the whole thing more groovy, they go so slow that even a distance of six or seven blocks might take the whole night! They go so slow that they are hardly even moving! All this time, there is heavy music and dumming going on all around them, and people are singing. No one will try to force them to go fast. If you try that, they will stop completely. The tiny steps and slow walking are almost like saying, "All we all glued here?" Then around one or two o'clock in the morning, something happens that not many people will know about. A woman on the new bride's side will secretly have a second manyo fanno cloth with them, and she will come near the manyo makan with it. Then she will flip that cloth on a different girl's head to fool the people, help the new bride escape from the crowd, and take her quickly to the new husband. The slow walking will continue through the village though, because the people think that the girl that they put the second manyo fanno on is the real bride!

When the new bride gets to the new husband's family compound, he is inside his room with one or two of his best and closest friends. He has been waiting back at his family compound this whole time with them. The manyo makan comes inside and puts the new bride's hand into the new husband's hand, and says, "Greet". Once they greet, the manyo makan tells the new bride to come lay on the bed while the new husband sits at the head of the bed. Traditionally, the new husband will have a sanke over their bed, which means mosquito net, even if there are no mosquitos. Then the new bride and new husband will go to bed. All the people who are on the way to the new husband's family compound keep drumming and singing and slow walking, though. By the time they arrive, it might be four or five o'clock in the morning. Those people will think that the new bride is just arriving with them, but by that time she has been there for a while.

•••••

Now it's Friday, and all the people who came with the new bride are inside the new husband's family compound. His family welcomes them and says, "Bride's children, here is your dinner!" Then they bring huge calabashes full of the food that they cooked the night before, for all of them to eat. People eat, eat, eat, and then it's time to go to sleep. That whole day, everybody is laid back and eating, sleeping and resting, and going to the mosque. Every compound in the new husband's village will host somebody from the new bride's side. Even if they have to give up their own room and sleep on the floor, they will do that, and all the houses in the village will be full.

On Saturday morning, everybody gets up and just hangs out and socializes with each other. After a while, the new husband's sisters, brothers, friends, and everybody else will gather in his family compound to greet the new bride. They will call out her name, but she won't answer. She will stay in the house under the sanke. The manyo makan will tell her, "Don't answer, they have to buy your mouth. They have to pay for your speaking." Then the people end up pulling out five or ten cents to give to her. Whatever they have to give is OK, and it's only the new husband's side of the family and his friends and neighbors that have to pay. She won't answer if they don't pay! They will give the money to the manyo makan to hold for her, and then the new bride answers them very softly. Then the new husband's side says, "Now we want to welcome the new bride and her children", and they will go get the biggest bull they can find, and kill it to feed everybody. Saturday is a very big eating time, and the big celebration continues all day.

On Sunday, everybody on the new bride's side goes back home except for the manyo makan and the dalindrila. The manyo makan stays for a week, to show the new bride how to be a wife, such as what to do and what not to do, and how to dress. In our tradition, the new bride also does not go outside the house for one week, and does not talk to anyone outside. The new husband also will stay inside. He will have two or three friends that will stay and guard him there, so he doesn't have to go outside. They can go buy things for him and for her, and bring them back. The manyo makan will also be cooking a lot of porridge for the new bride, and she puts a special thing in it. We have a type of spice that we call camare, made from a grass root that they dig. Whenever a woman is going to be married, they will make sure to gather a lot of that root for her. That is what is in the clay jar that the dalindrila carries on the slow walking. It reminds me of cinnamon, and it tastes so good. You can put it in cold water and it makes everything tastes good too. People say that when you eat it in porridge, it will keep your skin shiny and nice.

Every morning, the new bride will eat that porridge, and at the end of a week, she will cook her first meal in her new husband's house. We call that cooking bulufalo tabiro, which means, "Testing her hand cooking". It is a festivity for the new husband and all his friends in the village, who will be invited to taste the first food that she cooks. They all eat it and compliment her. They say, "Our new bride can cook very heavy. Our new bride, she can cook." After eating that meal together, she will start helping to cook food for the whole family also.

Traditionally, the women in every family compound all take their turns cooking breakfast, lunch, and dinner. The elder man's wife, his brother's wives, his sons' wives, and so on. So typically, the new bride won't be cooking every day, but when her turn comes she will cook. Also in our tradition, when you are a mother and your son marries a wife, you will never cook in the compound again. Your son's wife will now be taking your turn. When a woman becomes a wife, her husband's mother becomes a mother-in-law to her, and if her husband's father has more than one wife, they will become mothers-in-law to her also. So sometimes, all the elder women will all have daughter-in-laws who will do the cooking. There always comes a time when it is the children's turn, especially the sons in the family and their wives, to take care of their parents. The sons are the ones who will stay in the family compound with their wives for the rest of their life. The daughters might go get married and move to some other place a far distance from the family, and help take care of their husband's parents, so they cannot help their own parents every day in the same way the sons and their wives do. Our village thing is all about sticking together. Today it has changed in the big cities, but in the small villages it is still this same way.

In our tradition, we have a big celebration when two people get married, but we don't celebrate anybody's wedding anniversary as the years go by afterward. Also, usually the eldest son is the first one to get married, then the second son, and then the next son. It's the same way with the daughters, and the eldest gets married first. That's the intention of the parents, but in some cases it doesn't work out that way.

Every Mandingo area is different, and all of these marriage arrangements and celebrations are what happens in the area that I was born and raised in. What happens in someone else's area might not be exactly this same way, and I know there are many other places where even the marriage procession is very different than in my area.

MEETING PHILIP

In December of 1984 when I was in Gambia getting married, the band members in a group called Toure Kunda were living in Paris. They were three brothers from Cassamance, singing traditional Mandingo songs and playing guitar, drums, and keyboards. They also did original arrangements, and were famous in Europe for a long time. They asked Bill Laswell to produce one of their records, and Bill told them, "I want Foday to come play on your record". He talked to me about this before I went to Gambia for my marriage, but he didn't give me any details at that time. I knew well that it's very cold in Paris in winter, and I really wanted to spend the whole winter in Gambia with my new wife Bobo, who just came to my house in Brikama on December 20th. When Bill contacted me again to ask me to come to Paris, it was very short notice, but I agreed to go.

I flew up there on January 12th, 1985, but I didn't even get a visa before I left. Bill said I should get one at the airport, but I just went to Dakar to pick up my ticket and got on the flight. When I arrived at the Paris airport, one of the Toure Kunda members and their manager came to pick me. But at immigration, the people asked me to sit aside because I didn't have a visa, and said, "You can't go in to France. You should have a visa". I replied, "I know, but it's short notice and I will only be here three or four days", but they said, "No you cannot go in, we have to send you back to Senegal tonight on a flight". I said, "Good" because I wasn't that interested in going there anyway, except to work with Bill. If I went back home to Brikama, I wouldn't have to fight with the snow in France! Right then, the Toure Kunda people were looking for me and spotted me behind the glass in the immigration place, so they made a call to the foreign minister's office to get me the OK to go in. The immigration people said that I should come back to the airport the next day for them to stamp my passport, but I said, "No, once I leave this airport, I am not coming back until I go back to Gambia". So the Toure Kunda people took my passport back to the airport the next day to have it stamped. I just got married and I wanted to be home in Brikama and not in France, so I didn't put up with any wicky-wacky thing there. The Toure Kunda album I played on was called Natalia. We did the recording on January 14th, 15th, and 18th, and I went back to Brikama on the 20th and stayed in Brikama with Bobo until mid-April.

While I was there, Herbie Hancock and Tony Meilandt came to visit me, and we did a TV show for Jim Henson's Muppet Show. They arrived with a film crew on Friday February 8th, and filmed us in a big wooden canoe out on the River Gambia. I was playing kora and another guy was playing balafon, and Herbie was on the keyboard. A fourth guy was playing hand drums and other percussion. When I first got back to Gambia, I had also arranged with Radio Gambia to do a program while Herbie was there. The next day after that radio show was broadcast, a lot of Peace Corps volunteers from the U.S., both boys and girls, black and white, came to see Herbie at the Atlantic Hotel in Banjul. The whole hotel lobby was jam-packed, and he came out to greet them. Herbie and Tony stayed in Gambia until February 15th, but we didn't have time to travel into the rural areas.

•••••

While I was in Gambia at that time, I also met a guy named Mustafa Sissay while riding in a taxi car on the way back from Banjul to Brikama. I noticed that he had a kora in a bag and rasta dreadlocks. I thought he was a griot boy, but he was not, he just liked the kora. We greeted, and he told me he could play kora a little bit. He asked me if I could play, and I told him, "I can play a little bit". He asked my name then, and when I told him, right away he asked, "Ae you the griot who lives in the United States?" He wanted my address so we could write each other, and he was so excited to get it. Later on that same year, he happened to have chance to come to the U.S. He wanted to go to music school in New York, and he brought the kora with him. The school didn't work out for him though, maybe it was too expensive or something. He only stayed there two or three weeks, but while he was there, he happened to meet some students from the north side of Chicago who were going home for a vacation. He didn't even know them very well, but he told him he wanted to go with them, and asked for a ride. He showed them my address, and they gave him a ride all the way from New York to Chicago. They arrived on Saturday August 3rd, and I was in my apartment when my buzzer rang. I picked up the phone and he said, "It's me". I said, "Who"? Then I came downstairs and saw him, and my mouth was hanging open. I nearly fell down with suprise because he was just standing there with a duffle bag and a kora! So we went upstairs to my place, and I asked him, "What's happening?" He told me everything he was doing, but I was quiet. He knew nobody there but me!

I finally said, "Mustafa, I am scared for you. This is not like Gambia to show up at someone's compound. What if you arrived and I was not here? You don't know any other friends here in Chicago, and you don't see the danger. If I was in Europe when you arrived, you could die on the street here and wouldn't know even how to call for help. You are the luckiest human being in the whole world! If I was not here, what would you do?" Then he stayed with me for two or three weeks. I let him cool down at my place for one week, and then I said, "What do you want to do? People need to work here in the U.S., but you cannot play kora or drums. I don't know how to find you a job, because I never did a regular job like that. I play the kora. You have to go downtown to look for a job. Every day I will give you the train fare to go there. We will eat breakfast together before you go, and dinner when you come back".

During the time Mustafa was staying with me, I also went to see a documentary about Gambian griots at the Art Institute of Chicago on August 11th. Some moviemakers from England had gone to Gambia to make it, and it was called Born Musicians. I knew all the kora players and balafon players in that movie, including my grandfather Amadou Bansang Jobarteh and his son Sanjally, who are related to me on my father's side. Sanjally is now the father of Sona Jobarteh, the famous lady kora player. Also during his visit, I was booked as the opening act for John McLaughlin, who was doing a concert at the Vik Theater in Chicago on August 24th. I told Mustafa, "Let's go, you can see how the music thing goes here in the U.S.". We went to the theater and I played a solo kora concert to open the show.

During that same time, I knew three guys from Senegal who were living in Atlanta. The one I knew best is Mohammed Haidara, who was sent to the U.S. by a guy named Frances Senghor, the son of the first president of Senegal. Frances Senghor built a recording studio in Dakar, and sent those three guys to Atlanta to learn how to engineer and record. Three weeks after Mustafa Sissay arrived at my place, Mohammed Haidara and the two other guys came to Chicago to do something, and were staying at the house of a man named Ousman. I met up with Mohammed there, and we were talking. I asked him about the Gambians who live in Atlanta and the jobs they do, and I told him about Mustafa. I asked him to help, and he agreed. When I told Mustafa that it might be easier to find a job in Atlanta, he got ready to go there. When Mohammed and the other guys were getting ready to travel, I gave Mustafa some money to buy food and stuff, and took him to the place where those guys were staying. Mustafa stayed there overnight, and they all left together for Atlanta on Sunday, September 1st, 1985. I only talked to Mustafa once or twice after that, but never saw him again.

•••••

That same summer was the first time my mother ever touched a telephone with her hand. My mother Madame Jobarteh was about 70 years old at this time that it happened, on Tuesday, July 9th. The reason for our phone call was that during the time I was in Gambia earlier that year after getting married, she told me that she wanted to do the pilgrimage to Mecca, which is called the hajji. Before I left Gambia, I had prepared her trip and left the deposit money for her ticket. I said that I would send more money once the exact amount needed was known, so when the news came to my family about the total due for her trip, my good friend Buya Sillah went to the Banjul post office with my mother to call me. Even at that time in 1985, nobody in Brikama had a phone in their house, so they had to travel all the way from Brikama to Banjul just to make a call! Buya called me collect and said, "My man, you should call us back here at the post office. I am here with mom, and they say she has to pay $800.00 more, and you have to do this quick". Then he said, "Here is mom", and handed her the phone. When my mom got on the phone, she said, "Balla, is that you?" because she always called me Balla. The whole time we were on the phone, she was talking very loud because she was thinking that she had to shout for me to hear from thousands of miles away! After that conversation, she always liked talking on the phone to me. She liked hearing my voice, and I liked to hear hers too.

Soon after that, my mother left Gambia to fly to Mecca on Friday August 2nd. It was her first time on airplane, and she never thought she would ever get to go on a "flying boat" too! She was gone on her pilgrimage until August 29th, and I went to Gambia after she came back, to welcome her home. During the time I was there, two older women also came to my house to say hello. One of them said, "Thank you for paying for our hajji", and told me that she lost all her money on the way to Mecca. There was a big giant crowd of hundreds of people in the Gambia airport, and she was not used to that, so it was easy to get confused. In Mecca, both of these older women happened to be staying in the same tent with my mom. The second lady told me that she did not have enough money with her and it ran out quickly after they arrived. Then the women told me that every morning, my mom asked them, "What do you all want to eat?" and she fed them the whole time they were there. They were very lucky. God can do anything, so maybe God looked their way and fixed everything for them in that way. I sent my two brothers and my sister to the hajji too, but I have never been there. Whenever I bought their ticket and found out how much money it would cost for the lodging, food, and all that, I always gave them double that money to make sure they didn't run out. Even my mom came back with money after taking care of her two friends, and buying gifts for everybody.

•••••

On September 5th of 1985, my record with Herbie Hancock was released, called Village Life. I left Gambia and went back to the U.S. to do some concerts, and while I was in Chicago, I did a phone interview with a radio station in Santa Fe, New Mexico. The next day, I flew to Santa Fe and a good friend of mine named Jack Kolkmeyer picked me at the airport. He had booked a solo kora concert for me in Santa Fe on September 18th, and then at the International Lion's Den in Albuquerque on the 21st. One thing I always notice when I am in that area of the United States, is that the Native Americans there kind of remind me of the Fulani people called Lorobe, who are the cattle herders in Gambia. During the time I was growing up, the Lorobe people used a lot of beads in their clothing, necklaces, arm bracelets, and ankle bracelets. To me, those are very similar to what I see Native Americans do when they weave their beads. One other time when I was playing in Santa Fe, some Native Americans were there and invited me to go to their village. Their mud pueblo houses reminded me of the Fulani people too.

I went back to Chicago after those New Mexico concerts, and on October 1st, Mandingo Griot Society drove from Chicago to Minneapolis to play at Prince's club, which was called 1st Avenue. A good friend of mine in Chicago named J.C. Walton had a van, so we paid him to take us up there. He also liked African drums a lot, and we first met around 1982 when he was working with the Mantu Dance Group. They were the first Black American dancers that I saw in the United States who were trying to do African dance. I played with them at only a couple of their shows, but I became close with J.C. He was with them for many years and became a very good drummer, and at one point he changed his name to Manu. As soon as I met him, we became very close friends. He is from way out in the country in Yasou, Mississippi, and many things we do are the same because we are both from small villages in the bush: fishing and hunting of rabbits, deer, and other stuff. Whenever we see each other, we like to talk about those things, and our friendship became closer every year until it developed into the kind of thing we have now. Now we have played music together a lot for a long time too. He is my number one male friend since I came to the United States, and we can relate to each other very, very heavy. In fact, he is one person who I can talk to any time even now, and it doesn't matter if it's day or night. Sometimes I call him at three or four in the morning, and neither of us cares who is sleeping. He is the only person I know like that.

On that day in 1985, he was driving the band all the way to Minneapolis, but he hates cigarette smoking and all the band members smoked a lot! Everybody was smoking all the time, and every few minutes he would say, "I cannot breathe, you people are killing me!" Then we would say, "Roll the window down", but it was very cold outside and when that cold air came in the car, he rolled it back up. Then again the smoke made him say, "I cannot breathe!" and he rolled the window down. This happened over and over all the way to Minneapolis. It took us eight hours to get to the club, and then we went right into the club to set up and play. We played and played, and people loved us and danced. When we finished late at night, we hung out a little bit and then hit the road to go back to Chicago. On October 18th, we left Chicago again to go to Santa Fe for another big concert that my friend Jack Kolkmeyer booked. He put us in a fancy place to stay there, and that's when I happened to meet the blues musician who I had thrown out of his motel room by mistake in the middle of the night in Grinnell, Iowa!

In December, my Uncle Jali Tamba Suso and his good friend Jarju Kuyateh came to New York City to visit a friend there. My Uncle Jali Tamba is a great griot singer, and Jarju is a very good kora player too. I was in Chicago at that time, and they contacted me. Right away I started thinking about making a record with them, so I got in touch with the people at Flying Fish Records, and said, "This would be a great opportunity for three of us to record an album of traditional kora songs. So, are you all interested?" I knew that at that time, nobody would be able to hear anything like that music unless they went to Africa. Right away the Flying Fish people said yes, so I made the arrangements and flew Jali Tamba and Jarju to Chicago to do the recording. We recorded six traditional songs at Acme Studio in Chicago in one day, January 1st, 1986. Jali Tamba sang the vocals while Jarju played kora with me. Our album was released in 1986, and is called Mansa Bendung, which in Mandingo means "Welcome the King". In late January, I played a series of solo concerts starting at the University of Chicago on the 24th, Music Work in Atlanta on the 25th, and at SOBs in New York City on the 29th. On January 26th, I also did an interview with the Voice of America in Atlanta, and then I spent the rest of the winter back in Hyde Park.

●●●●●

In early May of 1986, Bill Laswell flew me back to New York to do some recording on Ginger Baker's new record, which he was producing. We spent May 6th and 7th in the studio, where I played kora, dusungoni, nyanye, kalimba, and other percussion. Ginger is something else. That album was called Horses and Trees, and it was the first thing I did with him, but after that I worked with him and Bill a lot. At the same time, I was also making plans to go to Gambia, so after a short time back in Chicago, I was back in the air, flying to New York to pick up the ticket for my flight to Gambia. While I was in New York, I met Philip Glass for the first time.

The way it happened was that on Monday, May 19th, I went to Celluloid Records to talk to a guy who worked there named Doug. That night, a friend of mine named Pascal, a French guy who also worked at Celluloid Records, came to my hotel. He said, "I want you to meet a friend of mine named Philip. He is getting ready to do a soundtrack for a film named Powaqqatsi. He has been all over the world but never to Africa. He needs a guide, and I recommended you to him." So me and Pascal, Philip's conductor Michael Riesman and producer Kurt Munkacsi, all took a taxi to Philip's house in Manhattan. We had a meeting in Philip's back yard, and I told him I could take them to Africa. They wanted to go to three places, so I suggested Gambia, Senegal, and Mali. The purpose of our trip was not to record or perform together, but for research on different kinds of music for the soundtrack of the Powaqqatsi film.

There is something very special about Philip. He is not afraid to collaborate with anybody from all over the world, with Ravi Shankar or with a didgeridoo player. He will find a way to write the parts for himself, and his partner would write theirs, and they would always make it fit. Once the sound comes together, it will say something, and you just have to listen. After our meeting, we exchanged music with each other. I gave him two of my Flying Fish records and he gave me two of his cassettes. The next day while I was on the plane to London, I was listening to his tapes on my Walkman with my headphones on. I layed back in my seat and listened to one cassette, first side A and then side B. Then I put the second tape in my Walkman and listened to side A and side B. After that, I said to myself, "Wow. This guy is not playing nothing!" Both cassettes sounded the same to me: da da, da. It took me a long time before I heard what Philip was playing. Later on, after listening to the tapes for a long time, I started to understand musically what he was playing, and it is like exactly how I play the kora! We keep repeating the same pattern over and over. No matter what we play, we always come back to that pattern. When he heard my playing, maybe that's why he liked it. Even now when he writes for his ensemble, I can hear that each person is playing a different pattern. You can hear a lot of things happening in the music, but it's all coming together in interesting patterns.

I stayed in Gambia from May 20th to June 29th, 1986, just hanging with my wife and family. Then I went back to Chicago, and in July, Mandingo Griot Society did a short tour in Santa Fe and Albuquerque again. Then we stopped to perform at the Indianapolis Black Expo on our way back to Chicago. I stayed in Chicago all summer long, preparing for two completely different trips to Gambia that would begin in the fall.

GRIOT TRAVELING

In 1986, I also met a guy in Atlanta named Rob Gibson, who was kind of a promoter. We talked about bringing some musicians from Gambia to the U.S. to tour with me, and I suggested my father's younger brother Surakata Suso, who plays the kora, and my eldest brother Mohammed Suso, who plays the balafon. Me and Rob arranged everything for the tour, with a whole lot of shows to play in the U.S. and Canada, jam-packed into one month. At this time, Surakata was living in the compound in Serekunda that I had first bought for my father in 1978, together with his brother Lamin and my blood brother Mohammed Suso and his family. Surakata is the coolest human being I have ever known. He never talks.

On Sunday, September 28th I flew to New York for two days, and then on to Gambia to bring Surakata and Mohammed to the U.S. After spending a few weeks in Gambia making the rest of the tour preparations and going to the embassy to get their passports and visas, we all left Gambia on Oct 20th and arrived in New York City the next day. Right away, we went to the Newark airport to fly to Atlanta. Rob Gibson picked us there, and invited us to stay with him and his wife in their big house. Rob is a nice guy, and he liked the music we were doing. Our tour began with a three-night performance from October 23rd to the 25th in an Atlanta concert hall called Stage Seven. On the 26th, Rob drove us to the Atlanta airport to fly to Austin, Texas to play at the University of Texas Performing Arts Center that night. The guy who was the promoter for that show was Steve Fields. He was a part of the university's Ethnomusicology Department, and later on I think he moved to Albuquerque, but we stayed in touch for a long time. The day after that show, we flew back to Atlanta, and then Rob drove us up to Chattanooga, Tennessee for a show on the 28th. On the 29th, he drove us back to Atlanta and we flew to Providence, Rhode Island to play a concert that night at Brown University. The very next day, we took the train from Providence to New York, and did a concert at a music place called Washington Square Church.

That concert was arranged by Robert Browning, who is the founder and director of the World Music Institute, and has been involved with many different musicians from all around the world for at least 40 years. Ever since I came to the U.S., I have played concerts for the World Music Institute many times.

Whenever Surakata and Mohammed were on an airplane with me, the flight attendants would come around to ask everybody, "Tea or coffee?" Those people never saw anybody ask for ten packs of sugar at a time, the way Surakata and Mohammed did! I had to watch them all the time and tell them not to take all the sugars in the plane! They never saw sugar in tiny packages before, only in 50-lb. bags. Mohammed had been to France in 1973 for a short time, but neither of them had ever been to the U.S. And neither of them could speak any English or had been around toubabs much. When we arrived in New York, they could hardly walk because they were in the traditional African dress, and the wind was blowing down the streets. It was their first time ever seeing a traffic light, and seeing so many people all around with noise everywhere. They did not know how to cross the street, with all the cars going by us. They just wanted to stand and watch, and not cross! Everywhere we went, they asked me, "Who owns all these cars? Who owns these planes?" I had to pull them along wherever we were going. It was a blown mind thing for them the whole time. Before we left Gambia together, they heard me explaining to them about the U.S., and they thought I talked too much, but I had to tell them, "This will be different than playing back home". After they got back to Gambia, they talked to their friends for at least two or three months about what it was like in the U.S.!

We were going to travel into Canada later on the tour, so the day after the Washington Square Church show, I went to the Canadian Embassy in New York to get visas for us. That night, we went to Philadelphia by train, and we were traveling with all our instruments so we had a whole lot of stuff to keep track of. When we got to our hotel in Philadelphia, I told them to wait inside the lobby while I took all our luggage into the hotel, one bag at a time. While I was doing that, the hotel people came up and start asking Surakata a bunch of questions, but he didn't know what to say. They asked him, "Who are you? What are you doing? Do you have a reservation?" That's the only time in my life I ever saw Surakata confused. When he saw me coming in the door with the next bag, he called out "Fodaymusa, come here quick!"

The next couple of days, we had some time off to just hang out in Philadelphia, then on Sunday November 2nd, we played at a music place there called The Painted Bride. Our Philadelphia promoter was a tabla player named Lenny Seidman, and he and his people also took us out for dinner before the show. In the restaurant, while we were waiting for our food, I told Surakata and Mohammed, "You two should come up with the song list that you want to play tonight". So they started talking. Mohammed would say a song name, and Surakata would say, "Maybe we shouldn't play that. It is kind of confusing for a listener because it has a 6/8 pattern, and hard for western people to listen to". Mohammed became very angry, but he didn't show it until later, when we went to The Painted Bride. Mohammed rushed in to get to the dressing room and Surakata followed after him, and I stayed behind to talk to some people in the club. By the time I got to the dressing room, they were fighting. Mohammed was yelling a lot and Surakata was just listening. Then Mohammed threatened to punch Surakata. I said to them, "I did not bring you here to go to war! This kind of thing doesn't go here. I am in charge, and if you try to make a war, I have your ticket and I will send you back home to Gambia". Then Mohammed became quiet. We played the show, and everything went OK. In fact, it was all very good. All these things were a big learning time for both of them.

The next day, Lenny came to our hotel and took us to the Philadelphia train station to go to Hartford, Connecticut. We stayed there overnight and then on November 4th, we played at the University of Connecticut Collective Arts Center. The next day, we flew from Hartford to Montreal. On November 6th, we played at a place called the Balattou Club, which was run by a Guinean guy named Lamin Toure. He was already in Montreal when I first arrived in the U.S., and opened that club a year before our show, but it is still there and now the longest-running African club in Montreal. While we were there, they did not put us in hotel. Instead, we stayed in a house with three or four bedrooms, so we each had our own room. We were off on November 7th and 8th, and when we woke up in the morning on the 8th, I saw that it snowed a lot and was very, very cold. Surakata and Mohammed didn't know anything about snow, and they didn't know about ice dropping on the ground and heavy cold. Snow was covering everything. I got up and cooked breakfast, and we ate. Then Mohammed said, "Let's go out and walk around". I replied to him, "Yes, but not right now", and he asked, "Why?" so I told him, "It snowed last night, do you see that white stuff?" He replied, "That's OK, no problem". Then I said, "Yes, it's a big problem because it is very cold. I am going to go out and buy you a long john pant and shirt, and then I will come back". I had clothes with me for that weather, but they didn't have anything but African dresses. Mohammed asked me again, "Why can't I go?" I told him that he must just wait for me to get back, and he was very mad. I went out and found a store, and bought long johns for both Mohammed and Surakata, and some chicken for our lunch. After that, I said, "Let's go outside" but Mohammed was so mad that he locked himself in his room. I cooked peanut stew and went to his room to call him to eat. He was so mad that he even said, "I don't want no food!" So Surakata and I ate the lunch. While we were sitting there, Mohammed opened his door and walked fast through the kitchen to go to the bathroom without even looking at us, then went back to his room and locked the door again. I gave Surakata his long johns to put on, and I went to Mohammed's door again, and said his name. He yelled back, "Why are you calling me?" I replied, "Let's go out now!" He came outside wearing his African dress and some slippers, and the wind hit him so big that he was shivering in a few steps and wanted to go back in. I went back inside the house with him and gave him the long johns to wear, and said, "See, I told you it is cold!" Then we all went back outside.

On November 9th, we played another show in Montreal, at a place called Cafe Campus. The next day, we flew to Newark and then to Santa Barbara, California, and then on the 11th, we performed a concert in a big hall at the University of California there. My long association with their Ethnomusicology Department and the Jazz Society was why they booked us there to play. The following day, we flew from Santa Cruz to

San Francisco, then to Newark, and then to Chicago. That was a very long and crazy day of flying! Now we reached the end of our tour, and Mohammed and Surakata stayed with me in my apartment in Chicago for another week before it was time for them to go back home to Gambia. On November 19th, we all flew to New York and then I put them on a plane for home.

The next morning I went over to Philip's house, to meet with him and his people some more about our plans for going to Africa together, and for me to be the guide on their trip. A couple of weeks later on Monday, December 8th, I flew from Chicago to LA with Mandingo Griot Society to rehearse with Herbie for a big concert called Jazz Africa. We rehearsed on Monday and Tuesday night, and then on Wednesday December 10th, we did the show at the Wiltern Theater in LA. It was Herbie, me, Adam, Hamid, Joe, Abdul, our drummer Aïyb Dieng, and a famous conga player named Aramando Peraza from the band Santana. That place was jam-packed, and all the people really liked our music. Some Hollywood people filmed the show with a bunch of cameras, and later on they put out an album and a video of it.

•••••

Sometimes people ask me if I ever felt a "culture shock" after coming to the U.S., the way Mohammed and Surakata did on this tour. But even though I grew up way out in the bush in Gambia, and many things were new to me when traveling all over the U.S. and Europe, playing in big clubs and concert halls with my band, Herbie's band, and many other famous people, it was never like a shock for me. The reason is because I got used to being around a lot of people from different countries when I was living and working in Dakar, and when I was teaching at the University of Ghana. I also heard many new languages in those places, and learned to understand them enough to be able to communicate. Even in my own country, there are so many different African languages spoken, so everyone is used to that too. In my childhood time, we had many neighbors and friends who spoke Fulani, Wolof, or other languages, which I also learned. I was learning English way back when I was a student in Sutukoba, and sometimes I was around other Gambians who could speak it well, since our country was a British colony. Once I got to Ghana, I also had a whole lot of English-speaking students, and a lot of the university people were speaking and writing English because it used to be a British colony too. I also got used to seeing a lot of toubabs in those places, so that wasn't a big thing for me to get used to either. By the time I started playing with Herbie, I had been on the road with Mandingo Griot Society for years, and used to playing with western musicians. I liked everything about it a lot. And we griots are travelers for hundreds of years, so that is also in my blood and a natural thing for me!

PHILIP IN AFRICA

A week after the Jazz Africa show, I left Chicago to fly to New York again, and meet up with Philip and his people to get ready for our trip. On Friday December 19th, I flew to Dakar with Philip and his girlfriend Candy Jernigan, Philip's son Zack who was a teenager, Philip's producer Kurt Munkacsi and his wife Nancy, and Philip's conductor Michael Riesman. The day we left New York, it was very cold. I was only wearing leather pants and a leather jacket, so I was freezing! We left Kennedy Airport on a late overnight flight, and I slept through the whole thing until they opened the door and it was morning in Dakar. It was so hot outside that the moment they opened the plane door, it was like fire coming in! As soon as we all arrived at our rooms in the Meridian Hotel in Dakar, I tore off my jacket and threw it on the bed! Then I picked up my video camera and started shooting a video, which I still have.

The next day, we took a Nigeria Airlines flight from Dakar to Banjul. The President of Gambia was supposed to travel on that same day, and at that time, our tradition was that griots would always accompany him whenever he went to the airport. They would be playing and singing anytime he flew somewhere, and they would be there again when he returned. Sometimes the Gambian National Troupe, which my father put together, also would accompany the president to and from the airport. So that day when we arrived and came out of the plane, there was a whole bunch of griots there, both men and women. One griot lady named Mamanding Kouyateh started singing my praise the moment she saw me. In our tradition, griots from the Kouyateh family sing praises to all kinds of people, but they can also sing and praise all the other griots, and when they do, the other griots give them money. Because I was just arriving and didn't have any Gambian currency, I pulled out a $100.00 bill and gave it to her. Philip and the others asked me, "What is this?" so I explained to them about the Kouyateh family, and they all started giving her a lot of bills too. I know that day she made a lot of money!

Mamanding Kouyateh knew me well before I came to the U.S., because her first husband Bajali was my very good friend, and a very good kora player too. When she first married Bajali, they would come to Brikama during the dry season between January and May in the early 1970s, to see me and do traditional singing and kora playing. Whenever they came to see me in Brikama, I would go around and around with them and my best friend Mohammed Camara. We went to places all over the Kombo District, to baby-naming ceremonies, weddings, and circumcision celebrations. At that time, Mamanding was a very good young griot singer in her mid-twenties. She and Bajali were from the village of Pachar, in a rural area on the west of Basse, near Bansang. As soon as we met each other, we started hanging out together and playing. We liked each other very quick. Sometimes when I was playing the kora, Mamanding would sing and Mohammed would tap the bottom of my kora with the tuning nail. Bajali was usually just sitting, because he was not healthy after he developed asthma a long time before. But we four always split the money equally that was given to us. Bajali was one of the best friends a human being can find. When I arrived in Banjul with Philip and all the others, Bajali had passed away from the asthma, and Mamanding was remarried to another man named Banna Kanuteh. Because of our long friendship, right away when she saw me get off the plane, she started singing my praise.

After we got all our bags at the airport, we went to the Hotel Fajara, which is on the Atlantic coast near Serekunda. Our arrangement was that anywhere we went on our trip, they had to pay for my hotel too. So they took a room for me at the Hotel Fajara just for me to have a place to rest, even though I was staying at my own home in Brikama. Then we all left the hotel and went to Brikama to see my family, and then to a big wrestling match in Serekunda. They never saw anything like that before. I took a video of that too, and then I accompanied them back to their hotel in Fajara.

The next day, we hired somebody with a passenger van to drive us way inland in Gambia, all the way to the town of Basse for the Youth Week Festival. That festival is a big, big thing, with traditional music, dancing, and drumming under the big tree in the bantaba in Basse. Griots were playing kora and balafon, and musicians were also playing the Fulani violin called the nyanye. A whole lot of people always come from all over the country to Basse for those two or three days, and in every corner of the town something is happening. This festival is mostly to bring a lot of young people together, but to bring all kinds of people together too. The roads from Banjul to Basse were not very good at all at that time, and it took seven or eight hours to get there because we also had to fix a flat tire outside a village called Kwinela. When we got to Basse, we went to a place to stay called the Apolo Hotel. Nowadays, there are some regular western-style hotels in Basse, but the Apolo Hotel was not like that. It was just some extra rooms in a traditional setting, and you had to put water in a bucket to take a shower. We stayed overnight there on December 22nd, and drove back to Fajara the next day.

In the morning on December 24th, I picked them at their hotel and took them to Serekunda again, just to walk around the town for a while. Then we all went to the Abuko Nature Reserve, which is full of so many birds and a whole lot of monkeys, deer, hyenas, and other animals too. Walking through the forest and grasses there is very different than places in the United States. Later on that night, we went to the U.S. Embassy in Fajara for a Christmas party. The people there invited us because Philip is famous and everybody knows him, and his sister was married to a guy who was involved with some kind of embassy stuff too. The next day was Christmas Day. In Gambia, even though the majority of people are Muslim, people will celebrate anything that comes. Whether it's a Muslim holiday or Christian holiday, people will celebrate, play music, and party. So on Christmas Day morning, I came to Fajara from Brikama and went to their hotel to say, "Let's go out to the market". Serekunda was really happening that day! Kankurans were doing the masked dancing just for the Christmas entertainment, singing, and dancing, and my friend Demba Njai was one of them. They were making the Bassang Kankuran and Jamba Kankuran, which we call the "fake kankuran" because they are not trying to scare anybody. Me and Demba Njai even talked to each other while he was a Kankuran. That is not something you can ever do with a Kankuran Wulen!

Then we went to my compound in Serekunda to visit my blood brother Mahamadou and his family. It is in the Churchill's Town area, and while we were there, we saw a group of Jola musicians and drummers and dancers on the street nearby. They were coming towards us, so I went and met up with the musicians and asked them where they were going. They said they were going to a traditional ceremony, but I told them, "My friends from America are here with me, and they want to see a lot of traditional music. Please stop here and make a circle, and play some music for them before you go". Then I went back in the compound and told Philip that we should pay those people, because I asked them to stop and play for us while they were going away from our area of town. So we paid them, and they formed a circle in the street. I also told Philip and everybody, "Once we are in the circle and these people are dancing, it's our tradition that whenever you have a guest in your music place, from time to time the musicians will come to you and hold your hand to bring you into the circle to dance. They know that you cannot dance in a traditional way, but they want to cheer you up and welcome you. So you gotta go in the circle to dance. You can't say, "Leave me alone", because that's a heavy disrespect. Just go in the circle and move a little bit, you don't have to know the dance." They all said OK, and I was happy because the drums the musicians were playing are my favorite Jola drums, called bougarabou. They are my favorite because the players have a syncopated rhythm, and you have to know that music to appreciate the rhythm. When I placed Philip and the others in the positions around the circle, the music started. One by one, dancers grabbed someone's hand and brought them inside the circle to dance. Kankuran were running around the outside of the circle too. I have a video of this, with all of them dancing. After that whole show, Philip and everybody else all laughed and Philip said, "Don't show this video to anybody in New York!"

On Friday December 26th, we were supposed to fly from Banjul to Dakar at one or two o'clock in the afternoon on Nigeria Airlines, stay overnight in Dakar, and then fly to Mali. But when we arrived at the Banjul airport, they told us that the pilots in Nigeria all cancelled their flights because yesterday was Christmas and they want to stay home and party. We said, "What kind of craziness is this? Tomorrow we are supposed to fly from Dakar to Mali. Now what should we do?" Philip asked me, "What else can we do to get to Dakar tonight?" and I said, "There is another way. We can go by road. First we will have to go to the Banjul port and take a ferry across the River Gambia, then we can catch a transport ride to Dakar". He agreed, so we went to the ferry terminal. By the time we got there it was sunset, and they told us the last ferry of the day had already sailed, and there would be no more ferries until tomorrow. Then I started thinking to myself, "What about a fisherman's boat to cross the river?" So I found some fishermen who said they could take us across the River Gambia. By that time, it was getting dark and we were all just standing and looking at their fishing boat with its small outboard motor. I said to Philip, "You are the leader of us, so if you say we should go, we will go. If not, we won't go". He asked me, "What do you think?" and I replied, "These people cross the river all the time".

Then Kurt said, "No way! I am not going in this boat, I am not going to kill myself." His wife Nancy said the same thing, and they left and went back to the Fajara Hotel. They forgot their money in a small bag, so Philip took a taxi to give that to them. That took a long time, so now it was getting really late. The five of us: me, Philip, Candy, Zack, and Michael Riesman got into the small boat with the three fishermen. It was pitch black out on the River Gambia, and you could not see anywhere. Near the back end of the boat there was a small hole, and one of the fishermen was using a container to bail water out of the boat the whole time we were going. I don't know why that hole was there! Waves were coming against the boat and bouncing on us, and we were all thinking, "Are we going to get to the other side or not?" Later, Philip said he was thinking that if anything happened to us, what would he tell Zack's mother JoAnne. It took around an hour to cross because the river is over three miles wide that point. That crossing point is not even the widest spot in the mouth of the River Gambia though, because just upstream it is over five miles to get across. Luckily we crossed OK! When we arrived at the Barra ferry terminal on the other side, it was almost the middle of the night, and we found that all the passenger cars and buses had already left the terminal. We got some dinner because we were so, so hungry, and then we had to hire a taxi to take us to Dakar. The taxi driver was speeding so fast, just flying down the road!

We got to the Hotel Meridian in Dakar just after three o'clock in the morning, but we couldn't sleep long because our flight to Mali was leaving in a few hours. We all just had time to rest a little while, and by eight o'clock we were flying. Kurt and Nancy stayed in Gambia while we left, and at ten o'clock on December 27th, we arrived at the Bamako, Mali airport. We went straight into the city to stay in the biggest hotel there. It was a very tall place, and our rooms were high up so we could look from our balconies and see the whole city. But first, we all slept a long, long time!

•••••

In Bamako on the weekends, there is always a lot of traditional music and marriage ceremonies going on. The next morning, December 28th, we went into one particular traditional area called Madina Kura, and saw drummers playing djembes, and a lot of people dancing and singing. A young friend I met in Bamako named Alhaji Sillah took us all around. There was a compound nearby where I could hear kora and balafon music, guitars playing, and two griot ladies singing, so we went over to see. When we got there, I looked at all the musicians playing and saw that one of the kora players was my cousin Musa Suso! He is known as Bolong Suso. Around that time, whenever I was in Gambia, me and my family would always talk about him, our cousin who left Gambia and said he was going to Tamba Kunda in the eastern part of Senegal. When he went there, everybody thought he would be gone for two weeks but he was gone for two years! Then we heard he went all the way to Bamako, but his wife was still in Gambia. That day at the compound in Bamako, I saw him but he did not see me, so I called his name. He looked at me, and right away he threw the kora down, and we greeted. Because I am older than him, he calls me Nkotoke. He asked me, "When did you come? Where are you staying? I will come to you after this is done". I told him, "I just came yesterday", and I told him where we were staying. I also told him, "The whole family is worried about you, and nobody knows what happened". He told me, "I will come to your hotel later, and we can talk then". While we were all there in the compound with the music, one griot lady grabbed Philip and one grabbed Candy to dance too. After that, we all went to several other areas to listen to music and then back to our hotel.

Quickly after we arrived, Bolong Suso came to the hotel. I picked up the phone and it was Bolong, down in the lobby calling. When he came up to my room, I told him, "Everybody is calling and talking about you, because you said you weren't staying away long, but now you've been gone a long, long time. All my uncles are talking, and everybody is talking because you left your wife behind". He replied, "When I came here, my intention was not to stay long. But when I arrived here, I could not leave. I'm kind of stuck because I do not have the fare to go home to Gambia". I asked him, "What do you mean?" and he said, "I cannot save money with the little I am making here". So I asked him, "OK, if you get the train fare now, when will you be ready to leave here?" He said, "I will leave tonight, brother!" Then I asked him, "That being the case, how much will it cost you to take the train from Mali to Senegal?" He told me, "10,000 CFA Francs will take me from Bamako to Senegal. That train leaves at 11:00pm". Then I told him, "OK, I'll give you 17,500 CFA so you can spend 10,000 for the train and the rest is for pocket money. But one thing I will tell you is this: Once I give you this money, if you don't go all the way there, if you stop part way, then I will never give you anything again or even look at you". He promised me and said, "I know what I will do when you give me the money". So I told him to come to my hotel room the next evening, because I needed to change my dollars to CFA before I could give him any money.

That next day, Monday December 29th, I went with Alhaji Sillah to exchange some money and go to the car park to get a van. We found a van driver there, and told him we needed a reliable van to take us to to the town of Sikasso the following day, because it is a very long drive, around 230 miles. We discussed the travels with him, and then we came back to our hotel. Bolong Suso came back to meet me that night, and I gave him the money, then he went back to the place he was living along with a lot of other Gambians.

In those days, a lot of Gambians got stuck in Mali, after trying to leave by foot to cross the desert to Libya, then to Europe. People who began traveling like this did not know about the desert, and a lot of people died on the way. Even today, people are doing this. When Bolong went back to his place and told those other Gambians that he was going back home, they all wanted to know who gave him the money. He told them, "My brother Fodaymusa". They asked him, "How can that be?" and he told them that I was there in Bamako. There were two other guys at that place who also knew me, and he told them where I was staying. One was my heavy friend Dembo Tamba from Brikama, who is known as Toboji Tamba. The other was Suleman Nyass, whose elder brother was my good friend Saana Nyass. By the middle of the day on December 30th, everybody came to that big hotel to try to find me, but I had already left to go to Sikasso with Philip and everybody else. The hotel people told them that we would be gone three days, so everybody scattered and went back home. Then a lot of them came came back later to wait for us.

The town of Sikasso is inside Mali, but almost to the border with Burkina Faso. When we got there, we went to the Solaghan Hotel, which was a lot like the Apolo Hotel in Basse: It was a two-story building but the rooms were very simple, and to take a shower you had to fetch water in a bucket. Sikasso also had a lot of different kinds of music there, especially dusungoni music. I like that kind of music a lot, and I knew that there were a whole lot of hunters there in Sikasso, so I went around with the van driver to try to find them. We finally found somebody who knew where we could find a singer. I asked him, "Can you put a dusungoni show together here for us? I am with some friends from America and they would like to hear that very much". He said yes, and so the next day we came back there again. In the Mandingo language, dusungoni means hunter's harp, so the hunters came to that compound, and they played dusungoni and danced. I videotaped some of that too. After that, there was a big balafon show that we went to. The sound and look and tuning of the balafon there is very different than the way it is tuned in Gambia, though. On the next day, Thursday January 1st, 1987, we all stayed in Sikasso at the hotel to rest and hang out. The next morning, we drove a long, long time, all the way from Sikasso to Segou, Mali. We spent the night there, and then drove back to our hotel in Bamako. That was a very long trip, almost 350 miles!

By the time we got back to our hotel, all those other Gambians were there, waiting for me. They called my room and I told them to come up, but I didn't know there were so many people! They all started talking, with everybody telling me their own story, such as "I want to go to Algeria" and "I want to go to Europe", but of course, I could not help everybody there. Toboji also said he wanted to continue traveling and try to get to Europe, but Suleman said he wanted to go back to Gambia right away. So I gave Suleman some money to go back to Gambia, and I took my friend Toboji aside and said, "Wait until I get back to the United States and then I will send you more money than I can give you right now". When I got back, I sent him the money, but he ended up staying in Mali for around three more years. Then he came back to Gambia, and is still there today. For many years, we have seen each other every time I am in Brikama. He had a tire place near the market, and I helped him buy the air pump to be able to fix the tires there, because he is my friend. In fact, when Emily and Uno came to Gambia to visit me and my family in 2010, I took them to his place and introduced them, and Toboji fixed a car tire for us.

On Saturday January 3rd, I went with Philip and everybody from Bamako back to Dakar by plane. The next day, they all flew back to the U.S., and I took Ghana Airways back to Gambia to be there for a while. This trip was the beginning of me and Philip getting to know each other, and soon afterward we began working together in the U.S. on the Powaqattsi movie soundtrack. Now we have been making music together for over 30 years.

That next Friday, my friend Stanley Jackson came to visit me again in Gambia. He's been to Gambia twelve times and always stays in my house. I call him Jack. When I first met him in Chicago, I had friends who asked me, "Why do you let this guy come all the time? He just is sitting there in your house." But I always told them, "I don't care. He holds on to me as his friend, and I hold on to him as my friend". Jack worked for Ford

Motor Company his whole life until he retired. Even if it was snowing out or any other storm, Jack wouldn't call and say that he can't come in, he would be there at work every single day. After he was there in Brikama with me and my family for a week, me and Jack flew back to Chicago.

Photos

1. My father Jali Saikou Suso in the early 1960's

2. My mother Madame Jobarteh in 1996

3. The village of Sare Hamadi, where I was born.

4. My teacher Jali Saikou Suso (in foreground)
in my first Brikama compound, at the 1988 baby-naming ceremony
for my daughter Nene.

5. The First National Troup of Gambia, founded by my father Saikou Suso in 1973 in the city of Banjul, Gambia.

Closeup -front row. L-R: Me with my kora, Jali Bakary Camara with his bolong, Abulai Samba with his kontingo, and my father Saikou Suso with his kora.

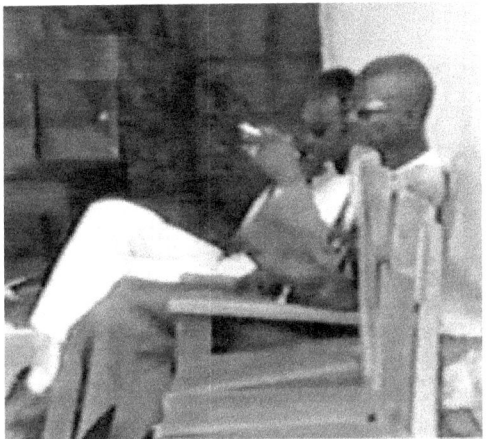

6. My father's brothers Lamin and Surakata Suso in my first Brikama compound, at the 1988 baby-naming ceremony for my daughter Nene.

7. My very good friends Demba Camara (R) and Wandifa Camara (L) in the town of Fatoto, Gambia in 2019

8. My very good friend Mohammed Camara in my first Brikama compound in 1996

9. My good friend Sekou Jatta from the village of Gunjur, in the early 1970's in Ghana

The Mandingo Griot Society

10. Mandingo Griot Society first promo photo, 1977
L-R: Me, Joe Thomas, Adam Rudolph, and Hamid Drake

11. Mandingo Griot Society performance in Grant Park, 1980. "Crazy Man" (me), with John Marsh in background

12. Philip Glass, Candy Jernigan, and Zack Glass watching a wrestling match in in the town of Serekunda, Gambia on December 20th, 1986.

13. Philip, Candy, Zack, and Michael Riesman in Segou, Mali on January 2nd, 1987.

14. With Philip in his Looking Glass recording studio in New York City, working on the soundtrack for Powaqqatsi on July 30th, 1987.

15. Taken on a rooftop in Brooklyn in the 1980s.

16. Bill Laswell at the VIP lounge in Narita/Tokyo airport, on our way to Bejing during the 1994 Flying Mijinko Band Central Asian Tour with Akira Sakata.

17. With Flying Mijinko Band members in Tiananmen Square, Bejing during our 1994 Central Asian Tour.

18. The Suso Trio with Manu Walton, me, and Abdul Hakeem, in 1995

19. Mandingo promo photo from the 1990s.
L-R: Hakeem Abdul, Hamid Drake, Joe Thomas, me, Koko Brunson, and Anindo

20. With Conrad Uno in his Egg recording studio in Seattle, taking a break during demo recording in 1995

21. With my son Basaikou in my second Brikama compound in 1996.

22. With my mother in my first Brikama compound in 1996.

23. With Bobo and kids in my first Brikama compound in 1996.
L-R: Basaikou, Mahame, Balamin (in Bobo's arms), and Fatou.

24. Playing music with Japanese saxaphonist Sakata Ikira at Goree Island, off the coast of Dakar Senegal, on December 25th, 1996.

25. Playing music with Akira Sakata and my family in my first Brikama compound, at the baby-naming ceremony for my brother Dembo's daughter Sendin, on December 28th, 1996.

26. With my blood brother Mahamadou Suso (L) and younger brother Dembo Kanuteh (C), at Sendin's baby-naming ceremony.

27. With my children in my first Brikama compound on July 29th, 1997. L-R: Basaikou, Fatou, Balamin, and Nene

28. Performing with Jack DeJohnette at the Jazz Festival in Austria on August 21st, 2002

29. With my good friend Paulo Sérgio Santos from the band Uatki, in Brazil in 2004

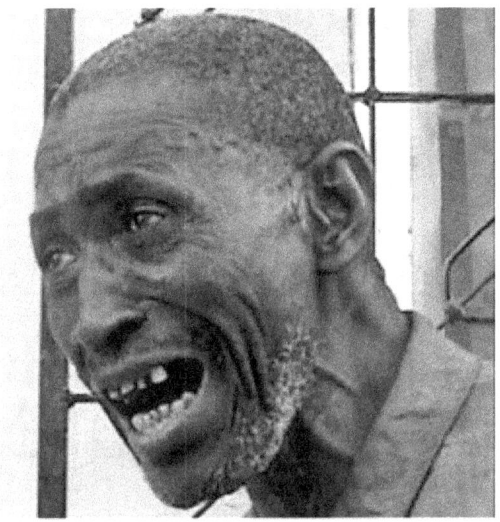

30. Jooka singer Mama Bisidi from Casamance, Senegal, singing in my Brikama compound

31. Jooka singer Suleman Jafunneh singing in his village of Bongeh, Guinea Bissau on February 16th, 2005

32. Jooka singer Nfamara Sanneh from Durubal, Guinea Bissau, singing in my compound in Brikama

33. My crazy car playing Jooka cassette with speakers on roof, surrounded by villagers in the Wuli District of Gambia in March 2005

34. My sister Dibba Sakliba in her husband's compound in the town of Lamin, Gambia on January 29th, 2006, at the celebration for her return from the pilgrimage to Mecca.

35. With Bobo, Emily, and Uno in my Brikama compound on December 23rd, 2010

36. At the end of a performance with Philip at the Carmel, CA Performing Arts Center on September 1st, 2012

37. Playing for my little gull at LaPush, WA on September 4th, 2013

38. Visiting with Emily's students at Magnuson Park Nature Knowledge Camp on April 16, 2015

39. Backstage with Iggy Pop at the Paramount Theater in Seattle on March 28th, 2016

40. In performance at Roulette in New York City on December 5th, 2016

41. At the town of Mandinga in Vera Cruz State, Mexico in December 2017

42. My beautiful wife Bobo in 2019

43. My daughter Nene in 2010

44. My son Basaikou in 2010

45. My daughter Fatou in 2019

46. Bobo and our son Balamin in 2019

47. My brother Dembo's daughter Sendin in 2019

48. My brother Dembo's son Mahame in 2019

49. My eldest brother Mohammed Suso's granddaughter, Makuranding Suso in 2019

50. Basaikou's good friend Ousman Kebbeh in 2019

51. Bobo's namesake, Bobodinding Guye in 2019

52. My namesake, Fodaymusa Walton in 2019

53. With my good friend David Braswell in Chicago in 2019

54. Finishing the book with Emily in her Arivaca, AZ studio in 2019

55. The River Gambia, near the village of Brefet.

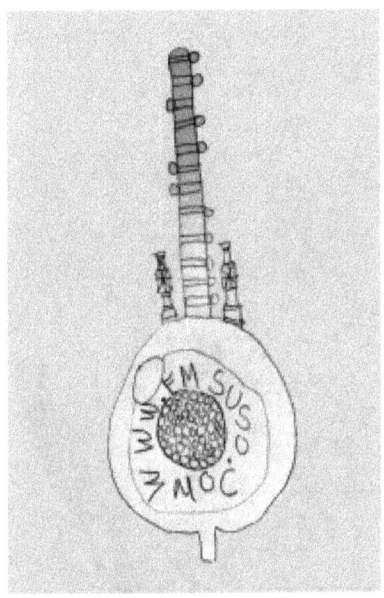

56. Kora drawing by one of Emily's students, April 16th, 2015

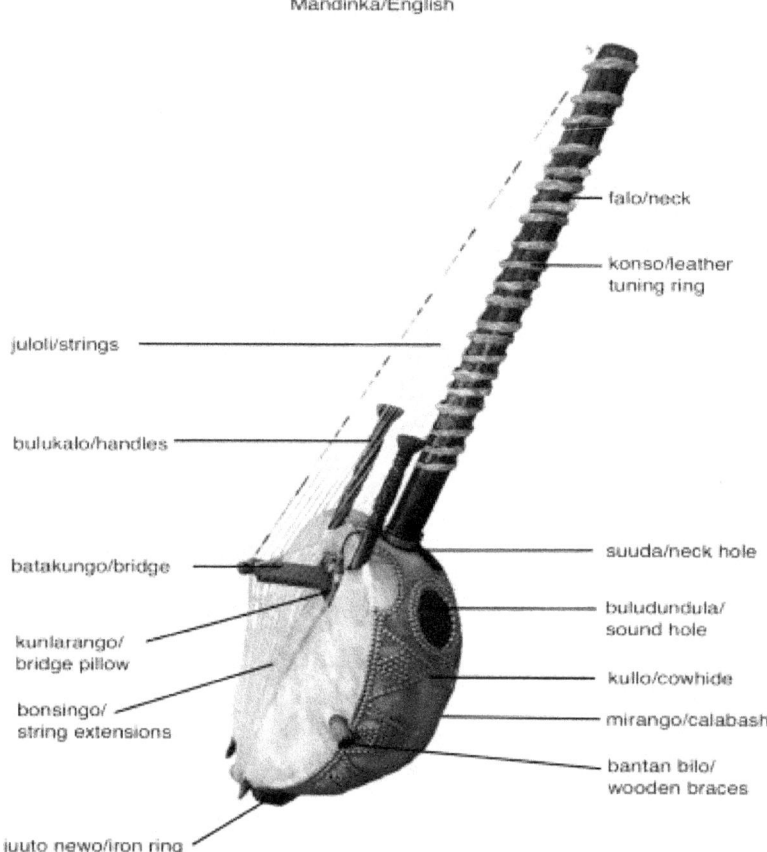

57. All the parts of a kora

ON THE ROAD, ALL THE TIME!

I stayed in Chicago for the first half of 1987, and there wasn't a lot of music going on for me or for Mandingo Griot Society, except a two-night stand that we played at the Field Museum of Chicago on February 7th and 8th. Also, the Jazz Africa record with Herbie came out at the beginning of the year, but the video didn't come out until some years after that. But a very big thing happened for me and Bobo in 1987: Our first child, a beautiful daughter we named Nene, was born in Brikama on Monday, July 6th! I was getting ready to go on a tour, so I had to stay in Chicago and couldn't go to Gambia. But by that time, there was a phone in my house in Brikama so they were able to call and tell me she was born. Because I was going to be traveling so much for a while, I held back her baby-naming ceremony until 1988.

•••••

I have been flying all the time for so many years, and experienced a lot of crazy things on planes. The way I am, I like to keep records of everything I do, and I have kept every single plane ticket that I ever used since coming to the United States for the first time. From 1977 to 2009, my regular flying tickets added up to 1634, and my tickets to go to and from Gambia were 98. In 2009, I just stopped counting them, but I still keep my airplane tickets. In fact, I will keep them all until the time comes when I cannot even fly anymore!

Also, every day since 1977 when I first came to the United States, I always use a daily planner as my journal. I buy one at the beginning of every year, and I always have it with me no matter where I am. Every night before I go to bed, I write down what I did that day. I never go to bed without doing that. That's why I can pinpoint the dates of everything I did in my life since 1976, or what happened to somebody else, if there was something special happening that day in the world, or any other important thing. Otherwise I could not remember these exact dates, but in this way, I can just look at my daily planner to see. It's all written down.

For a few years, I have said to myself, "Maybe I should just stop" but I never do. I might not buy a new calendar book at the beginning of the year, but right away I will start using a pad of paper to write every night, and then pretty soon I will go out and buy another daily planner book. I just gotta do it!

•••••

One crazy plane thing happened less than two weeks after Nene was born, when I was traveling to Dartmouth College in Hanover, Maryland on July 17th for a solo kora concert at at the Hopkins Center. To get there, I took a flight from Chicago to Kennedy Airport in New York, and then got on a small plane to Dartmouth. On the way, I didn't think we would survive! The plane was diving just above the trees, with passengers leaning from one side to another. I wasn't scared a whole lot, but I was thinking, "I hope no branch will grab this thing. If it does, maybe I won't make it". The plane was very small, and maybe that's why it got tossed around in the sky like that. I don't fly in small planes a lot, but something like that also happened one time when I was flying from Denver to Fort Collins, Colorado.

Many years before that while I was working for the Illinois Art Council, sometimes I would fly back to Chicago from Springfield on weekends, and take Osark Airlines to Midway Airport. At that time, Midway was a very small airport and Osark Airlines was the only airline company that flew from there, and it only cost $25.00 for a one-way ticket, and $50.00 for both ways. One day when we arrived at Midway and landed on the runway, all of a sudden "poom!" the pilot took off again. He got on the radio and told everybody, "I'm sorry, I didn't land in the correct place". Then we flew around and then landed again. Thanks to God no other plane was in our path.

One time in early 1984, I went to New York in January or February when a big snow was coming. We took off from Chicago and arrived late at night in Kennedy Airport. The heavy snow was piling up, and every time they plowed, our plane had to circle around and around without landing. Then the plane started making a shaking like a truck on a gravel road, and I was thinking that it was going to break into two pieces, but finally we landed. The next time something happened was after playing a show in Vancouver, Canada. When our Air Canada flight got back to Chicago, we couldn't land because of heavy rain. They came on the radio and said, "We have to go to Toronto". We arrived in Toronto, and then were going round and round there too, and couldn't land. They came back on the radio and told us, "Now we are going back to Chicago". Then when we got there, the Chicago people told the pilot, "No, you gotta go back to Toronto". We landed in Toronto and were there for two or three hours before they said, "Chicago is clear now", so we flew back there and finally landed.

Another crazy flying time was one time I flew from Chicago to London. On the way, we only flew about 45 minutes and then turned back to Chicago. They said to us, "The mileage thing stopped working on the plane". We came back, they fixed it pretty quick, and we took off again and landed at Heathrow Airport in London. I had to take a shuttle bus to Gatwick to catch my flight to Gambia, but by that time we were three hours late and my plane was already gone. So the Nigerian airline people said, "We can put you on a flight late tonight at 11:00 o'clock", and they put me in hotel to wait. At 11:00, I got on the flight to Kano, Nigeria. When we got to Kano, we flew to Lagos, Nigeria for a stopover, and many new passengers came on the plane. I smiled to myself and was thinking, "Now I am back in Africa", because I was watching what the passengers were bringing on the plane. All African style! Big baskets and calabashes full of tomatoes and onions, some even were holding chickens in a small cage made out of a basket. People came in like they just came from the market, with traditional and colorful clothes and hair. Nobody had to fit everything under their chair on that flight, they just came on in and set things down in the aisle of the plane, or held them on their lap. I was so happy, because I wished that all flights could be like that. From Lagos, we went to Abdijan Airport in Cote d'Ivoire, also called Ivory Coast, and most of the passengers with African style got off the plane there. More passengers came in too. Then we flew to Robert Field airport in Liberia, and some more passengers got off and came on. Then we went to Lungi Airport in Freetown, Sierra Leone, then to the airport in Conakary, Guinea, then to Dakar, and finally to Banjul. Whenever I fly, even today, I always like to sit by the window so I can fall asleep with no one bothering me to get out of my aisle. But that day when we finally landed in Banjul after a million miles of flying, I was so desperate to leave the plane! I didn't want to see any airplane. I wanted to kick a hole in the wall or punch the window to just get out! I was so tired of sitting in that plane, or even looking at that plane.

Another time, I flew from Chicago to Brussels on Sabina Airlines, on my way to Gambia. At that time, it was very common for Africans to meet in Brussels from all over Europe and the U.S. I was sitting on the plane by the window, with a young Gambian on the left side of me who was coming home from a school in an Asian country. The flight took off, and I fell asleep while the plane was still going on the runway. Around 20 or 30 minutes later, "poom!" the plane dove down hard and it felt like it hit something like a mountain. That young Gambian guy elbowed me in the stomach so hard! He apologized to me, and the plane got steady and kept going. Then the pilot came on the radio to say, "We have to go back to Brussels now. The plane has two engines, but we are only using one now, and the second one won't start again. We cannot get to Gambia with that one engine". When we got back to Brussels, we all left the plane and went to the terminal for one or two hours until they brought a new plane for us.

A long time ago, there also used to be a Ghana Airways flight that went from Chicago to Maryland, then to Gambia and on to Ghana. It was a very sweet idea when it started, because there was not so much changing planes, and I liked to fly on that airline. But one time taking a flight back to Chicago from Gambia, I went to the Banjul Airport at ten o'cock at night, but the plane didn't even come in to the airport until two o'clock in the morning. Around 45 minutes later, we finally got on board the flight. Then we sat in the plane on the runway until almost eight o'clock, before the plane even started to take off. We were going down the runway, then quickly we saw a whole lot of water pouring from the wings! Everybody was freaking out, and trying to stand up. But the pilot didn't even stop the plane, he just came on the radio and said, "I'm sorry, when they put gasoline in the plane, they filled it in a way that some got stuck and didn't go in. That is what is pouring from the wings, but don't worry. We gotta keep going to Ghana to fix it". That made everybody on the plane freak out. Gas finally stopped pouring from the wings, and we flew to Kotoka Airport in Ghana. When we arrived there, we got out and waited around while they checked the plane. When it was time to board the flight again, we stood in line for a long time. One old man even passed out. We finally took off and flew to Dakar, and were stuck there all the rest of the day on the runway, with the plane sitting there in the heat and our throats dry. We finally left at nine o'clock at night for Maryland. That's when I said, "I will never fly with Ghana Airlines again. I will walk or even swim to Africa!" Sometime after that, that airline fell apart and stopped operating.

Flying in America is not like anywhere else in the world, because it is so much more together here than anywhere else. Airport things in all other places, not just Africa, are not together like they are in the U.S. One thing that is funny to me now though, is that in my childhood time I always was dreaming about one day to be flying on an airplane. But now since I have done it so much and so, so long, and even though I still fly all the time for my work, right now I wish all my flights should be only one hour! If I could change everything, that is how I would make it.

•••••

Ok, now back to July 1987 after that crazy flying time from Chicago to Hartford, Connecticut. I performed at the Hopkins Center in Dartmouth on Saturday July 18th, then I left on Sunday to go to Jacob's Pillow, a performance place in the woods of the Berkshire Mountains in Massachusetts. There I met Lee Thompson, the director of Jacob's Pillow, and also her assistant Spider Kadelski, who now lives in Seattle. It is a big giant place, and people come there from all over the world. All the musicians stay in little cabins, and then play in the concert hall. All summer long they have a big dance festival there, even now, and I did a solo kora concert for them each day from July 21st to the 25th. At that time, there were two African dance troupes from Oakland, California there also.

One was a Ghanian dance troupe and the other was a Congolese dance troupe. Every day, all three of our acts would perform. There were some women from Swaziland there too, who won a contest and were brought to the U.S. to do an art tapestry for the Atlanta airport.

After spending about a week at Jacob's Pillow, I came to North Hampton, New Hampshire on Monday July 27th to play a show at a small but famous place called The Iron Horse. The next day, I played at the Night Stage in Cambridge, Massachusetts, and then I flew to New York to record with Philip. We spent July 30th and 31st in his studio, which is called The Living Room, to work on the soundtrack for the movie Powaqattsi. He was working on that music ever since returning from our trip to Africa together.

When I returned to Chicago, I did a solo kora concert at the Navy Pier on Sunday, August 9th as part of a big festival. A week later, I flew to Santa Fe, New Mexico to do a solo kora concert at the Center for the Contemporary Arts, then I turned and flew right back to Chicago to play a solo concert at the Ravinia Festival on August 17th. That festival is a big thing that happens every year at an outdoor performing center north of Chicago, with a covered stage and a giant grass amphitheatre. After that, I flew to Portland, Maine to do a solo kora concert at another big outdoor festival on August 21st. Then it was time to fly to Europe again.

On September 4th, I flew to Bern, Switzerland to do two solo kora concerts at the Gurtenbahn Festival on the 5th and 6th. Then I came right back to Chicago to work on a Mandingo band demo to give to a record company. On September 9th, we spent the day at Studio Media in Evanston, Illinois to start on that recording. A couple weeks later, I went to Greenwich, Ohio to play a concert in a college there on September 27th with two of my good friends: Manu Walton playing djembe and other hand drums, and a Senegalese talking drum player named Vuex Jobe. Manu is the same guy from the story about the Mandingo Griot Society band members smoking so much! We are heavy good friends, and always kept in touch since way back then. After I came back from Greenwich, I went back to the Evanston recording studio with Mandingo to continue making the demo, and stayed around Chicago for the rest of the year.

During that time, I was in the recording studio with my guys off and on a bunch of times to keep working on the demos. In all the years since we first put together the Mandingo Griot Society band, the other guys were also going off and doing stuff with other bands and other people, because they knew a whole lot of other musicians too. Near the end of 1987, I remember the day I was in my apartment watching TV and drinking tea when I saw that Harold Washington died. He was the first black mayor of Chicago. I never met him, but he lived in the Hyde Park neighborhood too, in a big building called Windemere House along the lake. It was Wednesday, November 25th, and when he went to his office that day, he had a heart attack. They took him to Northwest Memorial Hospital, but he died, and he was buried on November 30th at Oak Woods Cemetery.

•••••

1988 started off quiet for me too, with just a few shows. On February 10th and 11th, I was in Montreal to perform solo kora concerts again at the Club Balattou, owned by Lamin Toure. The next month, I flew to New York to do some more demo recordings on March 23rd and 24th. After going back to Chicago again for a while, I flew back to New York, and was going around and around to record companies with my demo tape. The only person I remember meeting with at that time was a guy named Duke Du Bois from GRP records. So many record companies that were around at that time are gone now! Also during that trip to New York, the world premiere of the Powaqqatsi movie happened on April 29th. Then on May 4th, I performed a solo kora concert at the Robson Center in Vancouver, BC as part of a benefit concert for the Canadian Red Cross. There were lots of other musicians performing there, including Paul Horn. Emily and Uno drove up from Seattle for that show, and we went out to dinner together.

I did a lot of recording with Bill Laswell that year too. We would record demos or other projects, not always for a particular company, but just to work on the music. From May 15th to 18th, we were in a New York studio that Bill rented. Then from May 21st-24th, I was recording as a guest artist on an album that Tony Vacca and Tim Moran were making. Tony is a percussionist and also plays the balafon, and Tim plays the saxophone and other instruments. Tim also fixes horns for people even today, and I saw a video of him on the internet doing this. After that recording was done, I went to talk with Philip's ex-wife Joanne Akalaitis about a project she was doing. She is a playwright and director, and she wanted to put on a play called "The Screens", which was about a revolution in Algeria. I went to her apartment, and she asked me if I could write music for it. She showed me a big book filled with scenes from the play, and when I saw that I said, "Yes I can do it". Then I came back to Philip's house where I was staying, and I thought I should ask him about it. I told him that Joanna talked to me, and I asked him if he knew any other musicians to work on it with me. He told me, "Oh, I can do it with you". I wondered if it would be a problem for him to work with me on the music, because it's with his ex-wife. But I was wrong about that, because Phillip is the nicest human being. We talked about it with Joanne, and she was OK with it too, so we all agreed that Philip and I would write the music for the play. It has many, many different scenes, and so writing all the music was a big thing for us to do.

In June, I flew back to New York to do more recording with Bill for my solo album called The Dreamtime. We recorded most of it at Platinum Island Studio that month, and finished it later that year at B.C. Studio. We recorded 11 songs with me playing kora and singing, and also playing dusungoni, nyanye, kalimba, talking drum, and karinyan, which is our metal scaper percussion instrument. That album didn't come out for two more years though.

I came back to Seattle again on Friday, July 8th, and Emily and Uno picked me from the airport. At that time, they were already in the house where they would live for more than 30 years. This trip was the first time I came to that house, but I came many times after that, and years later I even lived there with them for a while. A Nigerian guy named Patrick came to Seattle too, and took me up to Vancouver for another solo kora concert. He had also arranged for me to do a concert the next day, and took me on the ferry to Victoria and to a tiny island called Hornby Island. I played a solo kora concert in a small art center there, and then we went to someone's land that was filled with statues. As soon as you entered the gate, there were all kinds of big and small statues filling the land everywhere, all the way to the house and beyond! We spent the night there, and the next early morning we went back to Vancouver, then started to drive back to Seattle. I didn't know that Patrick smoked marijuana, and when we got to the U.S. border, they stopped us and searched the car. Then they grabbed him and the marijuana they found, and they took his car away. He was in jail there for two days or something like that, so he couldn't take me back to Seattle, but I had to come by bus to get there right away because on that night I was supposed to play at a big club in Seattle called the Backstage! Wow. That was a big worry thing. Emily and Uno picked me at the Seattle bus station and we got to the club just in time, where Dumi Mariare and his ensemble opened the show. For the next few days, I hung out with Emily and Uno and their house, and did some recording in Uno's studio. Then I flew back to Chicago on Wednesday, July 13th.

Back in Chicago, I decided to pierce my ear for the first time. On August 19th, I went to a place, and they pierced it and put in an earring. I wore that for a while, and then I got tired of it and took it off. Later on I tried again, but I still didn't like it. The next day, I flew to Jacob's Pillow in Massachusetts for their big summer festival again, and did a solo kora concert on Sunday the 21st. I spent the rest of the summer of 1988 just doing this and that around Chicago, and then I left on September 14th to fly to New York, just to stop there for a couple of days on my way to Gambia.

•••••

I arrived in Gambia on Sunday, September 18th for a nice long visit with my family. After about a month there, I decided to buy my first gun to use for hunting. I always loved to hunt ever since I was growing up and staying with the Yaffa family in Sutukoba, and my time with Balla Yaffa is still so clear in my mind even today. So I went to Banjul and bought a shotgun on October 17th, for $1,200 dalasi. I bought it from a famous Malian businessman named Alhaji Grigra, who lived in Gambia for a long time and everybody knew him. After that day, I went hunting out in the bush every day, or every other day, for about five weeks. There are a lot of rabbits out there in the bush, and I like it so much! On Tuesday, November 8th, it was time for the baby-naming ceremony for our first child, our daughter Nene. People knew her name before that day, but we still hadn't done the ceremony and celebration. Her real name is Sarjo, and she was named after my mother. Because in our tradition, we say, "The first child's name belongs to the father", I picked that name for her. But we call her Nene, which is the Fulani word for mother. A lot of griots, neighbors, and other people came by for a big, big party in my compound in Brikama, with a lot of cooking too. We were feeding hundreds of people that day! Later in November, I made arrangements for a driver to take Bobo and me and Nene on a trip to visit a whole lot of our Suso relatives. We left on November 26th and went to villages all around the Basse area, visiting the people. I hadn't been there for a long, long time, and all the people were happy to see me and Bobo with our little daughter. During that trip is when we stopped in the Fulani village and I met the elder man who knew my grandfather Jali Falai Suso, and he would not let me pay for the fresh milk for us. Later on, me and Bobo also drove to Senegal in my car with Nene, to visit all of the relatives in Bobo's family too and have celebrations with them too. Everyone was so happy to see us and welcome us, and Nene got to meet her grandmothers and even one great-grandmother. My family and Bobo's family are related on our grandfather's side, because Bobo's grandfather was the youngest brother of my grandfather Jali Falai Suso. Both of them were born in the village of Tambasansang, in the eastern part of Gambia, south of the River Gambia, but Bobo's grandfather had moved with his family to Cassamance many, many years ago.

We came back to Brikama on December 15th, and soon after that, Philip's son Zack Glass came for a visit all by himself for two or three weeks. In 1986, he was on the trip that I led for his dad and the other people to Gambia, Senegal, and Mail, and he liked it a whole lot. At the time of this trip, I think he was around 17 years old, and he had a lot of fun staying with us. I took videos of our time together in my compound with my friends and family too.

•••••

On Tuesday January 3rd, 1989, I was supposed to take Zack to Dakar to catch a flight to New York, but that flight was cancelled. Zack always calls me "King", and he was so excited to get to stay another day so he said, "King, one more night in Gambia, yay!" We called his mother Joanne Akalaitis to tell her that I would put him on another flight from Dakar. She was a little bit worried. I also told Philip, and he called his sister whose husband used to be an ambassador around the world. Then he told me to take Zack to the U.S. Embassy in Fajara to change his ticket. The next day, me and Bobo drove him to Dakar in my Puegot 504 car. We left Brikama and drove to the Banjul ferry place, and crossed the River Gambia to Barra. From there, we drove north into Senegal and came to a big town called Sokone. As we left the town, clouds of locusts came across the sky so we could not even see the sun. They were hitting the car, and smashing on the road and the windshield, and I couldn't even see the road to drive. I never saw anything like that before, and I told Bobo and Zack, "Roll up the windows, quick!" It was unbelieveable, and in all my life I didn't see locusts like that. Millions of them were covering the sky like a sandstorm! After we left Sokone, it was all over after only two or three blocks down the road.

Before getting to the Dakar airport, we stopped at the house of Bobo's Aunt Fatou in Pikine, just outside the main city, so that Bobo could stay and visit her for a few days. Bobo is from Cassamance, but after her aunt married a man from Dakar and moved to Pikine, Bobo came there and her aunt raised her up. That compound is where I saw Bobo for the first time. After we all visited there for a little while, me and Zack left so I could take him to the airport. I dropped him there, and stayed overnight in a Dakar hotel. The next day I started driving back to Gambia. When I was driving between Dakar and Mbour, I saw the locusts swarming again. This time, I could see them on the roadside as I was coming. I was thinking, "No, I am not going to slow down, I am going to fly through them." That was a big mistake. I pushed the gas pedal down and was flying down the road. When I got to the locusts, I hit them and started killing them, and right away my windshield was covered. There were millions of them again! All the glass was covered like nighttime, and I couldn't see anything. It's a good thing there was no other traffic, or it would have been a big problem! I thought if I went fast, I could get past them, but they covered my car like a dark blanket over all the windows. I could see nothing! I slammed on the brakes, so it is a good thing no one was behind me on the road too. Dead locusts were all over my car, everywhere. The brakes were smoking too! Then I came out of the car to see them, and I could not even recognize my car. I ran and got a big stick to scrape off my windshield, because my wipers were stuck like glue. Locusts were on the underside of the car and everything. Then I got back inside and drove very, very slow until I got to the town of Ngaingaye. I found some boys there to scrape and wash the car for some money. Soon there were 18-20 boys working on my car. They brought buckets of water and made it look like new again.

When I was young, sometimes I saw locusts out in the fields, and I know they make the farmers cry, because they can spoil all the crops and there's nothing they can do. But I have never seen that many locusts at one time. Then I drove the rest of the way to Kaolack, turned south and back down to cross the river and go to Brikama. The day after I returned, my friend John Crowley from New York came to my compound for a visit. This was his second trip to Gambia, and he was staying with some other friends for a while, and went to Benin also. The following Monday January 11th, Bobo came back to Brikama. Around that same time, my friend Mohammed Camara and his wife Fanta were about to have a baby. One day Mohammed told me, "If my wife delivers a boy, I will name it after you. If she has a girl, I will name it after my mother". I replied, "Now it's a competition between me and your mom, but I think I will win!" I returned to Chicago on January 19th, and on Thursday the 26th they had a baby boy. In our tradition, it's very common for us to name children after our friends, and when the baby-naming ceremony happened in Brikama on the next Thursday February 2nd, they named the baby Fodaymusa Camara.

•••••

After being back in Chicago for a short time, I flew to Albuquerque on Saturday, January 28th, 1989, for a solo kora concert at a place called the Kimo Theater. The next day, I went up to Santa Fe to see my friend Jack Kolkmeyer. It was his birthday, so we were celebrating and having fun. I played the kora for his party, and also did a guest spot on his radio program. On Monday, Jack took me down to the Albuquerque airport to fly back to Chicago. On February 10th, I flew back to New York to meet with Philip again about the music for The Screens. I stayed with him at his house until the 14th, and then I went back to Chicago to do some rehearsing with Adam, Hamid, Joe, and John Markiss for an upcoming Mandingo Griot Society show. We flew to LA on February 25th to do a concert at the California Institute of the Arts in Valencia as part of a student event they call a Mardi Gras party, and flew back to Chicago the next day.

Soon after we returned, I started working on writing a song for a guy named Lamin Mbasi Borjang, who lives in Brikama and likes my kora music so much. One day he even asked me, "Suso, can you compose some music for me?" The reason I composed a song for him is that he survived three big things that happened, and my song talks about how lucky he was. The first thing that happened to Lamin was while he was in England, working for a shipping company. This particular company shipped things to all kinds of different places, and sometimes those things were loaded in a truck, and then the whole truck was shipped to the destination. One of their ships sank with around 30 people aboard, and only six or seven people survived. Lamin was one of those survivors. He even showed me the hospital report so I could see what happened to him! The second thing that happened was when he was traveling in a truck in England, and an accident happened. One of his legs and one of his hands were broke, but the hospital fixed that also. The third thing happened again in England, when he was on another truck going to a remote area. The people loaded very heavy stuff and filled the truck all the way up, and he and some other people were sitting on top of the load. While they were going to take it someplace, the truck tipped over and two or three people died. He broke his two legs and one hand, and his jaw and collarbone. He was underneath that heavy load of stuff for many hours, stuck. The rescue people came to pull off the stuff, and found the other people who died before reaching him. Luckily he was still breathing. They took him to a hospital in London and he was there for a long time, and then took him to another hospital that specializes in his injuries. They put many irons in his legs and hand, and even in his jawbone. His legs became even more bowed than they were before, and he became shorter than before, so he had to wear a special shoe. It took a long time to recover, at least one or two years. That is why my song is about him being a survivor, because only God can keep you alive if you get hurt like that.

Lamin had married a toubab wife in England, and he gave her the Gambian name of Jaara Borjang. She was very smart, and he told me that she said, "Every month, the companies pay you some big money. This money will go a long way if you are living in Gambia. Maybe we should leave here and go to stay in Gambia". So they moved to Gambia and started receiving the money there. His wife gave him very good advice, because 5,000-6,000 British pounds a month is a lot in Gambia. Everything was going fine, but later on they divorced and she went back to England. It wasn't long after then that Lamin died. I knew him for a long time. He is from the area in Brikama called Sukuta kunda, one of the tradional areas of the town, and near the big mosque. The roads in that area have shells as their paving, and the houses there are older than any of the rest. When I first came to Brikama in 1971, that area was the main part of the town, and my brother Mohammed Suso's compound near the police station was at the very edge of town. In fact, there were only three compounds past his on the left hand side. When I would be standing in my brother's compound and looking over his wall, the bush was right there with monkeys jumping and eating fruits. Also, there were not many cars in Brikama at that time, and the car park was very small. When we walked to the big mosque, Sukuta kunda was on the left hand side and Sanneh kunda was on the right, along with a small marketplace that used to be the only one in Brikama. Across the street was a section called Suma kunda, and on the south end was a section called Mansaringsu. Near there are Foday kunda, Hawla kunda, Jatta kunda, and Borjang kunda, all named after the families who built them. These original parts of Brikama were built by the Sukuta and Suma families, and all those other families, so these areas will always be called by their names.

•••••

While I was back in Chicago in early 1989, my brother Dembo had a problem. While I was home in Gambia in 1988, my family had come to me to say that Dembo should travel. He wanted to go, so I said, "Maybe you should to go Germany. There are a lot of young Gambians there". Germany was good for work in those days, but Dembo had a visa problem, so I told him that he should go to Denmark first, then to Germany. Since 1968, when a lot of tourists from Scandinavia started coming to Gambia, there was never a visa problem between Scandinavia and Gambia. So I was thinking that Dembo should fly to Copenhagen, and then go by train to Germany. I paid for his ticket and gave him pocket money so he could go, and I told him that things are different in Europe than in Africa, where you can just be traveling easily from country to country. I told him, "In Europe, even if two countries house roofs are touching, but one is on one side of the border and one is on the other, you cannot just pass between them without the correct paperwork". At that time, I had a good friend in Copenhagen named Mamadou Camara, who I met there in 1982 while touring with Mandingo Griot Society. I told Dembo, "Mamoudou will pick you from airport, and have you stay there with him for a few days before taking you to the train to Germany". Dembo didn't follow that advice though. On Saturday, April 1st, Dembo left Gambia and went to Dakar, and stayed there for one or two weeks. Then he and bunch of boys he met in Senegal flew from Dakar to Rome. The authorities stopped some of them and said that they had to go back. Nobody among them even had a visa! At three or four o'clock in the morning that day, I was sleeping at my apartment in Chicago and my phone rang. When I said hello, Dembo said, "Brother, it's me. I am here at the Rome airport and they won't let me in". I said, "What? I didn't tell you to go to Rome. Let me talk to somebody there". I talked to the immigration people, and heard what was happening, then I told Dembo, "You messed up, and you didn't listen to me. You have to come back to Brikama". All those boys were in Rome until Tuesday April 18th, and then they were deported.

In 1989 it became even more popular for men to put holes in their ear, and a lot of artists did it. So in early May, I said to myself, "How about if I try again?" I went to a place to put the hole in, but again it didn't work well for me. My left ear seemed like it was heavier than my right ear, and when I was shaking my head it didn't feel right, so a few weeks later I just took the thing off. At the end of May, I went to Minneapolis, Minnesota with Philip for the auditions that JoAnne was doing for The Screens. She had decided to do the play at the Guthrie Theater in Minneapolis, and on May 31st, she had a whole lot of actors and dancers gathered there to try out for the play. She wanted us to help decide which ones to pick. One of the actors we picked was Don Cheadle, but at that time, he was young and nobody really knew him. I returned to Chicago on June 1st, and the following day I flew to Portland, Maine for a solo kora concert. Then I flew to New York and played another solo kora concert for Robert Browning and the World Music Institute at the Symphony Space on 95th and Broadway on June 3rd. The next day, I visited a friend of mine in Washington DC for a few days, then came back to Chicago and did solo kora concerts at Chicago Public Library Cultural Center on June 8th and at the Blues Fest at the Navy Pier on June

11th. I flew to New York again the following week, and from the 18th to the 29th, me and Philip recorded the music we wrote for The Screens, because we were not going to be playing it in person during the performances.

While I was in New York, I called Bill Laswell just to say, "What's happening, my friend?" He said, "Let's go out to eat", and while we were having dinner, he said, "I've got something to tell you. I saw this thing that looked like a kora in a store window in Chinatown, and it's made out of metal and called a Gravikord. It was made by a guy named Bob Grawi. Maybe you should check it". In fact, I already had met Bob Grawi some years before, because he was very interested in the kora. Bob told me that he looked at the kora in museums for years, and wanted to see if he could make something like that. The next day, I went to that store to look at it. The Gravikord doesn't have a body like a kora, it's just a metal frame. When I played it, I could see that there needed to be some changes on it. After I went back to Philip's house, I talked to Bill. He asked me, "What do you think?" and I told him, "I always like something new, but it needs some changes. And it costs $950.00 plus tax, and I don't think I want to spend that for it". Then Bill said, "I know, but don't worry about the price. If you like it, I will buy it for you". Then I called Bob Grawi and said, "I saw your Gravikord in the music store. It needs some changes, and I will buy one if you make them". He said, "Yes, I will do that. Come on over to my house and we will talk".

When I went to Bob's house, he had some Gravikords that were in progress and showed them to me. The changes I told him to make were to bend the handles a little closer to the body of the instrument, and to change the bridge. It looked like a bridge for an upright bass, so I told him, "I will draw a bridge for you to make, and show where the strings should lay in". I drew it for him so it looked exactly like a kora bridge. He said he would do those things, and I should come back to pick it up the next day. He made the bridge out of some strong and heavy material. Bill gave me a check to pay for it, and I gave that to Bob when I came to pick it up.

I came back to Chicago on July 1st with the Gravikord, and used it on some live shows. I also used it for the recordings of my 1990 album, New World Power. But I could not keep using that instrument, because when I played it, it felt like I lost the natural sound of the kora. It was a dry stick. I amplified it too, but when I was playing it, the strings sounded like I was hitting a gamelon or metal xylophone, with a harder sound. Bob Grawi tried to play it with his own music style, but I never saw anybody else play one. I kept my Gravikord for a long, long time, but when I moved to Seattle in 2009, a friend of mine asked me to give it to him so I did.

After a few weeks in Chicago, I flew back to New York, and on July 24th and 25th I recorded soundtrack music with a composer named Michael Small, who does a lot of soundtrack music. The movie was called Mountains of the Moon, and was about two of the English explorers who came to Africa in the 1850s. Then I came back home to Chicago for a few more weeks. In mid-August, I flew to Santa Fe to perform on the 11th and 12th at the Rainbow Warrior Festival, which was put together by Eliza Gilkyson. She is a very famous guitar player from that area, and she is still playing today. For that show, I brought Manu with me to play percussion and Abdul to play guitar. There were also Native Americans from the pueblo areas singing and drumming, and Tibetan monks chanting. The MC of the festival, who introduced everyone before playing, was Levar Burton. He was the actor who played Kunta Kinte in the movie Roots, and after we met, we talked a lot the whole time I was there. We also exchanged phone numbers and talked once or twice after that.

On Sunday August 13th, 1989 I flew back to Chicago and got the news that my first son was born! A midwife helped with the delivery at the hospital in Brikama, and everyone was doing fine. In our tradition, we say, "The second child's name also belongs to the father", so I named our son after my father, Saikou Suso. Also in our tradition, whenever we name a boy child after one of our fathers or grandfathers, we must put Ba before their name to show our heavy respect. Our word for father is Ba, so since our son was named after my father, we join those together to call him Basaikou. He just turned 29 last year. It's hard to believe! For a boy child that is named after one of our uncles, we put Kau before his name, which is our word for uncle. Later on, my blood brother Mahamadou Suso had a son who is named after our Uncle Boya, so he is called Kauboya.

On Thursday September 28th, I went to New York to go and talk to Bill. I had made a demo of a new song that I gave to him to listen to, and we also signed the contract for me to do a recording with him and some other musicians that became the New World Power album. In mid-October, I went to LA for five or six days, and met with a friend of mine from South Africa named Nicholas Pike. He plays the piano and is a film composer, and we played some music together. I think it was just for fun, and not a project. Two weeks later on Sunday October 29th, me and Philip met in Minneapolis again to see the premiere performance of The Screens at the Guthrie Theater. They used our recording of the music to accompany the play, and it was a big special thing that night, with a lot of people coming to that first show.

The next day I came back to Chicago, but right away I went back to New York again to record the New World Power album with Bill. Our first set of sessions was from November 3rd to the 17th. For some reason, I went back to Chicago on November 18th to do something, but I don't remember what! Then the next day, I flew right back to New York to work more on the record with Bill at B.C. Studio in Brooklyn on the 20th and 21st. We took off a couple days, and then we went to Platinum Studio to do more on Nov 24th and 25th. I took a break and went back to Chicago from Nov 26th to Dec 2nd, then I flew back to New York from December 4th to the 20th for more recording at Krypton Studios. During this time, we always did four or five hour sessions, instead of being there all day. We also spent more time on this album than any previous recording, because we were trying to do everything electronically, and it takes time to put those things together. I had to come up with all the parts to program on the machines too, including drums. On the recordings, I played kora, gravichord, and talking drum, and Bill played bass.

Jeff Bova played synthesizers, and Clive Smith & Nicky Skopelitis did a bunch of programming too.

•••••

On December 23rd, I came back to Chicago to spend a couple of weeks getting ready to go to Gambia. Every time I go home, I like to stay all through the dry season and come back to the U.S. just before the rainy season starts. In that season, it rains hard! It's like somebody is pouring a bucket on Gambia, and the weather is very hot too. So I left Chicago on Thursday January 4th, 1990 and flew to Frankfurt Germany, because I wanted to buy a dump truck and ship it to Gambia to start a business. My close friend Mohammed Camara had a brother in Frankfurt named Morro Camara, and he picked me at the airport and took me to stay at his house. The next day, me and Morro went around and around everywhere, looking for trucks. But the right one wasn't there for me. During that time, I also took a train to a German town called Ravensburg, to go and visit one of my brothers, Sefou Suso, on January 10th. He is the son of one of my uncles, and I hadn't seen him for a very long time. While I was back in Frankfurt, I decided to just cancel buying the truck, and to buy some more property in Gambia instead. I called my wife Bobo and my mom, and they said, "No, you should bring the truck and come". I flew to Gambia on January 18th, and when I arrived in Brikama, I told them, "You will see that I will get something way better than a truck".

On Tuesday February 6th, I bought my second compound in Brikama from a guy called Baba Sisay. At that time, people who wanted to sell their property would just tell everybody, and then the news would get around. Also, when people who wanted to sell their property heard that somebody was coming back to Gambia, they especially made sure everybody knew to inform them that it was for sale. Then if you wanted to buy it, you all would meet the owner and discuss the price. When that was agreed, you went together to the land office to buy the land and change the papers. There were realtor-like people in Gambia then, but in a town like Brikama you just went to the mayor's place or the area council to do it. It is changing now, but these middlemen can make a problem for it because they want a big cut. I didn't look around a lot before buying my compound. The land I bought was not even a block away from my own home compound that I bought in 1982, and where I was living with Bobo and my mom, and the rest of my family. Later on, my children Fatou and Balamin were born there too. I bought the land to build houses on, and then I hired the people to do it. It took some time, but as soon as houses were built, quickly they became full with tenants.

Around two months after I bought my second compound, Bill came to Gambia on his first trip, along with his girlfriend and a recording engineer named Billy Youdelman. The reason they came was to do recordings and photography for the album project called Ancient Heart: Mandinka and Fulani Music of the Gambia. They arrived on Friday, April 13th, and checked into the Novatel Hotel in Fajara. The next day, I picked them up and we went to look around Serekunda, Banjul, and Brikama, and then I brought them back to their hotel. On Sunday the 15th, I went back up to Fajara to pick them up, and took them back to my compound to record a group of griots there. The next day, we did more recordings at my compound, this time with Fulani musicians. Some of those musicians were from Guinea but lived in Gambia, and one of them was Juldeh Camara, who plays nyanye, a one-string violin. He became a very famous guy, and now lives in London and works a lot with a guitar player named Justin Adam. My wife Bobo also sang on it, my father's brother Surakata Suso and my blood brother Mahamadou Suso played the kora, and my elder brother Mohammed Suso played the balafon. Bill and everybody left Gambia to fly back to New York on Wednesday, April 18th, and I stayed another month with my family in Brikama.

●●●●●

For the rest of May, I was hanging in Chicago doing this and that, and then took a couple of quick trips. First I went to New York to do a solo kora concert on June 8th at a performing arts center called the Symphony Space, then returned for a gig with Mandingo at the Looking Glass

Club in Chicago on June 16th. On Friday, June 22nd, I got the news that my teacher Uncle Saikou Suso died in Gambia. I was thinking about him so much for a long time after that, because he was my teacher for all those years. On July 4th, another famous man in Gambia died. His name was Alhaji Mamodou Musa Njai, and his family was from the Basse area. He was a very famous businessman. He started his business selling kola nuts, then sold a lot of different things and became very rich.

On Monday July 23rd, the New World Power album came out on Axiom Records, which was part of Island Records. Me and Bill and the other guys in the band didn't go out on tour for it, but we did play a show on Saturday September 1st, at the Chicago Jazz Festival in Grant Park. The next week, I flew from Chicago to New York to work on a movie soundtrack for a guy named Philip Haas, who is an artist and filmmaker. He was making a movie called Magicians of the Earth: Seni's Children, about a woman named Seni Camara who was an artist that worked with clay, and made thousands of statues of people and animals. She was from a town in Cassamance called Binjona, and the movie was documentary of her life and work. It was very interesting to see and compose music for that movie. We went into Electric Lady Studio to work on it from September 8th to the 15th, and then I came back to Chicago.

Two weeks later, I was back in New York. So much flying! This time it was to record an album with Philip of the music we wrote for the play, The Screens. We started recording on Monday, October 1st and finished on October 4th. I got in touch with Bill while I was there, and on October 3rd I went to dinner with him and Tony Meilandt and Herbie Hancock. Then jumped on another flight back to Chicago!

Quickly, it was time to fly to San Antonio Texas with Mandingo for a concert on October 5th at the Caribbean African Festival. Then back to Chicago for another show at the Looking Glass Club, and a flight to Victoriaville, which is just south of Montreal, for a show at Canada Fest on October 8th. Then back to Chicago again on the 9th. Now when I think of these days, it's unbelievable to me! Back in Chicago, it was time to prepare for another trip to Gambia, but this time it was a quick visit. I left on Sunday November 4th and came back on Monday December 3rd. I knew that the year to come was going to be just as busy as the year before, maybe even more!

IN MANY WORLDS

On January 8th, 1991 I went to New York to record with Tim Moran and Tony Vacca again. On this record, Tim played saxophone and flute, Tony played balafon and other African instruments, and I played kora as a guest artist. This album was called Dance Beneath the Diamond Sky, and Don Cherry was a guest artist on it too. Our sessions were on January 9th to 11th, then I came back to Chicago and started recording a demo tape for myself of my solo kora music. On the 19th, Stanley Jackson took me to Park West in Chicago to practice with the Kronos Quartet, and later that day I did a concert with them there. That was the first time I actually played with Kronos, but a lot happened before that day which led up to that point.

Ever since I met Bill and we started working together a lot, he would always tell me, "Oh, it would be good if you could play with a group called Kronos". He said that many times, but I never asked him who they were, I just said, "Yeah, yeah, yeah". Then one time when I was in New York working in the studio with Bill and staying in Philip's house, I was standing in his kitchen with him and he said, "Tonight I am going to BAM in Brooklyn to see a group called Kronos Quartet". So right away, my mind went to this being the group that Bill was always talking about. Philip knew them very well also, and he had already written some pieces for them. So Phillip went to the concert, but I had to work in studio with Bill so I didn't go. After the concert, Philip went and talked to Kronos leader David Harrington, and David said to him, "We want to make a record with some African musicians, and we want them to compose some music for us. We just came back from Japan and bought a record there of a kora player, but maybe he lives in Africa. We would like that guy to compose a song for us". Philip asked David who he was talking about, and he could hardly pronounce my name, but Philip recognized it and laughed. David said, "What's so funny?" and Philip said, "That guy is in my house right now!" So David asked Philip to give me his number, and the next day I called him from Philip's kitchen.

David always talks so sweet, and that day he asked me to compose a song for Kronos. I asked him, "What is your instrumentation?" and he told me viola, cello, and two violins, so I knew right away that they played a classical type of music. So I said, "I need to hear some of your music before I say yes". Then David sent me two cassettes a few days later in Chicago. I was listening, listening, listening to the first cassette, and everything they are playing sounded OK, but I was not into it a lot. Then I listened to their other cassette with different songs, and what made me want to write for them was that they did the Jimi Hendrix song, Purple Haze! When I heard that, I was thinking to myself, "Aha! Yes, they will be able to do a song I compose. Even if I write a song with a beat, they will be able to do it". After that, me and David got in touch with each other again, and Kronos commissioned me to write a song. The piece I wrote for them is called Tilliboyo, which means sunset. After I wrote it, I took to a very good transcriber in Chicago named Ari Brown, who is a good friend of mine. He transcribed it to make sheet music for them to play, and then I sent them everything.

They began practicing on my piece in New York, and then happened to be coming to Chicago on Saturday, January 19th for a show at Park West. They contacted me beforehand to say, "We want you to do this show with us", and so we played that piece together. The next day, we went into the recording studio that is out at the place they do the giant Ravenia Festival every year, to record the song. Kronos put our recording together with songs they did with other African musicians I knew, such as Dumi Maraire, Hamza El Din, Obo Addy, and others, and made a record called Pieces of Africa that came out the following year.

From February to May of 1991, I was able to take it easy a little bit, which was good. At the end of May, I flew to Toronto to play a solo kora concert on May 22nd at their big annual festival of African music and culture. That was only a couple of years after that Afrofest first got started, and today it has kept going for over 30years. Some Gambians I know in Toronto came to my concert, and then afterward to my hotel for a visit. I flew back to Chicago for a few days, but then I got in a van with Mandingo Griot Society to drive back to Toronto again to play at that same festival on May 31st! The next day, we all played in Detroit at the Meadowbrook Music Festival. While we were there on Sunday June 2nd, the very bad news came to me that Philip's girlfriend Candy Jernigan died in New York from cancer. She was only 39. I flew to New York to go to her funeral and stay for a few days after. To be so young and pass away like that is very sad.

•••••

Later that summer, I went on my first tour with Bill and Ginger Baker and Anton Fier in Japan. We arrived there on August 14th to play at a giant event that happens every year in the city of Imabari. After we were there a couple of days, I bought a bunch of postcards and sent them to all my friends all over the world. We played the festival on Saturday the 17th, and they recorded us to make a live album called Imabari Meeting. The other bands at the festival were from Japan, and they were on that album too. One was even a reggae band! On the 19th, the same day we flew from Imabari to Tokyo, the news came on the TV to say that Gorbachov was being overthrown in Russia. The next day, we went into the Amuse Recording Studio in Tokyo to do some tracks. On that tour and in the following summer, we played in Tokyo, Nagoya, Kyoto, Imabari, Unsen, Osaka, and other places. I liked it very much. Everybody knows Ginger is a very good drummer and a little bit crazy. His way of playing drums is something else, and it was a very good experience working with him. I always call him "GB" whenever we are talking, and he became my friend. After our second tour, I didn't see him for a long, long time. Then one day in October 2005, I was walking on 3rd Avenue in Manhattan and saw him. We greeted each other, and I asked, "What are you doing here in New York?" He replied, "I am here for the reunion of my band Cream, tomorrow at Madison Square Garden".

On August 23rd, I left Japan and came back to Chicago for a week, and then flew to Seattle to perform at the big festival they have every year called Bumbershoot. I played a solo kora concert during all three days of the festival, including an outdoor show at the Memorial Stadium on September 2nd. The festival people put me in the Stouffer Hotel in downtown Seattle, and I was hanging out there with Emily and Uno a lot, and at their house. Also at that time, my friend Saikou Fatty was living in that area, and one day we went down to his house in Kent for a big meal with him and some other Gambians. When I first came to Seattle in 1979, there were only a few Gambians living there, and there were not so many even by this time in 1991. But now there are thousands! In fact, the Seattle area has a very big Gambian community, maybe the third biggest in the U.S.

I flew back to Chicago on September 3rd, and two days later I flew to Hartford, Connecticut for another show with Tim and Tony. We rehearsed a little bit and then on September 7th we played at the Iron Horse in North Hampton. The next day, we went to upstate New York and played at the Lake George Festival. After that, I went down to New York City to visit for a few days, and came back to Chicago on September 11th. After I was back for a couple of weeks, the sad news came that Miles Davis died in LA on September 28th.

On Thursday October 3rd, I came back to the northwest to play a duet concert in Olympia, Washington with Hamid Drake. We stayed with Emily and Uno at their house, and also did some recording with Uno in his studio on Friday and Saturday. On Sunday, Uno and me worked on the mixing, and I left that night to go back to Chicago. The very next day, the sad news came Adam Rudolf's mother Judy passed away. I liked that woman so much. She and her husband were my first hosts when I came to the U.S., and I stayed with them for nine months before I got my own place. The following weekend on October 12th, my favorite comedian passed away. His name was Redd Foxx, and he is my favorite comedian during my whole life, even now. I like everything about him, especially the crazy way he walks on his TV show. He never made a mistake and walked normal, he always walked the crazy way! I saw him one time in the LA airport, and he was walking normal and dressed very nice, with sunglasses, gold chain, and bracelet. I can see that in his regular life, he was dressing so sweet. But when he is on TV, that's when the craziness comes to him in every way!

The next Friday, October 18th, I stopped smoking cigarettes the first time. I said to myself, "I'm not going to smoke nothing. I promise myself I am not going to smoke". That smoking makes me blow my money a lot! When I was trying to quit, I would go buy a pack of cigarettes and smoke one or two of them, then throw the pack of cigarettes in the toilet. Then I would go buy another pack in a few hours. I could do that five times a day! Then I would start smoking again. It took a while after that for me to quit for good. On October 26th, I flew to Gainesville Florida with Hamid for another duet concert at The Gainesville Museum. Then I went right back to Chicago for another month before flying to New York to record with Bill on November 30th. That's when I had the amazing reunion with Stuart Sutton-Jones, while he was in New York and called my message machine in Chicago to try to find me, at the same moment I was walking down 14th St. in New York!

•••••

On Sunday December 1st, I flew to Gambia for another short visit, staying only just one month. I arrived back in Chicago on January 1st, 1992, and was there for the whole month. Then I flew to San Francisco for a big music seminar on February 13th and 14th. A whole lot of musicians were brought there, and we all stayed in one big hotel. At that seminar, I met Mickey Hart, the drummer from the Grateful Dead. He had been working with the Nigerian drummer Olatunji and was very interested in African music, so we spent a lot of time talking together. During the seminar, there would be two or three of us playing live music together and also doing a lot of talking, and one day I did a duet with a famous New Age guitar player named Ottmar Liebert. At the end of the seminar, a bunch of us jammed together to entertain the people, and I came back to Chicago on February 15th.

I flew to New York again on February 20th to rehearse with Philip for a couple of days, to do a promotional concert for The Screens album. On the 22nd, we left New York with Philip's producer, and another young composer named John Moran, to go to London for the first concert. We were there for only three days. The next month, I went back to San Francisco for a solo kora concert at the Hilton Ballroom on March 22nd. There was also a guy there from New York named Glen Velez, who played a concert with a round, framed drum. Also, there was a lady named Zelieka, but I can't remember who she was or what instrument she played. So much was happening, it was hard to keep track of!

I returned to Chicago on March 23rd, and Mandingo Griot Society played at a club there called the Hothouse on the 28th. That club was run by a lady named Marguerite Horberg, and she had it going for a long, long time before it closed. Even today, Marguerite is still putting on shows, and she called me a while ago to do a Mandingo Griot Society reunion. I told her I didn't think it was possible though, because we all live far away from each other and the tickets and concert fee will be too much for that little club. On April 10th, I flew to New York again to rehearse with Philip for another couple of days. Then on the 13th, we did a concert for the record release of The Screens, and a big party in Manhattan. A lot of people came to that show. Then I came back to Chicago again, and at the end of that month I remember being in my apartment watching TV with the riots happening in LA because of Rodney King getting beaten by the police.

The second time I tried to stop smoking was on May 21st. Every day, I wrote in big red ink on my journal pages, "No Smoking". But just like my trying to quite six months before, that lasted only about ten days, and then the smoking continued. I used to like to buy a whole carton of cigarettes when I smoked. Sometimes I would bring the carton home and then smoke only two cigarettes before I was thinking, "No! I can't keep smoking!" Then I would throw the whole carton away. And I wouldn't just put it in my own garbage can, I would take it outside and throw it in a big dumpster. Then later on, I would go down and try to get it out of the dumpster again because the smoking thing got me so bad!

On June 7th, Mandingo Griot Society went to Pittsburgh to play at the Three Rivers Art Festival, and came back to Chicago the next day. Then for the second half of 1992 and part of 1993, I was going on tour back and forth with Kronos Quartet and then with Bill and Ginger, along with playing a bunch of other concerts with Philip and other people. Each of their music was so different, and it was like being in many different worlds at once!

The Kronos Quartert CD called Pieces of Africa came out on earlier that year on Monday February 10th, but the first show I played that year with them was on Wednesday June 17th at Central Park in New York. Immediately, I flew back to Chicago and then to the west coast, because I was meeting Adam in Gaberville, California the next day to do a duet concert with him at the Reggae on the River Festival.

Then I had a week to get ready to go on tour with Bill and Ginger. On June 28th, I flew to Athens, Greece with Bill, Ginger, Bernie Worrell from Funkadelic, Nicky Skopelitis, and Aïyb Dieng. We played in an outdoor amphitheater in Athens, way on top of a big hill. It was a very interesting place. You had to walk a lot to get there, and the chairs were all different colors: white, green, red, and yellow. The people there liked that concert so much! A guy named Nicco was the promoter for it, and afterward he said "Suso, you should stay here for a few days so we all can get to know each other. I have a few friends for you to meet". I had to go to Switzerland to play with Kronos soon after that concert, so it was fun for me to get to stay in Athens instead of flying back to U.S. and then back to Europe. Every day, Nicco would come with his friend Wangeles to pick me at the hotel I was staying at, and we would go out to restaurants with Greek musicians who were playing. They introduced me to a famous musician there who played a Greek instrument called a bouzouki, which looks like banjo with a long neck. He could play that instrument very well! Nicco and Wangeles took me to lot of restaurants, and treated me very well the whole time I was in Athens.

Then on Saturday July 4th, they took me to the airport to fly to Geneva, Switzerland to play with Kronos at the Montreux Jazz Festival. A driver took me to the hotel, where Kronos had also brought Dumi Mariare and Hamza El Din to stay, because we were all going to play with them. On the 5th, we were all hanging out together and it was great. I went to Hamza's hotel room to talk with him for a long time, and then went into town with Dumi. The next day we performed, and the festival people made a big presentation in the ballroom of the hotel we were staying in. The host speaker was Quincy Jones, and the mayor of Montreux was there and gave him the key to the city. I flew back to Chicago on the 7th, and that festival time was the last time I saw Dumi and Hamza. A few years later Dumi died suddenly, and after some more time, Hamza also died suddenly. I will remember those great musicians for a long, long time.

On July 10th, I flew to Hartford, Connecticut with my friend and percussion player Manu, to do a daytime concert in a place called Bushnell Park. That night, I went to North Hampton and played with Tim and Tony at the Iron Horse again. After those few days on the east coast, I came back to Chicago on July 13th to get ready for another trip to Japan with Bill and Ginger.

This time, it was Bill and Ginger, me, Aïyb, Bernie Worrell, and a very funny guitar player from California whose name was Buckethead. On July 15th, we all flew to Japan and started our rehearsing. Our first show was in a tiny, tiny club called Tokyo PN on July 19th. The second show was on August 1st at a place called the Pitin Club. We played two shows per night and they paid us well, and they charged people a lot because it was so small. Bill and me were amazed together about that. Every day while we were in Tokyo, we were sleeping at our rooms in the Capitol Hotel in the daytime, and walking around at night, hanging out and eating in restaurants together. In Shinjuku, there was an Indian place called Taj, and an Indian restaurant called Moti. I liked Indian food a lot back then, and I like it the same today! On August 5th, we left Tokyo and took the bullet train to Kyoto. We checked into the Royal Hotel and did a concert that night, and the next day we went to Imabari to play in the festival for the second time. It was organized by a friend of ours named Toshnori Kondo, who is a Japanese musician and also from Imabari. The festival is not happening anymore, but in those days it was a big thing. They brought all the musicians to the city hall to meet the mayor of Imabari, and thousands of people came to hear us play. We flew back to Tokyo on Sunday the 9th, and two days later I flew back to Chicago.

On August 15th, I flew to Pittsburgh to play a duet with Manu at the Haramba Art Festival, and on August 28th, I flew to Germany to play two duet concerts with Philip in Frankfurt and Munich. I flew back to Chicago on the 31st, and Mandingo Griot Society did a concert at a festival in Rockfort, Illinois on September 5th. The big news for all of 1992 happened after I came back to Chicago though, when I got the call on Friday, September 11th that our third child was born, our beautiful daughter Fatou! Because I was doing so much traveling at the time she was born, we delayed her baby-naming ceremony and celebration until I came to Gambia in the first part of 1993.

On September 21st, I went back to New York to play with Tim Moran and Tony Vacca again in a club called Wetland, then down to Savannah, Georgia to play some more. For the rest of that year, I was just hanging in Chicago.

•••••

I spent most of January 1993 in New York, having some meetings and other stuff, but nothing big. Then on the 31st, I went back to Chicago to start getting ready to go home to Gambia. I arrived in Brikama on Saturday, Feb 27th, and after spending a nice week with my family, I got a call from Paul Horn, who is a flute player from Canada. We had met in New York some time before that, and he told me he wanted to come to Africa. We also made arrangements for doing a recording project with some musicians in Gambia, but we fell apart on one thing. When Paul called me at my house in Brikama, he said, "I am planning to come to Gambia, and I want us to finish our agreement about musicians and what we are going to do. And I need you to fully guarantee my safety". So I asked him, "What kind of safety do you mean?" He replied, "A guarantee that everything will be fine in Africa and be OK". I said, "How can I do that, when I cannot even guarantee that I will be here tomorrow? Anything can happen, and I can't grant your safety if I might be gone tomorrow". He insisted on this thing, so I told him, "Don't come, you should cancel your plans".

Gambia is very sweet in the dry season, and I like to be able stay there all the way from December to May whenever I can. But even if I can only go for a short time, I like to be there sometime during those months. In that year, my younger brother Dembo married his wife on Thursday April 15th, and she came to my compound in Brikama on April 17th to live with him, and with me and my family. Her name was Sula Sakliba, and she was from the village in eastern Gambia called Manjan Kunda. That is where all the people settled who followed my grandfather Jali Demba Jobarteh from Dabi, Mali a long, long time ago. The day Dembo's wife came to live with him in his compound was also the same day of the baby-naming ceremony for our daughter Fatou. Just like with Nene everybody already knew her name before the baby-naming ceremony. Because in our tradition, we say, "The third child's name belongs to the mother", Bobo named our daughter after her Aunt Fatou who lives in Pikine, Senegal, and raised Bobo there. In our tradition, we don't add anything in front of a girl child's name though, even if she is named after our mother, grandmother, sister, or aunt. Only with a boy child do we add Ba in front of their name if they are named after a father or grandfather, or Kau if they are named after an uncle. That day, we had a big celebration in my compound for Fatou's baby-naming, with singing and dancing and drumming all day too.

In May, Zack Glass came to visit me again for almost the whole month. Since I like hunting so much, I was planning to go on a hunting trip on the 27th, and he said, "King I want to go, I gotta go!" So I took him with me, along with my best hunting friends Lamin Jammeh and

Samba Saidy. I bought a bunch of food for camping, and we drove far inland to a place near Brefet where there are a lot of big islands in the River Gambia. We got in a wooden boat with a motor, and went to an island way in the middle of the water. We built a fire when we got there, and Lamin stayed there to keep it going. I put the light on my head to look for the deer and was walking in front, Zack was behind me, and Samba was following Zack. I liked being out in the bush so much, even though I didn't get any deer. The next morning, we left the island and went back to Brikama, and the following day me and Zack flew back to the U.S.

After a short time in Chicago, Mandingo Griot Society went to Chattanooga Tennessee to play a concert on June 11th at the Riverbend Festival. This concert was me, Adam, Hamid, and Abdul, along with an Ethiopian lady who was a singer, and somebody else on keyboards. Then on June 20th, I went up to Detroit to do a concert in downtown at a place called Chene Park, with Simon Shaheen on the oud, Aïyb on percussion, and Bernie Worrell on keyboards. Then I went back to Chicago to get ready for a European show with Kronos in Vienna, Austria. We flew there on July 5th, and played a concert at the Staatsoper Opera House on the 7th. After that concert, people came up to tell me that I was the first black person to ever perform in that place! I came back to Chicago the next day, and then I flew to the east coast on the 14th to play with Tony and Tim at a university in Newark, Delaware. Then back to Chicago for a week, before I flew to LA to do a concert with Kronos at the California Institute of the Arts in Valencia, and do a workshop there together the next day.

For all of August, I had the chance to be back in Chicago just hanging out, with only a couple music events at an African festival in Hyde Park. That festival began when a guy named Patrick Woodtor came from Liberia to Chicago, and opened an art and clothing store called Window to Africa. The store windows looked out onto Harper Square Court, in the center of Hyde Park. In 1993, Patrick started that small African festival, and he hired me to play the kora while a few young girls and boys dressed in African clothes walked around the courtyard for a fashion show. Mandingo Griot Society also played a concert there on September 4th. Every year, that festival got bigger and bigger, and eventually became the African Festival of the Arts. Patrick and other people worked hard to make it a giant thing, with all kinds of art, food, and music, and it is now held in Washington Park. Mandingo Griot Society played the festival two or three times after that, and I also played a concert there with Pharoh Sanders.

The week after that festival, I flew back to LA and did a solo kora concert at the Getty Museum on August 10th as part of a big music festival. I stayed in LA for a couple more days, and then flew back to Chicago for another month of free time. On October 10th, I flew back to New York and hung out for a few days rehearsing, and then played a World Music Institute concert on the 15th at the Washington Square Church with a guitar played named David Tronzo and a percussionist named Gordon Gottlieb. After a couple more days in New York, I went back to Chicago. All these times I was going back and forth to New York, and even today, I always stay at Philip's house. He gave me a key a long time ago and said, "When you are here, you don't need to stay in any hotel. Even if I am not here, you can just come on in and go to your room to stay as long as you want". Philip is something else.

On October 31st, I went to San Francisco to take part in the Composer's Forum at the very first Other Minds Festival. Philip was there too, along with Meridith Monk, Tom Baker, Trimpin, and many other famous musicians. The festival people also brought a whole bunch of us together to a place out in the country, to some big land that belongs to a rich man named Carl Djerassi. He had a daughter who died, and after that happened, he dedicated that land to her and built the Djerassi Resident Artists Center. It has performing places and places to stay, and everyone had their own room. We were there from November 4th to the 7th, and then we all came back to San Francisco for a big show at the Yerba Buena Center on the night of the 7th.

I flew home to Chicago on the 8th, and then right back to San Francisco again on the 14th to rehearse with Kronos to prepare for the next part of our European tour. After two days of rehearsals, I came back to Chicago for a while, and then flew to London on November 26th. This time, no other guest musicians from the Pieces of Africa album were there, it was just me and Kronos. Before most of our concerts, I would also have an interview with the BBC, with them asking me how I could write a composition for Kronos when I am playing a traditional African instrument, and other questions like that. Our first concert was on November 28th at the Huddersfield Town Hall, in a town near Manchester in Northern England. Then we drove down the east coast to play a show at the Corn Exchange in Cambridge on the 29th. Two days later, we played at the Royal Festival Hall in London, and then drove back north to play at the Royal Concert Hall in Nottingham on December 2nd. The last two concerts in London were at the Symphony Hall in Birmingham on the 3rd and the Newcastle Playhouse on the 5th. The next day we flew to Frankfurt, and after a few days hanging out there, we performed a concert at the Alte Opera House. On December 11th, I flew back to Chicago for a week.

Then on the 18th, I flew to Troy, New York, to rehearse with a band called Odadaa! which was founded by a famous Ghanian drummer and good friend of mine named Yacub Addy. I met him in New York many years before, I think it was sometime around 1979, while playing at the Bear Mountain Festival along the Hudson River. During that time, I was living in Chicago and he was living in Seattle, but he and his wife Amina moved to the city of Troy in upstate New York soon after that. We rehearsed for two days for a concert we would play together in early 1994, and it was very good. Then I flew back to Chicago to get ready to go home to Gambia.

• • • • •

On January 19th, 1994, a month after arriving home in Brikama, I said to myself, "I have tried many times before to stop smoking, but today is my final day. This is the day I will stop completely". For a few years before that, I was trying to stop smoking cigarettes many times, but I never could do it. That day, I was in my compound, sitting under the Mango tree with my good friend Mohammed Camara. I used to take a lot of Carlton Red cigarettes with me to Gambia so I wouldn't run out while I was there, and I pulled out my last pack. It had only four sticks left inside. At that time, I even had a fancy lighter, a very beautiful lighter, which I took with me to Gambia. I smoked two of the cigarettes, and I looked at those remaining two and then I gave them to Mohammed with the lighter. I told him, "Boy, from now on, you will not see me put the cigarette in my hand or in my own mouth, I will not do that. Even if somebody tells me that I gotta smoke a cigarette or I will die, I would rather die. I'm not going to smoke any more". He laughed and didn't believe me, but I was thinking of it as big serious stuff. Then I said, "We have known each other for a long time, you know me, and we joke a lot. But now you won't see a cigarette in my mouth any more". That was the end of it.

Every time I was in Gambia, me and Mohammed always spent the whole day together, and that next day he came to my place and said, "Boy, I don't have any cigarettes". He smoked Piccadilly European cigarettes, which are very famous in West Africa, and I always buy them for him. I sent somebody to buy a pack of Piccadillys and gave them the money for it. When they got back, Mohammed pulled out my lighter and put the fire on one of the cigarettes. I was sitting there next to him, but I wasn't even looking at him. Then he said, "Boy, are you serious? Are you not going to smoke any more cigarettes?" I replied, "I told you, for me to put a cigarette in my hand and put in my mouth, that is gone now. No, no, no, you won't see me doing that ever again. I tried many times to stop smoking, and I have blown a lot of money on cigarettes. This is it". He still didn't believe me. Each day after that until I left, Mohammed came to my compound and asked my mother, "Mom, did my man smoke anything since I left here?" and she would say, "No I did not see this". That's the time I stopped smoking with my mind and my heart, not just with my hand and mouth. Because of that, this quitting did not become so difficult.

I left Brikama on Wednesday January 26th, and then flew to San Francisco with Mandingo Griot Society on the 29th for a show at the Yerba Buena Center. A day or two after that, I started on a tour called The African Troubadours, for Robert Browning's World Music Institute, and in honor of Black History Month in the U.S. It was me, Yaya Jallow from Mali, Hassan Hakmoun from Morocco, James Makubuya from Uganda, and Adam Rudolph. Our first show was on February 1st at the Student Center at Colorado State University in Fort Collins, and then we went to Arcadia, California to perform at Humboldt State Univerity on the 3rd. The next three nights, we performed at the University of California at Berkeley, the University of California at Santa Cruz, and the University of California at San Diego. On February 7th, I went back to Chicago for a few days.

Then I flew to Wilmington, Delaware to join Tim and Tony for a daytime concert on February 12th, and returned to Chicago that same night. Soon after that, I flew to New York to play for two nights with my friend Yacub Addy's band, Odadaa! at the Symphony Space on the 26th and 27th. The following week, I started another tour with Kronos. I flew to Texas for a concert with them on March 6th at the Allen Theater on the University of Texas at Lubbock, and we all went to Austin the next day to perform at the Bass Concert Hall at the University of Texas. Right away after that, we flew to Wisconsin for a performance at the Cofrin Hall at the University of Wisconsin at Green Bay on March 10th. Then we flew to Ann Arbor Michigan for a concert at the Power Center at the University of Michigan on the 12th and to Iowa City for a concert at the Hancher Auditorium at the University of Iowa on the 14th. That was our last show of the tour, and I came back to Chicago the next day to prepare for another trip to Gambia.

On March 18th, the day before I left Chicago, my father's younger brother Lamin Suso passed away in Serekunda. That is who my son Balamin is named after. Exactly 40 days later on April 28th, my teacher's brother Lamin Suso died too. That was very heavy for me. I arrived in Brikama on the morning of March 21st, and stayed only until April 21st because I had so many music things going on.

When I arrived back in New York, it was early morning and I went to Philip's house. That evening, I met with a composer and violinist named Edna Michell, who asked me to write a piece for her, then I took Philip's son Zack to Mughal Indian Restaurant to get my favorite food. The next day, my friend Yakub Addy sent a car to Philip's house, to take me to New Jersey, and that night I did a concert with his band Odadaa! at Essex College. In those days, people would call me on the telephone and arrange all the concert things, and I always tried to do as much as I could before I left Chicago. But a lot of times, that was not possible, because there was just so much going on!

I went back to Chicago on April 23rd, and stayed a few weeks there. Then I flew back to New York to play with Kronos at the Alice Tully Hall in Lincoln Center on May 14th. Two weeks later, I flew to Allentown, Pennsylvania to play with Tim and Tony at the Mayfair Jazz Festival. Then right away, back to Chicago to prepare for a third trip to Gambia that year. This time, I was in Gambia from June 3rd to July 6th, then back in Chicago until the end of that month. Because I was so busy, I wanted to go to Gambia every time I had the chance, even if I could not stay there for a long time.

Sometime that year, a happy day came again when my brother Dembo and his wife also had their first child, a son. When it was time to do the baby-naming ceremony, Dembo named him Mahame. I cannot remember the exact day he was born, but I don't think I was in Gambia when that happened because I was so busy with touring.

On July 31st, I flew to LA, and Adam met me at the airport to drive up to Fresno and play a duet show at California State University the next night. Then I spent four days doing some classes there, playing and teaching kora with students playing their instruments. On August 5th, I flew back to Chicago for a couple of weeks to get ready for a big tour with a very famous Japanese musician named Akira Sakata.

•••••

All these years, I was traveling a whole lot. It's unbelievable! Every few words in these chapters, it says, "I'm flying", or "I'm playing", and always moving from one part of the world to another. This is what I did, going around the world many times. I did it so much that it got to the point of, "I hate to travel, I love to travel, I like to travel, I don't like", back and forth like that in my mind. Then I got to the point of thinking, "Wherever I am, it's OK as long as I am playing my music". This is why even when I was on the stage at that time, I didn't look at the people's faces a whole lot, I only looked at their heads moving. One day I was in Tokyo, another day in Frankfurt, and I didn't ever think about which place had more people coming to hear the music, I just played. In my childhood time, I was always fascinated with traveling, and that was my aim the whole time I was growing up, so I was happy to do it.

Our tradition back home is always for griots to do a lot of traveling, from one village to another over and over, and in Gambia you can be traveling in the same district for two or three months. But my griot traveling is about many countries. I go to one place, and they speak a certain language, then another place they speak a different language, and so on. To be able to do that, you have to make your ears used to all of it, and it's a whole lot to do, so you learn to just go with the flow. When you travel a lot, and you happen to go to any city or town that you have never been to before, the experience you have had makes it so you can know which direction to go. In every place we get to while I am on the road, I like to walk around a little bit, and where I grew up out in the bush, there is nothing like a street or a map or anything like that. But in all these traveling experiences, I learned how to find my way around a place even if I never was there before. I would just come out of the hotel and look at the movement of the people or the traffic in that city, and figure out where the downtown area was so I could go there. In that way, no matter where I was traveling, it was not easy for me to go and get lost.

One thing for me, when I am on the road, is that I am going to work. I am not going on holidays or anything like that. When the performance is done, I go back to my house or to my hotel, or go get dinner and hang with some friends, but no big party thing. I always say, "Don't try to do anything that is not like how you, yourself are. Just continue being yourself". The moment you forget who you are, you will lose your self-control. You will do something that is not good for you, and that's when you will have a problem. Don't say to yourself, "All those people are doing it, so I should do it too". If you're not into something, don't do it. People will ask you, but if you say no, they will leave you alone about that. Sometimes, people will say to me, "You don't drink? You don't smoke ganga?" I always say no, because I don't want to put any of that stuff in my body. I don't want to get drunk for anything. The only thing that gets me drunk is when I play my music. But I don't mean drunk the same as a person gets from alcohol. For me, it's something very different. I have had a kora in my hand now since I was almost a baby, and it's a natural thing for me to play it. I still like to play it so much, and to hear it whether it's just me playing alone, or with all kinds of other instruments and musicians. The way I feel when I play it is something else. That's why I always say that kora playing was a gift to me from God.

Also, the way I feel about playing music is because of the place I was born and the way I was raised. I have a strong faith in my heart. I learned this as a child, and it has stayed with me my whole life. So no matter what happens, nothing can change it. That's why I never do my music with anybody unless I know it will be good. No matter how famous they are, I don't want it to be a gimmick, and no one can buy me. That is why I like the people I work with. I have a faith, and I believe that my fate is not hanging on whether I do something with them. So I don't fall into that trap.

Another thing I do every day is to keep in touch with my family. Since the time when we got married, my wife Bobo has never been to the United States. She lives back home in Gambia, and I call her every single day. It doesn't matter where I am, in Europe, Asia, the U.S. or anywhere else in the world, I will be calling. To me, it's not a problem to be traveling like this and to have my family behind me, in my home. Griot families are used to that, and she is from a griot family so she understands that too. She doesn't say to me, "Wherever you go, I need to be there, I'm glued to you", because she knows it is our griot tradition to be traveling. Sometimes you can travel with your wife and family, and sometimes you don't. That's not strange to us, to see a griot traveling alone and the wife is at home. Me and Bobo talk about it, and we agree on that. It's good, and it's our way of life. She says, "You go, and anytime you can come home, you come". So I go to Gambia all the time, and any time I am not touring, I will just get in the plane and go.

In our years together we have four kids, two boys and two girls. Now they all are grown, but even with that, I call home every single day. I have been doing this for many, many years, ever since there was a phone in my house in Gambia. Years ago, before there were cell phones, I just used a regular phone to call my house and talk to Bobo, to my mom, and other family who were there. For many, many years, my phone bill was very high every month, around $500.00 to $700.00. In fact, my phone bill was always higher than my rent! If I saw a bill come in that was $350.00, I would say, "Wow, what's happening? This bill is so low!" In those days, every phone call was very expensive, especially to my country. Five minutes was $20.00. Also, the connections were not easy. You could call twenty times in a row and the call would go through only once, or maybe the call wouldn't even go through. After that, they came up with the phone cards, and I would buy a whole lot of those. At the end of a year when I counted up those $10.00 phone cards, it would be a lot of money. Nowadays, we use something called WhatsApp for $55.00 a month. If you have it, and whoever you are calling has it too, you can talk as many times as you want and for as long as you want, for that $55.00. I see now that a lot of people from foreign countries have it too, and it's a big thing. It makes a huge difference. You don't have to worry about how long your call is, and for us, it works very good.

THE FLYING MIJINKO BAND

In 1994, Akiria Sakata, a very famous saxophone player from Japan, put together a great group of musicans from around the world for a tour. The band members who were from Asian countries were: Sakata on saxophone, one Japanese guy playing double bass, another playing a Japanese flute, and another playing piano, plus a woman playing violin and three women playing hand drums and singing. The rest of us were: me playing the kora, Bill Laswell on electric bass, Nicky Skopelitis on electric guitar, Anton Fier on trap drums, and Aïyb on hand drums and other percussion. Sakata gave our group the name of Flying Mijinko Band.

He also got some big funding from the Japan Foundation to do the tour, and all our performances were recorded. Any place we went that had a Japanese embassy, they arranged everything for us: a bus to wherever we needed to go, a fine hotel, food, and everything. Later on, the Japan Foundation also produced a live CD from two of the last shows, called Flying Mijinko Band/Central Asian Tour. When they first contacted me to go on the tour, I wasn't sure. But when they told me that we would also go to Mongolia, I said yes because I had never met anybody from Mongolia, except one throat singer guy who was visiting Tokyo one time when I was touring there. But it turned out that our whole tour was amazing to me.

It began on Wednesday, August 17th and lasted until Wednesday, September 28th. We went to the cities of Tokyo and Hiroshima in Japan, Bejing and Hohot in China, Moscow in Russia, Tashkent and Samarkand in Uzbekistan, and Uulaanbaatar in Mongolia. We also had time to go out and explore those cities too. That was a very great thing about this tour! When we arrived in Tashkent, the capital of Uzbekistan, I left the hotel and went to the market with a translator, to look at all kinds of things they were selling there. My translator showed me one kind of bread they made which they said will last three years, and all you have to do is warm it up! It was round and big, and hard like a big plate. I didn't buy it, because my translator told me that the bread said 1992 on it and I was thinking, "Not me, not some two year old bread". Then we all went to Sammarkand, Uzbekistan in two big buses. On the way there, we came to a place on the roadside and our host said, "We are going to get some watermelon here". Farmers always bring their fruits to the roadside there, and the watermelon was in a pile like a mountain! The watermelon and grapes they had were unbelievable, extra sweet almost like honey. And the watermelon was a very, very long shape, but not round. I liked it so much that I kept a lot of seeds with me to take to Africa. Later on I planted them but they did not grow. Their grapes also were long and greenish-colored, and so sweet with no seeds!

We arrived in Samarkand on September 3rd, and we had the next day off, so I went sightseeing there too. First I went to the market with two translators: one was a Japanese woman, and one was a woman named Nasheba who was from Tashkent. When we arrived, everybody stopped everything they were doing in the market, and people flew to me and gathered around. Right away, I knew that they were not used to seeing black people. Everywhere I went in the town, all the people were following me. Nasheba said, "Look here Musa, look here at these people!" I had my camera with me, and I gave it to her so she could take pictures of me and the crowd. All the people in the whole market came and crowded me. Even some Uzbekistan army guys on a truck all came and crowded me to take a picture with them. The only word I could understand them saying was, "Muhammed Ali, Muhammed Ali!" which they were saying over and over. I have a video of this too! Those kinds of things didn't bother me, because I knew there were still places in the world where people never saw a living black person. On September 5th, we played a concert in Samarkand at the Registan, a very old, historic spot in the middle of the city. It is a giant public square surrounded by three big Islamic schools and other ancient buildings. It's so big and covered with mosaics, it's unbelieveable.

•••••

Then we flew to Moscow and stayed overnight, but we didn't play a concert there. When we came to the airport, it was very difficult to get to the outside because there were lots of people pushing everybody, and nothing was organized. We were lucky that the Japanese Embassy made things go quick for us! We stayed at the Hotel Ukrainian, which was across from President Yeltsin's office near the Moscow River. It was a very fancy hotel, and there were guards on every floor right by the elevator door, who were supposed to be watching the halls. Our guitar player Nicky Skopelitis closed his door and while he was asleep, somebody came into his room and stole his bag with his passport and $900.00. The next morning when we all woke up, we went and asked the hotel people to talk to the guard, and he said he didn't see anybody. We went looking, looking, looking all around, and finally somebody said they found the bag in the lobby with the cash gone. Luckily, the passport was still there.

In Moscow, they have stores when you can buy things only with American dollars, but no Russian rubles. You can see people standing in the square who are looking at everybody going in and out of those stores. They stand in front looking in, because they can't afford to buy anything in there. Those people might only make $40.00 a month, so it's very sad for them. When I was in Moscow sometime around 1982, it was a communist country and it took 250 rubles to equal one American dollar, but by 1994 it was 500 rubles for one dollar. I think those people should have stayed communist, because they tried to be capitalist overnight, and capitalism cannot happen that way. It's impossible, and it brought a big rate of crime in their country. Anyone who has the chance wants to leave there now.

The next morning, I left my hotel and came to a restaurant for breakfast and tea. While I was sitting there, a lady walked to my table and said, "How are you?" Where are you from?" I looked at her and asked, "What's happening?" and she replied, "I know you are not from here. Do you want a wife?" I said, "Why you asking me this? Get away, I don't want to talk to you". Then she walked into the restaurant kitchen. Not even a minute later, three armed men came in the restaurant, went into that kitchen, put handcuffs on her and a gun to her head and the chef's head, and led them both outside. I got out of that place quick and went to my hotel room. Later on I came down to get on the bus with everybody in the band for sightseeing, and we went to the University of Moscow and other places, then left to go to Mongolia.

•••••

When we arrived in the Mongolian capital city of Ulaanbaatar, we stayed overnight in a downtown hotel. Then they drove us to a camp-like place, and I liked what I was seeing everywhere. The walls of the Mongolian round tents had art on them, and everything inside was covered in red and blue designs. Inside each tent, there was a fireplace, and the chimney went way up though the roof. There were about 30 people in our group, so there were a lot of those round tents, which they call yurts. It all reminded me so much of my village in Gambia! I was also thinking about how different it is where I come from, and that from where we were, I wouldn't be able to even point to the direction of Africa. There was no forest or trees anywhere around us, just miles of short grass and wide, open space. From the camp place, I could see the men with camels, goats, and sheep far, far away.

The only problem I had that day was a very bad cold and headache. Everything else was so sweet. At nighttime, they put three of us in each yurt, with wooden beds to sleep in, and they built a fire for us. But that night, by around two or three o'clock in the morning, the fire went off and there was no other wood around for me to keep it going. I was getting so cold, sneezing with a running nose, and shaking. I tried to cover myself with all the blankets they had there, but no matter how many blankets I put on, I was still cold. I was in a big hurry for daytime when the sun would come up, and I was so happy when it started warming up a little bit outside.

In the morning, they organized a show for us in the camp, with traditional throat singers and a traditional fiddle-type instrument. A very good woman singer was there and sang for us. Around noontime, we walked a little way away from the camp, and they said that they would cook some meat for us. In fact, the whole time we were there, whenever they said, "It's time for food", our meal was only meat, for breakfast, lunch, and dinner. That day they killed a sheep, but they didn't cut its throat. They cut a hole in its chest, then a guy put his hand in and twisted the heart while holding the sheep's mouth and legs. The animal's heart broke and it died. I saw some ladies in our band who were crying, and some men with us who were looking very shocked. That didn't shock me though, because where I grew up in Gambia, the main hobby I enjoyed is hunting. In fact, I would like to be hunting in the bush every day. But the guys and ladies with us had never seen anything like that before, so it was a shock. After they killed that sheep, they skinned it. They took the skin off the meat in a perfect way, like a bag. The whole skin stayed together, with only the little hole in the chest. Then they cooked the meat in two different ways. Some of it they put inside the bag of the skin with some cut onions. Then they built a fire, and put some smooth rocks inside the fire until they became red-hot. They took those hot rocks and put them inside the bag of skin, and tied everything up inside so no steam could come out. They also lit another fire outside with a little gas torch, and burned all the hair off the skin while the stones were cooking everything inside. Their second way of cooking was inside a tall pressure cooker, but it was not electric. They put hot rocks on the bottom, then the meat inside with onions, and then more hot rocks on top until it was full. Then they closed the top very tight. I have a video of this too.

While the meat was cooking, I was saying to myself, "I am not going to eat this meat, it won't get hot enough to cook well". So I took a walk for two or three blocks away from the people, and layed down to think. All along our tour, the Japanese TV crew was filming and interviewing people, and they came over to interview me and ask me what I was thinking about. I replied, "I am just thinking about where I am now and where I was born. Here there are no trees, no tall grass, and no big leaves, and I like the way people are living here. In any place you go in my childhood part of Gambia, there are no crowded cities or anything like that, just how it is here outside Ulaanbaatar". After that, I came back to where everybody was, and the people told us that the food was ready. That meat tasted really, really good! I was so surprised how good it was. It's unbelievable! So I said to myself, "Well these people have been cooking this meat like this for a million years, so they know how to do it".

That night, even though I liked it so much in the camp, I told them to drive me into the city because I didn't want to stay there a second night. I told them, "I need to go to Ulaanbaatar because I am not recovered yet, and I can't be in the cold at night any more". So they brought me to a hotel in center of the city, next to the Red Square. My hotel was the only finished one I saw, but there was one unfinished hotel nearby. In fact, there was nothing much in downtown Ulaanbaatar at that time except people with cows or camels passing by. When I got to my hotel room, it was very different than in a typical western hotel, even though it was the #1 hotel. There was just a small day bed and TV, but when I turned it on, there was Ted Koppel on CNN! Right in the middle of Mongolia. I couldn't believe it! That was the first time I heard the English language since we started touring. For weeks, it was like I was in a bottle, but when I saw that Ted Koppel, I forgot about my cold and just watched the world news the rest of the night, because finally I could understand what was being said.

The next morning was Sunday, September 18th, and I went with Sakata, the road manager, and another lady named Cisco to a place outside the city where there was a weekly marketplace. I still had a cold, but I was feeling better. In that whole market, the people were looking at me too. That was a big crowd. Any direction I went, people were watching me. But I always say, "Once you travel a lot in the world, you will see a whole lot of stuff". On the way walking back to town, we decided we should get a taxi, so we started getting ready to do some flagging, but we didn't see any taxi. Then somebody there told us, "You can stop any car and they will pick you up, and then you can pay them". So we did that, and somebody stopped right away! We told them to take us downtown, and when we got there I bought a leather jacket for $200.00. It was a modern jacket, but it was made so good and looks good too. That was the only really big thing I bought on the tour, and I still have it!

• • • • •

The next day, we flew from Ulaanbaatar to Hohhot, China. When we came to the airport, we were in the waiting room and I was sitting on a sofa, near a picture of Genghis Khan on the wall. I didn't know it, but my foot was pointing to the picture, and somebody came and tapped my knee to say, "Will you bring your leg down?" I asked him, "What's happening?" and he replied, "Please take your foot down and don't point it to him, because he is our heavy leader". So I put my foot down because I respect their tradition. In Mongolia, they still respect Ghengis Khan as if he is still alive. I don't know about today, but in those days, they still had Ghengis Khan's picture on their currency, called the tugrik.

That day it was very, very cold out, but not just because I was sick. I don't know whether they didn't have heat, or they just liked to fly like that, but that was the coldest day I ever was inside an airplane. There were no lights inside the plane either. I asked for blankets and they gave me three of them, but for the whole flight I was just freezing. I could even see my breath! When we arrived at the Hohhot airport and they opened the plane door, all of us started coming down the outside staircase to walk to the terminal. The moment the Chinese people saw me, they all stopped everything to just look. They all followed me, just like at the market in Samarkand, to see what kind of passport I would pull out and what I would say. All the airport workers gathered around the immigration place to watch, and the immigration people kept looking back and forth at my Gambian passport and me. Then we got on the bus to come to the Zhaojun Hotel in the center of the city. The moment we walked inside, the receptionist and everybody else in the lobby were just looking at me too.

Later on, I came down to do some sightseeing, because there was all kind of games there, camels, shooting target practice stuff, and lots of other things happening. But the moment I arrived, people came all around me. I left the square and walked down the street just to see what would happen, and the people followed me in a big crowd! Whenever I stopped, they stopped, and whenever I walked, they walked. One time I stopped and pretended to look inside my shoulder bag, and the crowd gathered around me like a circle. I said, "Hey what's happening? What's wrong with you people?" Everybody just started laughing because they didn't understand what I was saying. I told them, "I'm from Africa", but they just laughed at anything I said! They followed me all the way back to the gate of the hotel, and then I went inside again.

On Tuesday the 20th, we were not playing a concert, but still in Hohhot, and I was walking around again. This time, only a few people followed me. I went to a department store that was selling suits, and bought one. I came back to the hotel to try it on, and the pants were OK, but I wanted the jacket to come to my knee and it was too short. By that time it was around four or five o'clock in the afternoon, so I was thinking, "I should go back there fast". I walked quickly there to tell them the jacket is too short, and I found one that was long enough. Luckily, they understood English there a little bit. The weather was really hot that day, and I was wearing a sleeveless t-shirt and jeans. While I was walking back, I saw people cooking corn over charcoal and said to myself, "I want to buy some of that, because that's how we do it in Gambia". A crowd came around me again, and a boy came up and wiped my arm and then looked at his hand. I said, "Hey, get away from me, what are you doing?" He wanted to see if my skin was painted and would rub off! In our whole group, my friend Aïyb and me were the only two black people. When I was growing up, I heard stories about this happening to black people, but this is the first time I ever had this happen to me personally.

When I came back to the hotel that evening, everybody told me that Aïyb got some kind of sickness and had to go to the hospital, but that it was no big thing. After dinner, me and Nicky and Anton said, "Let's go check on him" and we asked for directions. We got to the hospital, and Aïyb was in a room with a bunch of people, in a bed with wires hooked up to him. It was the wrong place though, because it was a hospital for people that went crazy! One guy there walked out the front door, and then came to the back door and asked to come in that way. The people there told him to go back to the front door, and that guy got mad and threw a big brick through the window. Luckily, it was a plastic window so it did not break. Then he started looking for another brick to throw, and all the nurses started running. All of a sudden Aïyb became a well man, and we cut all the wires off him and all ran back to the hotel!

On Wednesday the 21st, we played at the Ulan Red Color Theater in Hohhot, and all kinds of people came there to hear us. The next day we went to Beijing, and when we first arrived and I looked at all the people there, my impression was, "Do all those people have a place to live? Do all those people have a wife, mothers and fathers, sons and daughters?" I looked at how many bicycles were around Tiananmen Square, and wondered, "Do every one of these bike owners know which bike is theirs?" I was wondering this because I heard a long, long, time ago, even before I came to the U.S., that nobody owns a bike in China. People said that when you just see a bike, you can just take it, ride it somewhere, and then park and leave it. That was a fascinating thing to me.

In Gambia, we use a bike to transport things too, but China is #1 for that. My hotel room window looked down on a big street that was always full of people on bikes. There were also huge places where so many bikes were parked that I called them bike cities. I could see very few people who were walking. One day I was looking out of my hotel room, way, way down to the street, and I saw a guy on a bike that had two wheels in back and one wheel in front. He piled a big load on top of this bike, and it was unbelievable for me to see that a bike can carry it! He was pedaling, but he could only go slow because his load was so big. I opened my window and took a picture of this guy, because I couldn't believe he could even move his bike. Then I called a friend of mine named Alhaji Jawara at his home in Gambia, because when I first met him in 1972 or 1973, he went to China to take some kind of course and told me all about it after he came back. I called him and said, "Alhaji, I am in your city", and he said, "Who is this?" I told him it was me, and that I was in China. He said, "Wow", and I said, "You said there are a lot of people in China. I say to you, in ten minutes it's very easy to set your eye on one million people. The way the streets are filled, it's unbelievable. Men and their wives, all the kids, the grandparents, everybody is out there on the bikes. I think even a baby in the stomach here can ride a bike!" Alhaji was laughing to remember those bikes too.

All the Chinese cities I have seen have a big square in the middle, with a whole lot of buildings all around and facing it. Our hotel was next to a square like that too. The work that they were doing in that city was all by hand. Across from our hotel, they were building a very big building, and a whole lot of people, maybe more than a hundred, were digging holes by hand. I was sitting looking out my window way down at them when I saw some people bringing big cooking pots to the workers, and starting to dish out scoops of just rice for them to eat.

We all went to visit the Forbidden City also, to see the rulers, their kings, and their history. I liked that. Chinese people are something else. They are very hard workers and they stick together. You find them all over the world, because no place in the world is unfamiliar to them. They are used to everything, and nothing will be strange to them, even if on the right hand side of a street are all fancy buildings, and on the left hand side there are corrugated metal houses with tires on the roof. In every big city in the U.S. there is a Chinatown, and you can get everything Chinese there too, just like if you were in China. After just two days in Bejing, we flew to Tokyo and checked into the Prince Hotel in Shinjuku. We had Saturday the 24th off to do more sightseeing in Tokyo, which was very interesting too. Then on Sunday and Monday, we did big concerts for the Japan Foundation in their big building. There were a whole lot of people there, and the concert hall was jam-packed. On Tuesday we had another day off, and on Wednesday the 28th, I flew back to Chicago.

I wasn't there long though, because on October 6th I flew to San Francisco and did a concert with Kronos at the Stanford University Memorial Auditorium on the 7th. After flying right back to Chicago, for some reason I decided to fly to New York for a visit from October 12th to the 22nd. Then from December 11th-13th, I did a three shows in a row with a harp player, in Nashville, Phoenix, and San Francisco, and then I flew back to Chicago for a month. And the year of 1995 would begin with a big, big thing for me.

A CITIZEN OF THE UNITED STATES

I became very happy on Thursday, January 5th, 1995 because that's the day I became a citizen of the United States. Before that, I had a permanent resident green card ever since 1984, which my lawyer Ellen Armstrong from LA helped me to get. However, I was still holding only a Gambian Passport, and I still had to apply for a visa for many of the places I traveled to. The other band members would sit around waiting for me, and I had to go around and around and around to all kinds of embassies to apply for visas. So I said to myself, "I want to become a citizen of the U.S. because I have been living here now for almost 20 years".

To become a U.S. citizen, the government wants you to learn a whole lot about this country. The Chicago immigration office gave me a little book with a lot of questions and answers for me to study, and then I had to pass a test to become a citizen. I went in for the test on Tuesday May 30th, 1994, right in the middle of flying all over the place doing shows with Yakub Addy, Tony and Tim, and Kronos and taking my third trip to Gambia that year! I had to go in a little office with a guy who worked there and was going to ask me the test questions. I was doing a whole lot of studying to prepare, but was still a little worried because it was so many questions. That office guy gave me the test and signed my papers. Then the immigration people set the date of January 5th for me to come and become a citizen.

On that day, there were around 130 other people there too. We all went in a big room where there was a judge, and they called each person one by one, to come up to the front. They gave each of us a pamphlet and then we all went to sit down. Then everybody stood up and recited the words for swearing in, and they congratulated everybody. Immediately after that, I went across the street to to the passport place. I wanted to go to Gambia soon after that, and have a U.S. passport! I got the picture for it and brought it to the office, handed them the forms and everything, and my new passport arrived in less than two weeks. I've been using my U.S. passport ever since then, and I always renew it before it expires. I still have my Gambian passport, but I usually use the U.S. one to travel, especially when visiting a toubab county.

On Friday February 3rd, I flew to Gambia. Three weeks later on Sunday, February 26th, Bobo woke me up in the middle of the night because she was in labor! We had a new baby son that day! The next Sunday, March 5th, I named my son after my father's brother Lamin Suso, and to show our heavy respect we put Ba before his name to call him Balamin. Our baby-naming ceremony for him was done a week later on March 12th, with all the people gathered around and having a big celebration. I was happy I could stay in Brikama for the next few weeks.

After coming back to the U.S., I had some quiet weeks in Chicago before things got busy again. I flew to LA to play with Kronos on May 13th at the Schoenberg Hall on the UCLA campus, and then back to Chicago. A few days later I flew to Miami for a solo kora concert at the Colony Theater, then back to Chicago again. On Thursday June 1st, I flew to Seattle to do some recording with Uno in his studio. From June 2nd to the 8th, me and Uno worked on a five or six song demo of me playing solo kora and singing. Emily also sang on one of the songs, and their friend Jed played guitar on a song. On one other song, a pregnant lady named Toni sang on it, who was married to a Gambian guy I met in Seattle. I flew back to Chicago on June 9th, stayed there a week, and then flew to New York to do some more recording with Bill. On June 20th, I did some playing on somebody else's record, overdubbing kora tracks. After around a week in New York, I flew back to Chicago for the rest of June and July. On August 1st, I flew to New York again for about the millionth time! I was there for a week, and did some recording on Pharoh Sanders' record that Bill was producing, called Message from Home. On Saturday September 2nd, Mandingo Griot Society got together for the first time in quite a while to perform at the Rockford Festival in Rockford Illinois and at the Chicago African Art Festival on the 3rd.

The following Thursday, I went to Mexico with my trio: Manu Walton on conga drums and other percussion, and Abdul Hakeem on guitar. We did a very nice concert at Theatero Manuel Doblado in Leone, Mexico. The next month on October 8th, we played a fundraising concert in New York for one of our older African artists, named Alhaji Camara. The concert was for the World Music Insitute, and happened at the Symphony Space. Alhaji Camara is a very good drummer who came to United States in 1968 or 1969 with Ballet Africa from Guinea. He remained living in New York for all those years, and the fundraiser was for him to be able to go back to Africa to live in Dakar. After he returned, he didn't last a long, long time before he passed away. I came back to Chicago a few days later, and then soon after that, Mandingo Griot Society did another show, this time at the Stevens Center on the University of Notre Dame campus in South Bend, Indiana on October 26th. After two more months back in Chicago, I went home to Gambia on Monday December 18th.

•••••

Right after I arrived in Gambia, I bought a Toyota Corolla car to be able to travel from Brikama to Cassamance, and then to Guinea-Bissau. I wanted to talk to the griots in all those places, and make arrangements with them for recording and photography, before the time when Bill Laswell was going to arrive. We were working on a book and CD project called Jali Kunda: Griots of West Africa and Beyond. I came up with the whole idea for this project, to go around and record and photograph a whole lot of griots in Mandingo areas. Bill knew a guy from Elipsis Arts, the name of the company that published the book and CD project, and arranged for all that to happen.

I left Brikama the day after I bought the car, and from December 22nd to January 8th, 1996, I traveled to all these Mandingo areas to get things ready. On the 9th, I went back to Brikama because Bill was arriving along with a famous French photographer named Daniel Laine', and a recording engineer named Oz Fritz. On Saturday January 13th, we recorded Gambian kora players in my compound in Brikama, and the next day we also recorded Gambian balafon players in my compound. After a day of rest, we traveled to a town in Cassamance called Kolda, and on Wednesday the 17th, we recorded the Mandingo griots playing kora along with Fulani drummers there. Then we drove to Tabato in Guinea-Bissau, and recorded griots playing balafon there on the 18th. After that, right away we drove to Gabou in Guinea-Bissau, which is also called Chinchang Hok, and the next day we recorded griots playing kora there. On the 20th we came back to Gambia, rested again on the 21st, and Bill and all his people flew back to New York on January 22nd. In all, there were 11 kora players recorded including me, 20 vocalists including my wife Bobo, 7 balafon players, 2 nyanye players, and 8 drummers. I played percussion also.

•••••

After the Gambian military took over power in 1994, the first good thing they did in Brikama was to put streetlights there, all the way from Brikama College to the middle of the town on both sides of the street. On Monday February 2nd, 1996 they turned all the streetlights on at once for the first time. People were going crazy and hollering, and everybody came out to stand under the lights and look at each other. The whole village had a big celebration.

That same month, something big also happened in my family. In our tradition, when a man and woman marry and have children, but later on they divorce, the children will typically stay with the father. The reason we do that is because we believe every man should take care of his children. If the woman goes to marry another man, he should not have to take care of another man's children. Sometimes it doesn't happen exactly that way. Also in our tradition we also have child support, but it's different than in the U.S. Our child support is not based on a payment of money every month. Gambia is a farming country, so the child support is paid with crops themselves, not with money. When you work on your farm and harvest your crops, that is when you should go to the people taking care of your child and pay the child support. If you don't do that, and later on if you want to take the child and raise it yourself, the people will say no to you. They will say, "It doesn't go like that, because all the food the child ate all these years comes from us".

Many years before, my blood brother Mahamadou married and had a child, a boy named Kauboya. But when Mahamadou and his wife divorced, he did not keep their child. One day, my mother told me, "The child went with the wife. Mahamadou told her to take the child, because he doesn't want to". Then my mom said to me, "Go and get your son", because in our tradition he is my child too. So on Tuesday, February 6th, I sent two friends of mine named Balla Camara and Kausu Sisay to the village called Tambasansang, where Mahamadou's wife Fatou Kanuteh was living. Tambasansang is the same village where my father's father Jali Falai Suso was from, and Mahamadou's wife is a relative of ours too.

Mahamadou was mad about things, and he did not do anything to pay child support. So when Balla and Kausu went to Tambasansang to deliver my message to our elder people there, they said, "Before we let him go, you must pay the child support for our son Kauboya". So I paid all this and all the other necessary things. On February 7th, Balla and Kausu arrived back in my compound with Kauboya. I stayed there in Brikama for the rest of the month, and then flew to Chicago. Kauboya was around four or five years old at that time, and he has lived with us in our compound from that day on.

•••••

The rest of the Jali Kunda project was going to happen back in New York, including more recording for the CD, so I flew to New York to work some more on it with Bill and others at Green Point Studio, from March 22nd to the 30th. Philip played piano, Bill played bass, and Pharoh Sanders played saxophone. There was also a bunch of interviews done for the book, and many people also wrote pieces for it. The British singer Robert Palmer wrote the introduction, an American writer named Amiri Baraka wrote the liner notes along with my friend Kwabena Nketia from the University of Ghana, and Philip was one of the interviewers too. I did a lot of interviews for the written part of the book while I was in New York, and they also sent a woman named Iris Brooke to Chicago on June 2nd to interview me for a long time, and write a piece about my life for the book. Later that year, the CD and book set was released. The CD has 15 songs, and the book has over 100 pages.

On June 5th, I went back to New York for a big panel discussion at the St. Moritz Hotel, which was all based on African musicians and world music musicians. There were a lot of heavy musicians there, including Yakub Addy, Kwabena Nkatia, and David Harrington from Kronos. On the 7th, there was a big African Troubadors Concert at Town Hall in New York, with me, Adam Rudolph, Hassam Hakmoun from Morocco, James Makubuya from Uganda, and Yaya Jallo from Mali. I stayed in New York for another week to play a concert with Pharoh Sanders and his group at the Central Park Summer Festival on June 15th, and then I came back to Chicago for two months. On August 11th, I went back to New York for a concert with some other string players at Avery Fisher Hall in Lincoln Center, which was put together by the composer and violinist Edna Michell. That day, another very famous composer and violinist was there named Yehudi Menuhin. The event was a tribute concert for him, but I am not sure if he also composed some of the music we played.

After another month back in Chicago, I got the happy news on Tuesday, September 17th, 1996 that my brother Dembo and his wife had their second child, a little girl. They delayed the baby-naming ceremony until the end of December, when I would be in Gambia for another West African trip, this time with Akira Sakata. On October 2nd, the sad news came that Jali Sidiki Jobarteh, one of our very famous kora players who lived in Mali for a long time, died that day in Bansang, Gambia. That was the village he was born and raised in, and it was a shock to everyone because he had gone to Bamako, Mali for close to 50 years and had a big family there, and just recently came back for a visit. One day he was walking by the riverside in Bansang, and he suddenly had a heart attack and died. Jali Sidiki Jobarteh was also related to Amadou Jobarteh, who came to Seattle as a visiting professor for the University of Washington in 1987, and recorded with Uno in his studio during that time. A friend of Uno's named Jon Kertzer, who is an ethnomusicology guy, helped make that happen, and later on that music was released as a CD called Tabara.

I played with Kronos again at the Krannert Performing Arts Center on the University of Illinois at Champaign-Urbana on November 10th, and at BAM in New York on the 15th. That was the first time I ever played at BAM, which stands for Brooklyn Academy of Music. In between those two Kronos concerts, Mr. Kamasu from TV Tokoyo came to Chicago to meet with me about making a big West Africa music trip with Akira Sakata to Gambia, Senegal, and Mali.

SAKATA IN AFRICA

On Wednesday, December 4th 1996, I flew to Gambia so I could see my family for a few weeks before the tour with Sakata would begin. Then on December 24th, I went up to Dakar to meet all the Japanese people on the tour: Sakata, a video crew, an audio crew, and a crew from TV Tokyo. The next day was Christmas, and we all went to a Christian church in Dakar and watched them celebrating Christmas and singing songs. The Japanese TV people filmed some of that, and then we went to Gori Island, where millions of African people were brought to put on slave ships and taken to the United States, South America, and other places. We spent a lot of time looking around there, and then I sat on top of a giant old cannon and played my kora while Sakata played his saxophone, while the TV people filmed us. Afterward, we came back to the Taranga Hotel in Dakar.

On December 26th, we traveled to another village in Senegal called Mbambilor. Between that village and the Atlantic Ocean is a place called Pink Lake, where the salt comes up out of the ground. It is a very shallow lake filled with pink salt, and no life can be in that water there. There is a big layer of salt at the bottom of the water, and you can scoop it up like little rocks. A whole lot of people go to that lake and harvest the salt. They stand in the water up to their thigh or waist, with their buckets that are like a basket or sieve, and then they dump it into little wooden canoes. When the canoes are full, they pull them back to shore with a rope. When the people first scoop the salt into their bucket, it looks a little bit ashy. Then they take it to the shore to dump it, and everybody has their own little mountain of salt. The wind blows the ashy-looking stuff off, and the next day the salt is white like snow and it can be packaged. Anyone can go to Pink Lake to get this salt, women and men from any profession or family. People with big trucks will come there to buy salt from all the harvesters' mountains, fill up thousands of bags, and take it all over Senegal and neighboring countires to sell in the cities and towns. We don't have a lake like this in Gambia, so all our salt comes from Pink

Lake. In a place called Mopti in northern Mali, there is a salt place too, but they dig it up in big bricks from a dry salt lake to take to the market and sell.

The next day, we all flew from Dakar to Banjul. I took them all to the Novotel Hotel in Fajara, which is now called the Kombo Beach Hotel, then I went to my house in Brikama. Saturday, December 28th was the day of the baby-naming ceremony and celebration for my brother Dembo's daughter. They named her Sendin, after our mother's elder sister. The celebration was at my compound in Brikama where we all lived, and I played there with Sakata and some other kora and balafon musicians. Griot women were also singing, and the TV Tokyo crew filmed it all. The next morning, Sakata's people sent a car to pick me at my compound and take me to the Novotel Hotel, and then we all traveled back to Dakar.

•••••

On Monday, December 30th, we all flew to Bamako, Mali and checked into the Grand Hotel. The next morning, we went to the Mopti region of Mali, where the Dogon people live. We first went to one town called Sévaré, and then to another town called Sangha. The TV Tokoyo people rented a small plane with a pilot for us to travel in, but that plane only fit eight or nine people inside. They also hired a Malian chef to cook for us. That night we stayed in Sangha. There were tourists from all over the world staying in one of the two hotels there also, or camping next to them. I called the place we stayed, "The Stone Hotel" because the whole thing was made out of rocks. It's nothing like what we know as a hotel in the rest of the world. Even the windows were just a small round hole in the wall, around the size of a big plate. When the wind came in those windows it made a low, wooooooooooo sound. That hotel was built way up high on the side of a big hill, and in fact, whole towns are like that in the Dogon country.

On Wednesday, January 1st, 1997 the people of Sangha arranged a Dogon masked dance for us. The TV Tokyo crew filmed it, and I took a video of it too. The next day, we went to another Dogon village way high on the mountain, called Yougopri. Dogon country is something else. The people are farmers who like to live way up high, but all their farms are down at the bottom of the valley. They are the #1 onion growers in all of Mali. They can grow those onions even on hard rock! In fact, when you arrive, you can smell the onions before you even see them. The only difference between the Dogon people's onions and our Gambian onion is that their onion is a smaller size, but otherwise it's the same yellow onion.

Since Yougopri is way high, the young men from the village came down the mountain to meet us at the bottom and help us go up. They carried all our bags, the TV equipment, and everything else. When the rest of us were walking up, we could not carry anything. There was no road, only the places where the Dogon people's footprints were for thousands of years. While I was going up that mountain, I said to myself, "Even if somebody pays me twenty thousand dollars, I will never walk back up here! After all that climbing, we all got to Yougopri village on top. The whole time we were there, our chef stayed at the bottom of the mountain to cook the food. Whenever he was finished cooking, those young Dogon guys would run down to pick up the food and bring it up to us. I admired those guys so much who can go up and down the mountain like that! To them, it was nothing to climb up and down, over and over again in one day.

In Yougopri, all the houses were built out of rocks, and also built inside the mountain's rocks, like caves. The mayor's name was Abulai Dumbo, and we all went to his house, which was made inside those rocks. In front of the entrance, there was a rock overhang and a bench made from wood. The people welcomed us there with talking drums, the mayor and his son were playing drums made from a calabash, and his sisters and other women were dancing. Me and Sakata also played with them, but I played talking drum instead of kora. At the center of the village, there was a small gathering place, like the bantabas we have in Gambia. In the middle of that place, there was a big Fig tree and a lot of shade. But the fruit on it was different that the figs we have, it was very tiny. We all had a sleeping bag and a mat to sleep on in that gathering place, with the rocks up over our heads. The Japanese TV people were going around and around the village, taking pictures and filming.

Whenever I looked down from that village, I almost got dizzy. When you look out, you can see way way down for miles. It's unbelievable! Way above us, there was a tall cliff with holes in it. Whenever the Yougopri people die, they are taken up there to be buried. Young men make a way to climb up there, and then drop a rope down to hoist the body up for this burial. The TV people said, "Suso, we want you to play the kora way up high on top of that cliff", so we zig-zagged back and forth to get up there, and they filmed me playing. I was in a big hurry to finish though, so I could come back down again!

•••••

On Saturday, January 4th, we all left Yougopri and went down the mountain. We went to Sangha again, then went to Mopti and checked into the Kanaga Hotel. The next morning, we went to the marketplace in Mopti, and then got onto two big wooden boats with grass roofs, that they hired for a long journey on the River Niger all the way to Timbuktu. Many different boats of all sizes travel that river journey, which takes around three days. On the way, everyone has to camp on the riverbank, because in many parts of the journey there are no villages at all. For our journey, some people were with our chef in one boat where he was cooking, and Sakata and me and a few other people were in the other boat. We would all stop and get together to eat our food when it was ready. That first night on the boats, we arrived in Kokoye village and pitched our tent in somebody's compound. Kokoye is in the Bosso people's area, and they are a fisherman tribe. That night, I had a cold and headache, and I joined some of the Bosso people who had built a fire next to their house. I sent somebody to get a kind of tea called ataya, which is made from mint, and we drank it together. Some of the Japanese people joined us too, and it was a sweet thing.

On the 6th, we left Kokoye in our boats and headed for Timbuktu. After the whole day on the River Niger, we reached a town by the riverside called Niafunké. This is the town that Ali Farka Touré is from. I had a cold and headache that day too, and we pitched our tent on the riverbank at nighttime to sleep in our sleeping bags. We arrived in Timbuktu the next day, and for two days we went all around with the Japanese TV crew filming. On the 9th, we flew in a small plane from Timbuktu to Gao, and then to Kidal. Kidal is a far away town, near the northeastern border of Mali where it meets Algeria. That area is where the Tuareg people live. When we arrived in Kidal, there were Tuareg rebels in the desert who wanted Mali to be divided in two between eastern and western, and the guy we stayed with was the the leader of the rebels. That guy brought two cars, and took us out into the middle of the desert to the Tuareg people's camel dance. When we went driving out into the desert, we would see the rebels standing by the roadside, but they always recognized the cars of their leader, so they just waved and let us pass without stopping. At the camel dance, men were riding the camels all around in a big circle, and the camels were all decorated with a whole bunch of colorful stuff. Women were sitting inside the circle, playing hand drums, dancing, and hollering. I have a video of this too! I even climbed up on a camel's back and Sakata did too, and we rode the camels a little bit. Then we all came back to Kidal, to the rebel leader's house to stay overnight. That fighting is still going on there, even now after all these years.

On January 10th, we drove out to another part of the desert. It was very cold and dusty, so dusty that I was even in a hurry to come back to Bamako. The next day, we drove to Kidal, and took that small airplane to fly to Gao, then to Bamako. When we checked into Grand Hotel, I was so tired of the dust! Right away I jumped in the shower and washed, washed, washed until it was all off my body. The next day, we all left Bamako and flew to Dakar, and everyone else flew to France and then Japan.

I went home to Gambia and stayed in Brikama with my family for around two more months, and then came back to Chicago on March 27th. After I was home for a little over a month, sad news came to me again. My mom passed away suddenly in Brikama on May 1st, 1997. At that time, she was in her 80s. I was very glad that I was just there, and saw her almost every day for four months. Life is like that. You never know what is going to happen.

• • • • •

A few weeks later on May 18th, I did a solo kora concert at the Grusin Music Hall, on the campus of the University of Colorado in Boulder. Afterward, I flew back to Chicago and got ready to go to Germany on my way back to Gambia. On June 6th, I played a concert at the Frankfurt International Jazz Festival with Pharoh Sanders and a German bass player named Eberhard Weaver. On the 9th, I visited Augsberg, Germany, where my brother Sefou Suso lived, and stayed with him for a few days. Years later, he moved back to Gambia and died in car accident.

I left Germany and arrived in Gambia on June 15th, stayed in Brikama with my family until July 29th, then flew back to Chicago. A month later, Mandingo Griot Society got together again and played at the annual African Art Festival in Chicago, and then in early September I flew to New York and hung out with Philip until the 17th. On that day, my cousin Salieu Suso, who was also living in New York, went with me to Providence Rhode Island to visit a Senegalese friend, and I played a kora concert for him in his house. Except for another short trip to New York from October 22nd to November 4th, I was in Chicago for the rest of 1997.

JOOKA TIME

I also spent the first two months of 1998 in Chicago. Then on March 3rd, Manu took me to the airport to fly to New York for a month, so I could record six or seven traditional Jooka songs in Philip's 12-track home recording studio. I used a drum machine and then overdubbed the kora and all the singing, and then went back to Chicago.

Jooka is not regular kora music or singing. Jooka music is traditional farming songs for the people who were working out in the fields in olden days. The Jooka singer does not bend down to work, he walks in front of the men and sings their praises, how hard they work, how strong they are, and more. In those olden days, all people would be valued by their strength: a very strong farmer, wrestler, hunter, fisherman, king, or warrior. People also competed with each other on their strength for work. Work was what made somebody great, not how much money they had. You cannot chew a dollar bill to fill your stomach! In our tradition, we believe that everybody is equal on needing food, and that farming is the biggest thing in the whole world. It is very important to Mandingo culture. And all over the world it's like this too. Why? Because food is #1. Everybody is equal on that. A rich man cannot say, "Now I will never have to eat anything anymore". Even if you are president of the world, you gotta eat.

We Mandingos also have a saying "Anything you are able to save in this world, it's just the leftover of your stomach". For example, if somebody is starving to death and people bring one plate of food to that person, they would strip down naked if they had to in order to get the food. In fact, you can own a big giant house, but if you have nothing to eat for a long time and somebody comes along and says, "I will give you food if you give me your house", you will agree to that. If you have an airplane and that happens, you will give your airplane for one plate of food. You would give your car, or even a cruise ship in the ocean. Food is #1. The next big thing you need is where you sleep, and everything else in life comes after that.

While I was writing the songs, my mind went to the Jooka singers, because I remember them so well from my childhood time. Jooka music is all call-and-response. The Jooka singer calls, and the farmers in the field respond with one word or phrase. Each line of the Jooka singer's calls has different words anytime they open their mouth, but the farmers' response is always the same words no matter what the Jooka singer is singing.

In one of my Jooka songs, I wrote this response for the farmers to sing: "Traveler, traveler who will see the whole thing". And I sang the call, which was this:

"A group of strong farmers have a meeting"

"When they meet under the tree"

"They will ask each one of them to nickname their hoe"

"One will say, I'm strong, and my hoe is very strong, like a big scoop that can get the food from the boiling pot on the fire"

"One will say, my hoe is very very strong, it's like a scorpian that can make even grown men cry when it stings you",

"One will say, my hoe is very powerful, it's like an eagle that can snatch a fish from the middle of the ocean""

"One will say, my hoe is very very powerflul, like a flood that can wipe out the whole village"

It keeps going like that, because Jooka singers put a lot of words together to praise the workers. They sing about how they never get tired of working hard. And the men like to show each other how strong they are, and to work as hard as they can so they don't get left behind while working in the fields.

I wrote down the words to all the songs when I recorded the Jooka cassette. Later on that same year, I put that recording out on a cassette and took it to Gambia, and that cassette became very famous very quick. Usually Jooka songs are sung acapella by singers who also play a big bell in between their lines, and are not played or sung by a traditional kora player. So no one had ever heard my kind of Jooka music on a recording before, and my cassette became my biggest hit back home in Gambia, Cassamance, and Guinea-Bissau. It was much bigger than any record I made with anybody. Even though people knew me back home before this

Jooka tape, this music made a whole lot more people know about me. In fact, many people in Africa know me now only because of that cassette. Old men and old women will sometimes tell me that they never listen to any other music!

•••••

But before I could take my cassette to Gambia, I had a big concert to do with Philip in New York, of the music from The Screens. On May 4th, I flew there to rehearse with him and the other musicians for a couple of weeks, then flew back to Chicago. A month later on June 17th, I flew to New York again for two more days of reheasing, and then we performed an outdoor concert on Sunday, June 21st at the World Trade Center. It was Philip and his longtime collaborator Jon Gibson on flute, an Isreali percussion player named Zohar Fresco, and me. They set up a big stage between the two World Trade Center buildings for us to play on. Liz Thompson, the director of Jacob's Pillow in Massachusetts, is the person who arranged that concert. We became close friends back in 1987 and still keep in touch, and she has booked me and Philip to play together several times since this concert too.

On June 27th, we performed The Screens concert again at the Knitting Factory in New York, with all the same musicians. Then I flew home to Chicago, and made a quick trip to Indianapolis on July 2nd to take my Jooka recording to a manufacturing place. I had them make 5,000 copies for me. Later that month, my trio with Manu and Abdul played at the Artsgarden in Indianapolis on July 23rd, which is a great place inside a big glass dome. We stayed there overnight, and the next day I picked up my 5,000 cassettes from the manufacturer and went back to Chicago to get ready for my trip.

•••••

I arrived in Gambia on August 1st with my cassettes, and stayed until the end of October. When my cassettes hit the street, everybody wanted to buy them. People came to my compound and bought the cassettes all day long, and people even came from other countries to buy them. It was played on the radio in Gambia a whole lot too. Since Jooka is a traditional Mandingo thing, anybody who ever heard the Jooka music before liked it, because they had not heard anything like that for a long time. And the young people who never got to hear the Jooka music in the old days liked it because it was a new thing to them. People took those cassettes to their village and played them, and the other people liked it so much that they would even make copies on a boombox for all the other people in the village. Some cassette sellers in Gambia would buy two or three or four boxes from me, and each box had 30 cassettes in them. They would sell those cassettes in their stores, and then come back to find me and buy some more. Quickly, all the cassettes were sold. All the cassettes I made had my picture on them, but after I sold them all, some of those cassette seller people made more of their own copies to sell even without my picture. All those cassettes sold too.

While I was in Gambia, I also bought about eight koras and six balafons, and some small hand drums. Then I shipped them to the Gallery 37 Program in Chicago, where I was going to be an artist-in-residence and teach at-risk kids in an after-school program to play those instruments, and to do drumming and singing. Soon after I arrived back in the U.S. on October 30th, I made a short trip to Racine, Wisconsin to do a solo kora concert at the Prairie Performing Arts Center on November 7th, and then went back to Chicago. For the next two months, I was teaching the kids from that Gallery 37 Program in a few different schools in Chicago. I liked that so much!

•••••

On January 13th, 1999 I flew to New York again to rehearse for a concert with Kronos at the New Jersey Performing Arts Center. We did the concert on the 16th, and then I went back to Chicago for a month. On February 19th, I was back in New York to do a big benefit concert for Tibet House with Philip at Carnegie Hall. Philip helped to start Tibet House in 1987 as a cultural center for the Dalai Lama. Every year since then, he puts on an annual benefit concert there with a whole lot of other people. Our benefit concert was on Monday, February 22nd. Philip did a song with me called Spring Waterfall, which I wrote in 1996, and I also played some songs with Tre from the band Phish, and a Tibetan flute player named Nawang Khechog. Then I went back to Chicago for a week's time before leaving for Gambia, and I stayed in Brikama with my family for two months, from March to early May.

A few weeks after coming back to Chicago, I flew to Halifax, Nova Scotia to do two more concerts of The Screens with Philip, Jon Gibson, and the percussionist Zohar Fresco on May 28th and 29th. Our concert was in the Sir James Dunn Theater at the Dalhousie Art Center, which is on the University of Halifax campus. On the 30th, I gave a master class at that Dalhousie Art Center, playing the kora and talking to the students, and flew back to Chicago the next day. In the middle of June, I flew to New York just to hang around for a couple of weeks, then flew back to Chicago on July 3rd to spend a couple months there.

During that time, I was invited by a famous actress from England named Vanessa Redgrave to perform at a big concert event in Kosovo. She was working with the United Nations to arrange three days of music, theater, and dance performances to welcome the refugees back to Kosovo from all the nearby countries they went to during the big war that went on there for around ten years. On Friday, September 10th, I arrived in Skopje, Macedonia in the middle of the day along with Manu and Abdul. That night, we played a concert at the Universal Hall, and the next day we just stayed in our hotel room at The Continental. Philip was also there to perform, but as far as I could see, my trio was the only black musicians there. And besides Philip, everybody else was rock-n-rollers from England, Australia, and other places.

On Sunday the 12th, we drove from Skopje to the capital of Kosovo, a city called Pristina. Since the war had just ended there, they had to have the military people protect us. They put all of us musicians in two big buses, with the United Nations Peacekeeping Force in a jeep in front of us, and two big army tanks with machine guns behind us. As we were driving, we could see that most of the buildings had big holes in them everywhere. Then we played the big concert for the refugees there in Pristina. That concert was very good, and a whole lot of people were there. For those refugees, it might have been the sweetest thing they had seen in a long, long time because of all the fighting. After the concert, we all came back to Skopje with the jeeps and tanks escorting us again, and went back to the U.S. the next day.

After about a week or so back in Chicago, I flew to New York to rehearse for another big concert of The Screens with Philip, Jon Gibson, and a violin player named Ashley MacIsaac. We performed at the Metropolitan Museum of Art on September 27th to a jam-packed house. Afterward, I stayed on the east coast for another week, flew back to Chicago, then back to New York on October 11th to rehearse with Philip for another kind of concert. This was a benefit for an organization called Jewel Heart, which is a Tibetan Buddhist place that Philip is involved with. Our concert was on October 14th at a club in New York called the Fire House, and we did it with a modern dancer named Molissa Fenley who had worked with Philip for a long time.

On Sunday the 17th, me and Philip and Ashley flew to Ann Arbor, Michigan and played a concert together at the Hills Auditorium. Ziggy Marley was there also, and we tuned together and played a song his father Bob Marley wrote, called "The Redemption Song". After that show, I flew back to Chicago for a couple of weeks, and then took another flight to New York in early November for meetings with some recording studio people. Then when I was back in Chicago, I went into a recording studio on November 27th and 28th to record some demos.

For most of December and part of January it was Ramadan, so I had a quiet rest of the year. During Ramadan, you can travel and do whatever you need to, but you have to fast from before sunrise until after sunset. No matter what, you can't stop Ramadan, so it's good if you can stay quiet and have a laid back time. That being the case, many times I have to travel and do a lot of stuff, but I can do it since I am used to fasting for my whole life.

•••••

The year 2000 brought sad news to me several times. On January 16th, my friend Isatou Walker passed away from cancer, and her funeral was on January 20th. She was a member of Mandingo Griot Society for a few years in the 1980's, and I taught her to sing in my language so she could sing backup at our shows. I also translated the songs into English for her, so she would always know what she was singing about. On Thursday, March 9th, a very good friend of mine died in Brikama. His name was Kausu Sisay, and we first met there in 1971. Another good friend of mine in Brikama named Seni Sambou died two weeks later on Thursday March 23rd. He was my personal tailor for many years, and had sewed all the African clothes that I had with me when I first came to the U.S. in 1977, and that the Mandingo Griot Society members wore at our first shows. Then on Thursday, August 24th, Fatumata Sako passed away. She was the first wife of my teacher Uncle Saikou, and was there in Passamasi when I came to learn the kora and how to do griot traveling from my teacher. This year started with a whole lot of sad news. But sometimes life is like that. It's hard, but you have to take it.

A lot of other things happened this year too. On February 26th, I went into Philip's Looking Glass studio to do some recording. We recorded three solo kora songs with a guy called "Dante Dan" engineering. At the end of March, I flew to New York to meet with Philip and his manager, Linda Brumbach, and do a two-night performance of The Screens at the New Jersey Performing Arts Center in Newark with Philip. Afterwards, I flew back to Chicago to get ready to spend two months in Gambia with my family.

I arrived in Gambia on April 8th, and spent the first two days in Brikama. Then on Monday, April 10th, I started to go to Banjul with my friend Abulai Saidy. But that day was one of the most terrible days in

Gambian history, because of what we call the Student Massacre. Gambian students were protesting the government because of a boy being killed by the police earlier that year, and a girl being raped. The students did a big peaceful protest march from Brikama to Banjul that day. While they were passing through the Kanifing neighborhood in the north part of Serekunda, the Gambian security forces opened fire on the students, killing 16 people and wounding many others. Me and Abulai didn't know anything about that happening or we would never have tried to make our journey. I was driving my Peugot, and while we were going through the Tallinding neighborhood in the middle of Serekunda, we saw tires on fire in the middle of the street. We looked at each other and said, "Wow, let's take another route", so we went to the Bundung neighborhood, but the same thing was happening there. Then we tried to zig zag through the Dibba Kunda neighborhood towards Bakau, but by then the problem was everywhere. So I said, "Let's forget about going to Banjul and just go back home!" but we couldn't find a way to get to the main road to Brikama. Abulai was a cab driver and knew a lot of shortcuts, so he jumped and took the wheel. We began flying, zig zagging through Serekunda, turning left and right, left and right, until we got past Bakoteh and saw a road we could take to Yundum. We still didn't know exactly what was happening, but we knew it was something very, very heavy, and we were flying down the road as fast as we could. When we got back to Brikama, the moment we passed the police station, we turned right and headed down to my compound. When we got to the big open spot in front of the mosque, we saw a group of people walking down the main road towards the police station. We took a small side street to get to my compound, and parked the car. By that time, the students had arrived at the police station and we could hear the people hollering. Then we could see the flames of the fire, because they were burning down the police station. The next day, there were more protests in a lot of the rural areas, and more violence by the security forces, and a curfew was imposed. Nothing like this happened again in Gambia. I stayed with my family in Brikama for another month, and things began to calm down a little bit, but this was a very hard time in Gambia.

I came back to Chicago on May 7th, and on the 13th I drove to Wisconsin to do another concert of The Screens with Philip and Jon Gibson at the Weidner Center for the Performing Arts on the University of Wisconsin Green Bay campus. Then I spent most of the rest of spring and summer in Chicago. My trio with Manu and Abdul played a concert on July 20th at the Smart Museum of Art on the University of Chicago campus and on September 2nd at the annual Rockport, Illinois music festival. Then on October 20th, I flew to New York to meet with filmmaker Philip Haas about doing another project together. Some years before, I had created the soundtrack for his movie about a woman sculptor in Senegal. She was something else! From there I went to Lafayette College in Easton, Pennsylvania to do a master class for the world music students at the Center for the Arts. On November 3rd, Molissa Fenley accompanied me dancing while I played a kora concert there, and then I flew back to Chicago for the rest of the year.

•••••

In early January 2001, I decided to buy my first really good home recording studio equipment. For a long time, I used to have a little 4-track recording machine, but it started messing up so I stopped using it. So I went out and bought a 12-track Akai professional digital studio machine, an AKG microphone, and all kinds of cords and things like that, and took them home to hook them up. A few days later, I bought my first laptop computer, because I knew that communication things were all moving to the internet, and a computer is needed for that. I have a friend in Chicago who is a computer guy, and he showed me how to set it up, get online, and get email. For the rest of January, I spent a lot of time getting to know how to use my new recording setup because I was making plans for another Jooka cassette.

I still like to meet face-to-face with people instead of always talking on the phone or email, so I sometimes will go to New York for that, and to just check out what's happening around the town. So I went there for two weeks in February to do that, and to go to Philip and Holly

Critchlow's wedding on the 15th. Then from the time I got back to Chicago until the middle of April, I worked on recording the basic tracks and overdubs for a bunch of new Jooka songs with my new digital studio, so I could release another cassette.

On April 20th, I flew back to New York for Philip and Holly's big wedding celebration party at a big place on Houston Street in Manhattan. Then it was time to start getting ready for a long tour of The Screens. Over the next week, I rehearsed with Philip, Jon Gibson on soprano sax and flute, Yousif Sheronick on percussion, and Alexander Balanescu on violin. Then we flew to the west coast for the first leg of the tour. Whenever I talk with Philip about this music, we always say to each other, "The Screens music is magic", because people keep wanting to hear it even though we composed it a long time ago!

Our first concert was on April 28th at the Sunset Center in Carmel-by-the-Sea, California. The next night we played at the Music Recital Hall at Southern Oregon University in Ashland, and then went to Santa Barbara for a concert at the Lobero Theatre on May 1st. From there, we played the next two nights at the Mandeville Auditorium on the University of California at San Diego campus and at Freeborn Hall on the University of California at Davis campus. I flew back to Chicago for a few days, then we all met back up on the east coast to start the second leg of the tour. Our first concerts were on May 11th and 12th at the Lincoln Theater in Miami. Then from the 17th to the 20th, we went up the coast to Washington, DC for a concert at the Lisner Auditorium at George Washington University, the Sanders Theatre on the Harvard campus in Cambridge Massachusetts, the Flynn Center for the Performing Arts in Burlington, Vermont, and the Calvin Theatre in Northampton, Massachusetts. On May 21st, I flew back to Chicago for a week before we all met up again in New York, to fly to London for the European part of the tour.

We started with a concert at Bridgewater Hall in Manchester, England and at De Montfort Hall in Leicester on May 30th and 31st. Then back to London for a concert at the Royal Festival Hall and at Salisbury

City Hall on June 1st and 2nd. From there, we flew to Spain for one concert in Seville on the 3rd, then back to the U.S. for a two-night concert on the 8th and 9th at the Spoleto Festival in Charleston, South Carolina. It's a lot of traveling to do concerts on back-to-back-to-back nights like this!

After another break in Chicago, I flew back to New York and we all left together again for Spain. Our first concerts there were at the Teatro Jovellanos in Gijon and at the Kursaal Centre in San Sebastian on July 2nd and 3rd. In Spain, the places we played were pretty far apart, so we flew to most of them. On July 4th, we played at the Patio Collegio at Fonseca College in Salamanca, and on the 6th we went to La Palmas in the Canary Islands for a concert. Those islands are off the northwest coast of Africa, and I really liked it there! On the 7th, we went back to Spain for a concert at the Conde Duque in Madrid, and our last concert was at the Auditorio Parque Torres in Cartagena on Monday July 9th. That place was an outside stage with what looked like a university or a lot of old, big buildings around. The weather was killing me that day! We always played for 90 minutes, and it was just a little chilly before we started the show, but the sun went down about half way through, and my fingers and body were so cold by the time we were done, I could hardly play anymore. I wanted to just run off the stage at the end of our concert! On July 11th, I flew back to Chicago to spend the rest of the nice hot summer there.

A week later on July 18th, I got the sad news that my relative Boydarboe Suso had died in a car accident in Serekunda. Since we had a phone in our house in Brikama, I got the news from Bobo right away when it happened. A car hit him and he died. He was only a teenager around 16-18 years old, and a very bright boy who always had a happy face. My grandfather Jali Falai Suso and Boydarboe's grandfather were brothers, so Boydarboe's mother Marafin Suso and my father called each other brother and sister, and I called her my aunt. It was especially sad because Boydarboe was still such a young man when he passed away.

A NEW COMPOUND AND COLLABORATION

On Sunday September 9th, 2001, I flew from Chicago to Gambia, to begin looking for a compound in Brikama to buy for my friend Sorrie Camara. He lives in Toronto, but I have known him since we were children together in Passamasi. Sorrie is not a musician, but we became very good friends way back in those days and have been close ever since. For many years I used to always tell him, "Sorrie, whenever you have some money you should get a compound back home in Gambia". But he replied, "Two times I sent money to my relatives back home, but they just spent it". Still I kept telling him, "You must buy a place, or you will never have anything to show for all your outside traveling in the world".

Ever since I was growing up, I always saw people buying houses. Even when I was young, that was something I always paid attention to, and my mind went to that as something for me to do too. When I was first living in Chicago and told my friends that I wanted to buy a house back home in Gambia, they always asked me why. I have my own thinking when it comes to that. I asked myself, "If I can save even a small amount of money, what would benefit me more than anything else in the world? What kind of thing can money buy in this world that only gets more expensive as you get older?" My answer when it comes to this is that buying land will benefit me most in the future. Land and houses are the only things that will always have more value when they get older. Cars and trucks and airplanes are worth less even when they are 10 years old, but property is always worth more. So I would say to myself, "If I have it, my money will only go to property. Not a business, not a shop to sell anything, nothing like that. Because no matter how much money you have, even if you are a billionaire, you have to sleep someplace. It doesn't matter how rich or poor you are, you cannot live there permanently if that place is not yours". Whenever I bought a compound or some land to build on, I put my thinking on a balance sheet and checked it out, and came up with a solution about how to do it. Nothing beats that for me.

So in the summer of 2001, I told my friend Sorrie that I was going home to Gambia, and said to him, "If you trust me, I will buy a compound for you, and you don't have to give me a penny until I do it. I have a compound back home, and I want you to have that too. Otherwise when you go back home, you will have no place to stay. The Camara family compound will most likely be in a village, and maybe the family you know there does not know you anymore, so you couldn't live with them". Sorrie finally agreed with that, and when I got to Brikama, he called me and said, "Now I am going to send you the money". Then he sent me $10,000 Canadian dollars. Sorrie told me that he would be fine living anywhere, and that if I saw a compound that I liked, I should just buy it. So I began going around and around looking, and people came to me wherever I went, trying to sell me a compound. One of Sorrie's relatives tried to get me to buy a compound in Serekunda, because that is where he lived. But there the compounds are very small because it's a big crowded city. After a while looking, I told Sorrie, "The place I want to buy you a compound is in Brikama", and he replied, "You should buy it wherever you want".

One day, a realtor showed me somebody's land in Brikama near the big junction, on the right side of the road to Basse. On one part of the land they had built houses, and they wanted to sell the other part, which had no house on it. They sold that land to me for 95,000 dalasi, and I got all the papers correct for Sorrie. With the remaining money, I bought 350 bags of cement, and paid truck drivers to bring gravel stones and sand, and brickmakers to make bricks and build a fence all around the land. There were too many Mango trees on the land also, so I had some of them cut down to make room for a house, and had an iron gate built for the fence. Sorrie also sent more money to finish all of this work. I wrote down a list of everything I bought, and saved every receipt for every penny, and there was 835 dalasi remaining at the end. I put that money inside an envelope with the receipts and all the paperwork, and gave it to Bobo to save for Sorrie when he came to Brikama, because I had to go back to the U.S. A little while later, Sorrie arrived. He was so happy about the compound, it was unbelievable. When Bobo gave him the money and receipts, he put 3000 dalasi on top of that 835, and gave it to her. He said, "Take this. This gift is because your husband helped me a lot. If your husband didn't help me, I don't think I will ever get a compound". After that, Sorrie built a house there, and had some of his relatives living there. Now he goes there to visit, but he is still living in Toronto with his wife and children.

During all that time looking around and around with compound sellers, I saw the compound that I now live in with my family. One day, a compound broker named Caramo Minteh was showing places to me in an area around the Brikama Market, and he took me there. We were walking past the compound, and he told me, "Jali, this place also is for sale", but I replied, "The money Sorrie gave me is not enough for this, so we'll just be wasting our time". But Caramo persuaded me to go inside the gate to look around, and I said, "Wow, I like it a lot!" The land there, all the buildings on it, and the location, all looked so good. So went to look in all the rooms in the whole place. While we were looking, I said to myself, "I have the money in the bank to buy this". Later on we went back to my compound, where I had been living with my family since 1982. After dinner, I called my kids and my sister's kids all together and said, "I want to ask you people one thing, and you can answer however you want. Should we stay and live here, or should we move to another house?" Right away, they all jumped and said, "We should go, we should go!"

My mother told me I should never leave my first compound in Brikama because she liked it so much, but she had passed away so I couldn't ask her. So I called my blood brother Mahamadou in Serekunda and said, "I want to show you something". He came to Brikama the next day, and I told him I wanted to buy a new compound but wanted him to see it first. We went to the new place and walked inside to look around. He said, "Yes, OK, this place is good, but it will be expensive". I replied, "I know, but if I am able to get it, I will buy it".

The compound belonged to a businessman who took a loan from a bank, but he couldn't pay it back so the bank took the house back, and now they were selling it. They had been trying for a long time, but nobody would buy it. It was very expensive because the bank also wanted to make a good return. I said to myself, "My thing is different. My well-being is important, and my family wants me to get it". So I went back to see Caramo Minteh, and we went to the bank people together. Before we went, I knew I wanted to buy the house so I hired a lawyer named Mariama Denton to represent me. On October 1st, 2001, I paid cash for the compound, and took the money in a bag to the bank. My lawyer got all the necessary papers transferred, and then I hired a contractor named Sirifo Sanneh to remodel the compound. But he couldn't get started right away because there was a tenant living there with his family, a Senegalese tailor named Boylee. When I told that tailor that I owned the place now and said, "I need you to move because I am going to have some work done here", he became very arrogant and said, "I am not leaving".

Around that same time, I also decided to move from my first compound, up the hill into the second compound that I had bought in 1990. I had just finished remodeling this second compound, which is much bigger that my first one, and it now had three buildings. One building has eight apartments, and each one has a living room and one bedroom. The second building has three apartments like that, plus a shop on the other side. And the third building has three apartments that each has a living room and two bedrooms. It's very nice. So on Wednesday, December 26th, I moved my family into one of the two-bedroom apartments, including Dembo and Sula and their kids. The next day we had a big celebration there for all the wellwishers. On December 30th, I came back to Chicago with all the signed papers for the new compound. I told my brother Mahamadou to fight for me while I was back in United States, and get the tailor out of my new compound. He had to get the military people to come to the house and put him out on the street on January 8th, 2002.

•••••

After being in Chicago for a couple of weeks, I went to New York on Saturday, January 12th for a visit. I also wanted to buy an Eventide effects machine, and there is a big chain of stores in New York that sell used instruments, called Sam Ash Music Store. The Eventide is a pedal box I use when I play live, depending on what I am playing. It's not for playing a clean kora sound, but for people who want to hear anything new and original. I also wanted to get in touch with Jack DeJohnette while I was there. Back in June 2001, when me and Philip played the Royal Festival Hall in London, Jack was playing at a music festival that was going on there at that same time and came backstage to my dressing room with his promoter. I had heard his name, but only seen him playing drums one time before, when I was at the Woodstock Creative Music Studio with Mandingo Griot Society in 1980. But when we met backstage in London, Jack started singing the melody of the song Moonlight, which I recorded with Herbie in 1984, and said, "I like that song a lot. We should get together sometime".

So we exchanged phone numbers that day, and I said, "I come to New York a lot, so after I get back from Africa I will try to get in touch with you". So six months later when I went to New York, I called him. He said, "Come to Willow, it's right outside of Woodstock on the mountain". So on Tuesday January 22nd, I took a bus there and stayed with Jack in his house. He has a recording studio there, and the next day we starting recording together at two o'clock in the afternoon and played for about seven hours. On Thursday the 24th, we started recording at one o'clock and played for around five more hours. In these two days we recorded nine songs, and all were my original compositions except one. When me and Jack played together, it was like magic. Whatever I played, he played something against it, and we sounded like we were playing together for forty years. We mixed all the songs a few days later on Sunday the 27th, then I went back to Chicago.

Five weeks later, I went back to New York to do some recording with Philip at Looking Glass Studio on Saturday, March 9th. On that same day, a very good childhood friend of mine named Solo Wally passed away in Gambia. He was from the small village called Brifu, only one and half miles away from my village of Foday Kunda. In our childhood time, he was the champion wrestler of all the boys in his village, and I was the champion of my village. We were wrestling partners many times, and then we became very good friends and didn't wrestle anymore. I had not seen him for a long time because he went to Sierra Leone, Angola, and other areas, and I came to the U.S. He had a family, and later on they moved to Serekunda. I went to see him there a few years before he passed away, and he would also come see me from time to time in Brikama. We would laugh and talk of times past, when we were the leader of the boys in our villages, and meet together under the big tree for wrestling.

After me and Philip finished our recording, I went back up to Willow on March 16th just to visit Jack again for a few days. I made another trip to New York in April also, and soon after my return to Chicago there was very sad news from home. On Monday, April 29th, my brother Dembo's wife Sula Sakliba passed away suddenly while she was in labor, and the baby died also. They put Sula in an ambulance to take her to the big hospital in Banjul, but she passed away before they got there. The next day, they brought her body back to Brikama for the burial. By this time, Dembo and Sula also had third child, a girl named Jalikumba. Mahame and Sendin were also still very young when their mother died. Mahame was only around seven years old, and Sendin only five. That is very young to be without your mother. I am lucky that I had my mom for so much of my life. After Sula died, my sister Tita asked if she could raise Jalikumba, and she has lived with Tita and her husband in his compound in Brikama ever since then. Bobo became a mother for Mahame and Sendin, and they continued to live with my family, along with their father Dembo.

On June 2nd, I flew to New York and went straight to Jack's house in Willow. By that time, we had our recording in hand and a title for it: Music from the Heart of the Masters. On June 6th, we took the promo pictures for the record. Jack said he would put it out on his new label called Golden Beams, and then later another label came and licensed it to put it out. I flew back to Chicago on June 15th, and then flew to Oakland on Saturday the 19th to visit a friend of mine who is from my childhood village of Foday Kunda. His name is Tejan Singhateh, and he was living in Berkeley with his wife and family. A few days later I played a solo kora concert at the Summer Art Festival in Garberville, California on June 23rd, and then flew back to Chicago.

The music world is a small one sometimes, and something happened that summer which showed this very well. In 1997, I had met a promoter in Austria named Tomas Stousand when I played at the Frankfurt International Jazz Festival with Pharoh Sanders and Eberhard Weber. At that time, me and Tomas talked a little bit, and then other people there told me that he was the #1 promoter in all of Europe. So a while after I finished the record with Jack, my mind went to Tomas and I called him to tell him about it. I said, "I have a cassette to send you of kora music and drums". He asked me, "Who is the drummer?" When I told him it was Jack, he laughed. I asked him what was funny, and he replied, "I have been his European agent for 40 years". So I called Jack and told him about talking to Tomas, and he sent Tomas a CD. That guy went crazy, playing it all day in his office! He called Jack and said, "I want you both to come here to play at the Jazz Festival Saalfelden in Austria", and quickly he arranged it. In fact, the time between when I first called him and when we went to Austria wasn't even very long! Me and Jack met at JFK airport on Wednesday, August 21st to fly there, and our first-ever concert together was at that festival on the 23rd. It was just kora and drums, and it worked so well it was unbelievable!

I was back in Chicago until Saturday, October 12th, when I flew to New York again to do a music video with Jack at Big Mike Studio for something called World Link TV. Then on the 15th, I did some recording with Bill for a CD he was making with his wife Gigi. She is an Ethiopian lady and a good singer, and the CD was called Gold and Wax. Aïyb Dieng, Buckethead, Bernie Worrell, and a lot of other people were on that CD too.

Afterward, I flew back to Chicago to get ready to go to Gambia for the work to begin on my new compound. I arrived on Thurday Oct 31st, and exactly one week later, sad news came again. My mother's eldest sister Kanyo Jobarteh passed away. She lived in the village of Manjan Kunda, very near where she and my mother, and most of their brothers and sisters, were born. She had a very long life with many children and grandchildren.

On Tuesday, November 12th, I went with Sirifo Sanneh to buy equipment and materials for my new compound, and to get the work started. He had a lot of people working for him, and he was the manager of all their work. They did new mosaic tile on all the verandas and tile floors in all the inside rooms, all new windows, new bathroom fixtures, new electricity system and lights, new paint on everything, and more. I paid him for all this remodeling work, and he and his people worked on the compound for around three months. There were Mango, Avocado, and Coconut trees already growing in my compound when I bought it, and I added a lot of Banana trees too. During that same time, I helped a percussionist named Harris Eisenstadt come to Gambia to study drumming. Harris is originally from Canada but now lives in New York, and Adam introduced me to him some time before. On December 8th, Harris came and I got him a teacher named Jalaman Camara. Harris learned from him for a month or more, and then he went back to the U.S. During the month he was staying with me and my family, and all the way into February, I spent all my time seeing about the new compound.

•••••

Finally the day came for us to move in on Wednesday, Feb 19th, 2003. Dembo wanted to keep living in my second compound, so he stayed there but Mahame and Sendin moved to the new compound with me and my family, and Dembo comes there to visit almost every day. It was a lot of work to get settled in, but we were all so, so happy to have our beautiful new compound! I needed to go back to the United States at the beginning of March, but something very sad happened right before I was to leave. It was in an area just outside Brikama called Drumekolong, where there is a big Mango forest with thousands of trees, and that is where all the butchers go to kill their cows before they bring the meat to the Brikama market. On Friday, February 28th, a butcher from Mauritainia had a bull that he wanted to take to Drumekolong to kill. That bull was very hard to handle, so he and his brother asked some boys to help get it tied up and loaded onto a wagon. One of those boys was my relative Balla Kouyateh, who comes from another big griot family in Gambia. He was only around 20 years old. The bull went wild, but Balla and his friends helped the butcher get it tied up and put into the buggy to go to Drumekolong. When they got there it was evening time, so they decided to untie the bull from the buggy to leave it until morning for butchering. Everyone was backing away from the bull, and Balla bumped into a low concrete wall surrounding a well and fell in. He hit his head on the concrete on the way down and broke his skull. They took Balla to the hospital in Brikama but he died, and his friends and the butcher all got scared and ran away, afraid that people might say they were responsible for his death. I didn't hear about it until the morning, and I was told that they were going to take Balla's body to Banjul to do an autopsy. Right away I ran to the hospital to say, "Just leave him so he can be buried, don't take him to Banjul". We got the body and brought it to the house. We washed Balla and buried him. The butcher came to my house and offered me some money but I said, "No, you all ran away. It was Balla's time to pass away, so that's OK, but you should not have run away. You cannot give us any money that will bring him back".

After I left on March 2nd, I was back in Chicago until June. During that time, a big thing happened: I was watching TV on March 19th, and saw the war starting in Iraq, and that war is still going on now. Near the end of June, another big touring travel time began for me. I played at the Montreal Jazz Festival on June 26th in a club called the Metropolis, with a well-known jazz-funk trio named Medeski, Martin, and Wood, who play piano, bass, and guitar. The next night, I played with Jack DeJohnette at the Monument-National Theater. Afterward we both flew to New York and drove up to his place to record ourselves jamming in his studio on July 1st and 2nd. I don't know for sure if we released that music, maybe it was on The Ripple Effect CD. Then I went back to Manhattan to record on July 10th and 11th at a recording studio on Park Avenue, playing the kora and other instruments for the soundtrack of a PBS documentary film called Aids Warriors, with a producer named Ted Kuhns.

The following month was the African Art Festival at Washington Park in Chicago, and I brought Pharoh Sanders there to play with Mandingo Griot Society on August 30th. Then on Sunday, September 21st, I performed with Philip and Jon Gibson in a big concert for the Dalai Lama at Lincoln Center. It was for an organization called Healing the Divide that works to help the Tibetan people, and there were a bunch of other musicians performing there that I know also, including Kronos and Hamza El Din. Years later in 2007 after Hamza had already passed away, a CD came out of that whole concert.

After a week back in Chicago, I left for a European tour with Jack on October 6th. Every night we were in a different city, and sometimes even in a different country! Our first concert was in Oslo, Norway on October 8th at a big place called the Cosmopolite. The next night, we played in Malmo, Sweden at a jazz club called Jeriko. From the 11th to the 16th, we performed at Forteresse de Salses in Perpignan, France, the Middle Auditorium in Rome, the Stadtgarten in Cologne, and the Bayerischer Hof in Munich. Then on the 17th we went to a city in northern Italy called Rovereto, and perfomed at the Auditorium Felotti Polo Culturale. The next day we went back into Germany to do one night at the Odeon Theater in Goppingen, then to Fribourg, Switzerland the next night for a show at La Spirale, and back into Germany for a show at the Karlstorbahnhof club in Heidelburg on the 21st. Our last concert was on Thursday, October 23rd at the Teatro Comunale Mauro Bardusco in Cormons, Italy. The next day, I flew home to Chicago. It was good to get to rest a little bit there, because more traveling was coming again soon!

On October 30th, I bought my crazy car, the Toyota 4-Runner that I have now driven all over the place in West Africa. Before I left the U.S., I took a flight to Albuquerque, New Mexico on November 1st to perform a solo kora concert at the Outpost Performance Space, and came back on the 2nd. The next day, a friend of mine from Chicago helped me drive the 4-Runner from Chicago to New York so I could ship it to Gambia. We stayed overnight at Philip's house and then flew back to Chicago on November 8th. Why I didn't wait until I was leaving for Gambia to drive my car to New York, I just don't remember! On November 17th I flew to Gambia and picked up my crazy car and I still have it, even today. From that time on, I was at home in Brikama and traveling all around Gambia until flying back to the U.S. on March 14th, 2004.

ORION

The 2004 Olympics were held in Athens, Greece for the first time since 1896, and the Cultural Olympiad had commissioned Philip to write music, and perform it at a bunch of different places before the Olympics started. Philip had the idea of asking a whole lot of other people he liked to work with, to each collaborate with him on a song for it. He named the project Orion because it is the largest constellation in the night sky, and people from all different cultures in the world can see it. He asked me to work with him on the project, and also a Greek singer named Eleftheria Arvanitaki, Ravi Shankar who was the god of the sitar, didgeridoo player Mark Atkins, Wu Man, who plays a Chinese stringed instrument called the pipan, violinist Ashley MacIsaac, and a famous Brazilian band called Uakti. Uakti is a group of three musicians that Philip has known for many years. Their music is very different, very minimalist, and they don't play normal instruments. Every instrument they make is handmade from things like cans, wood, old shoes, dry wires, and plastics. You name it! Three of the band members will usually travel to play, and the fourth guy will stay in the studio back home, coming up with all kinds of ideas and making stuff from everything he can lay his hands on, even sound from water.

When Philip first asked me about this, I said to myself, "Wow, Herbie asked me to compose a song in 1984, and now Philip in 2004. It looks like I will be involved in Olympics music every 20 years. Sounds good". So perhaps in 2024 I will do this with someone else! I know that time flies, and that I will still be making music then too.

On Monday, April 26th, I flew to New York to do a duet concert with Philip at Town Hall in Manhattan. Then I stayed with him at his house for about a week to work on the Orion music before heading back home to Chicago. A few weeks later on Monday May 24th, we all flew to Athens. The Philip Glass Ensemble was very big: Philip, Ted Baker and music director Michael Riesman on keyboards, Frank Cassara and Mick Rossi on percussion; Jon Gibson on soprano saxofone, clarinet, and flute,

Andrew Sterman on flute and piccolo, and Lisa Bielawa, singer. All the collaborating musicians were there too, except for Ravi Shankar, who was not well enough to travel at that time. So his composition was performed by a very good sitar player named Gaurav Mazumdar. We all rehearsed together in Athens for a week, then we did the premiere concert at the Herodeon Theatre in Athens on June 3rd. That concert was recorded and later released as a live album in 2005. The Herodeon is the heaviest outdoor music place in all of Greece, a stone amphitheater that is almost 2000 years old, on the side of the giant Acropolis hill in the middle of Athens. It's unbelievable. The way we performed was that each of the guest musicians would play their piece, backed by the Philip Glass Ensemble. On June 4th, we performed the whole concert again at the Herodeon, and the place was jam-packed for both nights.

The next day, we all traveled away from Athens to the city of Thessaloniki, on the Aegean Sea. We got to have a day off there, then played a two-night concert on June 7th and 8th in another outside amphitheater called the Forest Theatre of Thessaloniki. It is up high on a hill overlooking the ocean and surrounded by mountains and big trees. Playing music in a place like that is something else! The next day, we traveled to Italy to perform at the famous Ravenna Music Festival on the 10th, at another big outdoor amphitheater called the Palazzo Mauro de André.

Something very funny happened in Ravenna too! The dignitaries who put on the festival told us before the concert that they were going to take us all out for a dinner after we performed. I was thinking it would be all Italian goodies, and I was rubbing my hands together about it. Before the concert, I was joking with everybody, "Hey, tonight we'll just be chewing after the music!" Then after the concert, the dignitaries took all of us to a fancy-looking restaurant with white tablecloths, napkins made into bow ties, and all that. The waiters were wearing a suit and tie, and there were three plates stacked up at each seating place, with lots of glasses and fancy silverware too. The waiter said, "We have a treat for you people tonight!" and so I was thinking of a lamb leg, roast chicken, and things like that.

We all sat down, and they started popping open all kinds of wine and tea. Then they brought the first course. It was cheese, and just looked like regular white cheese. We all ate some of that, and then they took our plates away. Quickly, they brought out the second course, a cheese that was a little bit yellow! Besides Philip, my best friends in that group were Paulo Santos from the band Uakti and Mark Atkins, who is an aboriginal man that always has a drink in his hand. When that second plate of cheese came to us, we three started looking at each other and making the eye. I looked at Mark and Paulo, and shook my head to say, "Let's get out of here". They were chewing the cheese, and they shook their heads at me to say yes. Then the third course came and it was cheese too, just a little bit more yellow! When they put that cheese down on the table, everybody sat back in their chairs and looked at each other. I just stood up and started walking out. Mark and Paulo and all the other Brazilian guys also stood up, and we walked outside. We went to the town square to check all around and see if there are any other restaurants there that are not just a cheese place. Then one by one, everybody followed me. When I found a regular restaurant, we ate regular food, not just cheese! I cannot live just on cheese! I don't even like it much! I worked like hell playing music all night, and I can't just eat cheese.

The next morning we left Ravenna to go to Lyon, France. On the night of June 12th, we performed the concert at another giant, 2000 year-old stone amphitheater called the Roman Theatre. I don't know how all these places can still be standing after all those years. The next day we flew to London for the last show of the tour, at the Barbican Centre in London on June 14th. Everybody else flew back to the U.S., but I stayed in London to visit a friend of mine named Bambo Jarra from Passamasi village for a few days. His mother is a very close friend to my sister Dibba Sakliba, who was married to my teacher Uncle Saikou Suso. I flew back to Chicago until the 19th.

●●●●●

FODAY MUSA SUSO A VILLAGE GRIOT BOY AND THE WORLD

In July, Ted Kuhn brought me back to New York to play music for the soundtrack of his new project for Frontline on PBS, a film called Ghosts of Rwanda. On July 11th and 12th, I recorded kora music in the same fancy studio on Park Avenue in Manhattan as the Aids Warriors soundtrack project we did in 2003. Then I came back to Chicago for one night, and then flew to Germany for two concerts of The Screens with Phillip and Jon Gibson. Our first concert was on the 17th at the Kampnagel Theatre in Hamburg, and then we flew to Copenhagen. That day in the Copenhagen airport, the three of us just sat on an outside deck of the first class lounge for a long time, watching the planes come and go, and talking and laughing. It was very sweet. Our second concert was on July 20th at the Concert Musik Teatret Albertslund in Copenhagen. Then the next day, we all flew back to the U.S.

A week later, I flew from Chicago to Troy, New York to work with my Ghanian friend Yacub Addy and his band Odadaa! again. We had a grant to write some music together for traditional drums and kora, and we worked in Yacub's house, writing and learning songs from July 28th to August 3rd, and I went back there on September 9th to work with them for a few more days.

On September 12th I flew back to Chicago to get ready to perform in concert with the Fulcum Point Art Project. It is a big group of musicians, and their founder and trumpet player Steven Burns commissioned me to write a song for them earlier that year. On September 2^{1st}, I also did a live radio show in Chicago as part of the World Music Festival and played the concert with Fulcrum Point at the Athenaeum Theatre that night. Soon afterward, I flew to Brazil to do some duet concerts with Jack DeJohnette. On Wednesday September 29th, we performed at the Direct TV Music Hall in Sao Paulo, then on the 30th at the Marina da Gloria in Rio de Janeiro, as part of the Phillips Music Festival. The next day, I flew to the city of Belo Horizonte to visit my good friend Paulo Santos and the rest of the guys from the band Uakti. We were just hanging in the city together for about a week, having fun, and then I flew back to

Chicago. Another time I went to visit them again, and they took me to the Ouro Preto region of Brazil, where they mine the Topaz stones. I like those friends very much.

JOOKA II

I spent the rest of October in Chicago, getting ready to go to Gambia to see my family and to do a tour with my second Jooka cassette. While I was recording this Jooka cassette, I decided to go on a big tour to eastern Gambia, Senegal, and Guinea-Bissau because those were the places my first Jooka cassette became such a big hit. I wanted all the people to see me, not just to hear my music, and I wanted to see them face-to-face, so they could say, "We met the guy who made this music".

One of the songs I composed on this Jooka cassette is for a man named Kamansa Jergu. He is not a king or a rich man, but is famous among the elders in the Foni District. He is one of the Jola people, owns a lot of cows, and he is very brave. The reason I composed the song for him is very simple: It was the time of my daughter Nene's baby-naming ceremony in 1988, and I wanted to sacrifice a bull for the celebration. Then people told me that for a baby-naming ceremony, it is better to kill a small animal, like a sheep or maybe a goat. So I decided to go and get two big sheep, because I knew a lot of people would be coming to my compound for the celebration. I got into my car to drive to the Foni District and towards the Brefet area, and I stopped at each village to ask whether there were people there selling sheep. But none of the sheep I saw were big enough, so I kept going. When I stopped at a village called Ndenbaan, I talked to a guy who asked me, "Did you just come from Brikama? You just passed by a village called Bajana, and there is a man who lives there called Kamansa Jergu. He owns a lot of animals, so go and ask him if he is selling sheep". So I turned my car around and went back to Bajana, and found Kamansa's compound near the roadside. We greeted, and I told him, "I am from Brikama, and I am a griot. I need a sheep for my daughter's baby-naming ceremony on the day after tomorrow". Then he took me behind the houses in his compound to look at his sheep, but I didn't see any there that satisfied me, because I needed the biggest one I can find.

He said, "OK, hold on. I don't have a sheep like what you are looking for, but let's go to the compound across the street". When we got to that compound, there were two of the biggest sheep I ever saw. Kamansa said, "They don't belong to me, but the owner is in the hospital in Banjul, and he told me that if I see anybody who wants to buy them, to bring them over to his place. I can sell them to you for him, and then I will bring the money to him in Banjul". The owner's family was also there, and they brought the sheep to the middle of the compound. I couldn't believe it, because I had never seen two sheep so big like this. I pointed to the biggest one, and told Kamansa that I wanted it. He said the owner wanted 950 dalasi for the biggest sheep and 850 dalasi for the other one. Today that is nothing, but in those days a sheep usually cost only 250-300 dalasi. Me and Kamansa talked back and forth about the price, and I told him I could pay 800 dalasi for the biggest one. He said, "OK, you can pay that". Then the owner's family said to me, "Hey, he said 950 for that one", but Kamansa told them, "Everybody quiet". Then he said to me, "You say you are a griot from Brikama?" I said yes, and he said, "Pay 800, and if the guy wants that 150 when he gets out at the hospital, I will pay it for you. You being a griot, I don't want to stand here arguing with you about this sheep". So I paid the money and left, and I never heard anything after that about the other 150. So now, whenever I pass that village, I stop to see Kamansa and say hello. Kamansa never had a bunch of cash money in his hand, but he does own a lot of animals. He is a high person in that traditional village, and people listen to him. In his house, there is always fresh milk or sour milk from his cows, and he always gives me a gallon.

That guy is very happening, and he has a big heart. When I decided to compose the song for him, I wanted to do it in the Jola rhythm, because Jolas have their own rhythm that is different than others. I imitated that Jola rhythm even though I was playing the kora on his song. I wanted to put some Jola words in the song too, but since I don't speak Jola, I asked a Jola friend of mine who lives in New York, "How do to you say this in Jola? How do you say that in Jola?" and I put those words in my song for Kamansa. That song became a big thing for Kamansa too, especially among the Jola people. They like hearing the words, and the dance rhythm of the Jola drums called bougarabou that I imitated in the song. Kamansa already had a name among the people, but he told me that my song made him more famous. Many Jola people who live in Gambia and

Cassamance came to see him, and the President of Gambia even sent him a free ticket to go Mecca for his pilgrimage.

• • • • •

Before I left Chicago, I had that same company in Indianapolis make me 5000 cassettes, and I arrived in Gambia on November 6th. The first few months I was there, I was mostly hanging in Brikama with Bobo and the kids, and my friends. While I was there, a very good friend named Bangaly Ketta came to visit me, but I was not expecting that. He is from Passamasi, but we had not seen each other since I left my teacher's compound there in 1971! For a long time, Bangaly was living in Sierra Leone and into the diamond business, so in fact we had never even been in Gambia at the same time in all those years! On December 21st, one of my cousins from Passamasi, but who now lives in Banjul, was visiting me in my house. I said to him, "Lamin, I didn't see Bangaly for a long time", and he replied, "Right now he is in our village!" So I called Bangaly on his cell phone and while we were talking, he told me that he was going back to Sierra Leone soon. I said to him, "Don't go yet Lamin, come here to Brikama for a few days and then you can go". So we spent three nice days together at my compound before he left.

By the time I was getting ready to leave Brikama for my second Jooka tour, some cassette sellers in Banjul and Brikama came to my compound to try to get me to sell some of my cassettes through them. I even talked to Ousman Ceesay, the most famous cassette seller in Gambia, in his shop in Banjul. He wanted to have all of my cassettes to sell, and said, "Jali, it will be difficult for you to go around to sell it". But I told him, "No, I am going to sell my own cassette, and it will be easy. You and me have two different ways of thinking: You are thinking that you can sell a lot of this cassette, give me some money, and take some profit. But the reason I want to sell my cassette is not just for the money, it's because I want to go to the places where the people are, so they can see me and hear the music too, and know, "This is our Jali who made this Jooka music". To me, it's not just the money". I wanted the people to see me, and me to see them too, and I didn't want other people to be selling the cassette for me without that.

So then I decorated my 4-wheel drive car with two big posters with my picture on them, glued to the windows. I attached two big loudspeakers on top of the car, one facing the front and one facing the back, with a cassette player wired to them. I took many, many boxes of cassettes in the trunk too. On Saturday, February 12th, 2005, I left Brikama with my friend Amadou Jallow, my good friend Bajo Jawara, and my cousin's son Saibo Koyateh. Amadou would drive slow through all the villages, and I would ride in the front passenger seat. Bajo and Saibo would sit in the back seat, and Saibo would be the one to sell the cassettes out of the trunk.

First we went to a whole bunch of cities and towns in Cassamance, and then we went all the way to Guinea-Bissau. In Cassamance, we arrived in Binjona, then went to Tanaf, then to many other villages. In every village as we were entering, I would turn the sound up. People would hear the music from the loudspeakers and quickly, quickly, all of them would come around and run up to the car. Right away that music became a big thing, and because of that, sometimes even today people call me Jooka jalo, which means Jooka singer. The radio stations in Gambia were playing it too. Then we crossed into Guinea-Bissau, and on February 14th, we went to a village there called Jali Kunda. Today it is a Fulani village, but many many years ago, I believe it was a Mandingo village because the name means "Home of the griots". I think maybe during the civil war in Guinea-Bissau, it was destroyed and the Fulani people came there and built up the village again.

There is a radio station there that is also called Jali Kunda, run by a Mandingo guy named Mamadou Sillah, but he is not the same man as from long ago at Radio Senegal. The Jali Kunda station played my Jooka cassette all the time, and it had a long signal so you could listen to it even all the way to Brikama. So before I left Brikama, I called him and told him I was coming. He asked me, "Please when you come here, make sure that you come to my village".

The Jali Kunda station itself was built by the Portugese after Guinea-Bissau was no longer their colony. They built a big camp-like place for the station, with a resturant, a bakery, a store, a farm seed building, and a small hotel. That whole place was inside a thick, thick jungle near the village of Jali Kunda. We arrived there around nine o'clcok at night, and we couldn't find it. I was looking at the map, and I happened to see somebody by the roadside named Sirifo. I said hello and told him what I was looking for. Sirifo told me that he could show me where it was, and he got in the car with us to go down the dirt roads through the thick jungle to get there. While we were going, I was saying to myself, "Wow, what kind of place can this be?" We finally drove into the camp place, and Sirifo got out and went inside, and then the people came out and welcomed us. Mamadou Sillah wasn't there because he was in the capital city of Bissau, but he told the people there, "The Jooka singer Mr. Suso will be arriving soon, and when he comes, you all should put him and his people in the hotel. Then take them to the restaurant and feed them". We were all so tired, so they showed us to our rooms in the hotel, and we stopped there to take a shower, then we walked to the restaurant.

After we ate dinner, I went inside the radio station to be interviewed by a Fulanese guy who could speak Mandingo very well. During the interview, he asked me, "Where will you go on your Jooka tour?" I told him I was there to see the people, and I told them the names of the villages that I would be traveling to. All the places I was going to were all on the same main road through Guinea-Bissau. By the next day when we left Jali Kunda to travel, news had traveled ahead of us and people in many of those towns and villages were just standing on the roadside, waiting, waiting, waiting for us to come!

In Guinea-Bissau, the people know the Jooka music even way heavier than in Gambia. They know it and value it very heavy. In fact, the best Jooka singers come from Guinea-Bissau throughout history. When I was a small boy, Jooka singers would come to my village of Foday Kunda. They would be traveling from village to village, and many of them would come from Guinea-Bissau. In our tradition, when a Jooka singer came, people in our village would also organize a show to happen at nighttime. Everyone would gather in the bantaba, and the Jooka singer would come.

They would have a school bell with a handle on it, and they hit that one time while they were singing and improvising the words. This does not happen at all anymore, and Jooka singing has disappeared in many, many areas. I think that even started to happen way back when I was still a young child. So many of the people in Gambia, Senegal, and Guinea-Bissau had not heard that kind of singing for a long, long time. During our time touring, some older people even told me that even if the president came to town, they wouldn't care and they wouldn't come out to see him. But they said, "We want to see you, because you did something that we thought we would never get to see. We never thought we would hear anybody singing Jooka music ever again".

One day while we were driving through the country, we came to a big village with a mosque by the roadside. It was prayer time, so I asked Amadou to stop the car so I could go inside to pray. When I got out of the car, I saw a guy looking at the car and at my picture in the window, and then he recognized me. He asked me, "Are you Mr. Suso the Jooka singer? I just came back from Gambia three or four days ago. Your cassette is very famous there, and it is already very famous here too". By the time I came out of the mosque, that guy had already gone into the town and told all the people about me. Quickly the whole street was jam-packed with people. When we started driving down the street, on both sides people were waving. I told Amadou, "Let's stop" and the moment we did, everybody gathered around us. Then I told him, "Pump up the volume". Everybody wanted to see me and touch my hand, saying wow, and wanting to talk. Older people and younger people, all of them were there. I gave my camera to Saibo and said, "Shoot us", so that I would always have a picture of this.

The following day, we went to a village called Bonjeh, because I knew of a traditional Jooka singer who lived there, an elder man named Suleman Jaffuneh. I know some people who are his relatives from Bonjeh, but now live in Brikama, and when they heard my first Jooka cassette, they told me about him and said that I should go see him. I remember so clearly the Jooka singers who came to my village of Foday Kunda when I was small, so it was very important for me to meet Suleman. His village was very far from the highway, and we drove for a long time to reach it.

When we got to his house, I asked his son about him, and he told me that Suleman was in another village in Guinea-Bissau called Sama Karantaba. But the son told me, "Since you have a car, I can go with your driver to get him and bring him back here if you want ". I was very happy to hear that and said, "Fine, that will be good!" My friend Amadou Jallow, who was driving my car, went with the son to get Suleman. They left around three or four o'clock in the afternoon, driving down a road that was just gravel. It was pretty far to get all the way to Sama Karantaba, so they didn't get back to Bonjeh until around nine o'clock at night.

Since the villagers knew my car and driver, the moment my car lights shined and they heard the engine sound, the whole village jumped up and started running. Then I knew that this guy Suleman is something else. He came and met me, we said hello to each other, and when we shook hands, he call me Karamoba, which means big teacher or highest teacher. It is a big respect name. I replied, "No, you are Karamoba". We said that back and forth to each other again, and then he said, "You took the Jooka song and made it popular among the people". Then I explained to him, "You are the one who made the words, and the roots of the whole thing. My reason to come to Guinea-Bissau was to meet the people, and especially to meet the people like you who are the traditional Jooka singers. The people I met in Brikama who are from your village are the ones who recommended you to me. Other people I have heard about, when I heard their music on a tape I was not impressed. Quickly those people will jump into singing about women, how beautiful they dress, and stuff like that. But I am looking for a Jooka singer who sings only about the bush, a farm, the crops, and tools. When I told this to your relatives, they said, "Suleman is your man". That is why I came here to meet you." He replied, "I hear what you say. Let's sleep and get up tomorrow, and see what we can do".

The next day after lunch, the news started going around that Suleman was going to sing. We came to his son's living room, and I told my cousin Saibo Kouyateh to use the boom box to record him. We set up my video camera, boom box, and microcassette. People were arriving even before Suleman started singing, and soon the whole living room and compound was jam-packed. When Suleman started singing, the words he said made my whole body start tingling, tingling. I almost cried to hear the words he was singing. He called, and everyone answered. It soon got too hot inside the room, so we went out under the Mango tree in his compound. The women lined up behind him while he sang. That day, Suleman sang! He sang all the way from lunchtime until five o'clock that evening. It was unbelievable!

•••••

The next day on February 17th, we left Guinea-Bissau and drove up to Cassamance. First we went to a town called Kolda, then to the big town of Ziguinchor, the place Bobo is from. We spent the night there with her family, and drove to Brikama the next morning. After a few days at home, I left Brikama with my little daughter Nene, my blood brother Mahamadou, and our driver Alhaji Suso, who is the son of my eldest brother Mohammed Suso. Alhaji lives with his family in one of the apartments in my second compound in Brikama. He drove us all the way to the Basse area, with my car jam-packed with Jooka cassettes. At that time, the road to Basse was very bad, with a lot of potholes and so much dust everywhere. The car we drove in was my own car, so I didn't want to be flying down the road. So we were going slow, slow all the way. We left Brikama at around eleven o'colock in the morning on the 23rd, and didn't arrive in Basse until five o'clock in the morning on the 24th.

When we arrived, I told Alhaji to take us to the compound of my good friend Mohammed Bayang. He is from Sare Hamadi, the same village where I was born, but we had not seen each other since our childhood time, for at least 40 years. Even so, me and Mohammed knew each other very well. He is older than me and was living in Sierra Leone doing the diamond business, and whenever I went to Basse I would go to his compound. He was never there all those times, but this time when my car stopped in front of his gate at five o'clock in the morning, right then he was opening the gate because he was going to the mosque to pray. I said hello to him and he said, "Who is there?" so I said, "It's me, Fodaymusa".

He couldn't believe it was me, he was so surprised! He said, "Come in, come in! I will go and pray, and then come back".

In his compound there was a big bentengo, a traditional seat in front his house, and I was so, so tired. But the weather was very hot even at that time of the morning, so I didn't want to go inside any room in the house. I just laid down on that bentengo and right away went to sleep. Nene came to lie down next to me too, and we all slept until the sun came up. In the morning, we all got up to take showers because we were so dusty from the drive. Then I headed to the radio station in Basse. By then my second Jooka cassette was already very famous in every part of Gambia, so when the radio station people heard that the guy who made that cassette was in Basse, they wanted to interview me and play my cassette. On the radio show, I said that I would be going to the marketplace with my cassettes, so afterward we drove to that area with the car full of them. Even by the time we arrived, people were already waiting for us.

During the whole tour, I would always turn the volume up and start playing the cassette when we arrived somewhere, and all the people came running, running, running once they heard that big boom, boom sound. While all the crowds were gathering in the Basse market and I was talking to the people, I felt someone pat me on the back. I looked back and it was my best childhood friend Demba Camara! He said, "I knew that you were coming to the Basse area, and I knew that you would not come without visiting Fatoto to see me. I want you to know that I already have a sheep for you that my wife Gundo is holding. I am going someplace right now, but I will be back tonight to meet you there". Demba is my very good friend ever since we met while I was studying the kora with my teacher. During that time, I took my kora across the river from Passamasi to Fatoto many, many times to visit him in his family's compound, Camara kunda. Over 100 people lived there when I was a child, and even nowadays it is the biggest compound in all of Fatoto, which is a large town.

When I was growing up, Fatoto was our "everything" town, the place to go for all the shops. So just before sunset, me and Nene, Mahamadou, and Alhaji all got back in my car and drove from Basse to Fatoto to visit Demba and his family. His wife Gundo welcomed us and cooked, and

Demba came back and joined us for dinner. Gundo also told me that she was holding the sheep for me. She is a very, very good wife and we are very lucky to have her, because she had triplets without taking any medication. She gave birth to them all in the house with the help of midwives, and with no hospital. God gave her those babies, and they all lived and are well.

During my childhood time while I was mastering the kora, the friendship between Demba and myself grew so much it is unbelievable. He is not from a griot family, but for my first Jooka cassette, I wrote a song for him called "Fatoto Camara Kunda". We are friends like that, and we will always stay that way. Now, all the old people in Fatoto, and even the babies who never saw me, have heard of me and know who I am. Everybody there calls me Camara Kunda Jalo and Demba's Jalo. So many people came by his compound and listened to the cassette on the boom box the whole evening, and me and my guys spent the night in Camara kunda.

The next day, we crossed over the River Gambia to go to Passamasi village and our Suso family compound, where my teacher Uncle Saikou's family is. There too, all the people gathered. The young people who had never met me were curious to come and see me, and to hear the cassette. The elder people knew me but hadn't seen me in a long while, and wanted to see me again. Everywhere I went, the crowds came! They were buying a lot of cassettes, and at the same time they didn't want the music from the car to stop, and were dancing all around the car! They are proud of me. First of all, I am their Jali and I came from there, so they want to see me. Second, they know I have been all over the world, and they are proud that I come back, and that I am keeping the Jooka music tradition going. They know, "Our Jali left here, but he didn't leave our culture. This is our tradition he is playing and singing, so let's go see and hear Fodaymusa". And third, they are proud of the Jooka cassette, and when they hear the music they want to buy it.

I still know the Wuli District like I know the palm inside my hand. Even if it's the middle of the night in any place there, I will know exactly where I am. When we left Passamasi, we drove to Tabanding. The moment we got to the bantaba, everybody came out running to see me, hear the music, and buy casssettes. After Tabanding, we drove to my village of Foday Kunda. It's not far, but we had to climb over a very big rocky hill to get there. At the top of that hill you can see for two miles or more, all the way down to Foday Kunda. There was no road for a car when I was growing up, but now there is a way to drive. The old road we use to walk on went almost straight up the hill, but the car road there now has switchbacks back and forth going up and down that hill. All around that road is filled with big rocks too!

As soon as we got to Foday Kunda, we went straight to Kamateh Kunda. The head of the family, Demba Kamateh, was there with his family, and all the villagers were gathered in his compound to see me and hear the music. My cassette was playing for hours, with people dancing and talking to me, and they were all very happy. Then we continued traveling to the villages of Brifu and Kanapeh, staying in each one only for a short time, with many people gathered as soon as we arrived to see me, hear the music and dance. Then we went on to the villages of Musa Kunda and Wellingara. We could only stay for one hour, or maybe even only 45 minutes at many villages we went to, and then we had to pass on. Every village wanted me to spend the night there, but if I did that, I would be on the road for a long, long time! At other villages we went to, the people there didn't know that we were coming, but when they heard the music playing from my car, right away they recognized the songs and came out dancing to meet us. Me and Mahamadou and Alhaji were taking videos and pictures, and talking to the people, which I like so much. I don't want to just grab their money, I want to see them and I want them to see me too. It's the whole thing. That's why I didn't want to just have the cassette sellers to be the ones to sell my music.

That day we also traveled to Borro Kanda Kasse. That is the village where my mother was born, so I have very, very deep roots there too. It was sunset when we arrived, and as soon as we got there, we went to the compound of Sefou Juwara. He was the chief of the Wuli District, which is comething similar to the governor of a state. We were playing the Jooka song I wrote about Sefou Juwara on the loudspeakers as we drove into the town, and the whole village came out to greet us. I even have a video of that, because people were going so crazy! It was unbelieveable. When we arrived at his compound, Sefou was so happy and the whole village was too. That whole night was full of a lot of talking, music, and dancing.

Sefou Juwara's father and grandfather were also the chief rulers of the Wuli District. His grandfather Kanda Kasse Juwara was the one who brought my grandfather Jali Demba Jobarteh from Mali to Gambia many years before, and gave my mother the nickname of Madame when she was a little girl. During the time I was a child around seven or eight years old, I visited there with my mother and saw Kanda Kasse Juwara while he was the chief. When he passed away and his son Kandara Juwara became chief, I was studying the kora with my teacher in Passamasi. Sefou is the son of Kandara Juwara, and he became the chief when his father passed away. Sefou was actually named after his grandfather, so his real name is Kanda Kasse Juwara, but he is called Sefou because that word means chief. Sefou Juwara is a few years older than me, the same age as my brother Mahamadou, and we knew each other growing up. He also has a half-brother named Bossy Juwara, who is my same age and now lives in Washington, DC.

We spent that night at Sefou's family compound, and he also gave me a bull and 500 dalasi. The next day, February 26th, was a more laid back day. First, we visited Manjan Kunda where a lot of aunts, uncles, and cousins on my mother's side still live today. We didn't do a big music thing though, because most of the people from Manjan Kunda had come to Borro Kanda Kasse the day before. Then we traveled to Sutu Konding village to stay with the Jatta family in their compound. When we arrived there, I told the family, "I need to go to some other villages with the music, even if I can only be there for 10 minutes, but then I will come back." They said, "But now we are worried you will not come back here. We want you to spend the night". I replied, "You all have a lot of villages around here that I want to go to, but I promise I will come back tonight". So to show them this, I left my kora and all our bags in Jatta kunda when we left to go to the village of Bajonkoto.

On the way there, we passed a village called Banny. The road went a little way behind the village instead of through the middle, but the people heard my music while we were passing. On the way back from Bajonkoto, we had to pas that same way again to get to Madina, and by that time, the people of Banny were all out and waiting for me. Everybody in the village was standing at the junction, waving me to go down the little side road to get the middle of Banny. They were all hollering, "Why did you pass us? Why are you in a hurry to get to another village?" That village had a whole lot of blacksmiths, and those people were even holding their iron tools in their hands and hitting them together while they were standing on the roadside! On my Jooka cassette, I wrote a song about blacksmiths called "Numutunkan Jalan", and they liked that song a whole lot. They were even hollering the name of that song to us at the junction! When we drove down that little side road into the bantaba, all the people were following us. Quickly, I told my guys to fast-forward the cassette to that blacksmith song, to play it for them. Then the people went crazy because they liked it so much!

After a little while in Banny, we drove to the village of Madina. That village has a lot of blacksmiths too, and on my cassette, I even mentioned the name of some of the elder blacksmiths from there. When we first arrived, I could see in the distance that the leader of all the blacksmiths was sitting on the bentengo in the middle of the village bantaba. His name was Babanding Kanteh, and his compound was right there, facing the bantaba. He stood up when he saw us coming, and started dancing to the music! Then he began walking to his compound, and we followed in the car. We parked and entered his compound, and all the people in the village came in too. The blacksmith families gathered around us, men and women and children. After a while I told them, "I came to my state of Wuli, and I came to see all the people. We stopped by special to say hello to you, but we will have to leave in a little while". The women then rushed in and gave me a whole bunch of traditional handmade cloths, and the blacksmith men gave me 600 dalasi. The third Jooka cassette I have now recorded has a song about that village and those people! In that song, I say the name of the men blacksmiths Mohammed Kanteh, Tombe Suso, and Burama Turay, and I talk about all the other blacksmiths there. I also mention the women Kumba Damba and Penda Kanteh. I know that when all the people in that village hear my new song, they will be so surprised!

After we left Madina, we drove back to Suto Konding to spend the night with the Jatta family. The following day we went to a village called Sarenjai, near the border of Gambia and Senegal. In my childhood time, that place was a small Fulani village, but later on for some reason it grew up and became big, with stores like a town. There is a big market there now called a luumo, which means weekend, and when I was small, that market was only open at that time. But now it is so giant, and people from Gambia, Mali, and Senegal all come there to trade and sell their goods. People built a lot of new houses, and even a police station is there now. That luumo in Sarenjai is now the #1 place around that area, and every day it is jam-packed.

We arrived there in the afternoon, and something unbelievable happened: I saw somebody who is my old friend, and that I had not seen since 1961 or 1962! His name is Daakumba, and he is a Fulani guy from a village called Chinchukoli. We spent a lot of time together in my childhood time, and he was my wrestling mate even though he is a little bit older than me. We wrestled each other a lot, and he was a very good wrestler too. Chinchukoli is not too far from Sarenjai, and so I was talking to people in the luumo about Daakumba. They told me, "He is here even today in this town!" and they went to look for him. After being there a while, I decided to go to a restaurant to eat some grilled lamb. At the same time, Daakumba was there in the luumo and saw my car with the loudspeakers on top, and he started asking the people who the car belonged to. They told him, "It's the griot who makes the Jooka music", and said that he could find me at the restaurant. So Daakumba came there in the middle of us eating. I was so happy! Even though we had not seen each other since our childhood time, Daakumba looked exactly the same! We grabbed each other, then I said, "How are you? How many years since I saw you?" and he replied, "Yeah, I didn't die, I'm still here – ha ha!" So we sat down to talk about our childhood times, wrestling matches, and all that. I couldn't believe that after all those years we found each other. Wow. He also got to meet my daughter Nene, my blood brother Mahamadou, and my brother Mohammed's son Alhaji, who were all there with me too.

Later on that day, we returned back across the River Gambia and spent the night in Basse. The next morning we left Basse and drove all the way back to Brikama in one day, with no stopping. We were flying down the road, trying to get back home fast no matter what happened to my car. All the cassettes were gone by then too. Since those first 5000 cassettes all sold right away, I had contacted the place in Indianapolis to send me another 2500, and those all sold quickly too because the second cassette was a big hit just like the first one! After three more weeks at home in Brikama, I left to come back to U.S. on Monday, March 21st.

CIRCLING THE EARTH

I wasn't in Chicago for long before it was time to do more concerts and touring. On Tuesday April 5th, 2005, I performed with Bill Laswell at the Channel 11 studio in Chicago. With us were my longtime Mandingo Griot Society drummer Hamid Drake playing traps, Pharoh Sanders on saxophone, a famous and really good Indian tabla player named Zakir Hussein, and some other guys on keyboards and horn. It was for a well-known PBS television show called Soundstage. There was a whole bunch of other musicians there also, including Bootsy Collins from Funkadelic, who played with Bill separate from us. Among them was Buckethead, a guy that me and Bill had played with a few times before. Buckethead is from California and he plays guitar in a very different way, with very far-out kind of music. He wears a bucket on his head with two holes cut in it to see out, but no one can see his face. He also has a bunch of different buckets for different gigs and what mood he is in. Sometimes you can see his face, but it's covered in white paint so you still can't see what he looks like. He can play good though, very fast and spacey. Only California can have this kind of a guy! I like him and his music a lot. A whole lot of songs were played by all these musicians with Bill, but they had to cut out a lot of them to make it into a TV show.

A month later on May 11th, I flew to New York to play some more duet shows with Jack DeJohnette, because our new CD called Music from the Heart of the Masters had just come out a few weeks before. On Friday May 13th, we performed at Joe's Pub, which is not a big, big place but it is very famous. Afterward I went back to Chicago for a few weeks, and then flew back to New York for two days to perform a concert with Jack at the Clearwater Festival in Hudson on June 18th.

On Tuesday, June 21st, I started another Orion tour with Philip and everybody else from all over the world that was on the previous tour. Whenever we do the Orion music, Philip and his people make sure to bring everybody there to play, even if it's just for one show and they live on the other side of the world. Our first concert was in the big grass amphitheater at the Ravinia Festival outside of Chicago, and then we all flew out to California to perform at the Costa Mesa Performing Arts Center on the 23rd. Then we took a break until the rest of the tour in the fall, so on the 25th I flew back to Chicago to stay for the next couple of months. Then it was off to Japan with Bill Laswell again!

I arrived in Tokyo on August 18th, along with Bill, Hamid, Herbie Hancock, Aïyb, and some other musicians. The Japanese people picked us up and took us to the fanciest hotel I have ever seen in my life, called the Hotel Nikko. It was something else. It was not in the middle of the city, and it seemed like it was inside the water and even turned in the air or something. The next day, I heard that Bill and everybody were going to move to a hotel in downtown Tokyo and I said, "I want to move somewhere else too, where all my other people are going". So we went to the Century Hotel in the middle of Tokyo, near Shinjuku. We just did one concert that time in Japan, at the Tokyo Jazz Festival on Saturday August 20th, and then we all flew back to the U.S.

I spent a few weeks in Chicago, and then I took a quick trip to New York on September 13th. I think it was for hanging out or having meetings, but not playing any shows. Then I spent a couple more weeks in Chicago before going back to New York on October 2nd for the rest of the Orion tour. The first four shows were at BAM on the 4th, the 6th, and the 8th. I stayed with Philip at his house for those days, and then we all left on the 9th to fly to Guanajuato City in central Mexico. It's a small city and at least 500 years old, but has a big international arts festival every year called El Cervantino. We got to explore the city on our first day there, which was very nice. Then we performed our concert at the festival on the 11th. The next day we flew back to Houston, and stayed there until the 14th when we went to Austin to perform at the Bass Concert Hall.

At that time it was Ramadan, so I waited until after the show to eat. Fasting is something I am used to, and if you didn't already know it was Ramadan, you wouldn't know it by how I was. People always ask me,

"How can you survive to be touring and not eating?" but that is nothing for me compared to when I was growing up. We would be working hard in the fields all day without eating or drinking one thing, and no one was ever going to say, "We will stop working because we are fasting for Ramadan". Ramadan comes in the middle of the farming season many years, and every day we still have to walk out to the fields far away from our village to do giant work all day. From early in the morning until the evening, we don't eat anything and we don't even drink any water. It doesn't matter if it's hot, and you are sweating and thirsty. One has to grow up with it and be used to fasting, and then it's not so hard. But if you're not used to it, then I know it will be very, very hard.

On Saturday September 15th, we all left Austin to fly to LA on our way to Australia. We got to LA around one o'clock in the afternoon, and we had a long layover until around nine or ten o'clock at night. The airline people told us that that no matter where we went in those hours, we gotta get back to the airport for our flight. So I just walked around the airport a little bit, and other people went into town. After a while, I told my good friend Paulo from the band Uakti, "I want to go to Chinatown to eat some good food before we fly tonight". So I rented a car and and we jumped in to go to my favorite Chinese place, called Chinese Friends. We ate a lot of food and then we went to the beach at Santa Monica. When the flight time was coming closer, we returned the car and went into the airport to board the plane.

In the Orion band, there was a keyboard player named Ted Baker and a drummer named Mick Rossi. On that flight, Mick was by the window and Ted was in the aisle seat, and sitting in the middle of them was one little old lady. Ted is a very big guy, I mean very big. That lady thought Ted and Mick were crushing her to death. I was sitting in the row behind them, and I could see her looking, looking, looking at Ted, but he didn't look at her. Then she said something like, "I gotta get out of here!" Then Ted just looked at her and said, "Hey lady, chill out". That made the lady stand up right away, and she called out to the plane people to say, "I can't sit here! You have to find me some other seat! I cannot sit here!" They told her that the plane was full and there was nowhere for her to move, so she said, "Then I will stand!" and she got out in the aisle to stand there. She wouldn't sit down even when they said, "You gotta sit down before we can take off". Then again Ted said, "Lady, chill out". I thought I would be laughing all the way to Australia! When Mick heard me laughing, then he couldn't help it and he started laughing too. It was a crazy situation. She argued back and forth with the plane people, and they kept saying, "Ma'am, please sit down, the plane is getting ready to roll, but we can't go unless you sit. Please, we beg of you, you gotta sit down".

She finally sat down, but she covered her face almost the whole flight so she couldn't see anybody. It was at least a 15-hour flight. I always go to sleep anytime I fly somewhere, so I was sleeping, sleeping, sleeping all the way to Melbourne. By the time we got there and I woke up to look at her, she didn't have a happy face. I don't think she will ever forget that flight in her whole life. Now I always say, "Lady chill out!" anytime I talk to Ted, and we have a big laugh. We arrived in Melbourne, Australia on October 17th and went straight to the Grand Hyatt Hotel. We had time off to do some sightseeing for a couple of days, and then did a three-night stand of concerts at the Melbourne Arts Centre from Thursday the 20th to Saturday the 22nd. During the daytime on the 22nd, I also did a solo kora concert in Melbourne. The following day, we all flew back to the U.S., and I came back to Chicago to stay until around Thanksgiving time.

•••••

On November 25th, I flew home to Gambia for a nice five-month visit. While I was there, I paid for my sister Dibba Sakilaba to make her pilgrimage to Mecca. She is from the Basse area, and was married to my teacher in Passamasi. Also, Dibba's mother and my mother are sisters, so we call each other sister and brother. Sometime after I came to the U.S. my teacher Uncle Saikou, his three wives, his three brothers and their wives, and all their children left Passamasi to settle in the village of Lamin, which is between Brikama and Banjul. It was around 21 people in all. Later on, my teacher passed away and so did two of his brothers and some of the wives. Dibba never had any children, and stayed with the rest of my teacher's family in Lamin, and at this time, only two of the wives and a lot of the children were still living.

I knew that Dibba wanted to make the pilgrimage so much. But it's expensive to go to Mecca, and it's a big thing to go. You need to have money for transportation, food, and a place to stay, which can be 3,000-4,000 dalasi per person. And when pilgrims come home, there is a big welcome celebration for them too. Usually the husband, children, or some close family will make that payment, but she did not have that, so I paid for her pilgrimage. She went to Mecca on Sunday, January 1st, 2006, and came back on Friday, January 27th. On Sunday the 29th, I did the big welcoming party for her. I bought a big bull for cooking at the celebration, and I have a video of that too. Dibba was very happy, and she said to me, "Brother, this a big thing you did for me. Even if you never ever do anything for me ever again, that's OK".

Afterward while I was still in Gambia, a bunch of my family and friends died. The first was one of my aunts, Marafin Sakaliba, who died in Serekunda on Monday, February 6th. Her father and my grandfather Falai Suso were brothers, and I went to Serekunda that same day for the traditional burial. Then on Sunday the 12th, my childhood friend Sarjo Kanteh passed away. We grew up and played together in our village Foday Kunda, and that is where he died. Two days after that, another friend of mine named Turo Jallow died. He was a singer, and his traditional drummers always played with him when he sang. That same day, another childhood friend of mine named Burama Darboe passed away in Detroit. We grew up together in Foday Kunda too. After I came to U.S., he came to live in the Bronx. I remember that one of the times while I was staying in Philip's house, I called to invite him to come by. That day, one of his friends brought him over because he didn't drive. Only a few days later on Saturday, February 18th, one of my neighbors in Brikama named Ebu Jardama died, and I went to that burial. The next month on March 19th, the wife of a good friend of mine passed away. My friend is very popular in Brikama because he owns the gas station, and it was his second wife Bintu that died. On April 15th, another neighbor of mine at my first small compound in Brikama passed away, named Sarjo Ley. This all was a very sad beginning to the year 2006, but that's how it is, and there's nothing you can do. A lot more people that I know died that same year too, but I don't want to list any more.

Whenever Gambian people die someplace other than Gambia, all the Gambians that live there will gather and tell the government people, "We want to bury him in the traditional way", and those people will say OK. Sometimes the Gambians will want to send the body back to Gambia for the burial also. In Gambia, even if somebody dies at two or three in the morning, the whole family gathers right away to mourn. Everyone in the whole family will be crying together in the compound. The only other time where there is so much loud crying is when there is a fire that everyone needs to help put out together. When somebody dies, quickly, the whole village will know what happened. Then we have a way to specially wash the body, put it in a white cloth, prepare the whole thing, and bury the person that same day or the next morning.

During the last five or ten years, some people who live close to Banjul or another big city might have an autopsy done to find out the cause of death for a person in their family, but most others believe that it is a waste of time. A lot of people even laughed when the autopsy thing first came to Gambia. Even now, many people will say, "What? Cut into the body? No way! If it's their time to die, then they just go, and there's nothing we can do about it. Since it cannot prevent death or bring them back to life, don't do any autopsy". Also, when the autopsy thing first came to Gambia, it was only to Banjul. So if a person dies way out in the Basse area or a small village, they are not going to send somebody 275 miles to Banjul for that. Another reason that an autopsy is not needed is that in Gambia, there are not a lot of people who die because somebody killed them. If a person is walking by, and a tree falls on them and they die, nobody is worried about being hit by a tree because of that. You cannot stop a tree from falling if it's the time for that to happen, so why think to have an autopsy. It's the same with a car accident.

Just before I left Gambia to go back to Chicago, I decided to buy a motor scooter for my son Basaikou. I brought it home, and the next day I tried to ride it myself. It was so sweet! After I drove once around the block, I said, "Tomorrow I am going to buy my own motorcycle". Even Bobo looked at me and said, "What? Why do you want this? You are going back to America in two days!" but I replied, "It doesn't matter. Even if I was leaving tonight, I have to have it". Bobo just said, "Wow." So I bought my own motorcycle, and for the next two days I was flying all over Brikama on it! Basaikou and his friends were riding his scooter too. My motorcycle is still there at my compound, but Basaikou's scooter is long gone now.

•••••

On April 25th, 2006, I arrived back in Chicago and had a pretty laid back spring and summer. The only show I did was a Mandingo Griot Society reunion concert on August 17th at the Made in Chicago Music Festival in Millenium Park. All the bands playing the festival were from Chicago or started there, and that was the first time Mandingo Griot Society played together in a long, long time. Everybody was there from the band, and it was good. In the fall, things got very busy again for me.

My friends from Uakti connected me with another famous musician in Brazil named Wagner Tiso, and he invited me to perform at a concert in Rio de Janeiro. Tiso is also an arranger, composer, pianist, conductor, writes film scores, and he wanted his band to play some of my music. So I had transcriptions made of some of my compositions, and sent them to Tiso ahead of time. On Sunday October 29th, I left Chicago to fly to Rio de Janeiro, and arrived the next morning around 9:30. They sent a car to pick me and take me to the Hotel Gloria, and they hired somebody named Celia Lopez to translate for me the whole time I was there. On the 31st, I started three days of reheasals with Tiso and around seven or eight other musicians who work with him a lot. Our performance was on Friday, November 3rd at a giant concert hall called Sala Cecilia Meireles. We played some of my compositions and some of Tiso's, and I think it was part of a festival because my friends Uakti were playing there too. The next day, I flew back to Chicago.

On November 16th, I rented a car and drove down to Champaign-Urbana, Illinois for some solo kora concerts at the Spurlock Museum of World Cultures, on the University of Illinois campus. This university knew me very well because of all the years I taught kids in the schools in that area when I first came to the United States. The Spurlock Museum has a big auditorium inside that is a great place for music. I played daytime shows there for the students from Urbana High School on the 17th and 18th, and they liked it very much.

Two weeks later on November 29th, I started a European tour with Jack DeJohnette and Jerome Harris, a bass player. Jack's son-in-law Ben Surman was our soundman. On the Ripple Effect CD that I did with Jack, Ben played keyboard, and his father John Surman played bass clarinet. Jerome is a very good bass player, and a laid back guy too. We did a very nice tour. First we flew to Frankfurt, Germany and then switched planes to fly to a city in Poland called Bielsko-Biala. That was the first time I have ever been in that country. On December 1st, we did our first show of the tour at the Bielski Centrum Kultury, a big concert hall in the middle of the city. The next day, we flew to the Netherlands and did a concert in Amsterdam at a famous hall called Bimhuis. That place is like a big glass house hanging over the water, it's unbelievable!

On Sunday, December 3rd, our agent hired a van and a guy to drive us to a town in Germany called Gutersloh, and we performed that night at a place called Jugendzentrum. The next day, we flew to Salzburg, Austria and played at the Jazzit Musik Club. On the 5th, we drove to Vienna to play at a place called the Porgy & Bess Jazz and Music Club, and the next day we flew to Frankfurt and then drove to another German city called Rüsselsheim am Main to play in a huge auditorium called the Stadttheater. On the 7th, we flew to Zurich, Switzerland and played at a jazz club called Moods, which is inside a big giant building that used to be a factory. On the 8th, we flew to Sacile, Italy, and then drove to Pordenone. On the 9th, we drove to Milan and checked into the Grand Hotel to rest, because we had two concerts to do on the 10th. The daytime concert was at the Milan Teatro Manzoni, and the nighttime one was at the Auditorium de Milano.

We had another long drive to Porto Sant' Elpidio on the 11th, and checked into the Royal Hotel when we got there. Our concert on December 12th was at a performing arts center called Teatro delle Api, which means Theater of the Bees. I don't know why it has that name, but I will always remember that place because that night the music was the best of the whole tour. In fact, I think that was the best we all played at any time I ever played with Jack! The reason is because when we played my song Makola Market, which is about a real market in Ghana, I came up with a new part right on stage. I looped that new part with my Boomerang pedal machine and then played on top of it. Jack was playing on top of it all with the drums and Jerome was doing a heavy bass thing. That was such a lucky night. At every place on the tour, we always recorded the shows, and then we each got a copy to listen to later. But even after listening to that tape, I cannot do that part again at any other show. I saved that tape even to today. That part was so good. I have to figure out that thing again!

On the 13th we drove to Rome for a concert at a huge outdoor place called the Auditorium Parco della Musica. We had a day off the next day, so we went around and around sightseeing to a whole lot of places. I always like to have the chance to walk around and get to know any city. That day, we even went to the Pope's place at Vatican City to look around. On the 15th, we drove to Forli, Italy for our last show of the tour, a concert at the Naima Club, and stayed at the Hotel St. Giorgio. Then I flew back to Chicago. Later that month, James Brown died on the same day as Christmas. That was very sad news for me, and for the whole world. He was still performing all the time even though he was getting older. That guy was something else.

•••••

On Wednesday, January 17th, 2007 I flew from Chicago to Gambia for another long visit. The following Tuesday, my good friends Lamin Guye and his wife Aminata Laam came to my compound to give me and Bobo their little girl to raise. I have known these friends for a long time, and they live not too far away from us in my compound in Brikama. They named their little girl Bobodinding, which means little Bobo. In our tradition, it's a common thing for a namesake to raise the child who is named for them. Sometimes the elder namesake will ask the parents if they can raise the child, and sometimes the parents will ask the namesake to raise it. Everybody was happy about Bobodinding coming to live with my family: Bobodinding, Lamin, and Aminata, me and Bobo, and all our children. I think Bobodinding was about five or six years old when she came to live with us, and she is still living in my house today. Now she is taller than everybody in the house! I also have seven kids that are my namesake, and named Fodaymusa. Some are living in Brikama, and some are in other villages or towns.

On Monday, March 5th, my drummer friend Harris Eisenstadt came to Gambia to visit me again, and to take more Mandingo drumming lessons from my friend Jalamang Camara in Brikama. During the three weeks Harris was staying with me in my compound, a very good person named Fakebba Sambou passed away on March 22nd. Fakebba had a small table in the Brikama market where he would sell one candle at a time, one pack of cigarettes at a time, or a little bit of kola nuts. He never had an extra dime, but one day many years ago he came to my compound at around seven o'clock in the morning. This was at my first Brikama compound, which was very small, and it must have been around 1998 or 1999, because Nene was still a small child. Fakebba had an old raggedly bike that he pedaled there, and he had a chicken with him. Bobo was outside fixing breakfast and he asked her, "Is this Jali Fodaymusa's compound? Is he around?" Bobo said yes, and told Nene to wake me. I heard him speaking to her because I was awake but still laying in bed, and then Nene ran inside the room to say, "Baba come out, a chicken seller is here". I thought to myself, "This person is here so early to be selling a chicken!" We greeted and then I gave him a stool to sit down, and I sat down too.

He said, "My name is Fakebba and I am from the Foni District. The only reason I came here today is that I heard your Jooka music and I like your traditional singing. I was born and grew up with that kind of thing. When I heard your Jooka songs and singing, I couldn't help it, I have to do something for you. I don't have anything, but today I am bringing you this chicken. That's all I can afford. I haven't got any money, but I want to give this to you to cook for your lunch or dinner. This is the gift I have for you".

This touched my heart a lot. That kind of thing is very rare for me since I settled in the western part of Gambia. Most people who are not my family or friends will come to my house because they have never seen me before, and only heard my name. Most of the time they ask me for something, like a cassette, money, or something else. But this poor guy didn't want anything from me, instead he took the last chicken he might have had and gave it to me. That feeling touched me so heavy that I decided to compose a song for him in 2004, and put it on my second Jooka cassette. Now that we griots don't have kings and warriors to compose for, we can compose songs for any people we want to. Being a known griot like I am, sometimes people will give me money and even though they don't come out and say, "Compose a song for me", I know that's what they would like. Once I sing a song about them, everybody will be hearing their name and that person will become famous. Other people will even travel to see that person. But before I compose a song for someone, I have to feel correct, and feel good inside about the person. Fakebba was one of those people. For me, it's not about how much money somebody will give me, but how their heart is and how they are inside.

•••••

A few weeks after Fakebba passed away in 2007, I went to visit my good friend Jimmeh Camara for a few weeks. I hadn't seen him since 1978, when we met during my first visit back to Gambia after I went to the U.S. At that time, I was staying in a small place in the middle of Banjul called Rest House. That was before I had any compound of my own, and before either of us were married. That place was a small, two-story building, and even today, the building is there but it has something else inside it now. I had a room on the second floor, and Jimmeh was visiting Banjul from Sierra Leone and had a room on the second floor also. Another Gambian friend named Ansumana Sankareh was staying in that place too. These two guys became my good friends, and every night after dinner on the veranda or my living room, I would be playing the kora. All three of us always had a lot of visitors coming to see us there too. Wow, those times, and the things that happened in that place, it was a trip. Then Jimmeh went back to Sierra Leone for the diamond business and Ansumana went to live in France. Many Gambians have been living in Sierra Leone since the late 1950's, and after Jimmeh went to Sierra Leone, we were never in Gambia at the same time again. I even forgot about him.

But then my Jooka cassettes came out, and Jimmeh heard them when he was visiting Gambia in early 2007. Those cassettes both became so famous. In fact, one night while I was in Seattle listening to the online Gambian newspaper, they were playing my Jooka music on that website, and the next day a friend of mine called me to say, "Jaliba, I heard your songs on the news!" When Jimmeh heard those Jooka cassettes, he started telling people, "I know this griot" and asking them where he could buy some cassettes for himself, and they told him that he had to go to Brikama. So he went there and came to my compound, but I wasn't there that day. Bobo was there, and he told her, "My people tell me that you have Jooka cassettes here", and he bought five of them. He also said, "When your husband comes back, please tell him to call me" and he left his name and number with her. After he left, Bobo called me to say, "I don't know when you are coming home, but somebody came here who says that he knows you, and he bought a bunch of your cassettes. He said you should call him, and here is his number". I asked her his name, and she told me it was Alhaji Jimmeh. In our tradition, Alhaji is added to your name after you complete the pilgrimage to Mecca, but since I didn't know Jimmeh had done that, I thought to myself, "I don't know anybody by that name".

I called the number anyway, and somebody in his family answered. I asked them, "Can I speak to Alhaji Jimmeh?" and then he came to the phone. Even after all those years, the moment he opened his mouth, right there I recognized him and remembered everything. It was like we have always been together. I said, "Jimmeh! How are you? Where are you?" He said, " I am in Serekunda! When are you coming here, when are you coming, when are you coming?" That guy, he can talk fast. He told me where he lived and exactly how to get there, so I went to his place with my blood brother Mahamadou. When I got there, I could see a whole bunch of stores there that all belonged to him, and behind them was a three-story building where he lived. The moment we saw each other, we grabbed each other and sat down a little bit to talk. He said, "Hey, my griot, long time!" and I said, "Our talking is not going to stop here. I will come and visit you all the way in Sierra Leone. Not now, but one day I will come there".

He told me all about his life, that he lived very far from the capital of Freetown in a town called Mbama Konta, and that his compound was big and full with people. He had three wives and lot of children, and some were married and living in Sierra Leone too. He also told me he owned houses in the Fajara area near Banjul, besides all the Serekunda properties. Then we went inside his house, and he brought out almost a pound of gold to show me. He said, "I can give you all this if you can bring it to the United States to sell, and then send me my money". I said, "No, don't give me your gold. I don't know anything about selling gold, and I still stick to my music. The cassettes you bought, that is my merchandise". Later on when I was getting ready to go back to Brikama, I told him, "I'm glad we saw each other and nothing bad happened to either of us, and that I know where you are living now". Then I told him, "I can't spend any more time here right now, so go inside the house and bring me some money". He came out bringing 5000 dalasi, all in a pack. Oh, that guy is something else.

A couple of years after that, while I was in Gambia again, I went to visit him in Sierra Leone. First, I flew from Banjul to Freetown, and stayed overnight in a hotel there. A lot of people know Jimmeh in Freetown, and he told them, "A friend of mine is coming, and he will spend the night here. I will pay for this hotel, and then in the morning, I want somebody to take him to the bus station to catch the bus and come to my house". So in the early morning, I heard a knock on my hotel room door and somebody's voice asking me, "Are you Alhaji Jimmeh's guest?" and I said yes. Then they took me to the first bus that went to the town of Bo, and I arrived around three o'clock in the afternoon. I didn't know where to get off the bus, but the guy that took me to the station had also told the bus driver, "This is Mr. Jimmeh's guest from Gambia, make sure to let him know where to get out at Bo". When I got up from my seat to come to the front of the bus, right away I saw Jimmeh standing there and asking the bus driver, "Do you have a guy here that came all the way from Gambia?" So I flew out of the bus, and we greeted. We got in his car and start going around that area together, and he introduced me to some older Gambians who had been living there a long time. Then we drove and drove, and finally got to his town of Mbama Konta. He has a very nice wife named Aminata Kurama, who is from Sierra Leone. I stayed with them for three weeks, and then I went to Sefadou, another big city in the Kono District of Sierra Leone. All the problems that people hear about with the blood diamonds and all that, come from that area because it is the biggest diamond-mining place.

When I got to Sefadou, I went to visit a Fulani guy named Samba Sabally, who I first met when I was studying the kora in Passamasi. Samba's family compound was only around a half mile away from my teacher's compound, and we spent a lot of time together. In Sierra Leone, Samba also had a lot of Gambians living with him in his house. I stayed with him for one week, then on Tuesday April 10th, I flew from Sefadou to Freetown, and then back to Gambia. I spent another six weeks at home with my family, then flew back to Chicago on May 22nd. Samba passed away in 2013 or 2014, but luckily we were able to see each other again during this visit.

After a few weeks back in Chicago, , I had another meeting in Chicago with the trumpet player Stephen Burns on Thursday June 7th. He was interested in working with me again to write some music together for his group called Fulcrum Point New Music Project. After that, from time to time he would come to my apartment with his trumpet to rehearse and write music together, and then we would have it transcribed.

⋯⋯

On Thursday, July 26th, my favorite uncle Aliev Suso passed away. He was the #1 kora maker in all of Gambia. Uncle Aliev didn't play the kora himself, but he was a master kora maker, and we griots could get any amount of koras we needed from him. He is originally from the Gambian village of Booraba, but lived near Serekunda in the town of Bakou for many years. When Scandinavian tourism first started in Gambia in 1968, he made souvenir koras to sell in the marketplace too. He was the first person to ever do that. He made miniature kora versions with seven or eight strings and not playable, and some that were larger with more strings. The small ones cost only around 5 dalasi, and he made many, many thousands of them. It seemed like everybody who was a tourist from Scandinavia took one home from Gambia as a souvenir, and wherever they went you could see them holding those little koras in their hand.

Other than the first kora I brought to the United States in 1977, which I built myself, Uncle Aliev built all the other koras I have ever had. Whenever I went to Gambia, I always went to visit him in Bakou and say, "I have something for you", because I would take plastic bags of kora strings and decoration nails to him from the U.S. I would give him all these kind of tools and supplies, and never ask him for a penny. So too, whenever I asked him for a kora, he never asked me for a penny. He built a lot of koras for me! Even now, I have five koras stored in Chicago in a friend's house that he made for me. But the last kora he built for me is my favorite, and the one that I take with me for all my performances all over the world. It is a very special kora and always sounds very sweet. I think it will be my last kora, because this is the kora I want to play for the rest of my life. The story of how I got it is very sweet too.

One time while I was in Gambia, I went to see Uncle Aliev and told him, "If you find a calabash that is sorongo and you build a kora out of that, it will be the sweetest sound of all koras." A sorongo calabash means oval-shaped, and it is very difficult to find. In fact, you would see at least 1000 round calabash before you would find one that is sorongo. So I asked him, "Please find one like that and save it for me, even if I am not in Gambia at that time". Then one day around 2005 or 2006 when I went home to Gambia, I called him to say, "Uncle, this is your son Fodaymusa from America. I have something for you". Then he said, "Me too, I have something for you". So I picked a date to come and visit him in Bakou, and we met at the tourist market near the big hotels, where he had his selling place. I pulled out my bags of nails and strings and gave them to him, and he pulled out that sorongo calabash. He said, "Here, I got it!" and I said, "Aha, this is very, very good! Go ahead and build a kora for me with this calabash. But once you build it, just leave it it plain like that. Don't put handles on it, because I will put the hole in it and take the handles off one of my koras in Chicago to use on this new kora. Then I will string it and decorate it myself". So he built this kora body for me, and after it was all dried, I had a cloth bag made to take it back to Chicago. After I got back to Chicago, I worked on it until it was finished, and decorated it with the nails and paint. I always did the nail design on my other koras too. It's a very strong calabash, and very rare, and my favorite of all koras. I was very lucky that Uncle Aliev found that sorongo calabash for me, because it was not too long afterward when he passed away.

A lot of people ask me why I always paint the back on all my koras. Nobody ever used to do this, but once I started doing it and other kora players saw it, painting became very popular. Now many players do it too. Here is the story of that first painted kora. When I first came to the U.S. in 1977 with the first big kora I made, I traveled around with it for many years. In all those years, I never had any case for it, because there was no kind of kora case to buy at that time. Every time Mandingo Griot Society would fly somewhere for a show, the airline people would say, "If it gets lost, we will pay you, but if it's spoiled during the flight, that's your own responsibility". Then the plane people would just lay it on the baggage rack and load it into the plane. I never worried about it because my thinking was, "It's my family instrument, so I know that I can get a new kora made for me if it breaks". I was always lucky with it for a long, long time too, until one flight from Hartford, Connecticut to Montreal, Canada around 1982. When I picked it up from the baggage place in Montreal, I could see that my kora had a big crack on the bottom, right along the line of the nails. Luckily the sound didn't change much because that calabash is very thick, and I played the show like that.

But when I came back to Chicago, I told my good friend Manu, "I broke my kora and I don't know what I can do to try to fix it". He told me, "You can fix it with fiberglass". At that time, since I had never worked with fiberglass, I didn't know that it was a liquid that can become hard like a rock. Manu knew all about that, so we went to the hardware store to get some. Then we took my kora to Washington Park, to fix it outside because of the way that fiberglass smells. I loosened the kora neck, and then the crack kind of came back together, so we put the fiberglass cloth and liquid on the outside of the kora to cover the whole crack. When it dried, I knew that the crack could not go anywhere now, and it was all fixed. But a few days later when I looked at that big patch, I started thinking that maybe I should paint over it. So I did it. I'm not a painter, but I painted it in a way that looked professional. Since then, I have always painted every kora I got, even a brand new kora that has nothing wrong with it. Now I always paint my website address on it too now, but back then in 1982 there was no computer thing, no internet, and no website.

After fixing my first kora in that way, I got a second kora, which I painted and used for a while. Then when I got my third kora, I decided to try to get a case for it. My friend John Crowley is very good at building things, and so he built me two different cases. The first one was made out of aluminum and very heavy, and had latches to lock it. The bottom part was flat and the top part was tall and fit over the kora. There was foam padding inside that fit the kora very nice too. In fact, it looked like a spaceship or a shiny metal tipi! That idea was very good, but the case was so heavy I could not travel with it. Then John made me a second case out of fiberglass. He measured the size of the kora exactly, made the case to be the exact shape of the kora, painted it black, and put a strap on it for carrying. It was very nice looking, and I traveled with it for a long, long time, but even that one was too heavy. Some time after that, when I was going to tour with Herbie in 1984, I told him that I needed a good case for my kora and dusongoni. So Herbie had two huge, heavy aluminum cases made with foam inside, for the roadies to carry and move around. At the end of that tour, he said I should keep those cases, but I said no and left them with Herbie. Those big cases I cannot carry, so I went back to using the fiberglass one.

Then a few years later, I was in New York talking to a musician friend about needing a case, and he told me that there was a lady in town who could make a bag for any kind of instrument. Her name is Kelly, and she had a very small office in Chinatown where she made her bags. My friend gave me her number and when I called her, she asked me where I lived so she could come see the kora. I told her Philip's address, and the next day she came to meet me there and measured the kora. Then she sewed a bag for it that was light and very strong, and padded very well. That bag helped me a lot. She made a bag for my dusungoni too. In the past 30 years, she has made me four kora bags, and each of them lasted for a long time. In all these years, I have also given a lot of kora players in the United States her number, and she has made bags for all those people too. She can make a bag for anything! At the time I first met her, her company was small, with just her and her husband working, but now it's called Undercover Bags and is very big. She moved it from New York to Massachusetts or Connecticut, and has people working for her. Once in 2015 when I was in New York, a friend of mine told me about a guy in San Francisco who could make a lightweight hardshell case for the kora. I still like my cloth case a lot, but maybe someday I will have that guy build something for me.

• • • • •

On Monday, August 13th, 2007, I went to New York for a couple of weeks, just for a visit and no concerts to play. I came back to do a solo kora concert at Columbia College in Chicago on the 28th, and a few weeks later I met with Stephen Burns again on September 17th to talk about plans for a perfomance together. It was Ramadan and I don't like to do a whole lot of stuff at that time unless I have to, so my activities were not super busy. On Wednesday, November 7th, I flew back to New York for the rest of that month, and went into the recording studio with Bill Laswell on the 21st. We recorded a new song I wrote, but we did not ever release on as a CD or anything. After I spent most of December in Chicago, I flew back to New York on December 27th to play for an African festival in a church there and then came back to Chicago on the 31st.

•••••

On January 23rd, 2008, Stephen Burns came to my place again for us to rehearse some songs, and on February 7th, he met me at a rehearsal place called Merit Music on South Peoria St. We rehearsed the songs there together with his band Fulcrum Point, and the next night we rehearsed again at the Chicago Youth Symphony on South Michigan Avenue. Then on the 10th we did a concert at the Harris Theater in downtown Chicago. That show was very good.

Two days later on Tuesday February 12th, I got a call from Brikama to tell me sad news from my eldest brother Mohammed Suso. Mohammed had three wives and a lot of children, and each one of those kids had their own children too. His daughter Mariama had a husband and two children, and she suddenly got sick and died there at his compound. In Mandingo tradition, his daughter is my daughter and his grandchildren are my grandchildren. For her to pass away so young was a hard time for everybody in the whole family, and all the neighbors too.

A couple of months later, I did another rehearsal with Stephen Burns at my apartment for a school concert at Leonard School and another school on April 1st and 3rd. Then I went to New York to work with Paul Simon on April 17th, for a big thing he was doing at BAM. He was playing a lot of the music he ever wrote during his life, in a bunch of concerts with musicians he had played with from all over the world. He was doing a kind of residency at BAM, and I think they were playing concerts for almost the whole month of April. Paul had one song he wrote called "Silent Eyes", and he and his people were talking among themselves to see if they could get a musician to play one particular part in that song. They were talking about all different instruments and players, and Steve Gorn, a very good Indian flute player and friend of Philip, suggested me. Then they all said, "Wow, yes let's have a him play a kora part, that is something different".

Many years before that, I had met Paul Simon when he came for dinner while I was staying at Philip's house. That night, we all ate together: Philip, his girlfriend Candy, his good friend who is called Stuck, Paul Simon, and his girlfriend Carrie Fisher. So all these years later when Steve Gorn mentioned my name, Paul said, "Oh yeah, I remember meeting that guy" and he called Philip at the beginning of April to find out how to contact me. When Paul called him, Philip was at the LA airport on his way to Australia. It was early morning in Chicago, and I was asleep when the phone rang and Philip said, "Hey Foday, it's me. I just talked to Paul Simon and he wants me to give him your phone number. He wants you to come and work with him in New York". I said OK, and by nine o'clock that morning, Paul called me. He said, "Foday, I want to bring you here. I want you to come and work with me here, and play the kora on one of my songs. Will you come?" I said, "Well, I'm not saying yes or no yet, because I gotta hear the music". I like to make sure it will be sweet before I say I will do anything. That's just the way I am, no matter who is calling. I want to put my music into something I can do well, not just throw something together and do it even if it doesn't work well. Once I know it will be sweet, then I will agree to do it. So then Paul said, "I will send you the song". He overnighted his CD to me with the song Silent Eyes on it, and I got it the next morning. As soon as it arrived, I put it on the CD player and listened to it again and again, and played my kora with it. By eleven o'clock that morning, Paul called me to see if I got the CD, then he told me the section he wanted me to play. He said, "Can you do it?" and I said yes. So he had the guy who was arranging everything at BAM call me to make arrangements for my fee, the flight, and other stuff. They wanted me to come and rehearse, then play for five nights.

I didn't know if it would actually happen though, because I didn't hear back from Paul's guy again for almost two weeks. Finally he called me at the middle of April to tell me that it was for sure. I arrived in New York on April 17th and we reheased from the 18th to the 22nd. Then we played the shows from April 23rd to the 27th, with the same two-hour show every night. I think Paul brought around 100 musicians there during that month. Each group of musicians played a bunch of shows, and then a new group would play the next ones. On the nights I played, there were a lot of people on the stage, but I did not know anyone else in the band other than Steve Gorn.

I flew back to Chicago on April 29th, and played another school concert with Stephen Burns and Fulcrum Point on May 6th at the Beasley School, not too far from my apartment in Hyde Park. A few weeks later on Saturday, May 24th, I did a solo kora concert at the Dominican University in River Forest, Illinois. Maurice Bibbs is the name of the crazy guy who booked me there. The reason I think he is crazy is that he sent a limousine to pick me and take me to the concert place, instead of just a car or a taxicab! On May 27th, I flew to New York again for a solo kora concert at the Gerald Lynch Theater in John Jay College, and came back to Chicago on June 2nd. During all this time since 1977, I never had a manager or agent that was booking me or my band, people just contacted me directly to ask me about playing for them. That's just how it is for me today too.

On Monday, June 16th at twelve o'clock at night, my good friend Manu Walton and his wife had a baby boy. Manu had gone to Gambia two times and married a wife from Serekunda. Her name is Amie Cissoko, which is the same last name as Suso. I was there in Chicago for the baby-naming ceremony the following Monday the 23rd, and they named the baby Ahmed Samba Walton. On the 26th, I did another concert with Stephen Burns and Fulcrum Point at the Garfield Park Conservatory in Chicago, and the next week on Wednesday July 2nd, I flew to Gambia. That was right in the middle of the rainy season, and it was raining so hard non-stop for two or three days after I arrived. I don't usually go to Gambia at that time of the year, because I like it better in the wintertime dry season, but I just wanted to see my family so much. From the Banjul airport to my house in Brikama, it was just pouring, pouring, pouring.

The whole time I was there it rained so much! Wow, it was a long time since I ever saw that much rain. I stayed in Brikama until Sunday, August 30th, and arrived back in Chicago the next day.

On September 13th, I did a solo kora concert at Mt. Holyoke College in Massachusetts, and then returned again to Chicago. About a month later on Thursday, October 16th, a very famous Gambian radio commentator named Alhaji Lalo Samateh died suddenly. He had his own national show on Radio Gambia about the news and many other things since that station was first created in the 1960s. He knew everything about the history of Gambia, and for all those years the whole of Gambia knew him and listened to his show, from the cities to the countryside and bush places. He was a very famous person to everyone.

OBAMA

On Monday, November 3rd, 2008, Barak Obama's grandmother died in Hawaii. I remember that because it was the day before the election when he became president. Obama was living in Hyde Park at the same time that I was living there, but I never saw him in person. He lived about six blocks from me, somewhere off 51st Street between Washington Park and my apartment. That whole year of 2008, even way before the election, police blocked the whole area around his house to guard him, so everybody had to detour around that. But one funny thing is that we went to the same barbershop and had the same barber too! The place was called Robert's Barbershop, and it was on 53rd and Harper, and then it moved to behind Blackstone and 51st Street. There were five barbers there who put that shop together, and I knew all of them very well, so whoever was not busy can cut my hair. One of those guys was also Obama's barber, and one time I saw him being interviewed on TV. The TV people were all over Hyde Park that year too, talking to everybody all the time. I used to tease that barber, "Oh, pretty soon you will be moving to Washington DC and the White House! You might be the new president's barber, but don't forget about me. Maybe I can come play for you while you cut his hair!" They didn't take him to Washington after the election though.

I have a good friend in Chicago named David Braswell, and he has been my good friend for a long time in Chicago, almost since when I first arrive in 1977. The first time I saw Obama on TV saying that he wanted to be the president, I was with David and some other friends. I told them, "This guy is going to become president", but David said, "Jali, don't you know the history here? That will never happen. No, no, no, that's not going to happen. There will never be a black president in the United States". I asked him why, and all those guys told me that no black American could be elected in this country. But again, I said, "Yes, this can happen. You are making a mistake. This guy will be the president here". They asked me why I thought so, and I said, "I know because of traditional knowledge. When I was growing up, the elder people back home would say that how a person looks can mean he will be a leader: his body structure, the kind of ears he has, the shape of his head, the kind of voice, and the way his mouth moves. They can see that on a young person and know what will be, and they don't have to know a person for a long time to see it. They will say that whenever you see these things on a human being, that person can be a ruler. They will be the leader of whatever group they're in".

I also told those friends that this is a special traditional knowledge, to know what is inside a person just by looking at them. And when that person opens their mouth, then you see more of the difference between them and other people. I said to them, "In our tradition, what makes people different is their look and their way of being, so when I see Obama, I remember what the elders say and I know he will be a ruler. He has that look". My friends all still said no to me. So when the election happened, I told David, "Do you see? Now what? Some things are meant to happen. Obama is a natural leader of human beings". He replied, "That blows my mind, I couldn't believe!" On the election night, there was a big celebration in Chicago, and Grant Park was jam-packed with the people who were so happy for him to be president.

On January 20th, 2009, I stayed in my apartment and didn't go anywhere, because the whole day I was watching all the Obama inauguration stuff on TV. People were so excited all over the city in Chicago, and because Obama lived in Hyde Park, there were a lot of people celebrating on all the streets around my apartment too. That was a very happy time.

•••••

When I first arrived in the United States, right away I saw so many people whose ancestors came here during the slave trading time. One time I said to myself, "I want to write a book, but not for reading. It will be a picture book and I will call it, The World Twins. I will take pictures of Black Americans living in the United States, and then match them with people living in Africa". The reason I thought of doing a book like that is because sometimes when I see Black Americans, I can almost tell which part of Africa they are from, even if they don't say a word. Sometimes I even see someone in the United States who looks exactly like one of my good friends back home in Gambia! But I didn't ever do that book.

My own belief is that there were a lot of Fulani people who were brought to the west as slaves. There are a few things I know that make me believe that. When I first came to the United States, I saw a lot of Black Americans doing something that traditional Fulanis did a long ago when I was growing up. Typical traditional Fulani men would make a comb out of bamboo to comb their hair, and leave that comb in their hair the same way that some people do now with an afro pick. But the big, big thing I have noticed is that the voice of the Fulani people and the voice of Black Americans sounds the same. The words are different, but the sound of their voice is exactly the same. For example, when I hear Black Americans talking but they are too far away for me to hear the words they are saying, and I can just hear the tone, rhythm, and pitch of their voice, it all sounds just the same as a Fulani voice. To my ear, Fulanis are the main tribe that has a voice to sound like that.

One other thing I will tell you is that, in the time before the slave trade started, and during the time it was happening, African kings had something built called a tato, which means war fence, around all their villages. The tato formed one big village out of all those smaller villages. It was a giant wall about six feet thick, made of mud and rocks and whatever they could find, and about 15 feet tall. The people with spiritual powers called the soothsayers would tell the king to use his most beautiful daughter as the tato pillar, and the daughter would volunteer for this. They washed her in a special way and dressed her, and then they built the thick wall on top of her and buried her in it. They had a strong belief that this tato would be a spiritual barrier and a physical barrier. But Fulani villages are known to be far away by themselves, in isolated areas so that their cows can have a lot of room for grazing. This is why I think that the slave traders caught a lot of Fulanis out in the bush. The white slave-trading people bought slaves from the kings, who had men that went out into the bush and captured people. Those men could not go and capture anybody without the king agreeing to it. But since Fulanis are isolated and out by themselves with their cows, there was nobody to protect them, and so they were most likely to be caught.

Fulani people are a big tribe in Africa, and you can find them in a lot of countries from Ethiopia all the way to West Africa: Gambia, Senegal, Mauritania, Guinea-Bissau, Guinea, Sierra Leone, Liberia, Ivory Coast, Burkina Faso, Mali, Ghana, Niger, Cameroon, and Ethiopia. Fulanis that have spread out to all these countries are still called Fulani, but have a lot of different names added to that, such as Lorobe Fulani, Pullofuta Fulani, or Tuklor, Gajaka, Matam, Anlunke, Hodobe, and Sabala Fulani. Some Fulani people are regular farmers, a lot of them are cattle herders, and some are very heavy Islamic scholars. I know about these things because my own village of Sare Hamadi was a Fulani and Mandingo village, named after the Fulani man Hamadi Baldeh who founded it. And I grew up with a lot of Fulani people as my friends, and traveled all over West Africa and know many different African languages too. A lot of people in Africa don't know that Fulanis are such a big tribe, because they usually only see a small Fulani village next to a big Sarahule village or a big Mandingo village. But I know Fulanis, and I don't think there is any tribe in Africa bigger than them.

•••••

My good friend David Braswell had a son named David too, and when he was a young boy, he had a sickness that made his skin scaly. He was crying all the time from it, and scratching until his skin would bleed. He was a small boy for his age too, and David tried everything for this sickness, but nothing would heal it. One day I told him, "I'm going to Africa soon, and I'm sure we have some herbs there that will help. I will bring some back with me". He said, "I've tried everything here and nothing works" but I replied, "The world is big, so it doesn't mean that there is just one place and one thing to try. If one doesn't work, then there are other places to go and things to try. In different places, the soils and the plants are different, and even the water is different". So when I went to Gambia, I talked to a lot of herbal people about the child's sickness. I didn't know the name of it, but one guy said to me, "Ah, I know what you are talking about". I said, "Do you all have anything for that?" and he said, "Yes, before you leave I will get something for you, and I will explain to you exactly what to do. If you do it in that way, you will get rid of this sickness". So just before I left Gambia, I went to visit that guy again, and he gave me the herb. When I got back to Chicago I took it to David and said, "This is what you must do every day: Give him some of this herb to drink every morning and evening. Also, give him a bath every morning and evening, and rub a lot of this herb on his body". It wasn't more than two months before the whole thing started changing. Now that boy is a grown man, and he is big and strong. He even came and visited me in Gambia one time! I still call him Young David, and he calls me Godfather. I will laugh and say to him, "Are you that same small boy?"

But in November of 2008, David Braswell started getting sick. On December 26th, me and Young David got together in Chicago to hang out a little bit and see what's happening with each other. By that time, David and his wife Marcia also lived in the same building as me in Hyde Park. His wife told me that David was very sick, and it was getting him way down. I was always wondering about that, but I thought maybe it was just because he was getting older. One day David even told me, "I will go to the Chinese doctor for it". His wife Marcia kept telling him, "Let's go to the hospital" but he wouldn't go, and they argued a lot about that. The sickness became much worse, and he became so skinny, almost like a skeleton.

On Tuesday, February 3rd, 2009, at around 9 in the morning, Marcia knocked on my door. She was very upset and almost crying, and she said, "Come see your friend". When I saw how he was looking, I said, "We are going to the hospital", but he was just going wild on me, saying, "Don't talk to me about the hospital, I'm not going!" Marcia also called Young David and his other son, and they came there too. But David just wouldn't listen to any of us. No one could tell him anything. I left for a little while, and then came back to the apartment and told him, "David, we are going to the hospital today. No matter what you do or say, today you are going". He said to me "Jaliba, don't take me to the hospital, I don't want to go". Then I told Marcia and the kids, "We are going to take your dad to the hospital, and even if he is going to die today, it will not be here in the house. We gotta go to the hospital". So Marcia called the ambulance, and quickly the people came and they put him in stretcher to take to Providence Hospital, which is the neighborhood hospital in Hyde Park. We followed the ambulance and got there at ten o'clock in the morning. Those people did what they could do for long time, and they put a lot of wires on his body. Then at three o'clock in the afternoon, they transferred him to Cook County Hospital. We followed the ambulance there. Those other doctors worked on him all the rest of that day there until very late in the night. They put a lot of needles and wires on him there too.

At around one or two o'clock in the morning of the next day, the doctor came out to talk to us in the waiting room, and said, "Now you can come inside to see him". When we came in his room, David was lying in the bed like a dead body, unconscious. I went to his head area, where he had all these wires coming out of his nose and hand, and a machine helping him breathe. I held his toe and put my hand on it. His wife and sons started crying, but I said, "No, don't cry. He will come out of this thing. Nothing is going to happen to him". I just had a feeling like that. But at that time, they all thought I was talking crazy. We went home at around two o'clock, and during that day Marcia came back to the hospital. David was getting better! Then every day the family would go see him, and sometimes I would go with them too. David stayed in there for two or three weeks, and he kept getting better and better until he came out of hospital and went back to his house. He said to me, "If not for you, I would be dead now" but I told him, "It was God who did that". Even today he is well. He is my good friend, and still always calls me Jaliba.

SEATTLE

The whole time I was living in Hyde Park, I found it to be the best place for me in Chicago. For all the 32 years I lived there, it was rare to hear or see something on TV about crime that happened in Hyde Park. I could go out at two or three o'clock in the morning, and still feel safe. Hyde Park is where the University of Chicago is, and it's a happening place, with a lot of students living from 47th Street all the way to 57th Street. There is also University of Chicago police and city police, so maybe that's another reason it is so safe, but to me, it always seemed like the people living there were more mellow and didn't want crazy stuff happening.

To move to Seattle first came into my mind in early 2009. I was thinking about it for a little while, maybe only two months. I was thinking, "I've been in Chicago for a long time now. Maybe I can try something new for a change. I don't want to go live in New York, and I don't want to go to LA. Maybe Seattle. It's far away, but maybe things will be different and it will be good to be there. I don't know much about the music scene, but I know that it's a pretty big city. Let me call my friends there, Emily and Uno. If they tell me that I should come, then I will go there".

So I called Emily to say, "I'm thinking about coming to live in Seattle, and I want to come there and look around a little bit". She replied, "That's great! Come and stay with us while you look around this town. When you come, your room will be here waiting for you". She also said that she was coming through Chicago on March 10th, on her way to see her family in Indiana. When she got there, we went to lunch together in downtown Chicago at my favorite Indian place, and then we were just walking around downtown together for a while. That's when I told her, "Hey Emily, I am coming to Seattle to live. I made up my mind that I want to come and live in Seattle, not just to look around". She asked me if I had a place to live, and when I said no, she said, "Your room is here. Come and live with us. You can stay as long as you want". That made me very happy, and I told my friends in Chicago. Some of them said, "Wow, we are so surprised about all this!"

On Thursday, March 19th, I went to New York again and did a duet concert with Philip at the City Winery on the 22nd, and came back to Chicago on the 24th. I started packing all the things that I wanted to take with me, and getting rid of the things I didn't need anymore. A month later on April 22nd, I called Emily to say, "I am coming to Seattle next Wednesday, April 29th" and she said, "OK, I will pick you up at the airport!" So on April 25th, I went and shipped all my boxes on Amtrak and addressed them to my friend Lamin Tourey, who was living near Seattle. I thought I would rent a car in Seattle and take them to his house, because he has a big basement. He was living in Lynnwood, but when I saw how far away that is from Emily and Uno's house, I decided that it would be better to put my boxes in a storage place closer to them.

•••••

On Wednesday, April 29th, I flew to Seattle and Emily picked me. I left my address book in the pocket of my seat on the plane, and something else too, like my watch. That address book had all my contacts for all the music I did for many years! I remembered it while I was still in the airport, and I tried to go back on the plane but they wouldn't let me. When I got to the car and told Emily, she said, "Let's go back and try some more. That is too big a thing to lose". But we couldn't get it. So I said to her, "That's how it is. Nothing I can do, but I know it will all work out OK". When we were driving to their house, I turned on my phone and saw that I also got a phone message from Amtrak, saying that my boxes arrivedat the train station. So the next day, Uno drove me to the University District to rent a U-Haul van there, and we went downtown together and took everything from the Amtrak station to a storage place in downtown Seattle.

I lived with Emily and Uno for two and a half months, but the whole time I lived in Seattle after that, their home was like my second home.

They gave me a key so I could come and go anytime, and wanted me to keep that key even after I moved to my own apartment. We always stick together, and so whenever I played music, they will come there too. I liked to cook for them, and we also went to eat Chinese food a lot. There is a place they like called the Yummy Café that is close to their house, and that was my favorite place for all the years I was in Seattle too. After a while, I asked Emily and Uno to help me find a place of my own, and Emily started taking me around the city so I could see the different neighborhoods. When Uno would be recording in his studio, me and Emily would ride all over the city, going here and there. One day in June, we found a very good place at 143rd and 15th Avenue Northeast, near the Lake City area. I liked that place very much, and they helped me to get it, and to move in the next month. That was very good.

Emily and Uno introduced me to all of their friends too. One of their friends, Nancy Guppy, asked me to play solo kora music on her TV show called Art Zone, on channel 21. We did that show on Tuesday, June 9th, and Emily and Uno came to the studio for the taping. One day not too long after that, I told Emily that I wanted to go buy a hat and get something written on it. So she drove me to a store at Northgate where they embroider words on the hats they sell. I bought one and had them write, "I just moved to Seattle" on that hat. And she decided to surprise Uno and buy him a hat that says, "I got to get my vitamin G" because he loves to play golf so much. He plays all the time! After that day, I was wearing my hat everywhere, and a lot of people stopped to talk to me everywhere in Seattle because of that.

Emily and Uno are the #1 fans of baseball. I never met anyone who likes baseball like they do. If you came to their house, you would see that they had hundreds of pictures of baseball guys, hundreds of caps, bat sticks, and balls. When you get there, you would know that you have come to a house of baseball. Their favorite team is the Seattle Mariners, and they have season tickets for that team. It's a heavy thing, and I am sure some big people at the Mariners know them too. Because of that, they held their 20th marriage anniversary in the Mariners stadium. Being their good friend and a griot, they asked me to be the one to read the ceremony to renew their wedding vows. It was a big thing. During the ceremony, I was wearing a big traditional African dress and hat, reading to them. All their family and friends were there, and their two friends John and Terese stood on the Mariners dugout with us. The sports people and TV people were there at the stadium covering it too, and they put a big picture of it in the Seattle newspaper! I have a copy of that paper still in a box. All kinds of people I know called me up after that, to say that this picture was in their newspaper too, so that story went all over the United States.

At that time, the Mariners had a very famous player from Japan, and every time he hit the ball, everyone shouted his name, "Ichiro, Ichiro, Ichiro!" I like that guy too. He could run very fast too. While Emily and Uno were doing their vows on the roof of the Mariners dugout, Ichiro ran out of the dugout to the field. He was running back and forth and doing some stretching, and he waved at us and was watching us. Then we all went to have a big party on the roof deck with all their friends and family. There was 100 people there, and Emily and Uno bought them all tickets to watch the game. All of this was very good. Even now, Emily and Uno keep going to the games, and they took me to some more Mariner games too. Before their big celebration, I had never been to any big stadium like that for baseball, football, basketball, or anything, even though I've been in this country for so long. I only saw those things on TV, but I knew that seeing it on TV and being there live to watch the game is a whole different thing. Everybody there is hollering for the team, and hey it's unbelievable!

When I came to live in Seattle, there were a whole lot of other Gambians living around that area too. Gambian men, women, and children lived in the south part of the city, and many in the north part near where I was living. As soon as they knew I was there, they were always wanting me to be at Mandingo ceremonies such as marriages, baby-namings, and any other kind of traditional gatherings because I am a well-known griot. Griots are always involved in these things, whether in Gambia or Seattle, or any other place in the world. Parents always want a griot to be there to announce the baby's name to the community, and to sing praises or play the kora at the celebration. That's just the Gambian style, no matter where we are. All those people knew about these traditional things and went through them when they were born, when they marry, and everything else, so they wanted this for themselves and their children too. Most of them are young people in their 20s or 30s or 40s, so a lot of them were born long after I came to the United States, but all those Gambians have heard of my name while they were growing up in Gambia. They know about me because of my music, even if they have never seen me with their own eyes.

As soon as I first arrived and was living with Uno and Emily, many Gambians came to see me. They were very happy to come to the house and say, "We came to meet our griot, who lives here now". In our tradition of griot traveling, people in every village would always feed the griot families during their time there, so these Gambians would bring big bowls of traditional food for me, and for my hosts Emily and Uno too. Even during all the years I was in Seattle, from time to time the Gambian men and their wives would also say, "We want to cook and take some food to our griot", and bring me a lot of traditional food to eat. So even though some things are different because of being in the United States, Gambians continue the traditions wherever they are. They just might have to change them a little bit, though. For example at baby-namings, the parents will usually have the ceremony in their apartment or house, with just the new mother and father and baby, their close family, the Imam, and a griot. But then the family will come to a nearby hall that they have hired, to have a big celebration with a hundred or more people, with music, griot singing and playing. Just like in our home villages, the place will be jam-packed and the celebration and music will go on all night long until morning. Just like in Gambia, people will stuff money in the griot's kora or in a bag while they are singing and playing. Sometimes I would bring my kora and play at these ceremonies, but not always. There would be other griots there sometimes too, like my brother David Suso, the griot that has lived in Seattle the longest.

Another thing that a griot does as his job is to be a mediator between people who are having an argument about something, to help them solve the problem. It can be between families, business people, or husband and wife. Long ago, my father Jali Saikou Suso did that a lot for the President of Gambia too. Also, it's very common for a griot to be sent as a songharo or messenger by the new husband's family, to meet with the new wife's family and help with the marriage arrangements, and to be at the marriage ceremony. A songharo doesn't have to be a griot, but many families will like to send a griot for this. All Gambian people like their culture a lot, whether they are Mandingo people, Wolof people, Fulani people, Jola people, or Serahule people. No matter where they are, they like to keep their traditions.

When I first came to Seattle in 1979 with Mandingo Griot Society, there were only three Gambians living there, but now there are 6,000! I can even remember that when we first played in Seattle, those three Gambians came to see us. I don't know how long they were living there before I came, but they saw my name on an advertisement for the show at a Seattle club and they came. Their names were Tony Lum, Mbaye Cham, and Eliman Cham, and after the show, they came up to talk with me. In 1980 or 1981, Eliman Cham moved to San Francisco and Mbaye Cham stayed in Seattle. He is still there today but he doesn't go to places with other Gambians much, so most people don't know him. Tony Lum moved to New York sometime later, and now he lives in Queens and works at the Brooklyn Museum. It's funny, because I had never seen him since 1979 and I didn't even know where he moved. But three or four years ago when I was still living in Seattle, I was talking to a Gambian guy on the phone who said, "Jali, there is somebody visiting me here, and while we were talking, we happened to talk about you. He is here in my house now, and is name is Tony Lum". On top of all that, when Tony got on the phone and told me that he was now living in New York, I asked him when he was going back, and he said it would be in five days. I said, "That is when I am going too". Five days later, we happened to board the same flight! He got on the plane before me, but when I was walking down the aisle, boom! I saw him sitting there, and I recognized him. I said "Tony!" and right away he jumped up, and we grabbed each other. From then on, especially since I started living on the east coast, we get in touch with each other from time to time and talk.

In Chicago, it's funny but I only did three baby-naming ceremonies in all the years I lived there. There were only eight or nine Gambians in

Chicago when I arrived there in 1977, but they didn't really settle there and all ended up moving away. Later on, more Gambians came to live in Chicago, but I didn't know them or mingle with them too much. There are a lot of Gambians in New York now too, many more than in Seattle. But when I came to the United States in 1977, the first place that Gambians started coming to live was Atlanta, because many people wanted to go to Georgia Tech University. Gambia is a farming country, so they went there to learn all about agriculture and then went back to Gambia to farm when they finished their schooling. At that time, nobody came to the United States to find work and live there, only to go to school. But later on, the main reason people started coming there was to find work, and that's how it is today. Many people come from Senegal, Guinea, and Mali too.

On Thursday, June 25th, 2009 we had a sad news day, because this is the day Michael Jackson died of a heart attack or something. He was still young too, with some little children. A couple of weeks later on Monday, July 6th, I rented a van to move all my things out of the storage place and out of Emily and Uno's house, and take them to my new apartment. After me and Uno got everything moved and I was taking the van back to the rental place, I got in an accident. Uno was driving his car ahead of me, to direct me where to go, and we went up a winding street called Ravenna Avenue. There was a garbage truck parked on the side of the street, and I put my foot on the brake pedal as I got close to it. But all of a sudden the driver backed his truck into me, because he didn't see me coming up the hill. Then he said I ran into him. The police arrived and talked to us. The van was damaged on the passenger door and the glass was broke, but luckily I had insurance and so it all worked out. The next day, I spent my last night at Emily and Uno's house before moving into my new apartment on Wednesday, July 8th. I like to do my important things on Wednesdays, because that's my favorite and lucky day for that.

On Saturday, July 18th, I flew to New York to rehearse for a concert with a guitar player named Joel Harrison and a banjo player named Tony Trischka. I knew Joel for a while, and he introduced me to Tony, and we rehearsed at Joel's house for our first show together. On the 21st, we did an interview and played some songs together in the studio at WNYC, a New York public radio station. The show was called Soundcheck, and they posted a video on YouTube of us playing. That YouTube thing had only been around for a few years back then, but there are so many videos of my music on it now, it's unbelievable. There are a lot of my daughter Nene's videos on there too. The next night, I played a concert with Joel and Tony at City Winery, and then a few days later on July 25th, I came back to Seattle for a few weeks.

Then on Thursday, August 13th, I flew from Seattle to Hartford, Connecticut. I went there because there is a Gambian professor at Yale University named Lamin Sanneh living there, and he is a way heavy history and religion scholar. A lot of people don't know him in Gambia, but he has a very heavy western education. He has been at Yale since 1989 and he is something else! At the same time, he is a typical traditional Gambian man, and into our culture so heavy. I first met him in 1976 when I was teaching in the African Studies Department at the University of Ghana. He was already a professor there, and we also happened to be living in the same area of South Legon. He found out that there was a Mandingo griot working at the university, and that's how we met.

Lamin Sanneh comes from one of the Mandingo royal families that we call nyanchos. Mandingos originally came from Mali, but during the Mali Empire we spread into eleven other countries in West Africa: Guinea-Bissau, Gambia, Ghana, Guinea, Sierra Leone, Senegal, Burkina Faso, Liberia, Niger, and Ivory Coast. The names of our five Mandingo royal families are Sanneh, Manneh, Sonko, Sanyang, and Manjan. Lamin Sanneh's family happened to come to the Kabou area of Guinea-Bissau, and they had kings after kings in their family there. In fact, Lamin is a descendent of Kelefa Sanneh, who was a warrior king. My great great great great grandfather Jali Madi Wulen Suso invented the kora during Kelefa Sanneh's rule, and he composed the very first kora song for him. In all traditional kora learning, the first song your teacher will always teach you to play is that very first kora song, called Kelefa.

So all this time after being at the University of Ghana together, here we are both in the United States. We got in touch with each other, and learned where we both had been living all these years, and Lamin Sanneh told me, "Fodaymusa, my son is going to get married on Saturday, August 15th. I like my family tradition very well, and I want to bring you to come here and play. We are the royal family and warrior kings of Kabou, and even though I live in the United States, I want to have a tradition for my son's marriage. I want to make sure that my son's marriage ceremony will still have our traditional instrument playing. I'm going to fly you here, the wedding will take place in New York City, and I would like you to play". So we made the arrangements for my travel and everything like that. When I arrived in Hartford, Lamin picked me and put me in a hotel. The next day, he took me to Yale to show me around the university and his office. He has written a whole lot of books about religion and tradition. On Saturday, we traveled to New York, driving in his car. Lamin has two children, a son and a daughter. He named his son Kelefa also, after his great great great great grandfather, and his daughter's name is Namunta. The place for the wedding was the Roberta Restaurant in Brooklyn, and that night I was playing, playing, playing at the reception there, singing and talking abut the Sanneh family, and all the royal family ancestors. Kelefah Sanneh married an American girl and lives in New York. He is a journalist, and he writes columns for the New York Times, so whenever you open that paper, you might see something written by him.

The next week on Wednesday, Aug 19th, I came back to Seattle. On September 21st I did a solo kora concert at the Triple Door in Seattle. It's a big, big club downtown, and Emily and Uno came to that show too. The next month on Monday, October 26th, Emily and Uno took me to a little village called La Push on the Quileute Reservation, to stay in a cabin on the Pacific Ocean. Before we left, I called one friend I have in Chicago who is always skeptical of things, even things he doesn't know. I told him I was going to La Push, and he said, "Who are these people? Are they black or white? How far away is that place? Is it a city?" I told him what I knew about the place, and he said, "I wouldn't go. Those people could kill you and throw you in the bush, or in the woods or something, and nobody would know". I said, "No, they are not going to kill me. I know these people and they are my friends. They are good people. You know me, I don't hang around with crazy people like that". He said, "Before you go, I want you to give me their phone numbers so I can call if something happens to you." I said, "No, I won't do that". When I called him after we got back to Seattle to say I'm OK, he said, "You were lucky". I just laughed, ha ha!

•••••

On the day we drove to La Push, Emily and Uno picked me at my apartment and we went to a place where there is a big ferry to cross the water from Edmonds to Kingston. Then we drove all the way to the Makah Reservation to the most northwest point of the United States. We stopped at the little town there, and got a permit to go and walk to a place that Emily and Uno called the "end of the world". To get there, we had to walk to a high place, way, way up high. From that point on, there is no land, only water, and big waves are hitting the rocks below. Down in the water, there are many, many kelp plants floating that look like a seal's head, and seals diving in the water too. We were looking down at them from the big cliffs we were standing on, and the thousands of yellow and red starfish that were all over the rocks. Those starfish didn't move even with the waves pounding on them, like they were glued to those rocks. All kinds of birds were flying all around, and we could see millions of them covering a big island way out in the water. It was very nice.

Then we drove to LaPush, and Emily and Uno got a cabin for us to stay in. They gave me the bedroom and they stayed on the living room bed. I never forget that. Our cabin was very, very nice. It had a whole kitchen, so it was easy to cook all the food we needed while we were there. There was a nice living room too, with couches and chairs and a table. The next day they promised me, "We are going to eat salmon. These people are good fishermen, and we can get fresh fish from them and cook it right that same day". So we all went down the street to the riverside, to look for a fisherman. We saw one Indian guy with his daughter in a big canoe, and he had three big salmon. We bought one of them and took it to our cabin, and we cooked it nice for dinner. The next morning I cooked the salmon eggs for them, and we ate them with our breakfast. Wow, we ate a lot of salmon on those two days!

After breakfast, Emily said, "We're going to put the leftovers out on the beach for the birds to eat". There were a whole lot of big trees behind our cabin, and we didn't know that an eagle was sitting in one of those trees looking at us. I walked with Emily down to the beach, and when she threw the fish head and bones and guts out on the ground, the gulls and crows came and started jumping around like crazy. Then right away, the eagle came down to get the head. In fact, as soon as that fish head hit the ground, the eagle arrived. The first time he came down, he missed it and just kicked it, and all the crows and seagulls went flying away, waaaaaa, waaaaaa. The second time he kicked it and poom! he picked it up and flew away with it. It's unbelievable! We were so amazed to see that. Another time too, around a year later, we went there to the same place and the exact same thing happened with an eagle. Those big birds are very smart!

In 2009, I also met a Seattle drummer named Barrett Martin. He came to visit some other musicians who were recording in Uno's studio, and so Uno called me to come downstairs and introduced us. We talked for a while, and Barrett told me he studied African drums and did a lot of playing around the world, and I told him about myself. Then I said, "I'd like to meet musicians in Seattle to put a band together". He told me, "I know a bass player named Keith Lowe and a saxophone player named Mark, who are really good. I will introduce you." Mark was working in a music school south of downtown, and we all began to rehearse there. Barrett would pick me at my apartment and drive us down there, and soon we had some songs put together. So I said, "Let's go to the studio to record." Uno agreed to do it, and we started recording some songs there in November. That same month, Uno and Emily took me to see a band called Red Dress at the High Dive Club in Seattle. All the guys in that band have been their friends for a long, long time, and they like the music very much. I liked it too!

⋅⋅⋅⋅⋅

On Friday, January 8th, 2010, I flew to New York for another trio concert with Joel Harrison and Tony Trischka. We rehearsed a little bit, and then did a show at a famous place called Le Poisson Rouge on the 10th. From there, I flew to Chicago on the next day to visit friends, and came back to Seattle on Wednesday the 13th. Later on, Barrett introduced me to a guy named Joe Doria who played a Hammond organ, and the five of us rehearsed some more. We played one show at a club in the Fremont area of Seattle, and after that I wanted to add Joe's playing to the recording.

So in March 2010, Joe brought his big Hammond organ to the studio and he played through Uno's big Leslie speaker. We had to take the door off the playing room to get that organ inside! We added more overdubs later in 2010, and then it was finished. I was thinking that maybe I will look around to see if I can get a record deal for us, but nothing came of that. That same month, I started working with Uno on a song I call Jooka Sataro. It's a long, long song, almost 17 minutes! We did a whole lot of different takes, and around five or six sessions together, maybe even more. We did it over and over all summer and fall, and still we didn't finish it. Uno still teases me about that, saying, "Maybe just one more try. Maybe it's too short!"

The next few months were pretty quiet, and then on Saturday, April 10th, I went back to New York for a big event. A woman named Susan Rockefeller made a movie called "Making the Crooked Straight", about a Jewish doctor from Brooklyn who goes to Addis Abbaba, Ethiopia to work with children who have a big hump on their back. Their parents cannot afford any treatment, so that doctor brings some of those children to the United States to do surgery for them, and has lot of those kids living with him in his house in Ethiopia. Susan Rockefeller used some of my music for the movie soundtrack, and she also wanted me to play my kora at a reception for the movie premiere, right before the movie was shown. The premiere was at the HBO Theater in New York, a big building on the Avenue of the Americas, and the reception was way, way up, on one of the top floors. After that, I stayed in New York for a few days, and then flew to Chicago to visit friends for another couple of days before going back to Seattle on the 17th.

Later on that spring, I met up with Susan and her husband David Rockefeller, Jr. while they were visiting Seattle. David and some other people had gotten together to take a ship called Ocean Watch all around the world in one year. They had left from Seattle at the end of May 2009 and came back to Seattle on June 17th, 2010. There was going to be a great big party for that arrival, and Susan and David welcomed me to come to that celebration. The ship was coming to the shore in a place called Shilshole, near a restaurant where Emily and Uno took me for dinner one time with their friends Ciscoe and Mary. Ciscoe is a guy who knows everything about gardening, and had his own TV and radion shows. He is something else. Susan called to invite me to go and see the Ocean Watch ship, and take a tour. Then the party happened at a big building with tall glass walls, called the Pacific Science Center. I did not play my kora, I just went to the party. Many official people from the City of Seattle were there too.

Sometime later in 2010, a woman named Nacha Mendez contacted me to ask me to play a track on her upcoming album. We had met each other in a very unusual way about five or six years earlier. I was at La Guardia airport on my way returning home to Chicago, and she was returning home from Europe to Santa Fe, New Mexico. We were checking our bags at the same time, and she asked me what I was checking, so I showed her the kora and we talked for a while. Later on, I think she checked me out on the internet or something, and found out who I was and about my music. Then she wrote a song called "Angelitos Negros" and sent the tracks to a studio in the University District in Seattle, where I recorded the kora track with a producer named Steve Peters. Later that year, Steve also contacted me to do a solo kora concert in Seattle at the Good Shepherd Center. It's an old building that used to be a home for girls, and the chapel on the fourth floor is a music space. The concert was on September 24th, and Uno and Emily came to see me with a lot of their friends.

On Monday October 11th, I went to Mexico City for another Orion tour with Philip. He met me at the airport, and from October 12th to the 14th we rehearsed with all the other musicians from around the world: Ashley MacIsaac on violin, Wu Man from China playing the pipan instrument, Mark Atkins on the didgeridoo, my friends Uakti on percussion, and the singer Eleftheria Arvanitaki from Greece. We performed a concert in León on October 16th, and two concerts in Mexico City on the 18th and 19th. The following day, I came back to Seattle. Three days later I flew to Oakland, California to play a solo kora concert at the Paramount Theater, then flew back to Seattle the next day to get ready for a special trip to Gambia.

EMILY AND UNO IN GAMBIA

I left Seattle on Wednesday November 3rd, 2010 and arrived in Gambia the next day. I spent the first few weeks with my family and visiting with friends, and then on Thursday, December 2nd, Emily and Uno arrived in Gambia for the very first time. In all the 30 years we knew each other, we had talked many, many times about them coming to Gambia, but now it was finally happening. Earlier that day, I went to Banjul and stopped at Latri kunda to see some friends on my way back to Brikama. Then I told my son Basaikou, "Get ready, we gotta go to the airport to go and get my friends Uno and Emily". Their flight came to Gambia from Brussels, and it was very hot that day. When their plane landed, I was just there watching passengers coming and coming off it, and I started wondering. Then I saw them coming through the customs line, Emily in front and Uno behind. We all greeted, and then me and Basaikou brought their bags to my car, and Basaikou drove us all to Brikama. When we came to the house, Bobo was ready for them with some nice big salad stuff for dinner. Every day, we went around and around, checking out all kinds of places in Brikama and meeting my friends. I know they liked it so much! We didn't even worry about toubabs eating at the table inside the house like they do in America. We all ate together outside. Every morning we would sit outside and break the fast together, sitting on the veranda by the wall, and we had our lunch and dinner there too.

Emily is very into the birds. She likes birds a whole lot, she likes books about birds, and she knows a whole lot about birds. In fact, she is a teacher of all kinds of things about nature. A long time before they came to Gambia, and soon after I arrived in Seattle, she went and got a book full of pictures of all the birds in Gambia. The day that Emily showed me that book, I was so surprised! I didn't know that anybody put together a book like that, and when I looked at it, I saw a lot of birds that I knew very well when I was growing up. Even though I never knew their names in English, I knew all their names in my language. I even saw almost all the birds in that book during my childhood time, and after I moved to

Brikama. Gambia is a small country, but the inland birds in the eastern part of the country are so different than the birds in the west. In fact, there are a lot of birds in Brikama that you will never see in the area I was born and raised in. I like that book a lot. It's fascinating, because when I travel around the world, I get to see a lot of birds and plants in different places. Even in the United States, the eastern birds are very different than the western birds. Also, some plants that grow in New York or Chicago cannot grow in Seattle, and some things that grow in Seattle cannot grow there.

I remember too, at nighttime whenever the moon came out, Emily liked to look at it, and Uno did too. One night in Brikama, we went to the telecenter to try to look at emails on the internet, and the moon was very big and bright. They had binoculars with them for watching the birds, and when we got back home, they let all my kids look through those at the moon and stars. They couldn't believe! By that time, my son Basaikou's good friend Ous was living with us also, and our compound was nice and full. There was Nene, Basaikou, Ous, Balamin, Mahame, Sendin, Kauboya, and Bobodinding. Fatou was living in Brikama with my sister Tita, and she also came over a lot. None of the kids had ever seen anything like those binoculars.

Me and Uno and Emily also went to a lot of places together. Sometimes we just walked around Brikama and I introduced them to many friends. A lot of friends and neighbors came to visit my compound too, so every day they were meeting people and people were meeting them. One night we drove to a town called Gunjur, which is on the west coast of Gambia by the Atlantic Ocean. We were just walking around a little bit close to the water, and saw something none of us ever saw before: millions of white butterflies flying around like a big tall cloud! Another day, Basaikou drove Uno and Emily and me to Brefet, which is by the River Gambia, and we hired some fishermen there to take us out in their canoe. There were a lot of birds in the trees by the edge of the riverside, even a big eagle on top of one tree.

We also went together to the Makasutu Forest where there are a lot of different water places. The people there paddled us to the other side of the forest in a big canoe, and we walked through the bush to visit a very wise old man named San. He is a Jola marabou, and he is the only one who can live in that forest. It was very good. Two times Uno and Emily went to see Nene and her band playing music in the Fajara area, and they liked that a lot too. We celebrated the Muslim New Year together, and all the kids from the neighbors around my compound came over for the special New Year cakes called kitimo that Bobo made. Later on, Basaikou and Ous drove Uno and Emily in my car to a fishing village called Tanji, where they stayed in a small hotel for one or two nights by themselves, going to watch the birds and monkeys, and all kinds of other animals in the bush. On the way there, I rode my motorcycle ahead of them the whole way on the highway, and Emily was taking videos of all that. Basaikou and Ous also took them to the Abuko Nature Reserve, which is a very heavy bird place. It was all very good the whole time they stayed with us. Then on December 21st, they left and came back to Seattle. I know someday they will be coming back to Gambia too!

●●●●●

I stayed in Gambia until January 25th, 2011, and the first half of the year was pretty quiet for me, just a little bit of this and that, and I was mostly in Seattle. On Saturday, May 7th, I played a solo kora concert at the Spirit of Africa Festival at Seattle Center, and there wasn't too much music going on the rest of summer. But on Sunday, June 5th, sad news came again. My dear sister Dibba passed away. She's much older than me, and her mother and my mother were sisters. She is so dear to me because of the way she is, very nice to everyone all the time, and everybody likes her a lot. Some years before, I paid for her to go and make her pilgrimage to Mecca, and she liked that very much.

On Monday, September 5th at 5:30 in the morning, Uno came to my apartment to take me to the airport on my way to Gambia. I stayed in Brikama only for a couple of days before I flew to Freetown, Sierra Leone. I spent the night there, and the next day I traveled to a city called Sefadou, to visit one of my cousins and his family. His name is Kandara Singhateh, and he is from my village of Foday Kunda but lived in Sefadou for many years. I was there at his place for two weeks. While I was there, I called home and Bobo told me that one of the daughters of my elder brother Mohammed Suso was killed in an accident on Friday, September 16th. It was strange, not a regular car accident. His daughter went to school in a village that is on the way from Brikama to Banjul. After school, the kids came to the street by the highway, waiting for the bus back to Brikama, and she was standing in front of a little store. Some driver was just flying down the road, and lost control of the steering. She saw it coming so she ran into the store, but the car went through the store and killed her. You might think, "How can a car push down the whole wall?" but those walls were made of mud blocks, and the car was going so fast that it just went right through them. The people who owned the store were inside there too, and they ran out the back door. She was only around 15 or 16 years old, and the car killed only her, but no one else. It was unbelievable.

A few days after that sad news, I left Sefadou and went to Mbama Konta to visit my friend Alhaji Jimmeh Camara. Just like before, I took a bus from Freetown to another city called Bo, and he came to meet me there with his car. We went to his compound and I stayed there for a while, then I left. That was the last time I saw Jimmeh. He passed away a few years ago, and before that he had sold all his properties in Sierra Leone and moved back to live in Gambia.

Those areas in Sierra Leone where Jimmeh lived are full of high, high mountains, and when I left his place, I hired a motorcycle taxi guy to take me to go back to Sefadou. That guy was driving crazy, taking me up and down the mountains on tiny roads! On Saturday September 24th, I left Sefadou and went back to Freetown, and then I flew to Gambia the next day. Whenever you go to Sierra Leone, the Freetown airport thing is not good. I like Sierra Leone, but I have difficulties flying out of there. If you are in the city, you have to drive all the way to the riverside and cross on the ferry, which takes a long time, and then you have to take a taxi to the airport. So if you miss that ferry, you will miss your flight. Even after you cross the river, it's a rushing, rushing, rushing thing to get to the airport because it is in Lungi, far from Freetown. I have been there many times, but the airport thing is just not sweet.

The war was terrible in Sierra Leone. People were killing other people, and cutting their hands off and their legs off. I don't know what caused the war to begin with, and made people become evil. Sierra Leone people are very hardworking people, and they are willing to work a lot to get what they need to live. But because of all the diamonds and gold there, all the foreign countries came there and fueled those things to become a big business. Other than money from that diamond and gold business, how can a rebel person in the bush get a bunch of guns and other stuff like that? When they saw that the government was there with all that money, all the people who were living way out in the country started saying, "Hey, wait a minute. What about us?" That kind of thing is always a big, big problem. That's the reason people even came up with the name blood diamond, because people used the diamond money to buy guns for the wars in all kinds of places, especially in Sierra Leone. Sierra Leone has a whole lot of diamonds. Liberia, Guinea, Zaire, Angola, Botswana, and many other countries in Africa all have a lot of diamonds too. But one thing is clear and for sure, which is that the Sierra Leone diamonds have more quality than any other place in the world.

That very bad war stuff happened long before I ever went there to see Jimmeh and Samba Sabally back in 2007. That war didn't last a long time like a lot of other African wars, but if it had, everybody in Sierra Leone would be dead. The people themselves of Sierra Leone are good. I know that, and I like that about them. To come out of all the hardship they got into, if these people were not strong, they would not be able to come out of all those horror things that happened there. The war made a lot of people move away from their villages, and Freetown is now full with the people 24 hours a day. It doesn't seem like those people even go to sleep anymore, and they are shopping and everything even in the middle of the night. The place I stayed in Freetown at the beginning of this 2011 visit was in the center of the city, close to the market. I was going to have to get up at six o'clock in the morning to catch my bus to Bo, but I couldn't sleep the whole night because the city was so full of noise and people.

In Freetown there were no taxi cars, only motorcycles. It seems like the motorcycle guys can ride those bikes even on the sky! And that was another way that things got pulled down in Sierra Leone during the war. There were a whole lot of rebels fighting in the bush, so to try and stop them, the government called them to come to the city to work instead of fighting. After the war was over, the government gave out thousands of motorcycles to those young men. So they said, "Hey, we can use these for taxis", so that how it got the way it is today. One of those motorcycle guys can put your load on his bike, and make you sit on top of that while they drive. If he could, he would take you to New York like that! Those guys are something else. Now things in Sierra Leone are better. People are trying to make a good life there, working hard to come out of the war thing. Also, many people who left have come back there now, and are helping other people with this and that, and bringing things to the country that they didn't have before.

• • • • •

On October 5th, I flew back from Gambia to Seattle. The next month I recorded a CD with my friend Gretchen Rowe. She lived across the street from my apartment in Seattle, and I met her because of a Somalian store in the Lake City neighborhood. The name of the store's owner was Abas, and he also had a very good tailor there working, who was from Cassamance. The tailor's name is Lamin Saidy, and one day he said to me, "I know somebody here who works in a school, and she can draw and do poetry. I will introduce you". Lamin also is friends with a whole family from Guinea, and that family also knows Gretchen. Lamin told those Guinean friends about me, and they told Gretchen. Then one day, the Guinean friends called me to say they wanted to visit me at my apartment. The whole family came over, and Gretchen was with them. We all talked and talked, I played the kora for them, and then they went home.

A few weeks later when I came home on the bus and was crossing the street, I heard somebody blowing a car horn who said, "Hey, hey, kora player!" to me. I didn't know anybody in that neighborhood, and so I was just standing and looking at her. Then Gretchen got out of her car and said, "I'm the one who came to your place with my friends", and then I recognized her. I asked, "How are you?" and she said, "I have some poetry I wrote that I want you to hear". We exchanged phone numbers and then later on I invited her to come over to my apartment so I could hear her poetry. She brought two or three notebooks full of poetry with her and I asked, "Can you read something to me?" so she read it. Then she said, "I wrote this, but I cannot read it strong" and so I told her, "If you are going to read, you must read it with the voice you have". Afterward, she asked me, "What do you think about this? Can you play the kora to this poetry?" and I replied, "Yes I can do it, and it can work. But it's going to be a lot of work. First of all, you have to use your strong voice. And then you have to be listening while I am playing the pieces of music". When she mentioned that she wanted to go to a studio to record it, I said, "If you practice enough and the thing is going well, I have a friend here who has a studio. That's where we will go if we are going to record it". I also told her that I didn't know anybody who would put out a CD like this. We practiced a lot for a long time, and then we went into Uno's studio from November 7th to the 14th to record and mix it, and Gretchen put out the CD herself. A friend of hers tried to be a manager for us, but then moved across the water to Port Townsend, where you have to take ferry to get there, so that didn't work out. On Saturday, February 25th, 2012, we did a concert at the Broadway Performance Hall in Seattle to celebrate the release of our new CD, called Koralations.

•••••

Earlier that year on January 1st, 2012, a very good friend of mine passed away. His name was Alhaji Muktar Sillah, and he was my neighbor in Brikama since 1982. The reason I remember his death is because he was a very good friend, a pure, traditional man, and an Islamic scholar. He had a lot of students living in his compound too. We became neighbors when I bought a plot of land next to his house for my first compound in Brikama. When I first built my compound, my mother was living there with my brother Dembo and my sister Tita, and one day Alhaji Muktar Sillah came to visit her while I was in Chicago. He told my mom, "Mother, now we have become neighbors, and you are an older woman just like my mother, so I will come and take care of you as my mom". Later on when I was talking to my mom on the telephone, she told me about it. In our tradition, that is what Mandingo people do, and if it's an older man, you will take him as your father. From that day on, Alhaji Muktar Sillah always called her mother, and I called him brother. We are not related in our blood, but we are related in that traditional way. He also has three elder brothers who I knew also, and in fact his eldest brother Alhaji Kausu Sillah was my friend before I ever came to Chicago. All these brothers are passed away now also.

A few years before he died, Alhaji Muktar Sillah had the chance to come to the United States. He was well known for spiritual works in Gambia, so word came around about him in Atlanta and other places in the U.S., and he went to Atlanta to visit some other Gambians there. Then a black lady in Chicago wanted to invite him to come to Chicago too. They talked to each other and arranged the whole thing, but I didn't know anything about it until he told me he was coming. I was still living in Chicago, and he called me to say, "Brother, I am here in Atlanta and I am coming to Chicago. Somebody invited me to come there". I said, "Brother, how long will you be here?" and he said, "I don't know, maybe two or three weeks, or maybe even one month". So I said, "OK, as soon as you get here, you should let me know". I didn't want to ask him all the details about why he was coming, but I was skeptical about it because I knew the lady who wanted to bring him there.

Alhaji Muktar and other Gambian people always just go by word of mouth, no contract or anything like that. So he came to Chicago, but it didn't turn out correct for him. When he came there, he was thinking that he would be doing some spiritual work for that lady, but he didn't know that she really wanted to marry him or something like that. He already had four wives and more than 19 children in Brikama, and he was not into that idea at all. He was just thinking that he would go to the United States for a few months, and then come back home. As soon as that lady knew that he was not into the idea of marriage, things started changing, and everything started going wrong for him. When I would be talking to him on the phone and ask, "How is everything?" he would just say "Hmm... hmm... hmm" but he didn't want to explain. But I live in the U.S. and I know the world, and I know very well how things are! Finally I found out that she would just leave him in the house and to go work, and that was it. He was stuck. He didn't know anything about going around Chicago or where to go, so he didn't even want to go around the block to find something to eat. Whatever she cooked for him, he had to eat. He doesn't drive a car, and he can't do anything about it.

As soon as I knew all about what was going on, I called my good friend Manu to ask, "Please go to Alhaji Muktar's place to pick him and bring him to my place". So Manu would do that, and we would all spend some good time together. One day I said, "Alhaji, you don't have to go hmmm... hmmmm, because I know exactly what is happening here. When you first told me you were coming here from Atlanta, I didn't ask you a bunch of stuff about that, and about that lady. I didn't want to say anything because I didn't want you to think I was holding you back. I knew that when you came here, things were not going to work out with that lady. And I know she told you not to tell me that you were coming to Chicago, and that she was the one bringing you here. She knows that I know her, and she knew that if you told me, I might tell you not to come". He was very quiet, so I knew what I was saying was true. I also told him, "I know something is wrong, and is not going in your favor. I know you are not happy where you are". He replied, "Exactly, exactly, yes! It's like somebody dropped me inside a big well and I cannot get out. My brother, I have to tell you, I'm stuck in a thing and I cannot come out." So I told him that I was getting ready to go to New York, and that I would take him with me. He said, "If I can even get to New York, that will be good. Two of my son-in-laws are living there". I said, " Yes, I will pull you out of this well. I know what you are going through, and that if somebody doesn't grab your hand and pull you out, you won't be able to get out of this well".

Then I told Manu about the whole thing, and he said, "Yes, I can see that". So I told Alhaji Muktar, "Here's what I'm going to do. I'm going to buy you a ticket from Chicago to New York. I will send my friend Manu to pick you from the house and take you to Midway Airport, where I will meet you. On the day we are leaving, you cannot tell her you're leaving, or tell her when or where you are going. After we get to New York, you can call her. If you tell her that you are going to leave before we go, and then she does something that will keep you here, then it will be your fault. Don't tell her nothing! I will meet you at Midway Airport and we will fly to New York. Drop the key under the door for that lady, and have your bag ready."

So Manu went and picked Alhaji Muktar after the lady went to work, and we met at Midway for the flight. By that time, he had already informed his son-in-law that he was coming. At that time too, Muktar was not well. He is a very tall and big man, and he has high blood pressure, and his health had been getting a lot worse in the United States. At the airport, he had to be in a wheelchair, and Manu was helping me to push. We got on board the flight. By then, he had already talked to his son-in-law in New York, who met him at LaGuardia and took him to his apartment in the Bronx. I went to stay at Philip's house. Muktar was there in New York for a few weeks, and then he went back to Gambia. I don't know what happened when he called that lady to tell her he was gone, but I do know he got away. Later on, the black lady passed away too. Before Alhaji Muktar passed away, I saw him a lot while I was in Gambia in 2011. In fact, any time I was in Gambia, it would be easy to see me sitting out in the yard in his compound, talking with him day or night. He is a #1 friend for that.

•••••

On Saturday January 28th, 2012 I flew from Seattle to New York to play a concert with Philip. We performed at Carnegie Hall with a bunch of different people on Monday the 31st to celebrate Philip's 75th birthday, and it was a big, big thing. I flew back to Seattle the next day, but a week later I flew back to New York to do a duet concert on February 7th with one of my cousins there, a kora player named Salieu Suso. I don't know why I didn't just stay in New York after the Carnegie Hall concert, but I guess maybe I was still enjoying all the flying! I played with my cousin

Salieu at SUNY Martitime College. That's where my friend Harris Eisenstadt works and teaches music, and he was the one who arranged the concert. After that, I did stay in New York for a while before flying back to Seattle. That springtime and summer were not very busy, so I had a lot of time for visiting friends and doing power walks, which I like. Some days I would walk for miles, up and down the hills, because Seattle is so full of hills. Some days I even walked all the way from my apartment to Uno and Emily's house, which is more than 6 miles!

I went to New York again on Wednesday, July 18th to rehearse with Philip for the Days and Nights Festival. That was the second year of this festival, which Philip founded, and all the concerts were held at the Sunset Center in Carmel and the Henry Miller Library in Big Sur, California. We rehearsed from July 19th to the 23rd and then I flew back to Seattle. On August 31st I back flew to Carmel, and the next day, me and Philip played a duet concert at the Sunset Center. Then I flew back to Seattle for a couple of months. On October 25th, I played with Philip and Adam Rudolph at the Kirkland Performance Center, which is near Seattle. Philip and Adam flew to Seattle early in that day so we could do a little rehearsal at the auditorium, and then we played the concert. Emily and Uno came to see us play, and after the show, I introduced them to Philip. That was the only time Adam met Uno, or saw Emily since all the way back in Mandingo Griot Society days. A few days later I flew to Santa Cruz, California to a solo kora concert at the Pacific Cultural Center on the 2nd. Then I flew back to Seattle on November 3rd, and stayed in Seattle for the rest of the year.

•••••

On Saturday, February 2nd, 2013, I went home to Gambia again, this time for three months. While I was there, my son Basaikou went to England to work and live. He is getting to be a grown man now, and he left Brikama to fly to England on Wednesday, March 13th. Bobo's brother Hatab Njai lives in London with his wife and children, and Basaikou went and lived with them when he first got there. Hatab and his family still live there, but after a while, Basaikou moved to another town outside of London called Leeds. On Tuesday, April 30th, I left Gambia and flew to Dakar, and stayed overnight with my longtime friend Abu Sidibeh, who lives near the airport. Two days later on May 2nd, I flew back to Seattle.

Something really nice happened later that month for Uno's mom, Marlys. On Thursday, May 23rd, she got married to a guy named Gary, and we all went to the wedding ceremony. She was in her 80s at that time, and the family made the ceremony very sweet. I was in Seattle during the rest of the summertime that year too.

●●●●●

Then on Tuesday, September 3rd, Uno and Emily took me with them again to the Quileute Reservation in La Push. This time we just crossed the ferry and drove to La Push to our cabin by the ocean, and didn't stop at that "end of the world" place. La Push is just a typical small Indian village. There is only one main street, and there is only one restaurant in the whole town. The restaurant is by the riverside, right before it goes into the ocean, and we ate at this restaurant every time we were there. This time, I also took my kora. After we got settled in the cabin a little bit, I opened the back door and started playing. While I was playing, a little gull came close by to the cabin. There was a bunch of seagulls flying around all the time, going left and right, but this one little gull came and stood still, listening to the kora. It even walked very near to me, and was just standing there while I played and played. It didn't go anywhere, but was just standing there looking at me and listening! That little gull stood in one place and didn't move at all. Emily and Uno were there too, and they saw it. It was just like a human being, walking very close to me and looking up at me. Usually, seagulls don't do that. Other seagulls were coming and going, and even making a noise, waaaaaa, waaaaaaa, before they leave, but this one didn't go. When I stopped playing completely, it flew away but it didn't go far. Then it came back as soon as I started playing again, and stood in the same spot. I could nearly reach out and touch it!

Around four or five in the afternoon, this old Indian man came up the beach, a little bit drunk. I was sitting there playing and looking at the big giant rock they call James Island, which is the Quileute chiefs' burial place. The man came over to our back patio to listen to me play, and I said, "Have you ever seen this instrument?" and he said no. He stayed and was listening to me for a long time, and told me that he liked the way it sounds. We talked together for a while longer, and then he told me, "We're going to have a gathering tonight in our village with drumming and singing, and you are welcome to come". So that night after dinner, me and Uno and Emily went to the community center in the middle of the village. The people were all gathered inside there in a big circle, and they introduced me to the audience and were very happy to see us. They invited me to come and stand in the middle of the people, and then in their tradition they gave me friendship gifts. One old woman took off her necklace of beads and put it around my neck. The old man gave me a bead necklace present too, and told me it was a symbol of peace. I still have those things today. I'm very sure that it's not a common thing to see African people mingling with Native American people on their reservation, and coming to their drum circle. The whole night was fascinating. In fact, the whole trip was like that.

The next morning by nine o'clock, the same little gull came back to our cabin. That was a surprising thing. Emily was outside and Uno was in the kitchen, and I was still asleep. As soon as I got up and came into the room, Emily said, "Musa, your friend is here". I said, "What?" and she replied, "The little gull is here again". As soon as I opened my mouth to speak, the gull came and stood even closer by the door, even before I played. There was a mark on her tail, and one or two feathers were missing, so we could identify her. It was the same one for sure! I took my time and made my tea, and all the time the gull remained, standing and waiting. It was unbelievable. So then I picked up the kora and went outside. All that time, the little gull stood and waited for me to play. It walked left and right, left and right on the patio, and then stood and watched me while I played. Emily took a whole lot of pictures of this. I played and played, and the seagull stayed and stayed. I've never seen anything like that before. After we got a salmon again and cooked it, we gave all the leftovers to that gull as a little reward.

Back home in Gambia when I was growing up, if something happened like that, the elder people in the village would come up with a kind of a theory. They would say, "This must be our dead relative who died many, many years ago, and is coming back in the form of this bird to check on us". So while I was playing, my mind went to this. I remember also that sometimes a dove would sit on top of a grass hut and start singing, and the parents would say, "Don't shoot this bird, it could be our relative who passed away". Mandingo people have a kind of belief that people can come back in a different form, like a bird or an animal, but not in a human form. So I started thinking like that, even though I am thousands of miles away from my home in Africa. Maybe this little gull is a dead relative of mine turned to be a gull, and that's why it came to stand and listen to the kora, and identified me just by the sound of my voice. Because it happened two days in a row! And on the second day, it got very, very close to me and was not even afraid. Especially since in Mandingo tradition the kora is attached to the spirits, I was also thinking that maybe a spirit that likes the sound of the kora transformed itself into a gull to come close to me, and pass by my feet almost like my pet. I said to Emily, "If I am playing anywhere else in the world and any seagull comes to me again, I will believe that this one is following me".

•••••

On Friday September 13th, 2013, a very important man from Gambia named Seni Singhateh passed away in Philadelphia. He was from my village Foday Kunda, and very well known all over the country. Seni was one of the few people in the whole Wuli District who went to school all the way through and graduated. Then he became a teacher in the first blind school in Gambia, which was in a town called Yorobel Kunda. The town is in the Fuladou District of central Gambia, near a bigger town that is called Georgetown. Toubabs first named that town McCarthy, then they changed it to Georgetown, but in our tradition, that town called Janjanbureh because it was founded by one guy whose name was Janjan and one guy whose name was Bureh. After a long time there, Seni left the blind school in Yorobel Kunda, and came to Bajul to work for the government. Later on, he moved to Serekunda. He had a son that moved to Philadelphia, and so when Seni got sick, that son brought him there to try to get well, but it didn't work.

On Saturday, September 28th, another good friend of mine named Alikalo Darboe passed away. We grew up together because he is from Brifu, very close to my village of Foday Kunda. He and his wife Anna used to live in Angola, and then they came back to live in Gambia. They died together because their house caught fire, and they didn't have a back door to their bedroom to get out. The fire started in their living room while they were asleep, and I think it was caused by electricity or something. In their house, they had iron gates by the front door just like I have at my house in Brikama, but I think they locked them. The fire woke them up and they were hollering, and the wife got up and ran out. Then she didn't see him, so she went back in and the fire burned her. She died in there, and he managed to come out, but he was burned very badly. They took him to the hospital and he died there only one or two days later. Then on Saturday October 12th, my blood brother Mahamadou Suso died in his house in Serekunda. He was sick for a long, long time.

Around this time was also when my friend Sekou Jatta started becoming ill. We met each other many years ago in around 1982 or 1983 when he came to New York, but he is from the village of Gunjur on the Atlantic Coast of Gambia. Before coming there, he had been living in Nigeria, Ghana, and Libya, and when we met, we two had a whole lot in common with our travel experience. He might be a little bit older than me, or maybe we are the same age, and we became close right away when we met. Sekou comes from a heavy scholar family. His father Kauomar Jatta was a very heavy Quranic scholar, and his mother's name was Jomma Jobarteh. His elder brother Kausu Jatta is a heavy scholar too, and still lives in Gambia.

When Sekou was in Nigeria and Ghana, he became a trader, and when he was first in New York, he worked for a record company called

HMV. He worked in the world music section of that company, but when the record company things started going way down, he didn't keep that job. After that, he began to do work for a security company that was hired by the people who build those big, big buildings in New York. They need people to guard their building supplies, which they store way out at the edge of the city. That security company had Sekou do the guarding, and he had to take the train for a long time to get to that storage place. It was just a big open space filled with stuff, with a barbed wire fence all around it, and he only had a little hut to stay in. It was always very cold and windy in the winter, and no trees for shade in the summer, and all kinds of dust was always blowing. Sekou never touched any of the stuff in there, but he had to walk around it all to check on it.

In just two or three years of working there, Sekou got some kind of chemical sickness. His body started itching all over, and then a kind of sore developed on his tongue. He was thinking that it was happening because his tongue was rubbing on his teeth, but it was cancer. He started going back and forth, back and forth to doctors for all kinds of tests, and then the doctors told him that they would do an operation that no person in the world had ever done before. The operation they did on him was to split his tongue and cut out half of it all the way into his throat, and also take out some stuff from both sides of his neck. Then they went and took some meat out of his right calf and measured it to fit the side of his tongue that was still OK, and sewed it on. Before the operation, the doctors told him that they could not guarantee whether he would survive it or not, but he said, "Yes, let's try and take the chance". It was very, very painful. They had to feed him through tubes for a long time. He told me that after the surgery, the new part of his tongue first became black and white and kind of shrank down, so it pulled the rest of the tongue to one side to make it shorter. Then his tongue became well. The doctors who did his operation even wrote a paper about the operation for some kind of medical journal because it was the first time it was ever tried on a human being.

Many years before Sekou ever got sick, there was one young toubab girl from North or South Carolina who came to New York, and he helped that girl so much. He helped her in her schooling, and to take care of her and make sure she was OK. So after he had the operation, her parents got him an apartment down there where they live, and for the past three years they have been taking care of some of his medical expenses. They are very good people. I have kept in touch with him through all this, and at first I could hear from the way he talked that it sounded like his mouth was full. But now, if you didn't know what happened to him, you wouldn't know from his speaking, but I can still hear it a little bit.

Sekou can eat regular now too, but he is still very skinny and he has more problems happening that the doctors can't figure out. They gave him all kinds of tests again, and all kind of medicines to try, but he told me that nothing works. The skin on his head is itching so bad, and he has bumps on it that look like snowflakes but are hard like a rock. So he has to shave his head every single day, and it takes him four or five hours to do that. Lately, that thing has come down on his arms and hands, and his legs and feet. This year, the bottom of his feet became dry like concrete, and very cracked and sore. He now has very heavy pain, like a nail or needles are pushing inside him. One day when I was talking to him just this past May, he told me that the doctors told him that they have to take out three of his back teeth because they are infected with radiation. The people he worked for in that storage place never paid him anything, or made a settlement after he became ill. I just have to pray for Sekou, that he can become well again and have his health back.

Near the end of October 2013, I flew to New York to play a solo kora concert at a place called Town Hall. It was part of a big, special concert called "In the Spirit" that Philip put together, with all kinds of musicians from all over the world. The concert was on October 24th, and afterward I stayed at Philip's house for a couple of weeks. On November 9th, I played a solo kora concert in a small place called The Riverside Café in Index, Washington. Emily and Uno drove me all the way there and stayed for the concert too. The lady who booked me for that concert had a special grant for that, and it was to bring world music to small towns, for people who did not have a whole lot of chances to see that. Index was one of my favorite places ever to play, because it is just a tiny village, and the café is just a small coffeshop. There is only one street in the whole town, and the vibe of the place is very good. It's in the woods, and there is a big river right next to the café, and the people are very nice. I want to go back to that place to play again.

●●●●●

At the beginning of 2014, the lady who had that grant drove me to some other little Washington town that was a very long drive away from Seattle, to play another solo kora concert. Then I played the last concert for her on Wednesday, February 12th in Duvall, Washington. It's a little town outside Seattle, in the eastern part of the county. Just like the concert in Index, I played in their performing arts center. The performing place is small but it is nice, and it was jam-packed, and the people liked my music a whole lot. Emily and Uno came there too, and invited their farmer friends Luke and Sarah. Luke was in Senegal for a while and can speak a little Wolof, which I can speak too. One time also, Uno took me way out in the countryside to visit their farm. They have a lot of crops there, and I liked that a lot.

On Monday February 17th, I flew to New York again. That early morning, a friend named Dan Rowe picked me at my apartment and took me to the airport. I first met him through his ex-wife Gretchen, who I made the Koralations CD with in 2011. At that time, I also found out that Dan is a very good piano player, and taught jazz in the Seattle Schools for a long time. Soon afterward, I went to his place and asked him if we could play some music together, but he wasn't sure. He didn't know the kora, and he said he thought the kora and his piano playing wouldn't work. But I told him, "This is your first time listening to the kora, and I know we can play together. The kora has 21 strings but the piano has a whole lot of keys, and me and Philip have been playing together for a long time." I tried showing him, but he was holding back. A lot of people know Dan as a very good teacher, and I knew he could play! Sometimes it takes a little bit of pushing and showing to give people the confidence, so I didn't give up, and kept taking to him about it. Finally he agreed, and we started rehearsing together a lot that year.

On Friday, February 28th, I went to see my friend Jack DeJohnette play a show with a lady named Aspranza Balding and some other musicians at Lincoln Center in New York. It was very nice and I'm glad I went, because I hadn't seen Jack in a long time. The next day I went to a live music place called Roulette in Brooklyn. A world music promoter friend of mine named Robert Browning was putting on a show there of Arab music, with a musician named Simon Shaheen who plays the oud, and who I played with many years ago. Robert put me on the guest list, and I'm glad I went there for a special reason. My good friend Stu was living in New York, but I had lost all contact with him many years before. The last time I saw him, he had some health problems with his knees, and I was worried about him. I think it was 20 years since I saw him, and in that time, his address changed, his phone number changed, and everything like that. I didn't know where he was, or if I would ever see him again. I would always think about him and hope he was OK, and that nothing happened to him. So there I was, sitting in the crowd, Simon was playing, and there were lot of people all around. During the first break time, when Robert Browning started talking, he said, "Thank you for coming out, and I'm glad to see you all supporting the music. I've been doing this for many years, and in fact, one of the people that I started worked with here long ago is here tonight", and then he mentioned my name. The people started clapping, and then Stu stood up. He was looking at me and rolling his eye! When I saw him, I just went up and we grabbed each other. He looked so good, with no braces on his knees and no limp. I couldn't believe! He changed completely, and his face was shining and his health was together. I kept saying, "Stu, what's up?" He said, "I'm fine" and I replied, "I know you are fine!" We exchanged numbers again, and now we keep in touch.

On Sunday, March 2nd, I went to visit my good friend Bill Laswell at his house, and then we all went out to an Indian restaurant on 6th Street. We were hanging out together for so many years, and at any place and any time, we went to eat all kinds of Indian food. I think if you put all together the Indian food we ate together, it would fill a semi-truck. Maybe even two trucks! He knows I like Indian food, and whenever I am in New York, I will call and say, "Hey, Mr. B! I'm in town". And the first thing he says is, "Which place do you want to go to today? There is a new one. It's very good and we should go there." Then he can tell me the exact address to meet him there! On Monday, March 3rd, I came back to Seattle for a while, and on Saturday April 26th, I flew back to New York again for a week. I think it was just to do some hanging out, not for a concert or anything. On May 3rd I flew back to Seattle for a couple months, and then I flew back to New York on Wednesday, July 2nd.

On July 18th, I went to see a friend named Ricky Gordon. Stu had introduced me to Ricky, and that night aound eight or nine o'clock, Stu and Ricky took me to Wynton Marsalis' house. I took my kora with me too. We all talked for a while, and then Wynton said, "Let's play some music together". I picked up my kora and he went to his piano. We played for a while and then I asked him, "Wynton, people know you from the trumpet, so please play that too". He said OK, and picked up his trumpet and started playing. Whoa, he can play! I told Wynton, "I want my friend Stu to shoot a little bit of video of us playing, because I want to put it on my Facebook page", and he said, "OK, no problem". So Stu made some video of us, but he didn't make it public when he put it on my Facebook page. We played together that night until one o'clock in the morning or later. Then Wynton said, "I'm hungry and I want to go get something to eat. Do you want to go?" and I said, "Yes, I am hungry too!" So we all went to some kind of Japanese restaurant not far from his place. After that, I was thinking that maybe Wynton was getting tired and he would want to go to sleep, but he said he wanted to keep going. So we came back to his place and even played some more together.

It's funny, that same time I was New York, I went to Chinatown and I found a yam that looked just like the thing we call bush yam at home in Gambia. It had a sign on it that was written in Chinese, so I couldn't read it, but when I saw the yam I couldn't believe it! Right away, I bought some to take it home to cook, and all night I was just eating that. When I put it in my mouth, I almost had a tear in my eye, because it's the same yam I remember. This reminds me of one thing I always say: "There is everything in the world. Whether you see it or you never see it, whether you know it or you don't know it, whether you hear it or you never hear it, everything is in the world".

So I called a friend of mine from Cassamance who now lives in Florida. His name is Morikebba Kouyateh, and he is a griot. We both are from the rural areas, and we will always talk about those things from back home, such as foods we remember. When I called him, I said, "Hey, I saw the bush yam", and he said, "What?" I said, "Yes I saw it, it's just a little bit lighter than the yams back home, but this is it". He couldn't believe it. So that day, I wrapped up one of those fresh yams very tight in a plastic bag and sent it to him. I know that as long as it's not exposed to the air, it can stay fresh for a long time.

Earlier in the year, me and Morikebba were even talking about that bush yam on the phone. He said, "Fodaymusa, when I go home and whenever I eat this yam, it's like I'm crazy." He said that one time when he went home, he landed in Dakar and then traveled to where he could cross the ferry into Gambia and go to Cassamance. And when he got to that ferry crossing, people were selling the bush yam. People in the interior of Gambia like to cook it, and then sell it in big plates. He said, "I was eating it like crazy, and people were even looking at me." He missed it a lot. Me too! I didn't eat that yam for many years.

When I called him after I found that yam, I said, "I'm going back to Chinatown tomorrow to buy more of this yam, and I will buy a lot. In fact, I will buy every bit of it and I will send some to you." But I went there the next day and it was gone. I told Morrikebba, "If I go to that Chinatown market again, and I see it there, whatever amount there is, I will buy all of it. Even if it's a big bucket, I will have to have it. It's unbelievable! It's God's creation, and maybe God didn't put it just in our area, maybe he put it all over the world. It might be different in each area, and maybe in China they even grow it. Maybe they don't even dig it as a wild plant in the bush, maybe they grow it in farms." Since then, I have seen that yam a few more times in Chinatown, and bought it. There is a special season for it, and it is only in the market at that time. I even found out that it is grown in Japan too. The world is something else!

I came back to Seattle on Wednesday, July 30th, and a few weeks later, me and Emily started writing this book! For many years before that, a lot of people have asked me, "When are you going to write a book?" but I would always tell them, "I play music. I cannot write a book." Then they would tell me that I can get somebody else to write it, and that I can just talk to that person. Even Philip told me, "Your book will be better than mine. You have all the dates for the stories in your life, from the journals you keep from the first day you came to the United States. You write every day, so it's important that you write a book."

So one day after I got back from New York, I went to talk to Emily about it. She is a good writer, and I told her that no other person could write this book with me. I asked her and she said yes, so we started on it. Our first day was on Monday, August 11th, 2014. From that time on, any time we had the chance, we came together at her house to write. I would be talking and flipping the pages of my journals, which I have been writing in since 1977, and Emily would be recording it on her computer and writing notes with a pen. Sometimes we would be inside the house, and sometimes we would go outside to be on their deck. They built a big beautiful garden at their house, and a whole lot of birds were always flying around when we were out there. Everybody I told about the book was very happy that I was writing it, and encouraged me to do it. Wow, time went by and was flying fast, and we were always working hard on it!

On September 4th, I flew to New York and stayed there until the 25th. I was in Seattle the whole month of October, and then I went back to New York on November 18th. While I was there staying in Philip's house, me and his young son Cameron made a song together. Cameron is into electronic music and is always programming drum machine, piano and other keyboards on his computer. He was young, but he could do it very well! So one day I said to him, "Let's do something together". I played the kora and he programmed his computer, and the song we made is called LT Groove. Cameron even made a video of it, which is on YouTube. On December 2nd I flew back to Seattle, and on December 18th I got the sad news that my very good friend Yacub Addy passed away in Massachusetts.

⋅⋅⋅⋅⋅

On January 21st, 2015, me and Dan Rowe went to Fastback Studio in Seattle to do a recording of our music. Some time after we first started playing together in 2014, a guy called Brian Jackson contacted me who wanted to represent me as a promoter and producer. He introduced me to the people at Fastback Studio, who were recording and videotaping musical performances and then posting them online. They wanted to do a recording with me, and I agreed to do it, but told them I wanted to have a copy for myself of what was recorded. Brian said yes, and the Fastback Studio people agreed to that too. Soon after Dan and I did the recording, I asked Brian about getting my copy, and he said he talked to the Fastback people. Then he told me that they said, "No, he cannot have a copy". I said to Brian, "How can that be? I cannot get a copy? I never heard anything like that." The next thing I knew, the Fastback Studio people had posted the video and recording on their website. So I told Uno, "Please call them and tell them that I did not give them permission to do that." He talked to them and they took it down, but still they left my photo on their website! So Uno had to call them again to get that photo taken down too. Their website is not going to do anything for me, because I was alive a long time before they made their website. Now every five or six months, I still go to their website to make sure they don't put me back on there. I might check that website for the rest of my life.

EAST COAST LIFE

I like Seattle so much, but after I was living there for about six years, I decided that I wanted to move to the east coast. Seattle is a much smaller city than Chicago or New York, which I like, but it's too laid back for playing my music, and too far away from other big cities where I play a lot. Ever since I first came to the U.S., I have done more music in New York than any other place, so I started thinking more serious about being close to that city. At the same time, the Seattle people who owned my apartment building wanted me to renew my lease for one or two years, and I didn't want to do that. So I asked Emily and Uno if I could live with them for a while again. They said, "Yes, of course! Your room is still here, and you can stay as long as you like". On Thursday March 26th, 2015 Uno came to my apartment to pick me with all my stuff. I had some boxes that I put in a storage place, and I took all the rest to their house. April 1st was my first night to sleep in my room there again.

One night during that summer, I was in New York, sitting outside with Zack Glass on the front stoop of Philip's house because it was so hot. Many people were passing by us, and a guy passed by around ten o'clock who was carrying a guitar. I called out to him and said, "You play music? Can you play some for us?" His said his name was Karl, and he sat down and played a few blues songs, which were very good. I told him that I play music from Africa, and then I went upstairs and brought my kora down. He had never seen a kora before, or knew anything about it. Then I tuned my kora to his guitar, and we started playing together. As soon as we started playing, all the people passing by stopped to hear us. There was a whole wedding party there, with the bride still in her wedding gown, and they even started dancing and throwing money at us! We played on the front stoop for two and a half hours! Then I told Karl, "Let me give you my number, and you can give me yours". Later on that year, when I was booked for a solo kora concert show in December at Roulette in Brooklyn, I called and asked him to come and sit in with me. The next year when he got a show at the B.B. King Blues Club in Manhattan, he asked me to sit in with him too. It was very, very good. All this because he happened to pass by that night when me and Zack were on the front stoop, and I said, "Come on over". Since then, me and Karl see each other every time I am in New York.

On August 29th, Emily and Uno hosted another big party at their house, and asked me if I would play my kora. That day it was very rainy out, so we set everything up for the concert inside, and I cooked a big pot of peanut stew and a big pot of red stew for all the guests. All their friends and neighbors came, and the house was jam-packed! Every room was full. That was the third or fourth time I did that kind of thing at their place in Seattle. Maybe even more than that! Most of the times, I played out on their deck and the whole back yard was jam-packed. Every time, the people liked my music a lot and it was very nice.

Later on that summer, Philip asked me to play at his Days and Nights Festival again in California. On September 25th, we played together at the Henry Miller Library with a Dutch harpist called Lavinia Meijer, and the concert was called "Poetry and Music Under the Redwoods". While we played, a very famous poet named Jerry Quickley recited his poetry. The Henry Miller Library is a really nice environment to play, because the stage is outside under the tall trees. I would like to play there again too! In the middle of December, I went back into the studio with Uno for more recording. This time, it was just me playing solo kora and singing, and we finished seven songs. That was the one of the last things we recorded in his studio, and Uno said he likes it the best. In all our years of recording, he never charged me one penny! Uno is something else.

●●●●●

In early February of 2016, I went to New York again to rehearse for the annual Tibet House concert at Carnegie Hall. The concert was on February 22nd, and that is when I met the American punk rock singer Iggy Pop. Me and Philip performed a concert together again with Lavinia Meijer, and Iggy Pop was singing with us. Sharon Jones also performed, with the Patti Smith Band backing her up. Sharon Jones was amazing. It is sad that she passed away later on that year, so young. Iggy was also the very last act, and he dedicated his performance to David Bowie, who had passed away just a month before. At the end of it, he got everybody up dancing like crazy for the song Jean Genie. Later on, Iggy contacted me to say that he would be traveling to Seattle for a show at the Paramount Theater on March 28th, and invited me to that show. His people put me on the guest list, and I asked them to put my friends Uno and Emily on that list too. At the show, Iggy was jumping all over the place, dancing and singing so well! He had a famous guitar player in his band named Josh Homme, and they played another David Bowie song to end the show. Iggy also left backstage passes for us, so we went up to see him in his dressing room after the show. He asked me a whole lot of questions about the kora, and about Mandingo people in West Africa, and we all talked together for a long time.

I was doing a lot of flying back and forth to New York in all of 2016, visiting people and checking out things, just to see where exactly where I might want to live. Now when I look back at all the years since I came to the U.S., I think to myself, "If I added up all the time I spent flying back and forth to New York, it would be about a year of my life!" Finally I decided it was time to just move there, so on November 9th I flew to New York again. I stayed at Philip's house for a while, then I went to North Haven, Connecticut to stay with my good friend Asher Delerme. We have known each other over 40 years now, since we met in Ghana in 1976 while I was teaching at the university. Right away when I decided to move to the east coast, Asher invited me to come and stay with him at his house in North Haven. He has a lot of instuments at his place, so we started playing together whenever I was visiting there, and it was very sweet. We like each other's playing so much! We have played together many times, and he has always been very dedicated to playing with me, so one day I said to him, "Let's make a band together." So we formed the Suso Quartet: me, Asher on percussion, Jordan Janez on bass, and Dan Rowe on piano. Me and Asher and Jordan rehearsed together a lot in North Haven, and then we went into a local recording studio and made a demo of around eight songs. I sent those files to Dan in Seattle so he could rehearse the songs too. Then in April 2017, Dan went to Uno's recording studio in Seattle and laid down the piano tracks for all the songs. The Suso Quartet hasn't done a whole lot yet, but I like the way we sound very much.

•••••

On March 12th, 2017, I went from Asher's house in North Haven to New York for the Glass @ 80 concert at National Sawdust in Brooklyn. This was another World Music Institute concert, and the band was me, Philip, Asher, and Jeffrey Ziegler on cello, who used to play with Kronos. That was the only show I did with Philip in 2017, but for the first time in many years, we started making plans to record together again. Many times over the past 10-12 years we said to each other, "Let's make another record" but it didn't happen. That changed one night when I happened to be staying at Philip's house on the same night as Leo Heiblum, who is another one of Philip's friends that stays at his house whenever he is in New York. Leo is a very good musician and composer from Mexico, and he looks like a hippie with a big beard and big hair. That night, he was in his room playing a small Mexican guitar called a jarana, and when I heard it, I came down to listen closer. The song he was playing sounded just like a traditional kora song, so I said to him, "I will go get my kora, and we can play together on what you were just playing." When we played, it sounded really good! Afterward, I went to Philip and said, "Now is the time. You should come downstairs and listen to us." When heard us play, he said, "Let's talk." The next day, me and Philip talked about this very good chemistry that happened, and about the two of us making a recording with Leo playing jarana and Asher playing percussion. We started making plans, and in May, we all rehearsed together for two days. Then in early June, we went into New York University's state-of-the-art recording studio for three days to record nine or ten songs that I composed. Me and Leo also recorded the traditional Mexican song that we first played together at Philip's house. Leo sang it in Spanish, and I sang in the Mandingo language. Then Leo took the tracks back to his recording studio in Mexico City and mixed it there. Our new band is called the Suso/Glass Quartet.

Leo's main work is writing music for film soundtracks, and he has won many awards. He knows everybody in the Latin filmmaking industry, and everybody know him. When we first met, he told me that was also putting together the music for the Fenix Film Awards ceremony that was to be in Mexico City in December 2017. While we were doing our recording sessions, we were talking together about filmmaking too, because people are always telling me that I have such interesting stories and I should make a documentary movie of my life. But I don't know anything about the movie business, so I never talk to people much about it. Leo told me, "You should come down to Mexico City so that people can see you face-to-face, that's better than a lot of words. I will also see if you and Natalia Lafourcade can play here at the awards ceremony." Natalia is a very famous singer and songwriter from Mexico, and has won a lot of Grammy awards. Then after Leo returned to Mexico, he called me to say, "Everybody is excited for you to come here." He gave Natalia some of my music to listen to, and she said that she would like definitely to play with me. I asked to hear some of her music too, and she sent me some songs to listen to. I picked one of the songs that I thought would work the best for us to perform together, which is called Hasta la Raiz, because the kora tuning and the part I composed for it fit very well.

At the beginning of December 2017, I flew down to Mexico City for nine days, and they put me in a big hotel. I rehearsed with Natalia and the band for a few days before the awards show. Then the night before the show, Natalia and her band did a concert in a brand new, big auditiorium building, and she asked me to come see it. She reserved seats near the stage for me and Leo's nephew Alan, who was my driver while I was in Mexico City. The place was jam-packed, and the band played a long time. I began to get tired and left before it was over, but she didn't see that because of all the stage lights. So towards the end of her show, she began talking about me, and the performance we were going to do together at the awards show the next night. She even introduced me to the audience and asked them to give me a big hand. The spotlight was shined on where I was sitting, but I was gone! Natalia told me about this the next day, and she was laughing and told me that she understood, so we laughed together about it.

The next afternoon, we did our soundcheck at a big, historic theater called Teatro de la Ciudad, where the awards ceremony was held. Then there was a red carpet event in front of the theater, with photographers everywhere shooting pictures, and the whole street was jammed with people. That night, our performance started with Natalia's band and Leo on stage playing, and I was behind the curtain. I came onstage playing my kora for the beginning of the song, and then Natalia came out singing. The show was very good. The song me and Natalia played together was one of her big hit songs, but the way I played the kora against it, everybody said that the song had never sounded so good.

Ever since I first met Leo, and he knows how much I like the jarana, he would always say to me, "There is an old man in Vera Cruz named Don Andres Vega Delfin. He plays the jarana, and I want to take you there to see him." So one early morning a few days after the concert with Natalia, we drove down there. It was eight hours on a regular highway and two more hours on a dirt road filled with potholes, to get to Don Andres home in the village of San Miguel. On the way, a funny thing happened. Leo had also been telling me that there was a town in Vera Cruz called Mandinga. So while we were driving to San Miguel, we came to that town. Leo told me, "Look, here is the sign for that town, Mandinga". I told him to stop the car and take a picture of me standing next to the sign, because I wanted to be able to tell people that this is the place in Mexico where the Mandingo people settled. Although I have been all over the world, I have never seen that village, but I know the history of it. Our history tells us that there was a prince of Mali 734 years ago named Abubakari Keita. He told his people that he wanted to see what was behind the ocean, so he and his men made forty big wooden boats, and they put all the food and everything else they needed into those boats, and pushed them out into the sea. The waves took them all the way to Mexico to the mouth of a big river, and it was too far to sail back, so they settled there.

In that village, I saw black Mexicans who speak Spanish, but they have African features. There were also big carved stone heads with

African features, and carvings in the rocks. Then we saw a restaurant called Mandinga, with a palm leaf roof. I told Leo, "Let's stop. I want us to eat here." While we were eating, a Mariachi band with guitar, violin, harp, and accordian players came by and played for us. Leo speaks perfect Spanish, so I told him to ask the musicians, "Why is your town called Mandinga?" They replied, "The people who built this town came from Africa, and they are called Mandinka." I believed that from them, because in fact, the village of Mandinga is at the mouth of a big river. So I said to them, "If I tell you that I am a Mandinka, will you believe me?" They said, "We don't know." So I said, "I bet you have never seen an African person come to your town and tell you that they are Mandinka." They said, "No, never!" Then I said, "Your town's name is the tribe I came from, a tribe from West Africa. I know about my people who sailed to Mexico hundreds of years ago, and you are the descendent of those people". Then I told them that I was a musician, showed them my card, and told them about my instrument. They never saw a kora before. I also gave them some money, and then we drove the rest of the way to the home of Don Andres.

He and his wife have 17 children, and all are artists. The boys play the jarana and the girls are singers. Andres is a player! One kind of kora tuning goes so well with the jarana, and we played together. Anything he played, I could play the kora with that. I liked his playing very much, and playing music with his children too. It fits together so unbelievable. When we played together, it was like we played together for many years. We stayed there with Don Andres' family for three days. Me and Leo stayed at the home of Marta, one of his daughters who lives just across the street. Two of his sons' houses are also right next door to him. They are all such nice people. During our visit, I also started talking to Leo about the idea of bringing Andres up to play at Philip's Days and Nights Festival in California, so that me and Andres can play together again there. Andres was 87 years old, but he was so strong that sometimes he even got up to dance to the music! Me and Leo said to each other, "This would be good". When I got back to New York, I talked to Philip in his kitchen about bringing Andres to that festival sometime. Philip liked the idea too, and I think it will happen. Sometimes I still call Marta's phone from my house. I will just say, "Marta, this is Suso!" and she will say "Hey, Suso!" but I cannot speak Spanish and she cannot speak English. One of Andres' sons lives in Mexico City and his wife can speak English, so sometimes I call him to give a message to Marta. That grandson plays percussion on the jaw of a horse, with all the teeth in it. It makes a great sound!

•••••

At the beginning of 2018, I flew from New Haven to Chicago to visit my good friend David Braswell for two weeks. I have known him for all the years I lived in Chicago, but I hadn't seen him since I moved to Seattle in 2009. It was very nice. Then on Wednesday January 31st, I flew to Tuscon, Arizona to visit Uno and Emily. Uno picked me at the airport and we drove down to the small village of Arivaca, which is very close to the Mexico border. Uno and Emily bought a house and some land there in 2016 while I was still living with them in Seattle, and the next year they liked it so much that they sold their Seattle house and moved down there to spend all their wintertimes. I hadn't seen them since I moved to the east coast, and also I wanted to keep working on the book in person with Emily.

I was there in Arivaca with them for the whole month of February. Their place is very nice, and the way it was built makes it look like a compound. They have a beautiful big yard, and when you are there, you can be looking at a whole lot of birds, deer and other animals, and a lot of big, tall trees all around. It's in the warm desert but with lots of grasses all around too. It's the kind of place I like. Uno and Emily already knew a lot of people in that village, because they went there many times before to see the birds. They asked me if I wanted to play a concert while I was there, just like I used to play at their place in Seattle. I said yes, so we had an outside concert in their compound on Sunday February 18th. Uno went and borrowed a bunch of chairs from the community center, and set them up in the yard so it looked like an amphitheater. He set up mics and a PA on the patio, and everything was very good. They invited everybody in the whole village to come, and the yard was full. I played the kora on the stone patio, and all the people were sitting out in their big yard. I liked it so much because it was outside and a free show for everybody, just like a traditional village. The audience just comes and sits down all together to listen to the music, and then people walk up to the griot and give any kind of gift they can give, for the music and history they hear. Almost nobody in Arivaca had ever seen a kora before or knows what it is, and when I played they really liked it. Everybody was so quiet and listening very well, and it was reminding me a lot of griot traveling back home.

While I was there, we did a lot of stuff. One day, Uno and Emily took me to a very tiny town on the Mexico border called Sasabe, where only nine people live! We also had a big dinner for some of their Arivaca friends a few times, and one of those people was a guy named Dan Kelly. He invited us to come to dinner at his house too, and when we got there he showed us this crazy ATV car called a Polaris, that a friend had left at his house. Dan invited me to go on a ride in it with him, so a few days later, we went in that Polaris way down a small road until it turned to dirt, and we went over big rocks and everything. I fell in love with that car! I told him, "Maybe someday I will buy a car like that to take to Africa". He let me drive it too!

On Sunday, February 25th, Uno and Emily took me to a very famous town called Tombstone. It is famous for all the cowboy things that happened there, and Uno and Emily know that I like cowboy and western movies ever since I was growing up back home in Africa. Wow, the day we got to that town, we saw a lot of places that look the same way they did 150 years ago! You can find out all about the real cowboys who were there back then, who passed through, and who did what. Even the people working there all dress like they did in the old days, with cowboy clothes and horse buggies rolling down the street. That town became very famous because of a big cowboy gunfight that happened there a long time ago. When you say Tombstone, everybody knows what you mean, because there are a lot of movies that were made there about that gunfight and that town. We went to a place where we could shoot the big old pistols, which were very heavy but had fake bullets. We saw guys at the OK

Corral doing a play about that gunfight, and other stuff. Tombstone is now a tourist town, and when we got there the streets were jam-packed with people, but in the evening when we were leaving to go back to Arivaca, the town became completely empty like nobody ever lived there. I enjoyed that very much!

The whole time I was in Arivaca, it was very sweet. On many days, I worked on the book with Emily in her little studio house out in the yard, and after I came back to North Haven, we also recorded some more on the phone. In that village of Arivaca, they also have one small bar called La Gitana. That's the music place for the whole village, and they have bands play there sometimes, but also on many nights musicians just gather there to jam. I went there a lot with Uno and Emily to see all different kinds of music being played, and they introduced me to all the musicians there too.

One night, I met a guy named Glen Moore, who plays upright bass very well, and used to be in the band called Oregon. This was the first time I met him, but many years ago when Mandingo Griot Society was touring the west coast a lot, I got to know their percussionist Collin Walcott. Now Glen lives in Arivaca too. I talked to him for a long time, and he invited me to come to his house and jam. So one day Emily drove me over to his compound, where he has a studio. I tuned my kora to fit his bass, and we jammed together with a friend of his named Rob Withrow, just for fun and to put some ideas together. It sounded very good. There are a whole lot of good musicians in Arivaca. At the Sunday night jam, Emily got up to sing too, and the people liked it very much. I met a lot of the people in that village during my time there, and they all welcomed me very nice.

Around a month before I went to Arivaca, I got an email from an organization in Toronto, Canada called the Glen Gould Foundation. Glen Gould was a very famous pianist who passed away a long time ago, and after that, this foundation was formed in his honor. Every two years, the foundation gives an award to an outstanding artist, and they have a special way to pick the winner. They pick ten jurists who are all different kinds of artists, and those people will discuss and debate which person should get the award. When they first contacted me to come there and be a jurist, I asked them to explain it to me. They said that I would come there to Toronto and meet with the other jurists to pick somebody for the award. They also said all the nominees will have their picture and a lot of bio information in a big book, and all the jurists will have their bio and information in that same book too. They said they will send it to me, and we jurists will read from that book to help us choose the winner. Since I know that everything is about the computer nowadays, with download this and that, I told them, "I hope this is not all going to be reading a whole lot from a computer, because I am not into that. I just want to know from the start how it will be, and for you to know about me before I say yes". They said, "No, no, it's not like that, it will be face-to-face meetings for all the jurists. You will be meeting together to talk, and then chose the artist to win the award". They made everything very clear, so I said I would do it. It was a very big honor.

A few days before I left for Arivaca, the Glen Gould people sent me that big, thick book with 83 nominees to read about, and so I started reading it and thinking about the people. Even though Glen Gould was a pianist and composer, all kinds of artists can be nominated for the award: a singer, photographer, painter, musician, composer, dancer, or other kind of artist. You have to be a special artist, not just to be good at what you do, but also to cross over into another art or break new ground in your art and do it better than anyone else. The leader of the jurists was Viggo Mortensen, an actor who is also a writer and musician, and the other jurist people were famous painters, movie producers, writers, composers, and singers from all different parts of the world. When a friend of mine in Chicago saw the picture of us all, he said, "Suso, are you in the United Nations now?" and I told him, "Yes, I am in the United Nations of Music". The Glen Gould people flew us all up to Toronto in April, and we jurists went through a long process from April 11th to the 13th to choose just one artist for the award, and we decided to give the Glen Gould Prize to the great opera singer Jessye Norman.

After the Glen Gould event was over, I went back to North Haven, Massachusetts for a while. Then on Monday July 9th, 2018, I left there to move back to Chicago. I was thinking, "This is the place I lived when I first came to the United States, so maybe I should go back there again to live". I brought almost all my things to Chicago, and am still living there right now, but not really settled. The rest of 2018 wasn't too busy, but I made some trips to New York and other places, and played some concerts from time to time. Then on Friday January 4th, 2019, the new CD called "Introducing the Suso/Glass Quartet" came out, and we shall see what will happen next.

A VILLAGE GRIOT BOY

We griots are the oral historians of the people, not just musicians who play the kora. I am a traditional griot, and I can play 111 traditional songs that cover all five areas in West Africa where traditional kora music is played: Gambia, Senegal, Guinea-Bissau, Mali, and Guinea. When you play traditional songs, those are just the way they are. Many of them were written hundreds of years ago and have been played millions of times by griots. Traditionally, when griots sit down and play these songs, there is no rehearsal. Someone just calls out the name of the song, and either you can play it or you cannot play it, and that's it. There is nothing happening like talking with each other about how the song should be. It's the song. And the heavy history that goes with it is very important. Because of that tradition, the main beats are always the same, and the main song is played by everybody, with some of the griots taking turns to improvise on top of that.

Today, some people just play the kora without that history part, but the true tradition of being a griot is to know all those songs. That's why it takes a long time when you go to study with your teacher. To play the instrument might not even take a long time, but to study the history and know it by heart will always take a long time. If you are a griot, you can show up in any crowd and take it by storm just by talking to them. People will stand and listen to you, and you don't even have to play your instrument. Just what you are saying is so important to the people, more important than playing the instrument. That's the heavy way to be a griot. Those days are gone now, and you don't see that much today.

Today, young griots might learn to play the kora in their own house, or they might get a teacher and pay them fifty dollars a month. But if they learn in that way, they will not be able to learn the history that goes with the songs. If you don't learn to be a griot in the traditional way, you might be able to play the kora but you won't know much about the history. You might just play some music, but not the traditional kora songs. In fact, when you ask some young kora players today, they might not even know the names of the traditional songs! They might call a song by one word that is in it a lot, but that word is not actually the name of the song. That's a big problem.

Each of the traditional West Africa kora areas also has different styles and tunings on the kora: Two are common in Guinea and Mali, and three are common in Gambia, Senegal, and Guinea-Bissau. So if a griot comes to Gambia and doesn't know the Gambian tuning and style on the kora, he cannot play it. It's the same with Mali style, you have to know it to know how to play it. To western ears, all the styles are complicated, but most western people prefer Mali style because it is played slower and with a 4/4 beat, which is easier to listen to. Kora players from Gambia, Senegal, Guinea-Bissau, and Guinea usually play a syncopated rhythm such as 6/8. They can play a 4/4 beat too, but they play it aggressively and fast, and can also sing and play at the same time, and recite the history of the people. In Mali, the griot women sing while the men play the kora quietly. Men there cannot sing and play the kora at the same time. Sometimes I see western writers say that the best kora players are in Mali. But not us griots, we know. There is a Mandingo saying that means, "People don't know which of the doves are male or female, but the doves know".

When I was growing up, I didn't want to limit myself to just one of those styles. I learned to play every one of those tunings and rhythms, so that when I play any style, you will think I came from that region. This is something I mastered before I started playing rock and roll, or jazz style on my kora. I can play my own original compositions, or I can sound like I never left Africa. And one thing I believe is that anything you are gifted in will be easy for you. I believe I was gifted to be a griot and a musican. With the kora, dusungoni, nyanye, balafon, and drums, I believe I have that gift. I am a musician, not just a kora player. Once I hear any song, I can start to play it.

I do not disapprove of playing something different and original on the kora, and playing with all kinds of western instruments and music styles, because I myself do that. Before me, I don't think anybody did it. When I came to the United States in 1977 and formed the Mandingo Griot Society, it was the first kora band anywhere in the world. I had the idea to go and play the kora in a different way, in a country where koras didn't come from, where they have never seen it, and where they don't know what it is. When I came to the U.S., my band members told me that the name Mandingo Griot Society would be very difficult for western people, and that people would not remember it. I told them, "If we don't do well, no one will remember us. But if we play good, people will remember our name". I came with that idea, and we were one of the first world music bands. Then I did my original music for so many years, right up to today. So a new way of playing the kora, that's OK with me.

Today though, you can hear a lot of young people who learn the kora, and right away they have a new sound on it. They might hear my music and want to do something like that too, but they don't understand that before I played my own songs or other types of music, I learned the tradition very heavy first. There is nothing wrong with playing new styles on the kora, but I don't like it that many young kora players today cannot play even five traditional songs very clearly. I think it's best to know and learn traditional songs first, and then do other stuff. What I look for is this: Try to play the traditional songs until you know those very, very well, then go and play anything else you want. Our griot tradition is very important. If you do it in that way, you will always be able to go back and play the traditional kora songs, and you will never forget them.

I have a very different thinking about many other things too. First of all, I believe that everything has a time. This is my heavy belief. And until the time comes for that thing, you will not be able to do it, but nothing can stop it once it comes. It has a time. And I believe also that anything a human being can do or can get is already decided. The creator will make that. That means you don't have to kill yourself doing things, but you don't have to lay back and do nothing also. It's just that no matter what you do, you will get what you are supposed to get, and you will do what you are supposed to do. For sure, your destiny will push you to get it. If it's not for you to get, you won't get it. People who force things, those are the people who will end up losing everything. If you are not meant to be a millionaire but you go around and rob and cheat to get a million dollars, you will end up getting killed or in prison for your life. In this world, somebody can be on the street with a jackhammer, lifting big loads and doing back-breaking jobs, but still not making enough money, and somebody else can be wearing a suit and tie in an office with the cool air and everything, making a whole lot of money. The one on the street is much stronger and working harder, but the other person is making all the millions. All people need to try, but the creator is the one who will make things happen for you. Also, 50 people can be in the same classroom learning the same subject, but they will all end up different, and two people can be the same car and have an accident but only one is killed. It's not because anybody is smarter or better, it's just their time and their destiny.

This is my heavy belief, and this is why no matter what happens, you don't see me complaining. I am alive, and when you are alive, anything can happen. Everything will stop the day you die, but as long as you are breathing, something will happen. What will happen, I don't know. Nobody has anything when they come into this world, because everybody comes in empty-handed. Nobody even has clothes, and they have to wrap us up in a blanket when we are born. When a baby comes into the world crying, no one can know what that baby can do 40 years later, how long they will live, or anything. The baby could be a millionaire or the baby could be a street person, it could be a criminal or a policeman, a blind person, or anything else.

I remember the day I was leaving Ghana to come to the United States. I had a lot of Ghana money, which is called cedi, but that money cannot be spent anywhere else. No one can change that money outside Ghana either, so I went to buy a lot of African clothes to spend it. I had a lot of my friends telling me, "Don't go to America! Don't go to America!" especially when I told them I was going to Chicago. They said, "Don't go there, they will shoot you!" but I told them, "If it's my time, then I will die, even if it's right here in Ghana, in my bed. If it's time for me to die, then nothing can make me stay here on this earth. That's how it is". When I got to London, I had nothing in my pockets. I did three or four concerts there, and when I arrived in the United States I had $900.00. That money carried me all the way to today!

The kind of faith I have, it is so deep, it's too, too, too, too much. But that's how it is. It's unbelievable. Sometimes I have nothing, and sometimes I have a whole lot of money. If I have to spend all of it, that's OK, but my faith never lets me down. When I went home to Gambia in 1983,

I took all the money I had with me. I moved out of my Chicago apartment when I went to Gambia, because I didn't know when I was coming back. I had to wait for my papers to come, and the immigration people told me it would be between three months and six months before I knew what would happen. Later that year when I came back to Chicago, I only had $600.00 left. I talked to my friend Manu and asked him, "I came back now, but I don't have my apartment anymore, so I don't have any place to stay. Can I stay with you?" He said, "Yes, man! You know my house is full, but for you I have room. Even if you have to sleep on the floor, you can stay". I was there at his house for five or six days, and then we talked to another guy we know named Moses Norman, and he said, "Yes, I have a place with two bedrooms, you can come and stay here". I told him, "Moses, I just came back from Gambia and I don't have any money, so I can't pay you anything now", but he said, "One thing I will tell you is, don't worry about that". So I said, "Thank you very much! I know something will happen, and I know I am not going to be like this forever unless I die tomorrow morning. Something will change. When that happens, you will see it". He told me again, "Don't worry about that. I've known you since you came to this country, we are friends, and hey". So I moved in with him, and every month he paid the rent, phone bill, and everything. At that time, he was working for Commonwealth Edison, the light company, so he had enough money for all that.

I didn't have anything change for me for many months. Some days I would just take $3.00 to spend to put some food in my mouth, but even with that, I still had a strong feeling. You would never see me down. I was always thinking, "If God says this is how it will be until I die, that's how it is". I have a strong faith, and I never reget or worry. If anything happens to me, I will take it very easy and say, "God the creator has done a lot for me all my life". Moses did not worry either, and every month paid the rent and phone bill, even though I was the only one making long distance phone calls. He was patient and didn't worry.

At the end of that year, that's when I took off. I made a demo tape, and I told my friends that I was going to New York to look for some kind of thing. By that time, I had only $400.00. I took $150.00 to buy my airline ticket, and I took $100.00 to New York with me in my pocket. I took a nighttime flight because that was the cheapest flight, and it was snowing hard when we arrived. The plane was shaking hard like we were on a gravel road. All the other times when I flew and there was a problem, I didn't worry, but that time I thought I wasn't going to make it. Eventually we landed, then I went to my friend John Crowley's house in Brooklyn, and spent the night. When he went to work in the morning, he dropped me in Manhattan. All I had with me was a list of record companies, such as Island Records, CBS, Electra, Nonesuch, and others, and a bunch of cassette tapes. I didn't have any appointment, I just went to their address and handed them the tape, and after I left they just threw my cassette inside their big basket at the door. But that day is when I happened to go to Celluloid Records and met Jean Karakos. He called Bill Laswell and introduced me to him. I was so happy when Bill said, "I think we can do something together".

After that meeting, at first nothing happened. I went back to Chicago, and my money was drying up fast. I only had $16.00 left. Then one day Bill called me to say, "We want to bring you to New York to play on the recording for Herbie Hancock. My guy will call you tomorrow to talk about what the fee will be". The next day that guy told me they would pay me $3000.00. When you have $16.00 and somebody says they will pay you $3000.00, what can you say inside except, "Wow". But since I never like anything to take me by a big surprise or to act crazy, I just replied, "Let me talk to my people here, and then I will call you back". I called back the next day and said, "OK, yes I will come", and they sent me the plane ticket. I played on the record, and they gave me $3000.00 plus $50.00 per diem for the five days I was there. When I came back to Chicago, I was in a big, big hurry to get to my friend Moses' house. When I got there, I put my bags down and we greeted, and he asked how my trip was. Then I said, "Come and sit down. All these nine months I have been here, you are the one who has been paying all the rent of $300.00 a month. Now I can pay". I counted all the money out in front of him, $150.00 for every month I was there. Then I told him, "You have been paying for all the phone bills and everything, even though I am the one making the outside calls", and I gave him all the rest of the $3000.00 too. That day, I was so happy in my heart!

From there, everything changed. I got my own recording contract, I went to meet Herbie in LA, and went on tour with his band. Since then, I have worked with all kinds of musicians from all over the world and played in many different places. The music business is not like an everyday, 9 to 5 job. Sometimes it goes up, and sometimes it goes down. You just have to keep going, going, going on it! Have a good heart and keep your head together, and do your thing. When you keep searching and keep trying, something will happen. Because God says that, "I owe that to a human being that keeps trying. As long as I put you on the earth, keep trying".

Later on in 1984, I was thinking to move in to my own apartment again, and I went to the apartment building owner in Hyde Park who knew me from all the years before when I lived in his building. He told me, "Anytime I have an apartment for rent, I will let you know", so pretty soon I moved back there. That is the apartment where I lived all the way until 2009. Then when I came to Seattle, it was because something told me inside that it was the time for this, and it was the same when I decided to leave and go to the east coast, and to come back to Chicago. That's how it is for me.

I am a village griot boy, born in the small village of Sare Hamadi in the Wuli District of Gambia, and I have been traveling all over the world playing music for close to 50 years. Today, I am thousands of miles away from Sare Hamadi and Foday Kunda, and back in Chicago. I always say, "If nothing else, then I do see the world!" I am very happy that I have written my autobiography, and I thank everybody I have met along the way, and all the people who read this book. May you all get enjoyment from it, and reading about the knowledge I happened to gather through my life. This is where the journey brings me so far, as I am sitting here on May 6th, 2019.

Acknowledgements

I would like to thank my very good friend Conrad Uno for all the work he did for this book: creating the cover design and layout, helping me choose pictures from my videos and still photographs to use inside it, and managing all the publishing details. Special thanks to my wife Bobo Suso, for standing by me with all the world traveling I do, and all her support for so many years. Special thanks to all my children too, and to my father's brothers Lamin Suso and Surakata Suso.

Foday Musa Suso

May 6th, 2019

I would like to thank my brother Daniel Bishton, my good friend Cindy Current, and my husband Conrad Uno, whose feedback, support, and insightful questions about the first draft of this book was a great gift. Special thanks also to Conrad Uno for his patience and steadfast encouragement over the past five years, as this book came into being.

Emily Bishton

May 6th, 2019

Discography
Foday Musa Suso 1977-2019

Listings in bold font are detailed within the book

Artists	Title/Description	Year	Record or Film Co.
Foday Musa Suso	Sounds of West Africa: The Kora & The Xylophone	1977	Lyrichord
Foday Musa Suso	Kora Music from The Gambia: Foday Musa Suso	1978	Folkways Records
Mandingo Griot Society	Mandingo Griot Society	1979	Flying Fish Records
Foday Musa Suso	Soundtrack for the TV movie, Roots: the Next Generations	1979	David Wolper Productions/Warner Brothers
Mandingo Griot Society	Mighty Rhythm	1981	Flying Fish Records
Various Artists	The Official Music for the XXIIIrd Olympiad in LA	1984	CBS
Herbie Hancock	Sound System	1984	Columbia Records
Foday Musa Suso	Hand Power	1984	Flying Fish Records
Mandingo	Watto Sita	1984	Celluloid Records
Various Artists	Afro Trance-Cosmic Communication	Bootleg	Cosmic Communications
Mandingo	Harima 12"	1985	Celluloid Records
Various Artists	New Africa	1985	Celluloid Records
Foday Musa Suso and Herbie Hancock	Village Life	1985	Columbia Records
Toure Kunda	Natalia	1985	Celluloid Records
Various Artists	Trilogy	1985	Celluloid Records
Various Artists	New Africa	1985	Street Sounds
Foday Musa Suso, Tamba Suso, and Jarju Kuyateh	Mansa Bendung	1986	Flying Fish Records
Ginger Baker	Horses and Trees	1986	Celluloid Records/RCA
Foday Musa Suso and Herbie Hancock	Jazz Africa (album and film)	1990/1991	Verve Records/Lorimar Pictures

Artist	Title	Year	Label
Foday Musa Suso and Phillip Glass	Soundtrack for the movie, "Powaqqatsi"	1988	Golan/Globus Productions
Foday Musa Suso	Julu Kemu	1989	Rhizome Sketch
Material	Seven Souls	1989	Virgin Records
Foday Musa Suso	Soundtrack for the movie, "Mountains of the Moon"	1990	Polydor Records
Mandingo	New World Power	1990	Axiom
Mandingo	Powerhouse 12"	1990	Axiom Records
Foday Musa Suso and various artists	Ancient Heart: Mandinka & Fulani Music of the Gambia	1991	Axiom/Mango Records
Various Artists	The Lyrichord World Music Sampler	1991	Lyrichord
Various Artists	Imabari Meeting	1991	Meldac
Autonomous Zone	The Map is Not the Territory	1991	Meldac
Herbie Hancock	The Very Best Of	1991	Columbia
Various Artists	Celluloid/Our World of Music	1991	Celluloid
Various Artists	Ear Magazine Presents Absolut CD #3, Improvisation/ Composition	1991	Ear Magazine
Foday Musa Suso and Philip Glass	The Screens	1992	Point Music
Foday Musa Suso	Soundtrack for the documentary, "Magicians of the Earth: Seni's Children"	1992	Fernando Trueba Prod. Cinemato-gráficas/ Milestone
Uatki/Philip Glass & Foday Musa Suso/John Moran	Point Music	1992	Point Music
Kronos Quartet	Pieces of Africa	1992	Elektra/Nonesuch
Various Artists	3000 Series Compiler 1	1992	CMP
Various Artists	Hörbeispiele Zu Volker Schütz Musik In Schwarzafrika	1992	Institut Für Didaktik Populärer Musik
Various Artists	Deutsche Grammaphon London Records Philips Classics Verve Ecm Antilles	1992	PolyGram Classics & Jazz
Philip Glass, David Bowie, Brian Eno	"Low" Symphony	1993	Point Music
Various Artists	Sounds of Africa	1993	Sounds of the World
Nicky Skopelitis	Ekstasis	1993	Axiom

Umar Bin Hassam	Be Bop or Be Dead	1993	Axiom
Hideo Yamaki	Shadow Run	1993	Mercury
Material	Live in Japan	1993	Restless Records
Various Artists	In Defense Of Animals - Benefit Compilation	1993	Restless Records
Various Artists	Wings Around Africa	1993	Intermusic S.A.
Foday Musa Suso	The Dreamtime	1994	CMP
Flying Mijinko Band	Central Asian Tour	1995	The Japan Foundation
Various Artists	Nouvelles Musiques Pour Le 21ème Siècle	1995	Point Music
Foday Musa Suso and various artists	Jal Kunda: Griots of West Africa & Beyond (album and book)	1996	Ellipsis Arts
Pharoh Sanders	Message from Home	1996	Verve Records
Various Artists	La Strada Per La Libertà - Strange Fruit	Unknown	Nuova Iniziativa Editoriale
Possession	Off World One	1996	Sub Meta
Various Artists	Breaking The Barriers Of World Music - The CMP Story Volume Two	1997	CMP
Various Artists	Paraísos (Lo Mejor De Las Nuevas Musicas)	1998	Divusca
Various Artists	The Verve Album	2000	Verve
Philip Glass	Philip On Film - Filmworks By Philip Glass	2001	Nonesuch
Various Artists	Jazz Funk	2001	Jazz & Tʒaʒ
Various Artists	Drum & Tribe Cyber Jam Vol. 2 African Breakbeats	2001	Jazz Flame
Philip Glass	The World of Philip Glass	2002	Decca Records
Various Artists	Auszüge Aus: Neue Welt (Streifzüge Durch Die Avantgarde)	2004	Decca/Universal
Foday Musa Suso and Jack DeJohnette	Music from the Heart of the Masters	2005	Kindred Rhythm/ Golden Beams
The Ripple Effect	Hybrids	2005	Golden Beams
Foday Musa Suso and Philip Glass	Orion (Music for the XXVIII Olympiad in Athens)	2005	Orange Mountain Music
Pharoh Sanders	Anthology	2005	Universal Classics & Jazz

Various Artists	Cool Summer Vol 4 - June 2005	2005	Jazziz
Foday Musa Suso	The Two Worlds	2006	Orange Mountain Music
Gigi	Gold & Wax	2006	Palm Pictures
Ginger Baker	Dust to Dust	2006	Brook
Various Artists	Healing the Divide: A Concert for Peace and Reconciliation	2007	Epitaph/Anti Records
DJ Spooky That Subliminal Kid	Afrique Universelle - La Biennale Di Venezia	2007	Synchronic
Herbie Hancock and Bill Laswell	Technovoodu: Astral Black Simulations	2007	Not on Label
Foday Musa Suso	Soundtrack for the documentary, "Making the Crooked Straight"	2010	HBO
Foday Musa Suso and Nacha Mendez	Angelitos Negros	2011	Not on Label
Foday Musa Suso and Philip Glass	Philip Glass Recording Archive, Vol. 6: The Music of Philip Glass and Foday Musa Suso	2011	Orange Mountain Music
Foday Musa Suso and Gretchen Rowe	Koralations	2012	CD Baby
Herbie Hancock	The Complete Columbia Album Collection, 1972 - 88	2013	Columbia
Various Artists	Change the Beat: The Celluloid Records Story, 1979-1987	2013	Strut
Method of Defiance	Phantom Sound Clash Cut-Up Method - One	2014	M.O.D. Technologies
Carmen Staaf	Day Dream	2017	Tone Rougue Records
Various Artists	Soul Of A Nation (Afro-Centric Visions In The Age of Black Power)	2017	Soul Jazz Records
Suso/Glass Quartet	Introducing the Suso/Glass Quartet	2019	Orange Music

Photo Credits

1. Unknown
2. Dembo Kanuteh
3. Foday Musa Suso
4. Foday Musa Suso
5. Unknown
6. Foday Musa Suso
7. Unknown
8. Foday Musa Suso
9. Unknown
10. Unknown
11. Unknown
12. Foday Musa Suso
13. Foday Musa Suso
14. Unknown
15. Unknown
16. Foday Musa Suso
17. Unknown
18. Unknown
19. Unknown
20. Emily Bishton
21. Daniel Laine'
22. Dembo Kanuteh
23. Dembo kanuteh
24. Japanese TV film crew
25. Japanese TV film crew
26. Unknown
27. Unknown
28. Unknown
29. Paulo's wife
30. Foday Musa Suso
31. Foday Musa Suso
32. Foday Musa Suso

33. Foday Musa Suso
34. Foday Musa Suso
35. Basaikou Suso
36. Unknown
37. Emily Bishton
38. Emily Bishton
39. Emily Bishton
40. Jack Vartoogian
41. Leo Heiblum
42. Fatou Suso
43. Emily Bishton
44. Emily Bishton
45. Sendin Kanuteh
46. Ousman Kebbeh
47. Fatou Suso
48. Ousman Kebbeh
49. Alhaji Suso
50. Balamin Suso
51. Fatou Suso
52. Damian Sutton
53. Banny Harris
54. Conrad Uno
55. Emily Bishton
56. Emily Bishton
57. Emily Bishton

Student Writings

In 2018, I came to the 4th & 5th grade classroom of my friend Gretchen Rowe at Sacajawea Elementary School in Seattle Washington, to play the kora and talk about my life to her students. Afterward, Gretchen asked them to write about their thoughts and feelings:

•••••

"Do you like African music? If so, have you heard of the kora? Could you, in your wildest dreams, think of an African boy growing up to be a famous kora player traveling around the world giving concerts anywhere and everywhere? Foday Musa Suso was that boy and become a part of African music history. He was born in 1950 in the Mandingo Tribe, Gambia, Africa. Foday started learning kora at a young age, and was taught by Sekou Suso. In Foday Musa Suso's tribe, the teacher would make the intermediate kora player play for the elders to see if the kora player was ready. They would say, "He is ready," or "He needs more time." Foday got it on his first try. In Foday's life, he learned how to play 11 other instruments, taught kora for 3 years in Ghana, and has played with many other musicians in the world. When Foday plays, it makes me feel like I just need to stop everything and listen. If it is fast-paced, it makes me want to get up and dance. Foday's music, no matter what instrument he's playing, is so beautiful that I can't describe it. It feels as if he can fit his kora into everything. It seems that he throws himself right into it all. When I hear his music, I fall into a pit, and all that's in that pit is me and his music. Foday's slow music with the kora will always soothe what I would call the unsoothable."

Elizabeth

•••••

"Do you like music? Foday Musa Suso does! He plays the kora. The kora is a really cool and traditional instrument from the Gambia. It has 21 strings. Foday had to work really hard in the fields for his kora teacher, but he got an excellent kora education and became a world renown musician."

Ryder

"I know Foday's music would make me happy when I'm sad, because the sometimes the rhythm is upbeat, and that makes me happy and excited. When I'm feeling down, the music brings me back up, and when he's playing more of the low beats, it calms me down from everything. Foday Musa Suso is a very talented musician."

Aisha

•••••

"Do you play an instrument? Foday Musa Suso learned to play an instrument called the kora as a young boy. But, not only did he play it, he became world famous for playing the kora! Foday Musa Suso was born and grew up in a small village in Gambia. As a kid, he loved the kora. Even before he could hold his dad's kora, he loved to play with it and pull the strings. When Foday started to learn to play it, he had to move to his teacher's house. He worked for him in exchange for being taught how to play the kora. In order to graduate, he had to pass a final test, which was to play for the village elders. If they thought that he was ready, he would graduate. If they thought he wasn't, he would have to go back and have more teachings. His hard work paid off, and he passed on his first try when he was 18 years old. Later, Foday moved to Chicago and soon after started a band called the Mandingo Griot Society. He taught himself how to read and write English. Since then, Foday has traveled all over the world and has also played with many famous musicians. Now, he is one of the most famous kora players ever, and you can probably see why Foday Musa Suso is famous."

Milo

•••••

"Have you ever heard of the kora? Well, if you haven't, today's the day. I'm going to tell you about a very special world famous kora musician named Foday Musa Suso. Foday was born in Gambia and worked on farms. When he was young, he got very interested in learning the kora, and started learning how to play the kora from his teacher Sekou Suso. Foday never gave up. Instead of paying for lessons like we do in Seattle, Foday took several jobs working for his teacher. He watered, planted crops, and kept the baboons away. He also had to make his own kora, which is very hard, especially at that young of an age.

Auna

•••••

"Have you ever wondered how a young boy could grow up to travel all over the world doing what he loves, playing music? He is a man that can play 12 different instruments. Man, I wish I could play that many instruments. Well, anyway, I'm talking about Foday Musa Suso, a well-known kora player. Foday was born on February 18, 1950, in a small village called Sare Hamadi, in the Wuli District in eastern Gambia. He is part of the Mandingo Tribe. Foday started learning how to play the kora while he was living with his master kora teacher named Sekou Suso. Foday was taught to play kora in the village of Pasamasi. Foday's father sent Foday to Sekou Suso, because fathers aren't allowed to teach their sons to play the kora. Foday had to practice playing the kora for years. It was hard, because kora students also had to work for their teacher – like farming throughout the day and practicing kora during night. After Foday practiced and practiced, he had to play his kora in front of the elders who knew the song that Foday was about to perform. Then, the elders would tell Sekou Suso if Foday passed the test. Guess what! Foday passed the test on his first try. I'm proud of Foday. Other students had given up because it was too hard, but Foday didn't quit, because he is not a quitter. Did you know Foday is also a self-taught student? For example, he taught himself how to read, how to write, and all the things you do in school. Foday went to Chicago when he was 27 years old and lived there for 31 years. Chicago is where he created the Mandingo Griot Society with percussionist Adam Rudolph. He has at least 1500 plane tickets from traveling. Currently, Foday is 69 years old and is still performing."

FODAY MUSA SUSO A VILLAGE GRIOT BOY AND THE WORLD

Aisha

• • • • •

"Have you ever wondered how a boy from a small village in Gambia was able to travel the world as an adult? Have you ever heard of an instrument called the kora? Foday Musa Suso was that boy, and he is a world renowned kora player. Foday has been playing since he was very young, what a champ! This man has learned his talents in the Wuli District. After years of work learning to play the kora, he became an oral historian. He learned to play and sing at the same time. He had to make is his instrument by hand using fishing line as strings, and a gourd as the base of his homemade kora. Did you like my story? What was your favorite part?"

Andre

• • • • •

"How did someone who grew in a small village in Gambia become world famous? Read about Foday Musa Suso to find out. Foday was born in Sare Hamadi Village in Gambia. He was born into the Mandingo Tribe. He didn't go to an organized school, so he is self-taught in English. When he was young, he started learning the kora. His teacher demanded a lot, and many students quit because of this. Foday was one of the few who didn't quit. Apart from the kora, Foday can play eleven other instruments. Foday has performed on every continent in the world except Antarctica. Foday says it's not what your talent is, but how well you get along with the people in each country."

Noah

Mandingo Glossary

- **Alibala:** The destroyer. A deadly disease that struck Gambia twice in the mid-1950's, and killed many children.
- **Amuta:** Catch him. Commonly said to dogs to urge them to hunt.
- **Ansimbo:** New men coming home. The big celebration for all the new men who have just come home from manhood training.
- **Ansindong:** The special dance done by the new men who have just come home from manhood training.
- **Ataya:** A strong, sweet tea made from mint.

- **Baba:** Your born father.
- **Badomora:** Mothers' spending. Money that is given by the family of the groom-to-be to the mother of the bride-to-be, as part of the marriage arrangements.
- **Bakeba:** Elder father. A title for any of your father's elder brothers.
- **Balafon:** A traditional Mandingo griot instrument made with wooden keys like a xylophone, with round gourds hanging beneath each of the keys.
- **Bantaba:** Village square.
- **Bantan bilo:** The wooden braces inside the body of the kora.
- **Bantang:** Silk Cotton Tree. Bantang Ba is a big Silk Cotton Tree.
- **Barinkekido:** Brothers' gun. Money given by the family of the groom-to-be to the brothers of the bride-to-be, as part of the marriage arrangements.
- **Barungo:** Strong dance. The dance done by the uncircumcised boys in the village at a celebration done on the night before the circumcision ceremony.
- **Batakungo:** The bridge of a kora.
- **Bembo:** A Gambian fruit that is smaller than a grape and

grows on a vine.
- **Bentengo:** A traditional couch-like seat, usually placed in front of a grass hut or in the village square. A large one is called a jarri benteng.
- **Bombolo:** A traditional log drum, used by young men while guarding farms from wild animals.
- **Bougarabou**: Jola drums that are played with a syncopated rhythm.
- **Buko:** A small grass tent with no walls.
- **Bulakalo:** The wooden handles on the body of a kora.
- **Bulefule tabiro:** Testing her hand. The first cooking that a new bride does for her new husband and all his friends.
- **Buludundula:** The sound hole in the body of a kora.
- **Bulufilo:** Nighttime fishing.
- **Bulukuo:** The day they are going to wash. The first time that circumcised boys take a bath after their wound is healed.
- **Bunkun passing:** A carving made from the Bunkun tree, for young men who have just come home from manhood training to keep in their pocket in case its needed.

- **Calabash:** A gourd that is cut in half when dried, and used for making instruments, bowls, and other household items.

- **Camare:** A spice that tastes like cinnamon, and is traditionally put in porridge for a new bride to eat to keep her skin shiny and nice.
- **Chamfuro:** The time during during the celebration done the night before the circumcision ceremony, when strong young men enter the dance circle to pick boys up and carry him towards the waana.

- **Dalindrila:** Someone to help you get used to a new place. A young woman who accompanies a new bride on the walk to her new husband's compound.
- **Daa:** Giant catfish that live in the River Gambia.

- **Dimbaya:** Family
- **Dolingo:** A fishing hook.
- **Duma kereng:** Ground squirrel.
- **Dundungo:** A traditional drum made from wood, with a head on each end, and played with a stick.
- **Dusongoni:** Hunter's harp. A traditional instrument made from a small, round calabash, with a long, thin neck, and 4 strings.

- **Easilobula:** Now we open the road for you. The time when a prospective bride's family agrees to open marriage negotiations with a prospective groom's family.

- **Fadomoro:** Fathers' spending. Money given by the family of the groom-to-be to the father of the bride-to-be, as part of the marriage arrangements.
- **Fadondiko:** Father's dress. Money given by the family of the groom-to-be to the father of the bride-to-be, as part of the marriage arrangements, and used to buy material to make a special shirt for him.
- **Faijo:** a big round net that has a rope in the middle.
- **Falo:** The neck of the kora
- **Fanding:** The word for stepfather, used as the title for your father's younger brothers.
- **Fenkengo:** A small clay jar.
- **Fina:** A traditional singer that recites from the Holy Koran or sayings from the prophet Mohammed at traditional ceremonies
- **Findo:** A crop commonly grown in eastern Gambia that has a very small, round grain.
- **Fudo:** A cloth wrapped around something to carry, to make a bundle.
- **Fufu:** A traditional Ghanaian food, also called banku.
- **Futuio jabajibongo:** Watering the onion. Marriage arrangements that are made by two families far ahead of the

time when the marriage is to take place.
- **Futunafulo:** The marriage money, paid by the husband's family to the wife's family. Traditionally it is naninintala, which is 4 dalasi and 50 bututus.

- **Griot:** A West African traditional oral historian.
- **Gyil:** A traditional instrument of the Lobi tribe from Northern Ghana, and similar to the balafon.

- **Haridino and sauta:** Kora tunings from Mali and Guinea.

- **Jali:** Griot. Used as a title in front of a griot's name.
- **Jalinding:** Young griot.
- **Jumas:** Friday prayers at the mosque.
- **Jungo:** A big tree at the edge of the river where groups of fishermen gather.
- **Jutu newo:** The big iron ring at the bottom of the kora neck, which the strings are attached to

- **Kafo:** A group of similar-age boys or girls from the same village, formed during their childhood and continuing throughout their lives.
- **Kanbanibungo:** Young boys' room. A very big grass hut in the family compound where all the boys in the family live after they completing manhood training.
- **Kankuran:** Masked dancers that are traditionally made by the men's secret society to be protectors from evil spirits or from bad people.
- **Karamoba:** Highest teacher.
- **Kekuta:** New man. The temporary name given to a newborn male child from birth until he receives his permanent name.
- **Kenke:** A traditional Ghanian food
- **Kasketo:** A round, cloth hat, usually worn by white people in Africa.
- **Kansolo:** Grass cutter. An animal that looks like a beaver but

- eats tall grasses and has a small tail.
- **Kantary benteng:** A guard tower built in the middle of a farm, where young men spend the night guarding crops from wild animals.
- **Keike**: Mister. A greeting to a man
- **Kewulo:** Men's secret society.
- **Kingo and sampintango:** The two special ansindong dances done by the new men after they return to their village for the celebration.
- **Kombo:** Sunset.
- **Konso:** Leather tuning rings on the kora neck that the strings are attached to.
- **Kontingo:** A traditional Mandingo griot instrument with a body made from a long carved log and covered with goat hide, and a small neck with five strings.
- **Kora:** A traditional Mandingo griot instrument with a body made from a half of a large, round calabash with a cowhide stretched across it, and a strong wooden neck made from a small tree with 21-strings.
- **Kosso:** A small fish found in the River Gambia, with fins on its sides and top that are very sharp and can break off in your skin.
- **Kullo:** The cowhide stretched across the body of the kora
- **Kunjeh:** A small, pear-shaped Gambian fruit.
- **Kunlarango:** The little pillow under the bridge of the kora
- **Kupanpang:** an eastern Gambia native plant with milky sap in its leaves, used to make wulenmindo.
- **Kutiro:** A small traditional wooden drum, with an animal hide stretched over it. Similar to a djembe, and played with a stick or by hand.
- **Kutifingo:** A small, round Gambian fruit that grows on a tree, with a big seed inside. Also called simbong.

- **Mako:** A traditional yellow corn, also called toubanyo.
- **Mankaro:** Antelope
- **Manyafing:** Black ants that bite.

- **Manya wulen:** Red ants that bite.
- **Manyo:** New wife. A bride-to-be or a newly-married woman.
- **Manyoke:** New husband. A groom-to-be or a newly-married man.
- **Manyo dingoli:** Bride's children. The people from the bride's village who will accompany the bride on the walk to the new husband's compound.
- **Manyo fanno:** Bride's cloth. A piece of white cloth that covers the bride's head during the marriage and the slow-walking to her new husband's compound.
- **Manyo makango:** The elder woman who will stay very close to the new bride during the walk to the new husband's compound, and for a week afterward.
- **Manyo tulungo:** The traditional Mandingo celebration for a new wife.
- **Manyo yenyengo:** Walking slow with the new bride. The slow walking with tiny steps, to bring the new bride to the new husband's compound.
- **Marango:** Carved round sticks used during manhood training, for percussion instruments and for discipline.
- **Mfama:** Father.
- **Mirango:** the gourd or calabash that a kora body is made from.
- **Mono:** A cooked porridge, made from finely-powdered millet.
- **Musubungo:** Women's house. A very big grass hut in some family compounds with many beds inside, where all the wives in the family live.
- **Musukuta:** New woman. The temporary name given to a newborn female child from birth until she receives her permanent name.

- **Na:** Your born mother, who gave birth to you.
- **Nabba:** Elder mother. Any wife of your born father who he married before he married your born mother.
- **Nanding:** Stepmother. Any wife of your born father who he married after he married your born mother.

- **Nkotoke:** elder brother.
- **Nammo:** A type of lake or pond fishing done with a long rope that has one-foot long lines hung on it a foot apart, with a hook tied to the end of each line.
- **Nonkonla:** The day we will announce the marriage plans to the public. Also called futusito, which means, Tieing the marriage tight.
- **Numo:** A blacksmith who does circumcisions.
- **Numoli:** A blacksmith family.
- **Nyancho:** A Mandingo royal family.
- **Nyanye:** a one-string violin and traditional instrument of the Fulani people

- **Panketo:** A small, round pound cake.
- **Pasajo:** A traditional mattress made from a large jute peanut bag, and stuffed with small dried grasses.
- **Passingo:** A special sign language used to communicate without words.

- **Saata:** A traditional white corn.
- **Sanjano:** The time of year for digging peanuts, and harvesting other crops.
- **Sanke:** A mosquito net.
- **Santo kereng:** tree squirrel.
- **Seema:** In eastern Gambia, the name for the elder man who is in charge of watching over all the boys who are to be circumcised, and during their manhood training. In western Gambia, he is called ansimba.

- **Silifata nonkong:** A small amount of money paid by the new husband's family and representatives to the new bride's family, during the slow walk to the new husband's compound.
- **Simba:** A special tool for digging peanuts.
- **Sondiro:** To show you something about the Kankuran. A ceremony for men to learn the symbol language of the

Kankuran Wulen.
- **Songharo:** The messenger or negotiator for the groom-to-be for all the marriage planning and preparation.
- **Sorongo:** Oval-shaped.
- **Sorro:** A double-headed fishing spear.
- **Sunjulo:** A 6-10 ft long rope with a stick on the end, used by fishermen to drag daa out of the water.
- **Sunkang:** an animal in the raccoon family, but much bigger, and a longer tail, with spotted, long hair. It lives in an underground burrow or inside a termite mound.
- **Sunkutumuto:** Go get the bride. In traditional marriage preparations, the time when a prospective groom and his host bring the prospective bride to the host's compound so they can talk. Also called musukammo, which means, Go bring the woman.
- **Suto doling fayo:** Night hook fishing.

- **Tabunlo:** A large traditional wooden drum with a single head, used only for communicating important news in a village.
- **Tato:** A long, heavy war fence, that kings had built around multiple villages in their areas in order to protect them.
- **Taye:** An animal that is black with a bushy tail and white spots, in the same family as raccoon but doesn't climb trees.
- **Tenda:** A crossing point over a river.
- **Tikingo:** An electric fish found in the River Gambia that is round like a blowfish, but doesn't have any spines. Frequently caught in the same places where sokoro, binteko, and kulun domo fish live.
- **Toma:** Namesake.
- **Tomora:** A kora tuning that is used in western Gambia and the Casamance region of Senegal. Also known as silaba.
- **Toronkoso:** A traditional team game with bamboo sticks and a round ball.
- **Toubab:** A white person.

- **Waana:** The place where the new men will be. The special place outside a village where circumcision and manhood training is done. Also called jujuo.
- **Wato:** a wild cat with a big neck and spotted body that climbs trees.
- **Wlubobasang:** A traditional multi-colored corn.
- **Woroto:** A tool for cutting grain, with a curved blade like a sythe.
- **Wulenmindo:** A mixture of crushed black ants, red ants, hot pepper, bees, and kupanpang leaves, fed to dogs to make them better hunters.
- **Wusungo:** A net that is like a long basket, made from woven bamboo.

www.ingramcontent.com/pod-product-compliance
Lightning Source LLC
Chambersburg PA
CBHW071144070526
44584CB00019B/2653